to discriminate on a most particular level between objects previously viewed as identical or hopelessly uninteresting ∙ This increased perception pays the student for his work & as an added attraction ∙ he has acquired a pleasant skill ∙ ¶ Calligraphy is the art of writing beautifully ∙ & with delight ∙ and can be the province of every man who has mastered the more difficult art of expressing himself through written symbols ∙ The student is his own teacher ∙ and as such will learn only what he teaches himself ∙ This book can smooth his path ∙ preventing time-consuming & discouraging errors ∙ but can do little else ∙ Ability is best obtained through practice ∙ the more (within reason) the better ∙∙ The ability to do calligraphy well is in direct proportion to the time spent in doing it ∙ Work carefully & deliberately ∙ as haste is the enemy of good workmanship ∙ People who run for buses will never make calligraphers ∙ ¶ This book is large so that the letters will be clear & the same size as the student's ∙ It should be used as a writing pad ∙ with the student's work opposite the page he is studying ∙ For this purpose ∙ a fold-out writing guide is provided in the back ∙ so that any page in the book can be copied without inconvenience ∙∙ ¶ In this third edition I hope to have removed the more glaring errors of the preceding ∙ & though new mistakes may be found ∙ the generous reader will pardon them and me ∙

abcd defgghijkklmnopqggqzrstuvrwwwx
yyz3z ∙ ABCDEFGHIJKLMNOPQRSTUVWXYZ ∙
abcdefghijklmnopqzrstuvwxyz ∙ & ∙ 1234567890 ∙

THE
PUSHCART PRIZE:
BEST OF THE
SMALL PRESSES

♭ ♭ ♭ THE PUSHCART PRIZE:

An annual small press reader assembled with founding editors Anaïs Nin, Buckminster Fuller, Ishmael Reed, Joyce Carol Oates, Leslie Fiedler, Nona Balakian, Paul Engle, Reynolds Price, Len Fulton, William Phillips, Tom Montag, Ted Wilentz, Rhoda Schwartz, Richard Morris, Leonard Randolph, Hugh Fox, Harry Smith, Gordon Lish, Daniel Halpern, Charles Newman, H.L. Van Brunt, Paul Bowles, Ralph Ellison, (and the 400 editors and writers whose names follow . . .)

BEST OF THE SMALL PRESSES

BEST OF THE SMALL PRESSES

EDITED BY BILL HENDERSON

First Edition 1976–77

THE PUSHCART PRESS

THE PUSHCART PRIZE: ✶ ✶ ✶

Endpapers:
from An Introduction To The Elements of Calligraphy,
by David Lance Goines,
Saint Heironymous Press.

ACKNOWLEDGEMENTS

"Musical Shuttle" by Harvey Shapiro © 1975 by *Sun*, reprinted by permission of the author and Sun press.
"Pricksong" by Marilyn Coffey © 1975 by *Aphra*, reprinted by permission of *Aphra*.
"Power" by Adrienne Rich © 1975 by *The Little Magazine*, reprinted by permission of the author and *The Little Magazine*.
"Peace in the Near East" by Gerald Stern © 1975 by *American Poetry Review*, reprinted by permission of the author and *American Poetry Review*.
"The Artificial Family" by Anne Tyler © 1975 by *The Southern Review*, reprinted by permission of the author and *The Southern Review*.
"Encounters with Ezra Pound" by Charles Olson from *Charles Olson and Ezra Pound: An Encounter At St. Elizabeths* by Charles Olson, edited by Catherine Seelye © 1975 by The University of Connecticut. All rights reserved. Reprinted by permission of Grossman Publishers, a division of Viking Penguin Inc. and *Antaeus*.
"Cordials" by David Kranes © 1975 by *TriQuarterly*, reprinted by permission of *TriQuarterly*.
"Fiction Hot and Kool: Dilemmas of the Experimental Writer" by Morris Dickstein © 1975 by *TriQuarterly*, reprinted by permission of *TriQuarterly*.
"Song of The Soapstone Carver" by Sheila Nickerson © 1975 by Sheila Nickerson, reprinted by permission of the author and Thorp Springs Press.
"Stationery, Cards, Notions, Books" by Harold Witt © 1975 by E. V. Griffith, reprinted by permission of E. V. Griffith and *Poetry NOW*, from *Poetry NOW*, Vol. II, No. 2 (issue 8).
"The Pilot" by Naomi Lazard © 1974 by *The Hudson Review*, reprinted by permission of *The Hudson Review* and the author from *The Hudson Review*, winter 1974–75.
"Funeral" by Clarence Major © 1974 by Barlenmir House, reprinted by permission of Barlenmir House, published in 1975.
"I Wish You Wouldn't" by William Gass © 1975 by *Partisan Review Inc.*, reprinted by permission of *Partisan Review* and the author.
"Falling Toward Thanksgiving" by David Weissman © 1975 by David Weissman, reprinted by permission of Raincrow Press.
"Spring" and "Silence" by Michael Hogan © 1975 by Michael Hogan, reprinted by permission of Cold Mountain Press and Unicorn Press.
"The Griots Who Knew Brer Fox" by Colleen McElroy © 1975 by Colleen McElroy, reprinted by permission of *Yardbird Reader*.
"The Monster" by Ronald Sukenick © 1975 by Ronald Sukenick, reprinted by permission of *The Iowa Review* and the author.
"Some Questions and Answers" by Saul Bellow © 1975 by Saul Bellow, reprinted by permission of *Ontario Review* and the author.

Acknowledgements

"I Come Home Late At Night" by Patrick Worth Gray © 1975 by *Blue Cloud Quarterly*, reprinted by permission of *Blue Cloud Quarterly*.

"Lost Colony" by Marvin Weaver © 1975 by *St. Andrews Review*, reprinted by permission of *St. Andrews Review*.

"The Spring" by H. L. Van Brunt © 1975 by H. L. Van Brunt, reprinted by permission of the author and The Smith press.

"Like A Good Unknown Poet" by Art Cuelho © 1975 by Art Cuelho, reprinted by permission of Holmgangers Press.

endpapers are from *An Introduction to the Elements of Calligraphy*, by David Lance Goines © 1975 by St. Heironymous Press, Inc., reprinted by permission of St. Heironymous Press, Inc.

"Whitman's Song of Myself" by Robert K. Martin © 1975 by Partisan Review Inc., reprinted by permission of *Partisan Review*.

"Take Me Back to Tulsa" by David Ray © 1975 by *The Chariton Review*, reprinted by permission of *The Chariton Review*.

"A Chronicle of Love" by H. E. Francis © 1974 by *Kansas Quarterly*, reprinted by permission of *Kansas Quarterly* from the winter 1974–75 issue.

"Retarded Children in The Snow" by Michael McMahon © 1975 by *Aspen Leaves* reprinted by permission of Aspen Leaves Literary Foundation.

"City Joys" from *City Joys* © 1975 by Jack Anderson, published by Release Press, reprinted by permission of Release Press.

"Autumn Evenings" by John Beauvais © 1975 by John Beauvais, reprinted by permission of the author.

"The Human Table" by Marvin Cohen © 1975 by Marvin Cohen, reprinted by permission of Latitudes Press.

"Late Track" by Jane Bailey © 1975 by *Montana Gothic*, reprinted by permission of *Montana Gothic*.

"Popocatépetl" © 1975 by The Sunstone Press, reprinted by permission of The Sunstone Press.

"The Mother In Law" from *Tales of Beatnick Glory* (Stonehill Press) by Ed Sanders © 1975 by *Center* and by Ed Sanders, reprinted by permission of *Center*.

"Nothing Very Much Has Happened Here" by Rhoda Schwartz © 1975 by *The Word-Smith*, reprinted by permission of *The Word-Smith*.

"Science and The Compulsive Programmer" by Joseph Weizenbaum © 1975 by Partisan Review, Inc. reprinted by permission of *Partisan Review*.

"Father of the Bride" by Jack Pulaski © 1975 under this title by *Goddard Journal* and Jack Pulaski, reprinted by permission of *Goddard Journal* and the author.

"Grandparents" by Howard Zimmon © 1975 by Howard Zimmon, reprinted by permission of The Seamark Press.

"Five Black Poets: History, Consciousness, Love and Harshness' by Eugene B. Redmond © 1975 by *Parnassus: Poetry In Review*, reprinted by permission of *Parnassus: Poetry In Review*.

"The Death of Yury Galanskov" reprinted by permission of AIUSA from *A Chronicle of Current Events Number* 28 to 31 © 1975 by Amnesty International.

"Is Don Juan Alive and Well?" by Arnold Mandell © 1975 by Ontario Review Press, reprinted by permission of Ontario Review Press.

"Lynda Van Cats" by Alexander Theroux © 1975 by *Antaeus*, reprinted by permission of *Antaeus*.

"The Dog" by Avrom Reyzen © 1975 by *Antaeus*, reprinted by permission of *Antaeus*. Translation © 1975 by Joachim Neugroschel.

"The Elephant" by Drummond De Andrade © 1975 by *Ploughshares*, reprinted by permission of *Ploughshares* and Mark Strand, the translator.

"Alcohol and Poetry: John Berryman and The Booze Talking" by Lewis Hyde © 1975 by *American Poetry Review*, reprinted by permission of *American Poetry Review* and Lewis Hyde.

"Lecturing My Daughter In Her First Fall Rain" by Tom Montag © 1975 by Tom Montag, reprinted by permission of Pentagram Press.

"Style 3" and "Style 5" by William Wantling © 1975 by William Wantling and Second Coming Press, reprinted by permission of Second Coming Press.

"The Flowering Cacti" by Gene Fowler © 1975 by Gene Fowler, reprinted by permission of Second Coming Press.

"At Dawn In Winter" by John Glowney © 1975 by *Anaesthesia Review*, reprinted by permission of *Anaesthesia Review*.

"Number 17 From *The Lives of the Poets*" by George Mattingly © 1975 by George Mattingly appeared previously in *Breathing Space* by George Mattingly (Blue Wind Press) and is forthcoming in *Sweet Dreams* (Seamark Press), reprinted by permission of the author.

"The Day of the Night" by James Scully from *Santiago Poems* © 1975 by James Scully, reprinted by permission of Curbstone Press and the author.

"Veterans Head" by Diane Chapman © 1975 by *Xanadu*, reprinted by permission of *Xanadu*.

"The Hallucination" by Joyce Carol Oates reprinted with permission of *Chicago Review* © 1975 by *Chicago Review*.

"Missing The Trail" by David Wagoner reprinted with permission of *Chicago Review* © 1975 by *Chicago Review*.

"Broken Portraiture" by Bruce Boston © 1975 by *Gallimaufry*, reprinted by permission of *Gallimaufry*.

untitled poem by Laura Pershin © 1975 by Cosmic Information Agency, reprinted by permission of Cosmic Information Agency.

"Bad Poems" by Michael Dennis Browne © 1975 by *Dacotah Territory*, reprinted by permission of *Dacotah Territory*.

"Steelmill Blues" by Steve Packard © 1975 by *Liberation Magazine*, reprinted by permission of *Liberation Magazine*.

"Black Money" by Tess Gallagher © 1975 by Tess Gallagher from *Stepping Outside*, 230 copies published by The Penumbra Press, January 1975, reprinted by permission of The Penumbra Press.

"The Death of Sun" by William Eastlake © 1972 by William Eastlake, reprinted from *The Far Side of the Storm—New Ranges of Western Fiction*, Gary Elder, editor (San Marcos Press, 1975) with permission of Gary Elder and San Marcos Press, E. W. Tedlock publisher, and by permission of the author.

"Cloe Morgan" by Karl Kopp © 1975 by *Newsart/The Smith*, reprinted by permission of *Newsart/The Smith*.

"Intro" by Harold Brodkey © 1976 by Harold Brodkey, from *A Party of Animals*, Farrar, Straus and Giroux. First published in *American Poetry Review*, 1975 reprinted by permission of *American Poetry Review*, the author, and the author's agent, International Creative Management.

"Hurry" by Octavio Paz reprinted with permission of *Chicago Review* © 1975 by *Chicago Review*.
"Afrikaan Bottles" by G. K. Wouri reprinted by permission of *The Cimmaron Review* and Oklahoma State University Regents.
"A Postscript to the Berkeley Renaissance" by Jack Spicer © 1975 by Jack Spicer estate, reprinted by permission of *ManRoot* and Robin Blaser.
"So Much Water So Close to Home" by Raymond Carver, first published in *Spectrum* Winter, 1975, Vol. XVII, © 1975 by Raymond Carver.
"Variations on *A Mound of Corpses in the Snow*" by Stephen Berg from *Grief* by Stephen Berg © 1975 by Stephen Berg. All rights reserved. Reprinted by permission of Grossman Publishers, a division of Viking Penguin, Inc.
"A Liberal's Auschwitz" by Cynthia Ozick, reprinted by permission of *Confrontation* and the author.
"Now I Am Married" by Mary Gordon, reprinted by permission of *Virginia Quarterly* and the author.
"Beautiful People" by John Bennett and "Experimental Language" by Tony Quagliano reprinted by permission of *Ghost Dance*.
"Xenia," Eugenio Montale, poems from *Xenia* as translated by Jonathan Galassi are published by permission of Arnoldo Mondadori Editore, Italy and New Directions, New York. © 1975 *Ploughshares*. All rights reserved.

Also from
THE PUSHCART PRESS

THE PUBLISH-IT-YOURSELF HANDBOOK:
Literary Tradition and How-To
(seventh printing)

This book is for Anaïs Nin

♨ ♨ ♨

LITERATURE
AND
BREAKFAST CEREAL
INTRODUCTION

THINK YOU KNOW WHAT'S HAPPENING in literature today? Maybe you've been missing something.

"Approximately 2,000 alternative publishers now exist in the United States and their number is mushrooming," announced *The New York Times Book Review*. Most of these small independent presses have appeared in the last decade. During the same period many large commercial publishing houses have been absorbed by conglomerates more interested in parking lots, television, motion pictures and it was gravely rumored for a forthcoming takeover (and gravely denied) in breakfast cereal.

Not since the Paris of Hemingway, Pound and Joyce has so much talent been invested in small presses in every country of the world. The modern small presses publish because of enlightened individualism or, in a few instances, sheer cussedness. They also answer a variety of situations, such as political oppression—the Russian *samizdat* network that nourished Solzhenitsyn for instance—or because of commercial exclusion: the American do-it-yourself tradition that encouraged Anaïs Nin and Stewart Brand and small press immortals such as Thomas Paine, Edgar Allan Poe, Walt Whitman, Stephen Crane, Upton Sinclair, and Carl Sandburg.

The result is a galaxy of important authors that most readers have never head of, let alone read. *The Pushcart Prize* is the first and only collection that annually will bring to a general audience the finest in short fiction, non-fiction, poetry, translation and literary what-not—the classics of tomorrow by today's multitude of small press talents.

Even the most avid reader could not have hoped to keep up with the activity of small presses in the past year. Consequently he or she may have overlooked the publication of Michael Hogan by Greensboro, North Carolina's Unicorn Press, Austin Texas' Cold Mountain Press and New York's *The American Pen*. Hogan, a winner of the American P.E.N. prize for writing by prisoners, lives in the maximum security ward of Arizona State Prison. Up in Cambridge, Massachusetts, *Ploughshares* was publishing Eugenio Montale a few months before he was named winner of the Nobel Prize for Literature.

In Philadelphia, the fiction news of the decade continued with the publication in *American Poetry Review* of the introduction to the novel in progress by Harold Brodkey. From New York, via London's Amnesty International and the Russian underground arrived *A Chronicle of Current Events, Numbers* 28-31, long suppressed by the KGB. All of the above are represented in the following pages as are H.E. Francis' "A Chronicle of Love" from *Kansas Quarterly* (one of Pushcart's favorite short stories) and Colleen J. McElroy's "The Griots Who Knew Brer Fox" from *Yardbird Reader* (one of several near-perfect poems) and "Science And The Compulsive Programmer" by Joseph Weizenbaum from *Partisan Review*, a nicely proportioned essay of crucial importance.

If you are looking for names you will find Octavio Paz, William Gass, Joyce Carol Oates, Saul Bellow and others. But the limelight belongs to the unknown writers. There's plenty of sorrow here, but lots of love, a few bitter sweet laughs (see David Kranes' "Cordials" from *TriQuarterly*) and a charming trifle or two like Alexander Theroux's "Lynda Van Cats" from *Antaeus*.

The small presses in this volume range from the widely known like *Chicago Review* and *Partisan Review* to those of recent repute such as *Antaeus* and *TriQuarterly* to those of limited fame like *Ghost Dance* and *Xanadu*. In addition about sixty other small presses are reprinted in our final choice, a choice which certainly must be considered "a" best and in no case "the" best. Despite the fact that more than 400 people helped collect this book, any selection from over 2,000 small presses is bound to be limited. For instance, the term small press includes a host of publishing endeavors from one person self-publishing outfits (not to be confused with vanity house ruses) to university literary journals to book presses turning out several titles a year. Some could not be included because of space limitation. An excellent essay by W.S. Merwin "Aspects of a Mountain" nominated by Reynolds Price from *Shenandoah* would have required a fifth of the book to reprint and regretfully had to be excluded for shorter essays of equal worth. Not included also are reviews (with one exception), propaganda, or many presses of special or local interest like *Living In The Ozarks Newsletter*, published by Joel and Sherri Davidson of Pettigrew, Arkansas. Also absent here are portions of valuable informational books like *Foxfire* (a folkloric small press creation now distributed by Doubleday) and *Rain*, a Portland Oregon journal that gathers sources and methods of environmental improvement, and *A Directory of American Poets*, an annual listing of the names and addresses of active poets.

Beyond these distinctions, the only criteria is that the final selections represent what is well thought and well expressed. No literary mafia has trafficked here. In fact some of our founding editors aren't speaking to each other. Good. No school of style, idealism or politics dominates. Financial backing depends entirely on Pushcart's other publication, *The Publish-it-Yourself Handbook: Literary Tradition and How-To*, now in its seventh printing. We require no governmental or foundation grants to continue assembling and printing this collection every year as planned.

The Pushcart Prize is awarded with the widest possible democratic participation. About a year ago we contacted small press notables Anaïs Nin, Buckminster Fuller, Charles Newman, Daniel Halpern, Gordon Lish, Harry Smith, Hugh Fox, Ishmael Reed, Joyce Carol Oates, Len Fulton, Leonard Randolph, Leslie Fiedler, Richard Morris, Nona Balakian, Paul Bowles, Paul Engle, Ralph Ellison, Reynolds Price, Rhoda Schwartz, Ted Wilentz, Tom Montag, and William Phillips and asked them to assist us as founding editors— without remuneration of any sort—by sending in their nominations of the best from the small presses they read, and also by commenting on the final selection. (They could also nominate pieces from their own presses, up to a maximum of six, like all other editors). Next we announced our plans to the *COSMEP Newsletter* (Box 703, San Francisco, California. The Committee of Small Magazine Editors and Publishers is *the* small press organization in the United States, 950 members strong and surging). Full page ads followed on the third cover of *Publishers Weekly* and in *Small Press Review*, requesting nominations from editors. Finally 2,400 nomination invitations were mailed directly to small press editors (again a limit of six "best" from each press). The 3,000 incoming nominations from all sources were screened by Bill Henderson and Poetry Editor H.L. Van Brunt. Our pick was submitted to the founding contributing editors for final approval.

What happens next, we hope, is a variety of response, and suggestions for next year's collection (October 15 is the deadline each year, for the pick of that calendar year). Certainly not everyone will agree with our choices of a best and it just wouldn't be an alternative movement of any worth if some individuals didn't disagree.

"The Prize" in the title is publication in Pushcart's edition and a pro rata share to both author and press of the entire Pushcart profits. That way nobody is going to get rich but nobody will be left out either.

The real prize is recognition to those authors and editors who for too long have labored in anonymity. This book is for them with love and respect.

And to you, the reader, we hope this book will offer at least some idea of why today's small presses are important to the good health of our culture—a culture too often dominated by big bucks conglomerates and rumors of breakfast cereal takeovers.

Bill Henderson
THE PUSHCART PRESS

𝆕 𝆕 𝆕

SMALL
PRESSES CONSIDERED
FOR THIS BOOK

Western Humanities Review, *The American Pen*, *Margins*, Cities Investigation, *Bachy*, *Nimrod*, *Ghost Dance*, *th unita gargoyl*, *Aldebaran Review*, *West Coast Poetry Review*, *Montana Gothic*, *Vagabond*, *Hudson Review*, *American Poetry Review*, *Gray Day*, *TriQuarterly*, *Antaeus*, *Fiction*, *New Letters*, *Paris Review*, *Modern Poetry Studies*, *Ontario Review*, *Canadian Fiction*, *The Little Magazine*, *Fiction International*, *Southern Review*, *Shenandoah*, *St. Andrews Review*, *Sewanee Review*, *Iowa Review*, *New Poetry*, *Alcheringa*, *European Judaism*, *Chicago Review*, *Virginia Quarterly*, *Paintbrush*, Black Sparrow, Second Coming, *Black History Museum Newsletter*, *Yardbird Reader*, Folder Press, Latitudes, *Ararat*, *Pembroke*, *Twentieth Century Literature*, *CoEvolution Quarterly*, *Massachusetts Review*, *Samisdat*, *ManRoot*, *Stoney Lonesome*, *Colorado Quarterly*, *Kansas Quarterly*, *The Blacksmith*, *The Literary Tabloid*, *Diana's BiMonthly*, *Kosmos*, *NewsNovel*, *Apocalypse*, *Truck*, *Art and Archaeology Newsletter*, *Seer Ox*, Renaissance Press, *WIP Magazine*, *Huron Review*, *Reason*, *Ball State University Forum*, *Harvest*, *Eternity SF*, Knollwood Publishing Co., *Tractor*, Ithaca House, *Bartholomew's Cobble*, *Living In The Ozarks Newsletter*, LP Publications, Sunstone Press, *The Texas Slough*, *Zahir*, *Speakout*, Proexistence Publications, St. Mawr Jazz Poetry Project, *Dramatika*, Glass Bell Press, Barlenmir House, Bureau of Common Sense, Bakke Press, Holmgangers Press, Canterbury Press, Arica Press, Stroken Press, *Greenfield Review*, *B and R Samizdat Express*, *Mouth of the Dragon*, Pale Horse Press, *The Fountain*, *Xanadu*, *Metamorphosis*, *Confrontation*, Assembling

Press, Druid Heights Books, Lame Johnny Press, *Beyond Baroque*, *Center*, river bottom press, *Pembroke Magazine*, Cross Country, Litmus Press, Sun Books, *Golgonooza*, Times Change Press, *Yellow Brick Road*, *The News Circle*, Cat's Pajamas Press, Telepoem, Yellow Jacket Press, *Northwest Review*, *Gay Literature*, Community of Friends, *San Jose Studies*, Westernlore Books, *Unexpected*, *The Voyeur*, Puckerbrush Press, Curbstone Press, *Ploughshares*, *Primavera*, The Countryman Press, *Resources*, *Sparrow*, Pleasant Hill Press, Chandler and Sharp Publishers, Printing Arts Press, *Stone Country*, Bellevue Press, *transken*, Great Lakes Press, Ox Head Press, *Blue Cloud Quarterly*, *Star West*, The Press of Arden Park, Copley Books, Solar Age Press, *White Pine*, Berkeley Poets Cooperative, Illuminations Press, *Purr Magazine*, *St. Croix Review*, *Vile Magazine*, Neo-American Church Press, Pitcairn Press, *Manuscripts*, *Cosmic Circus*, Smoking Mirror Press, Carpenter Press, *Modularist Review*, Bardic Echoes Brochures, *Aspen Leaves*, *Chariton Review*, *Mountain Summer*, *Cimarron Review*, *Beloit Poetry Journal*, pulpartforms, *Tales*, *Nitty Gritty*, Dragon's Teeth Press, Energy Blacksouth Press, *Painted Bride*, *Momentum*, From Here Press, Scrimshaw Press, *Literary Sketches*, Seven Stars, *Rain*, *California Bard*, *Burning Deck*, Treacle Press, *Skywriting*, *Mustang Review*, Cold Mountain Press, Pentagram Press, *Kayak*, Ventura Press, *Quartet*, Ash Lad Press, *Crow's Nest*, Salt Lick Press, Capra Press, Linden Publishers, *Open Places*, *Ann Arbor Review*, *Lowlands Review*, *Wetlands*, Magic Circle Press, *Nausea*, *Coldspring Journal*, Stone Marrow Press, *Kil-Kaas-Git*, *Southern Humanities Review*, New Spirit Books, Ragnarok Press, Pilot Press Books, *New Worlds*, Atlantis Editions, New Rivers Press, Artists and Alchemists Press, Queens College Press, Unicorn Press, Occum Press, Smyrna Press, *The Niagara Magazine*, *Inlet*, Babbington Press, Parallax Press, St. Heironymous Press, *Dacotah Territory*, San Marcos Press, *Moons and Lions Tailes*, Angst World Library, Pigiron Press, *Some*, Peace and Pieces Foundation, Release Press, Box 749, Cellar Press, Pulse-Finger Press, *Intermedia*, Maine Editions, *Scree*, Hard Pressed, *The Smith*, *Oyez Review*, *eddy magazine*, Toothpaste Press, Quick Books, Pocket Poetry Press, *Gallimaufry*, *Dadazine*, Valley Editions, *Paunch*, *The Remington Review*, *Chelsea*, *The Newsletter*, *Street Cries*, *Oz Publications*, *Wine Rings*, *Pearl*, *Off Our Backs*, Raincrow Press, Rootdrinker, Vehicule Press, *New Writers*, *The Spirit That Moves Us*,

Mt. Alverno Press, Cleveland State University Poetry Center, Out of the Ashes Press, *WomanSpirit, Bleb, Aspect, Hawaii Review,* Hector and Hector, *Open Cell,* Copper Canyon Press, Alternative Press, *Duck, Nostoc, Story Quarterly,* Hibiscus Press, Cosmic Information Agency, Prescott Street Press, *Jambalaya, Pequod,* Resources For Community Change, Street Press, *Mosaic, Outworlds, Panjandrum, Other Voices, Caim, Poet Papers,* Iris Press, *The Blacksmith, The Literary Tabloid, Aleph,* Reed Cannon and Johnson Press, Tin-Tan, Malki Museum Press, *Big Moon, The Word-Smith, Carolina Quarterly,* Fiction Collective, BkMk Press, *Obsidian,* Black River Writers Press, *Black World, Synergy,* Sand Project Press, *Poet and Critic, Puddingstone, Schist, South Dakota Review, Sequoia, Stile, Tawte, Telephone, Unmuzzled Ox, Lunar Retorno, Anesthesia Review, Ark River Review, Big Scream, Black Maria, Cafe Solo, The Cape Rock, Chernozem, Concerning Poetry, Poetry Northwest, Speciala, Crow's Nest, Cutbank, The Dragonfly, Endymion, Epoch, The Falcon, Cottonwood Review, Gravida, Hiram Poetry Review, Isthmus, Invisible City, Lake Superior Review, Lucille, Moving Out, New Orleans Review, The New Moon, Mana Magazine,* Second Back Row Press, Juniper Press, *Red Fox Review, Southern Poetry Review, Ark River Review,* Micah Publications, Abraxas Press, Star Book Store and Valley Publications, Lillabulero Press, Soft Press, *Dogsoldier, Bravado, Creative Computing, North American Mentor Magazine,* Nebula Press, *Modernismo, Cage and Doorkey, Hyacinths and Biscuits, Modern Prometheus,* Unity Press, *Northern Light, Liberation, Happiness Holding Tank, Puerto Del Sol,* Glide Publications, Third World Communications, Paradigm Publishing, R.V.K. Publishing, *Applegarth Follies, Spectrum, The New Moon,* Peace Press, *The Stone,* The Boston Critic, 13*th Moon, Nairn, Alternative to Alienation,* University of Missouri Press, Canadian Fiction Magazine, The Fault Press, Dryad Press, Jamima House, Leland Enterprises, *Pequod,* Cherry Tree Press, Trinty Press, *Poetry NOW, Panache,* New York Zoetrope.

THE
PEOPLE WHO HELPED
MAKE THIS BOOK

EDITOR and PUBLISHER: *Bill Henderson*

POETRY EDITOR: *H.L. Van Brunt*

FOUNDING EDITORS: *Anaïs Nin, Buckminster Fuller, Ishmael Reed, Joyce Carol Oates, Leslie Fiedler, Nona Balakian, Paul Engle, Reynolds Price, Len Fulton, William Phillips, Tom Montag, Ted Wilentz, Rhoda Schwartz, Richard Morris, Leonard Randolph, Hugh Fox, Harry Smith, Gordon Lish, Daniel Halpern, Charles Newman, Paul Bowles, Ralph Ellison.*

DESIGN & PRODUCTION: *Ray Freiman & Company*

ROVING EDITORS: *Ben Pesta and Carole Dolph*

EUROPEAN EDITORS: *Kirby and Liz Williams*

AUSTRALIAN EDITORS: *Tom and Wendy Whitton*

JACKET DESIGN: *Barbara Lish*

SUSTAINING CONTRIBUTING EDITORS: *Rochelle Holt, Tristine Rainer, Eric Greinke, Rochelle and Robert Bonazzi, Elliott Anderson, Merritt Clifton, Paul Mariah, Richard Pflum, Claudine Seever, Tom Ahern, Kosrof Chantikian, Darlene Wheeler, Tom Smith, David Wilk, Otto Reiss, Michael McClintock, K. Michael*

McKenzie, Larry Brenner, Frank Hamilton, Robert Poole Jr.,
Merrill and Francis Rippy, David Lenson, Maryland Lincoln,
Frederick Mosey, Stephen Gregg, Robert Knigge, John Bennett,
Lynn Shoemaker, John M. Bennett, Rod Steier, Joel and Sherri
Davidson, Diane Pike, Arleen Lorrance, Jody Ellis, James
Normington, Charles Taylor, Stewart Brand, Raymond Smith,
Diane Kruchkow, Steve Kowit, John H. Kennedy, Erin St. Mawr, J.
Pyros, Margaret Kaminski, Barry Mirenburg, Catherine McEver,
Anne Cotterill, Gary Elder, Joe Kimball, Ellie Flatto, Irving
Stettner, Joe Bruchac, Richard Seltzer, Andrew BiFrost, Joseph
McLaughlin, Ames McDaniel, Charles Fishman, Tom Fallon,
Martin Tucker, Henry Korn, Linda Hasselstrom, George D. Smith,
James Krusoe, Alexandra Garrett, Carol Berge, r.c. halla, Norman
Macleod, Bob Galvin, Jim Mele, Ken Norris, Charles Potts,
Aethelred and Alexandra Eldridge, Tommy, Robert Matte Jr., Paul
Cook, Joe Hajek, John Jacob, Loren-Paul Caplin, Maryann Travers,
Michael Strelow, Daniel Curzon, Moses Yanes, Arlene Okerlund,
Paul Bailey, N. Ballentine, Janet Ruth Heller, Peter S. Jennison,
Richard Gardner, Felix Stefanile, Eugene Boudreau, Jonathan
Sharp, George Myers Jr., Judy Neeld, Gil Williams, Ken Saville,
Jacques LesStrang, Don Olsen, Br. Benet Tvedten OSB, Leon Spiro,
Budd Westreich, Jack Frazier, Carlo Giovanni Cicatelli, Charles
Entrekin, Norman Moser, Linda and Geraldine King, Angus
MacDonald, Anna Banana, Jack Call, John Marten, Paul Lutz,
David Plumb, David Green, Bob Fox, Roger Charles, Garland
Burnette, R.C. Morse, Clarence Weaver, John Stafford, Andrew
Grossbardt, Don Keck Du Pree, Clinton Keller, Marion Stocking,
Walt Shepperd, Barry Glassner, W.R. Wilkins, Cornel Lengyel, E.
Ethelbert Miller, Louise Simons, William Mohr, William Higginson,
Mary Lewis Chapman, Richard Soos Jr., Steve Johnson, Elizabeth
MacGavin, Keith Waldrop, Bruce McPherson, Martin Grossman,
Marjorie Appell, Ryan Petty, Michael Tarachow, George Hitchcock,
Raymond Barrio, Richard Costa, Bill Romey, A.D. Winans, B.M.
Bennani, Bern Porter, Paul Fericano, John Haining, Noel Young,
Eleanor Bender, Fred Wolven, Tom Whalen, Ann Scott Gray,
Mabel Johnson, Thomas Zawyrucha, Valerie Harms, Leo Mailman,
Pamela Beach Plymell, James Bertolino, Tamara Smid, David
Jeffrey, Robert Miller, Sal St. John Buttaci, C.W. Truesdale, Adele
Aldridge, Anne Demerle, Elias Bokhara, Neil Baldwin, Joseph
Harkey, Richard Uhlich, Douglas Flaherty, Courtney Murphree,

*Mark Vinz, E.W. Tedlock, H. Schjotz-Christensen, Balthazar
Kahn, Jim Villani, Harry Greenberg, Alan Ziegler, Larry Zirlin,
Maurice Custodio, Francine Ringold, James Boatwright, Mary
Maud Ferguson, Douglass Turner, Orion Roche, Harley Lond,
Steven Cook, Kirk Robertson, Martha Ann Whitmore, J. Rutherford
Willems, Civia Cohen, Allan and Cinda Kornblum, Harold
Schneider, Ben Nyberg, Joel Scherzer, Robbie Rubinstein, Richard
Marsh, Mary MacArthur, Bill Gaglione, Seymour Mayne, Arthur
Efron, Joseph Barbato, Dean Maskevich, Sonia Raiziss, Sidney
Bernard, Robie Woliver, Ann Menebroker, Karl Kempton, Joan
Smith, Alan Basting, Martha Rosler, Alan Casline, Si Dardick,
Constance Glickman, Timothy Erwin, Morty Sklar, Michael Ford,
Leonard Trawick, Ruth and Jean Mountaingrove, George Ryan, Ed
Hogan, Gary Kissick, L.I. Hamilton, Normon Solomon, Milton
Loventhal, Sam Hamill, Ken and Ann Mikolowski, Sonya and Lynn
Grow, Marshall Brooks, Tom Bracken, Thalia Selz, Pamela Painter
Skeen, Margaret Wensrich, James Davis, Vi Gale, Mark Rudman,
Don Murray, Graham Everett, David Gast, Bill Bowers, Dennis
Koran, Charles Upton, Bernard Taylor, Muriel Ashley, James
Taylor, Patricia Wilcox, John Judson, Karen Rockow, James
Coleman, Guy Owen, A.G. Sobin, Arthur Vogelsang, Jonathan
Katz, Roberta Kalechofsky, Warren Woessner, William Griffin,
Henry Roth, Bob Burns, Robert Sward, William Hudson, Marc
Rangel de Algeciras, David Ahl, John Westburg, Ken Stange, John
Weber, E.V. Griffith, Jane Card, Paul Foreman, R.H. Alcott,
Stephen Levine, George Amabile, Paul Loeb, Vickie Leonard,
Chuck Sphar, Daniel Quigley, S.P. Stavrakis, Ralph Culver, Mick
Fedullo, Jeffrey Greene, David Sears, Warren Werner, Jill
Jamieson, Marcus Louria, David Marovich, Harold Moskovitz,
Richard Jorgensen, Anita Silvey, Ellen Marie Bissert, Bill Halloway,
Elouise Loftin, Merrill Leffler, d.h. Sullivan, Albert Drake.*

✹ ✹ ✹

NOTES ON PRESSES AND CONTRIBUTORS

The American PEN (156 Fifth Ave., New York, N. Y. 10010) is the literary publication of the American branch of P.E.N. international and is issued quarterly under the direction of several distinguished editors. For information about Michael Hogan see the listing of Unicorn Press.

The American Poetry Review (401 S. Broad St., Philadelphia, Pa. 19147) began publishing in 1972. A poetry-oriented magazine in tabloid format, it has the largest circulation for a magazine of this type. LEWIS HYDE is a translator and works as a counselor in the alcohol ward of the Cambridge (Mass.) Hospital. HAROLD BRODKEY is the author of *First Love And Other Sorrows* and a novel, *A Party of Animals*, forthcoming from Farrar, Straus and Giroux. GERALD STERN's books are *The Pineys*, *The Naming of the Beasts* and *Rejoicing*.

Amnesty International Publications (53 Theobalds Rd., London, England WCIX8SP and 200 West 72nd St., New York, N.Y. 10024) works in behalf of intellectual and political prisoners in both the communist and non-communist world. The *samizdat* writers publish throughout Russia, often communicating by typewriter in a chain letter distribution.

Anaesthesia Review is published by The Trouser Press (732 S. Forest, Ann Arbor, Mi. 48104) and was begun for "purposes of personal aggrandizement, but the means may redeem our uncertain ends." JOHN GLOWNEY is a student at The University of Michigan, where he has won awards for both his poetry and fiction.

Antaeus (1 W. 30th St., New York, N.Y. 10001), now in its fifth year, publishes on a quarterly basis an international assemblage of fiction, poetry, essays, art and literary documents by both known and unknown authors. AVROM REYZEM (1875–1948) excelled in brief delicate tales that drew on a wide human comedy of Jewish life. ALEXANDER THEROUX is the author of *Three Wogs* and is a lecturer at Harvard. CHARLES OLSON (1910–1970) was called by William Carlos Williams "A major poet with a sweep of understanding of the world, a feeling for other men, that staggers me."

Aphra (P.O. Box 893, Ansonia Station, New York, N.Y. 10023) is a feminist literary magazine which has been published since 1969. MARILYN COFFEY is a feminist, humorist and poet.

Aspen Leaves (P.O. Box 3185, Aspen, Colo. 81611) features poetry, fiction, essays, reviews, interviews, and graphics and is supported by private donations and grants through The Aspen Leaves Literary Foundation. MICHAEL MCMAHON lives and works on a farm in New Hampshire and his work also appears in the Spring 1976 issue of *Aspen Leaves*.

Barlenmir House (413 City Island Ave., New York, N.Y. 10064) has published several dozen books of poetry in its Gallery Series since 1973 and specializes in fine binding and printing. CLARENCE MAJOR was born in Georgia and lives in New York City. His work has appeared in over 100 journals and books.

Blue Cloud Quarterly (Blue Cloud Abbey, Marvin, S.D. 57251) is published by the Benedictine monks of the Abby who work among the Indian people on four reservations in the Dakotas and specializes in Native American themes. PATRICK WORTH GRAY teaches at the University of Nebraska and has published poetry in *Saturday Review*, *Many Smokes*, and *The Lamp In The Spine*.

Blue Wind Press (1206 Spruce, Berkeley, Ca. 94709) was founded "because there wasn't anything on tv." The press publishes medium-sized editions of quality paperback and clothbound fiction and poetry by unknown writers and "works by better known authors that are too interesting for larger publishers." GEORGE MATTINGLY is the author of three books and "currently feeds his landlord as a freelance graphic designer and typographer."

Center (% Carol Bergé, Thomas Jefferson College, Allendale, Mi. 49401)—"no magazine offers more wealth of imagination or variety of talent" said *Margins*. ED SANDERS is the author, among other books, of *The Family*, and was described by Charles Olson as "the finest young poet in America."

The Chariton Review (Northeast Missouri State University, Kirksville, Mo. 63501) publishes semi-annually and features poetry, fiction, reviews, parts-of-novels and translations under the editorship of Andrew Grossbardt. DAVID RAY is professor of English at the University of Missouri, Kansas City, and is editor of *New Letters*.

Chicago Review (University of Chicago, Chicago, Ill. 60637), now in its 30th year of continuous publication, brings together "distinguished work by established authors and younger, less-known writers. Each issue offers new poetry and fiction, unconventional essays and discerning reviews, plus a generous selection of graphics." OCTAVIO PAZ, a critic, poet, and editor, is currently a visiting professor at Harvard. DAVID WAGONER's eighth novel, *Tracker*, was recently published by Atlantic-Little Brown. JOYCE CAROL OATES is a winner of The National Book Award for fiction and is also a frequent contributor to small presses. STEPHEN BERG is a founding editor of *American Poetry Review*.

Cimarron Review (203 B. Morrill Hall, Oklahoma State University, Stillwater, Ok. 74074) publishes a variety of fiction, poetry and non-fiction. At last report, G. K. WUORI lived in West Lafayette, Indiana.

Cold Mountain Press (4406 Duval, Austin, Tx. 78751) publishes poetry, art, photos, post cards, broadsheets and pamphlets. For Michael Hogan's bio see Unicorn Press.

Cosmic Information Agency (P. O. Box 24, E. Lansing, Mich. 48823) publishes *The Lansing Star*, a bi-weekly news/art tabloid for students at Michigan State University and Lansing Community College. "We own ourselves and make our plans as we go along." LAURA PERSHIN is a recent graduate of Michigan State University.

Curbstone Press (321 Jackson St., Willimantic, Ct. 06226) specializes in young American poets and translations of poetry. Founded by Alexander Taylor in 1973, the press has a leftist orientation but publishes non-political books too. JAMES SCULLY is author of *The Marches* and *Avenue of the Americas* and wrote the selected poem while in Santiago de Chile on a Guggenheim grant in 1973–74.

Dacotah Territory (P.O. Box 775, Moorhead, Minn. 56560) was begun in early 1971 "to export some of the tremendous literary energy and talent of the Upper Great Plains, but also to import the best work from anywhere." A chapbook series was started in 1973 and ten titles have appeared so far under The Territorial Press imprint. A Native American anthology is planned for 1976. MICHAEL DENNIS BROWNE teaches at the University of Minnesota and is the author of the poetry collection *The Wife of Winter* (Scribners) and the long poem *Sun Exercises* (Red Studio Press).

Gallimaufry (359 Frederick, San Francisco, Ca. 94117) edited by Mary MacArthur, was established in 1973 as a bi-annual journal of contemporary literary creations. The press also publishes a chapbook series. BRUCE BOSTON's first collection of stories is *Jackbird* (Berkeley Poet's Workship and Press). He is a Yaddo Colony Fellow and assistant editor of *The City Miner*.

Ghost Dance (ATL, EBH, MSU, E. Lansing, Mi. 48823) is edited by Hugh Fox and says "we are trying to avoid repeating ourselves, want newer and more innovative work." TONY QUAGLIANO publishes widely in the small presses. JOHN BENNETT is editor of *Vagabond*.

Goddard Journal (Box 595, Goddard College, Plainfield, Vt. 05667) is a production of "304 Publications", an assortment of students, faculty and "other deviates" at Goddard College and has been published since the 1960's. JACK PULASKI's fiction has appeared in *The Iowa Review* and *Ohio Review*.

Holmgangers Press (22 Ardith Lane, Alamo, Ca. 94507) "sent out our first Holmganger in 1974 and we're still on the dodge," says editor Gary Elder. ART CUELHO edited *Blackjack Magazine* and is "a good unknown poet."

The Hudson Review (65 E. 55th St., New York, N.Y. 10022) publishes poetry, fiction, translations, essays, literary criticism, chronicles of music, art, photography, theater, film and dance, reports on cultural developments from many countries, and book reviews. NAOMI LAZARD teaches poetry at New York's 92nd Street YMCA and is the author of *Cry of The Peacocks* (Harcourt), a collection of her poetry.

The Iowa Review (The University of Iowa, Iowa City, Iowa 52242) is now in its seventh year and publishes poetry, fiction and criticism quarterly. RONALD SUKENICK's most recent novel *98.6* was published by The Fiction Collective.

Kansas Quarterly (Kansas State University, Manhattan, Ks. 66506) is a continuation of *Kansas Magazine* first published in 1872 and devoted to short stories, poetry and an infrequent drama, with alternative issues featuring art, history and literary criticism. H.E. FRANCIS lives in Huntsville, Alabama and won the 1973 Iowa Short Fiction Award, the annual *Kansas Quarterly* Award for "A Chronicle of Love" and will be featured in *The O'Henry Prize Collection* 1976 for the same story.

ManRoot (P.O. Box 982, South San Francisco, Ca. 94080) "is involved with issues" and recently devoted an entire issue to the poetry of the late JACK SPICER. Spicer's poetry was also celebrated in 1975 by the publication of *The Collected Books of Jack Spicer* (Black Sparrow).

Montana Gothic (Black Stone Press, P.O. Box 756, Missoula, Montana 59801) is an independent journal of poetry, literature and graphics founded in 1975 in response to the "ascendency of the imagination in Montana." JANE BAILEY's first book, *Pomegranate, Erotic Poems*, will be published by Black Stone Press this year.

Latitudes Press (3514 Lafayette Ave., Austin, Tx. 78722) was founded by Rochelle and Robert Bonazzi and specializes in innovative fiction, primarily by younger American writers. MARVIN COHEN is the author of six books—four collections of fiction, a novel and a meditative book on baseball.

Liberation Magazine (339 Lafayette St., New York, N.Y. 10012) is in its 20th year of publication as "an independent radical monthly publishing articles, fiction, poems and graphics and working toward a more human society." STEVE PACKARD lives in Chicago and teaches in a free school. A former member of Newsreel film collective, he is writing a book about his experiences in the Movement.

The Little Magazine (P.O. Box 207, Cathedral Station, New York, N.Y. 10025) publishes poetry, fiction, reviews, parts-of-novels, long poems, enjoys a circulation of about 900 and comes out four or five times a year. ADRIENNE RICH lives in New York, is the author of several poetry collections and won The National Book Award for Poetry.

Ontario Review (6000 Riverside Dr., E. Windsor, Ontario, Canada N8S1B6) was founded in 1974 as a "North American Journal of the Arts" with particular interest in poetry, fiction and essays on the humanities. SAUL BELLOW has won the National Book Award three times. ARNOLD MANDELL is Chairman of the Department of Psychiatry at The University of California at San Diego.

Parnassus: Poetry In Review (216 W. 89th St., New York, N.Y. 10024) is a general review of poetry published from the Parnassus Book Shop. EUGENE B. REDMOND has been poet in residence at Sacramento State College. He is the author of *In A Time of Rain and Desire* (Black River).

The Partisan Review (Rutgers University, New Brunswick, N.J. 08903) has been an American literary press fixture for several decades. William Phillips, Linda Healey, and Steven Marcus are the principal editors. JOSEPH WEIZENBAUM and ROBERT K. MARTIN teach at universities, as does WILLIAM GASS, who is also the author of *Omensetter's Luck*, *In The Heart of The Heart of The Country* and other books.

Pentagram Press (6820 W. Neil Place, Milwaukee, Wis. 53209) will soon have over 20 titles in print since its founding in 1973. TOM MONTAG is the editor/publisher of *Margins*.

The Penumbra Press (Box 12, Lisbon, Iowa, 52253) was founded in 1971 and operates from a country house near Lisbon. Its primary objective is "to continue the tradition of fine printing through publication of contemporary poetry and short fiction." TESS GALLAGHER has been published in *Antaeus*, *The American Poetry Review* and *The New Yorker*.

Ploughshares (Box 529, Cambridge, Mass. 02139) is an independent literary journal serially edited by New England poets and writers to reflect different and contrasting points of view. EUGENIO MON-

TALE won the 1975 Nobel Prize for Literature. CARLOS DRUM-MOND DE ANDRADE is the most distinguished living Brazilian poet.

Pitcairn Press Inc. (388 Franklin St., Cambridge, Mass. 02139) was set up in 1975 by the author, JOHN H. BEAUVAIS, to publish his first book of poems, *A Flight Of Arrows*, where the selected poem appears.

Poetry NOW (3118 K. St., Eureka, Ca. 95501) is an eclectic poetry journal appearing six times a year in tabloid newspaper format. HAROLD WITT's poetic epic about small town America, *Winesburg by The Sea*, will be published in 1976 by Thorp Springs Press.

Raincrow Press (2903 Marshall Ave., Cincinnati, Ohio, 45220) published its first book in 1975, DAVID WEISSMAN's *Falling Toward Thanksgiving*. Founding editors are Alan Basting, Joseph Darwish, and Christopher Smith.

Release Press (200 Carroll St., Brooklyn NY 11231) founded in 1973 initially published pamphlets of poetry and drawings and then expanded into "all matter of printed paper from postcards to full size books." *City Joys* is JACK ANDERSON's third collection of poems. He was the recipient of a National Endowment for the Arts creative writing fellowship in 1973–74.

San Marcos Press (P.O. Box 53, Cerrillos, NM 87010) prints and publishes from a small ranch about twenty miles south of Santa Fe. WILLIAM EASTLAKE is the author of three novels and the forthcoming *Dancers In The Scalp House* (Viking).

St. Andrews Review (St. Andrews Presbyterian College, Laurinburg, N.C. 28352) was founded in 1970 and is published twice a year. MARVIN WEAVER lives in Fayetteville, N.C. and heads the city's arts council. In 1976 St. Andrew's Press will publish his first collection *Hearts and Gizzards*.

The Seamark Press (Box 2, Iowa City, Iowa 52240) has been publishing since 1968 and specializes in poetry, translation, fiction and essays, and in pamphlets and books designed, typeset and hand-printed by a staff of two. HOWARD ZIMMON "Can't find a thing to say about himself."

Second Coming Press (P.O. Box 31246, San Francisco, Ca. 94131) published five books of poetry in 1975 on a grant from the National Endowment for the Arts and will do several more in 1976. GENE FOWLER is an ex-San Quentin convict whose work has appeared in numerous small presses. The late WILLIAM WANTLING died in 1974 at the age of 41 and was widely published in the small presses of the early 60's.

The Smith Press (5 Beekman St., New York, N.Y. 10038) is under the editorship of Harry Smith with Sidney Bernard and publishes *The Newsletter on The State of The Culture, The Smith* magazine, and *Newsart* as well as various books, such as H.L. VAN BRUNT's *Indian Territory* and *Uncertainties*. Poet KARL KOPP recently moved from Arkansas to New Mexico: "I will have to play an ever more active role inside a deeper community than I have yet known."

The Southern Review (Drawer D, University Station, Baton Rouge, La, 70803) was first published at Louisana State University from 1935 through 1942 under Robert Penn Warren and Cleanth Brooks. The magazine was re-established in 1965 under Lewis P. Simpson and Donald E. Stanford. ANNE TYLER's novel *Searching for Caleb* has just been published by Knopf.

Spectrum (P.O. Box 14800, Santa Barbara, Ca. 93107) is a literary magazine put out by the University of California at Santa Barbara, staffed by students and presenting both student and professional work. In 1972 and 1973 it was awarded first prize in the College Literary Magazine Competition sponsored by the Coordinating Council of Literary Magazines. RAYMOND CARVER has appeared in *Esquire, Harper's Bazaar, Iowa Review, December*, The O'Henry Prize collections and is the author of the McGraw-Hill/Gordon Lish book *Will You Please Be Quiet, Please*.

Sun Press (456 Riverside Dr., New York, N.Y. 10027) issues *Sun* magazine twice yearly and beginning with the publication of *Lauds* by Harvey Shapiro has published eight books to date. HARVEY SHAPIRO has published six collections of poetry, conducted poetry workshops at Columbia and Yale, received a Rockefeller Foundation Fellowship and edits *The New York Times Book Review*.

The Sunstone Press (P.O. Box 2321, Santa Fe, N.M. 87501) has issued fifty titles since its founding in 1971.

Thorp Springs Press (2311-C Woolsey, Berkeley, Ca. 94705) "publishes the best contemporary poetry, fiction, and drama available" and has done so for six years. SHEILA NICKERSON, a native New Yorker, has lived in Alaska since 1971 and has published several volumes with Thorp Springs.

TriQuarterly (101 University Hall, Northwestern University, Evanston, Ill. 60201) features poetry, fiction, articles, art, photos, cartoons, interviews, satire, criticism, parts-of-novels, long poems, collages, plays and concrete art under the editorship of Elliott Anderson. DAVID KRANES lives in New Hampshire and is the author of *Margins* (Knopf). MORRIS DICKSTEIN is the author of a study of Keats, won a Guggenheim fellowship and is at work on a book about the 1960's.

Undine (244 Fifth Ave., New York, N.Y. 10018) is a literary magazine done in calligraphy. For HARVEY SHAPIRO see Sun Press.

Unicorn Press (P.O. Box 3307, Greensboro, N.C. 27402) was founded in 1966 and since then has published nearly one hundred books, plus broadsides and postcards. MICHAEL HOGAN was born in New England and is now a prisoner in the maximum security block in Arizona State Prison.

Word-Smith (1817 S. Vogdes St., Philadelphia, Pa. 19143) publishes "the best poetry, fiction and criticism received and offers readers a variety of examples of language under maximum pressure to tell the truth." RHODA SCHWARTZ's published volumes include *In the Cannibal Hut* and *The Burned Letters of Felice to Franz*.

Xanadu (1704 Auburn Rd., Wantagh, N.Y. 11793) is published twice a year since 1974 and holds no allegiance to any clique or school, according to editors Charles Fishman and George William Fisher. DIANE CHAPMAN's first book *Final Degree* was recently published. She is editor of *Sandcutters* poetry quarterly.

Yardbird Reader (P.O. Box 2370, Station A, Berkeley, Ca. 94702) is a division of Yardbird Publishing Co., founded in 1972 to encourage black, feminist, third world and experimental writing. COLLEEN MCELROY is in the English department at the University of Washington, Seattle.

CONTENTS

xxxii   *Contents*

THE
PUSHCART PRIZE:
BEST OF THE
SMALL PRESSES

CORDIALS

fiction by DAVID KRANES

from TRIQUARTERLY

nominated by Gordon Lish

It WASN'T UNTIL THE WAITRESS brought her Benedictine and she felt her first contraction that Lynn even thought of herself as being pregnant. She was anatomically thin and had managed to conceal the fact for well over seven months, with a regimen of boiled turnips and cold consommé—and the reminder was badly timed to say the least. She had wanted to sleep with David Marker from the moment she and Jack had spent a Saturday with the Markers sailfishing three months ago out at Wildwood, but there'd been interferences at just about every point. She had called him; he had called her; they had tried one afternoon at her apartment only to find her son Adam home from Hotchkiss as a surprise. Fall in New York is a difficult

time to have an affair: everything starting up, schedules over-
crowded again; and so this evening was to have been an island for
both of them.

"Something the matter?" David asked her.

She smiled. "No."

"You winced."

"Just anxious, I guess."

"As am I."

She rubbed the knuckles of his hand, climbing each ridge, knead-
ing the loose skin in the depressions with her forefinger and thumb.

"Do you want to leave now?" he asked.

"Let's finish our drinks," she said, her eyes partly on her watch,
wondering when the next contraction would come. It came seven
minutes later. She drained her glass: "All through," she said.

David smiled, breathed in his Drambuie and drained it. "Let's
go," he said.

He helped her on with her coat. "Where are we . . . ?"

"A friend lent me his studio."

"Where?"

"Rowayton."

"That's an hour."

"Fifty minutes. And it's a nice Indian summer. We'll drive with
the windows down. Sea smell's an aphrodisiac."

"I don't need an aphrodisiac." Her voice was surprisingly soft and
quiet.

David nodded to the maitre de, and pushed the door open; she
went out. "It's a great place—this place—this studio."

Lynn breathed the late September West 52nd Street smells, and
felt another contraction coming on.

When they cloverleafed onto the Merritt Parkway, the tugs were
coming regularly, just under five minutes. Both the front windows
were down. David had the heater on, her coat off. She had her face
against his neck, her jaw pressed there. She'd worn no bra—she
didn't really need to—and he was moving the tips of his right middle
fingers over the nipple, under her burgundy knit.

"You're perspiring," he said, trying to make it sound playful.

"Yes." She bit at him. "It's the heater. The blower's going right up
my dress." She knew, in fact, it was probably lactating.

"Rowayton?" There was a hum in her voice.

"There are fourteen-foot ceilings," David traced her neck. "And a fireplace."

"Had you planned on using the fireplace?"

"For a fire, sure; not for us."

"I don't know if I can wait." Lynn felt her body tightening again, watched the speedometer climb from 70 to 85.

"You'll love it," David said to her; "it's on the shore. You can hear the ocean. Waves. It's a great rhythm. Great keeping time to. Natural. Nothing rushed." He let his hand slide slowly down to her leg. She picked it up, kissed it. She looked at her watch: three minutes and twenty seconds; she picked up and kissed his hand when she felt the next contraction again; three minutes and fifteen.

"How long until we get there?" she asked him.

"Twenty—twenty-five minutes." He played with her nipple again. She held her breath. "You're really remarkable," he told her. "I've been clawing half New York's concrete for three months."

"Me too," she said. "I've been having the most amazing fantasies."

"I'm not very good at waiting," David told her, then smiled.

"Nor am I." She thought about it; it was true. "I wait for very few things."

"Waiting fantasies are strange." He began to slide his hand down to her abdomen. "They make you feel almost adolescent." She picked his hand up again, kissed it, checked her watch. "Your heart's jumping."

"There's a motel in Mamaroneck," she said.

"One quarter hour, *max*," he told her. The pains were coming every two minutes plus.

When they pulled in beside the studio and cut their lights, Lynn's spasms were only a minute, or slightly more, apart. Like a school-boy, David started to undress her in the car; she put two hands against his chest: "Let's go inside."

He smiled; "O.K.," then kissed her eyes, let himself out, and walked around to her door. She could smell the sea, as he'd predicted, and it smelled as though her own body had become huge, grown unlit and infinite and moved outside to become anatomy in the night around her. She became her own child briefly—undelivered though dependent and scared. She thought of when she was fourteen, parking out near Coney Island with a boy named Arnold, the "Tennessee Waltz" on the car radio, how her whole mouth had trembled, how her thigh muscles had gone slack. She heard the door button click, felt the sea wind against her hair, smelled the blown redolence of herself.

Lynn didn't like being aggressive. She had always hated that role, it ruined everything; but she pulled David inside and when he wanted to get a fire going, she said *no*.

"Why?"

"Please."

"Lynn, that's the whole . . ."

"Afterward!"

"I may want to sleep."

"Please!"

"O.K."

She pulled him to the bed.

She had continually fantasized David's undressing her, three months lived it in her mind: its being gentle, slow; kisses, where he placed them, breast, belly, hip; when they came. And so against her better judgment she let him, let it work out, let the mind come true. True: she stood there, in the dark, arching, moving, turning slightly for him on the balls of her heels. And David carried it off: it was worth the concealment, worth the pain. The hands played, the kisses came on time, in form. She felt the zipper on her dress move down, slipped her arms out, felt the dress fall around her hips. She felt her water break. "David," she said, and pulled him in.

She dug at him, made his shoulder bleed, bit his face. It helped to get the pain out. He was trembling, "Jesus! Jesus-God! Jesus, Lynn," he said. "God, come on! Off our feet! Off our feet! Talk about adolescents! God!"

"Then get undressed," she told him.

"You!"

"David . . ."

"Do it. You—"

His jacket was already off. His neck was moving on its base; his breath, heavy, wet. "Christ, you're incredible! You're incredible!" he said.

She couldn't help it. They were somewhere between twenty and thirty seconds apart now, and the pain and pressure was too much. She grabbed the collar of his shirt and tore, ripped it down, spread it, snapping all the buttons in a line. They landed, light as crickets, on the rug. "Fantastic!" David was moaning. "Oh, fantastic! Wow!"

She yanked his belt. "Oh, God!" She felt it uncinch. She broke the button above the fly and heard the zipper whine. The pants fell past his knees.

"O.K." she managed, her voice strained and tight, "You do the rest."

"No. Please." He was rocking. "You. The shoes!"

"David . . ."

"O.K. I'm sorry," He stepped out of things. "I'm sorry." He let other things drop. She saw his shape sit on the bed's edge, pull his shoes off. She didn't know how she was going to make it as she removed her panties and came close.

He pulled the bedspread down. She found a wastebasket and slid it beside the bed. She moved against him, kept his hands on her back, pressing her whole anatomy hard, violently down, against, trying to create hard enough pressure to displace some of the pain. She screamed. She dug in. She fought against him with her fists and knees. He kept bellowing sounds to match hers, saying things like: *God*—he thought his fantasies were pretty advanced, but—*Jesus*—he realized now that they were—*Christ*—naive. But as they tore and fought against each other, Lynn felt herself giving way and knew that what she'd hoped for was impossible. She could not last. She could not hold out.

She slid down his body slowly, marking it with her teeth, clearing herself as where she could. When the baby came, it came easily and she was able crudely to slice the cord, get everything in the wastebasket and cover it with the bedspread without really losing much of the rhythm of the foreplay. She submitted to David pulling at her, at her shoulders, slid back up along him, joining, both of them, three minutes later, coming almost together under the bloodsoak of sheets.

David lay with his head off the far edge of the bed, making sounds. Lynn played one hand over his ribs, blew breath gently against his sweat. She could smell herself—herself, the ocean and her own birth, but could not keep them apart. She thought she heard a steamer, way out in Long Island Sound. Shortly afterward, when David showered, she took the basket out to the small pier of the studio front and emptied it into the sea. Standing there briefly, she tasted herself again, her own fetality, felt the darkness—warm, salty, moist, in membranes layered out and out around her. The moon, real and untelevised above, seemed a strange opening in space, a place she might ultimately move to, go. She ached, but could not feel her body. It was an abstract ache, one in air.

Inside, they came together one more time: much quicker, less violent, more studied, more synchronized. David did not shower. Instead, he dressed himself hurriedly and lit a long cigar.

"Did I hurt you?" he asked. "I'm always afraid . . . "

"No," Lynn reassured him from the bathroom. She stopped herself with toilet paper, pulled on her panties, and dropped her dress over her head. "No." Somehow it was true.

"Hey—you start?"

"What?"

"Your period start?"

" . . . Yes."

In the car, on the way back to Manhattan, they talked enthusiastically about St. Croix.

Her husband, Jack, was sitting on the long couch going through briefs in his blue bathrobe when she came in. There was a small snifter of crème de cacao on the coffee table to his right. They said hello. She kissed him on his forehead and hung up her coat.

"Where you been?"

"Theater."

"What'd you see?"

"*Long Day's Journey.*"

"How was it?"

"Fantastic.' ' She straightened her hair.

"Great play." Jack wrote a sentence in the margin of his brief.

"There's some triple sec there, if you want."

"Thanks."

"Picked it up on the way home."

She poured a cordial glass half full. The smell of orange reminded her somehow of Christmas, kumquats from Florida fruit packages she had bitten into in lost distant Decembers as a child. She crossed the room. She stood in front of their window wall, looking out. The lights beyond, below, all the bunched thousands of them, looked like perforations. She stared at the reflected milk stains on her dress, her reflection seeming to spread out across the perforations to surround her until, searching the distance, she was gone.

"Did you find it?"

"Hmmm?"

"Find the triple sec."

"Yes. Fine. Thanks."

"See the letter from Ad?"

"No. What's he say?"

"They beat Taft 21 to 20. He pulled a ligament in his knee. He's been having whirlpools. Nothing serious. They took X rays at the Sharon Hospital. He's seeing Cynthia Kaufmann this weekend. Listen—do you want to?"

"Hmmm?"

"You at all horny?"

She pressed the cordial glass against her lips. The fruity taste rose up, viscous, wet; it made orange seeds of her eyes. "Maybe later," she said.

"Can't hear you."

She took the glass away, wet her lips. "Maybe later."

"Sure, O.K."

Her eyes watered. She experienced the only moment akin to incest she had ever felt. She thought of her son, Adam, in the whirlpool. Her knee hurt.

MISSING THE TRAIL

by DAVID WAGONER

from CHICAGO REVIEW

nominated by Joyce Carol Oates

Only a moment ago you were thinking of something
Different, the sky or yesterday or the wind,
But suddenly it's yourself
Alone, strictly alone, having taken a wrong turn
somewhere behind you, having missed the trail,
Bewildered, now uncertain
Whether to turn back, bear left or right, or flounder ahead
Stubbornly, breaking new ground out of pride or panic,
Or to raise your voice
Out of fear that screaming is the only universal language.
If you come to your senses, all six, taking your time,
The spot where you're standing
Is your best hope. When it first dawns on you you're lost,
You must memorize everything around you, scouring
That place for landmarks,
For rocks, bushes, or trees you'd know again in the dark,
For anything unmistakable to return to,
Or some ragged signal
That can reestablish your eyes, even the shirt off your back,
While you branch out from there, the trunk of your life,
In all directions,
Trying to stumble once more across the vaguest of trails
You may want to follow again for some strange reason
Toward somewhere or other
You may now (having been lost and found) barely remember
Wanting to get to, past the middle of nowhere,
At your wit's end.

b b b

THE ARTIFICIAL FAMILY

fiction by ANNE TYLER

from THE SOUTHERN REVIEW

nominated by Reynolds Price

THE FIRST FULL SENTENCE that Mary ever said to him was, "Did you know I have a daughter?" Toby was asking her to dinner. He had just met her at a party—a long-haired girl in a floor-length gingham dress—and the invitation was instant, offered out of desperation because she was already preparing to leave and he wasn't sure he could ever find her again. Now, how did her daughter enter into this? Was she telling him that she was married? Or that she couldn't go out in the evenings? "No," said Toby. "I didn't know."

"Well, now you do," she said. Then she wrote her address down for him and left, and Toby spent the rest of the evening clutching the scrap of paper in his pocket for fear of losing it.

11

The daughter was five years old. Her name was Samantha, and it suited her: she was an old-fashioned child with two thick braids and a solemn face. When she and her mother stood side by side, barefoot, wearing their long dresses, they might have been about to climb onto a covered wagon. They presented a solid front. Their eyes were a flat, matching blue. "Well!" Toby would say, after he and Samantha knew each other better. "Shall we all *three* go somewhere? Shall we take a picnic lunch? Visit the zoo?" Then the blue would break up into darker colors, and they would smile—but it was the mother who smiled first. The child was the older of the two. She took longer to think things over.

They would go to the Baltimore Zoo and ride the tiny passenger train. Sitting three abreast on the narrow seat—Toby's arm around Mary, Samantha scrunched between them—they rattled past dusty-looking deer fenced in among the woods, through a tunnel where the younger children screamed, alongside a parade of wooden cartoon animals which everyone tried to identify. "That's Bullmoose! There's Bugs Bunny!" Only Samantha said nothing. She had no television set. Bugs Bunny was a stranger to her. She sat very straight, with her hands clasped between her knees in her long skirt, and Toby looked down at her and tried to piece out her father from the curve of her cheek and the tilt of her nose. Her eyes were her mother's, but surely that rounded chin came from her father's side. Had her father had red hair? Was that what gave Samantha's brown braids that coppery sheen? He didn't feel that he could ask straight out because Mary had slammed a door on the subject. All she said was that she had run away with Samantha after two years of marriage. Then once, discussing some earlier stage in Samantha's life, she pulled out a wallet photo to show him: Samantha as a baby, in her mother's lap. "Look at you!" Toby said. "You had your hair up! You had lipstick on! You were wearing a sweater and skirt. Look at Samantha in her party dress!" The photo stunned him, but Mary hardly noticed. "Oh, yes," she said, closing her wallet, "I was very straight back then." And that was the last time she mentioned her marriage. Toby never saw the husband, or heard anything about him. There seemed to be no visiting arrangements for the child.

Mornings Mary worked in an art gallery. She had to leave Samantha with a teen-aged babysitter after kindergarten closed for the summer. "Summers! I hate them," she said. "All the time I'm at work I'm wondering how Samantha is." Toby said, "Why not let *me* stay with her. You know how Samantha and I get along." He was a graduate student with a flexible schedule; and besides, he seized on every excuse to entrench himself deeper in Mary's life. But Mary said, "No, I couldn't ask you to do that." And she went on paying Carol, and paying her again in the evenings when they went out somewhere. They went to dinner, or to movies, or to Toby's rambling apartment. They always came back early. "Carol's mother will kill me!" Mary would say, and she would gather up her belongings and run ahead of Toby to his car. When he returned from taking her home his apartment always smelled of her: a clean, straw smell, like burlap. Her bobby pins littered the bed and the crevices of the sofa. Strands of her long hairs tended to get wound around the rollers of his carpet sweeper. When he went to sleep the cracked bell of her voice threaded through all his dreams.

At the end of August, they were married in a civil ceremony. They had known each other five months. *Only* five months, Toby's parents said. They wrote him a letter pointing out all their objections. How would he support three on a university grant? How would he study? What did he want with someone else's child? The child: that was what they really minded. The ready-made grandchild. How could he love some other man's daughter? But Toby had never been sure he would know how to love his *own* children; so the question didn't bother him. He liked Samantha. And he liked the idea of her: the single, solitary treasure carried away from the disaster of the sweater-and-skirt marriage. If he himself ever ran away, what would he choose to take? His grandfather's watch, his favorite chamois shirt, eight cartons of books, some still unread, his cassette tape recorder—each object losing a little more worth as the list grew longer. Mary had taken Samantha, and nothing else. He envied both of them.

They lived in his apartment, which was more than big enough. Mary quit her job. Samantha started first grade. They were happy but guarded, still, working too hard at getting along. Mary turned the spare bedroom into a study for Toby, with a "Private" sign on the door. "Never go in there," she told Samantha. "That's Toby's place to be alone." "But I don't *want* to be alone," Toby said. "I'm alone all day at the lab." Nobody seemed to believe him. Samantha passed the doorway of his study on tiptoe, never even peeking inside. Mary scrupulously avoided littering the apartment with her own possessions. Toby was so conscientious a father that he might have written himself a timetable: At seven, play Old Maid. At seven-thirty, read a story. At eight o'clock, offer a piggyback ride to bed. Mary he treated like glass. He kept thinking of her first marriage; his greatest fear was that she would leave him.

Every evening, Samantha walked around to Toby's lab to call him for supper. In the midst of reaching for a beaker or making a notation he would look up to find her standing there, absolutely silent. Fellow students gave her curious looks. She ignored them. She concentrated on Toby, watching him with a steady blue gaze that gave all his actions a new importance. Would he feel this flattered if she were his own? He didn't think so. In their peculiar situation— nearly strangers, living in the same house, sharing Mary—they had not yet started to take each other for granted. Her coming for him each day was purely a matter of choice, which he imagined her spending some time over before deciding; and so were the sudden, rare smiles which lit her face when he glanced down at her during the walk home.

At Christmastime Toby's parents flew down for a visit. They stayed four days, each one longer than the day before. Toby's mother had a whole new manner which kept everyone at arm's length. She would look at Samantha and say, "My, she's thin! Is her father thin, Mary? Does her father have those long feet?" She would go out to the kitchen and say, "I see you've done something with Toby's little two-cup coffeepot. Is this *your* pot, Mary? May I use it?" Everything she said was meant to remind them of their artificiality: the wife was someone else's first, the child was not Toby's. But her effect was to draw them closer together. The three of them formed an alliance against Mrs. Scott and her silent husband, who lent her his support merely by not shutting her up. On the second evening Toby escaped to his study and Samantha and Mary joined him, one by one, sliding through the crack in his door to sit giggling silently with him over a game of dominoes. One afternoon they said they had to take Samantha to her art lesson and they snuck off to a Walt Disney movie instead, and stayed there in the dark for two hours eating popcorn and Baby Ruths and endless strings of licorice.

Toby's parents went home, but the alliance continued. The sense of effort had disappeared. Toby's study became the center of the apartment, and every evening while he read Mary sat with him and sewed and Samantha played with cut-outs at their feet. Mary's pottery began lining the mantel and bookshelves. She pounded in nails all over the kitchen and hung up her saucepans. Samantha's formal bedtime ritual changed to roughhousing, and she and Toby pounded through the rooms and pelted each other with sofa cushions and ended up in a tangle on the hallway carpet.

Now Samantha was growing unruly with her mother. Talking back. Disobeying. Toby was relieved to see it. Before she had been so good that she seemed pathetic. But Mary said, "I don't know what I'm going to do with that child. She's getting out of hand."

"She seems all right to *me*," said Toby.

"I knew you'd say that. It's your fault she's changed like this, too. You've spoiled her."

"*Spoiled* her?"

"You dote on her, and she knows it," Mary said. She was folding the laundry, moving crisply around the bedroom with armloads of sheets and towels. Nowadays she wore sweaters and skirts—more practical for housework—and her loafers tapped across the floor with an efficient sound that made him feel she knew what she was talking about. "You give her everything she asks for," she said. "Now she doesn't listen to *me* any more."

"But there's nothing wrong with giving her things. Is there?"

"If you had to live with her all day long," Mary said, "eighteen hours a day, the way I do, you'd think twice before you said that."

But how could he refuse anything to Samantha? With him, she was never disobedient. She shrieked with him over pointless riddles, she asked him unanswerable questions on their walks home from the lab, she punched at him ineffectually, her thumbs tucked inside her fists, when he called her Sam. The only time he was ever angry with her was once when she stepped into the path of a car without looking. "Samantha!" he yelled, and he yanked her back and shook her until she cried. Inside he had felt his stomach lurch, his heart sent out a wave of heat and his knees shook. The purple marks of his fingers stayed on Samantha's arm for days afterward. Would he have been any more terrified if the child were his own? New opportunities for fear were everywhere, now that he was a family man. Samantha's walk from school seemed long and underpoliced, and every time he called home without an answer he imagined that Mary had run away from him and he would have to get through life without her. "I think we should have another baby," he told Mary, although of course he knew that increasing the number of people he loved would not make any one of them more expendable. All Mary said was, "Do you?"

"I love that little girl. I really love her. I'd like to have a whole *armload* of little girls. Did you ever think I would be so good at loving people?"

"Yes," said Mary.

"I didn't. Not until I met you. I'd like to *give* you things. I'd like to sit you and Samantha down and pile things in your laps. Don't you ever feel that way?"

"Women don't," said Mary. She slid out of his hands and went to the sink, where she ran cold water over some potatoes. Lately she had started wearing her hair pinned up, out of the way. She looked carved, without a stray wisp or an extra line, smooth to the fingertips, but when Toby came up behind her again she ducked away and went to the stove. "Men are the only ones who have that much feeling left to spare," she said. "Women's love gets frittered away: every day a thousand little demands for milk and bandaids and swept floors and clean towels."

"I don't believe that," said Toby.

But Mary was busy regulating the flame under the potatoes now, and she didn't argue with him.

For Easter, Toby bought Samantha a giant prepacked Easter basket swaddled in pink cellophane. It was a spur-of-the-moment purchase—he had gone to the all-night drugstore for pipe tobacco, seen this basket and remembered suddenly that tomorrow was Easter Sunday. Wouldn't Samantha be expecting some sort of celebration? He hated to think of her returning to school empty-handed, when everyone else had chocolate eggs or stuffed rabbits. But when he brought the basket home—rang the doorbell and waited, obscured behind the masses of cellophane like some comical florist's-messenger—he saw that he had made a mistake. Mary didn't like the basket. "How come you bought a thing like that?" she asked him.

"Tomorrow's Easter."

"Easter? Why Easter? We don't even go to church."

"We celebrated Christmas, didn't we?"

"Yes, but—and Easter's not the question," Mary said. "It's the basket." She reached out and touched the cellophane, which shrank beneath her fingers. "We never *used* to buy baskets. Before I've always hidden eggs and let her hunt for them in the morning, and then she dyes them herself."

"Oh, I thought people had jellybeans and things," Toby said.

"*Other* people, maybe. Samantha and I do it differently."

"Wouldn't she like to have what her classmates have?"

"She isn't trying to keep up with the *Joneses*, Toby," Mary said. "And how about her teeth? How about her stomach? Do I always have to be the heavy, bringing these things up? Why is it you get to shower her with love and gifts, and then it's me that takes her to the dentist?"

"Oh, let's not go into *that* again," Toby said.

Then Mary, who could never be predicted, said, "All right," and stopped the argument. "It was nice of you to think of it, anyway," she said formally, taking the basket. "I know Samantha will like it."

Samantha did like it. She treasured every jellybean and marsh-mallow egg and plastic chick; she telephoned a friend at seven in the morning to tell her about it. But even when she threw her arms around Toby's neck, smelling of sugar and cellophane, all he felt was a sense of defeat. Mary's face was serene and beautiful, like a mask. She continued to move farther and farther away from him, with her lips perpetually curved in a smile and no explanations at all.

In June, when school closed, Mary left him for good. He came home one day to find a square of paper laid flat on a club sandwich. The sight of it thudded instantly against his chest, as if he had been expecting it all along. "I've gone," the note said. His name was nowhere on it. It might have been the same note she sent her first husband—retrieved, somehow, and saved in case she found another use for it. Toby sat down and read it again, analyzed each loop of handwriting for any sign of indecision or momentary, rever-sible anger. Then he ate the club sandwich, every last crumb, without realizing he was doing so, and after that he pushed his plate away and lowered his head into his hands. He sat that way for several minutes before he thought of Samantha.

It was Monday evening—the time when she would just be finish-ing with her art lesson. He ran all the way, jaywalking and dodging cars and waving blindly at the drivers who honked. When he arrived in the dingy building where the lessons were given he found he was too early. The teacher still murmured behind a closed door. Toby sat down, panting, on a bench beneath a row of coat hooks. Flashes of old TV programs passed through his head. He saw himself blurred and bluish on a round-cornered screen—one of those mysteriously partnerless television parents who rear their children with more grace and tact and unselfishness than any married couple could ever hope for. Then the classroom door opened. The teacher came out in her smock, ringed by six-year-olds. Toby stood up and said, "Mrs.—um. Is Samantha Glover here?"

The teacher turned. He knew what she was going to say as soon as she took a breath; he hated her so much he wanted to grab her by the neck and slam her head against the wall. "Samantha?" she said. "Why, no, Mr. Scott, Samantha didn't come today."

On the walk back, he kept his face stiff and his eyes unfocused. People stared at him. Women turned to look after him, frowning, curious to see the extent of the damage. He barely noticed them. He floundered up the stairs to his apartment, felt his way to the sofa and sat down heavily. There was no need to turn the lights on. He knew already what he would find: toys and saucepans, Mary's skirts and sweaters, Samantha's new short dresses. All they would have taken with them, he knew, was their long gingham gowns and each other.

🔥 🔥 🔥

THE GRIOTS WHO KNEW BRER FOX

by COLLEEN J. MCELROY

from YARDBIRD READER

nominated by Ishmael Reed

There are old drunks among the tenements,

old men who have been

                                                              lost

forever from families, shopping centers

starched shirts and

                                                    birthdays.

They are the griots, the story tellers
whose faces are knotted and swollen

              into a black patchwork
              of open sores and
              old scabs; disease
              transforms the nose
              into cabbage; the eyes
              are dried egg yolks.

They grind old tobacco between scabby gums
like ancient scarabs rolling dung from tombs

in their

                                        mother country.

In this country, they are scenic, part of the

view from Route 1, Old Town.

Don't miss them; they sit in doorways
of boarded houses in the part of town
that's nested between wide roads, roads
named for English kings and tourists.

> These old men sit like moldy stumps
> among the broken bricks of narrow
> carriage streets, streets paved with
> the Spirit of '76, the Westward Movement
> and Oz.

The old men never travel the wide roads;

they sit in the dusk, dark skinned as Aesop,

remember their youth. They chant stories

to keep themselves awake another day,

> tales of young girls bathing in kitchens
>
> before wood stoves, smells of
>
> > the old South,
>
> or Northern tales of babies bitten by rats,
>
> women who have left them or how they
>
> were once rich.

They'll spin a new Brer Rabbit story for a nickel;

tell you how he slipped past the whistle-slick fox

to become

> the Abomey king.

But you must listen closely,
it moves fast, their story;
skipping and jumping childlike,
the moral hidden in an enchanted forest

                                 of word games.

         These stories are priceless,
         prized by movie moguls
         who dream of Saturday matinees
         and full houses.

You have to look beyond the old men's faces,

beyond the rat that waits to nibble the hand

when they sleep. The face is anonymous,

                       you can find it anywhere

but the words are as prized

as the curved tusks of the bull elephant.

🔥 🔥 🔥

THE DEATH OF YURY GALANSKOV

by THE RUSSIAN *SAMIZDAT* UNDERGROUND

from A CHRONICLE OF CURRENT EVENTS, 28–31

published by Amnesty International

nominated by Pushcart Press

(editor's note: what follows is a preface by Amnesty International in London and New York. The sub-headline "A Chronicle of Current Events" begins the portions from the Russian underground)

PREFACE
by Amnesty International

A Chronicle of Current Events *was initially produced in 1968 as a bi-monthly journal. In the spring of that year members of the Soviet Civil Rights Movement created the journal with the stated intention of publicizing issues and events related to Soviet citizens' efforts to exercise fundamental human liberties. On the title page of every issue of* A Chronicle of Current Events *there appears the text of Article 19 of the Universal Declaration of Human Rights, which calls for universal freedom of opinion and expression. The authors are guided by the principle that such universal guarantees of human rights, and similar guarantees in their domestic law, should be firmly adhered to in their own country and elsewhere. They feel that "it is essential that truthful information about violations of basic human rights in the Soviet Union should be available to all who are interested in it." The* Chronicles *consist almost entirely of accounts of such violations.*

Although the Constitution of the USSR (article 125) guarantees "freedom of the press", the Soviet state officially reserves for itself and for officially-approved organizations the right to decide what may or may not appear in print. Since 1930 publishing has been a virtual monopoly of the Soviet state, and printing has been a complete monopoly. In the past decade and a half many Soviet citizens whose writings have not been published through official channels have reproduced their work in samizdat *form. These* samizdat *("self-published") writings circulate from hand to hand, often being re-typed on the chain-letter principle.*

In an early issue it was stated that "the Chronicle *does, and will do, its utmost to ensure that its strictly factual style is maintained to the greatest degree possible. . . . " The* Chronicle *has consistently maintained a high standard of accuracy. When any piece of information has not been thoroughly verified, this is openly acknowledged. When mistakes in reporting occur, these mistakes are retrospectively drawn to the attention of the readers. Furthermore the* Chronicle *frequently reproduces without any editorial comment official documents such as governmental edicts, bills of indictment, protocols of searches, investigation officials' reports, etc.*

In February 1971, starting with number 16, Amnesty International began publishing English translations of the Chronicles *as they appeared. Publication of the* Chronicles *ceased temporarily after issue number 27, dated 15 October 1972, as a result of a KGB operation known as Case 24 which was aimed at the journal's suppression. The* Chronicle *reappeared in the spring of 1974 when numbers 28–31, covering the period from October 1972 to May 1974, were distributed in Moscow.*

This book is a translation of copies of the original typewritten texts of these numbers . . .

Amnesty International

A CHRONICLE OF CURRENT EVENTS

Everyone has the right to freedom
of opinion and expression; this
right includes freedom to hold
opinions without interference and
to seek, receive, and impart
information through any media
and regardless of frontiers.

*Universal Declaration of
Human Rights, Article 19.*

Number 28   31 December 1972

This issue contains material more than a year old, and that fact has
naturally had an influence on its selection and on the length at which
it is presented. The reason for the break in the *Chronicle's* publication was the KGB's repeated and unequivocal threats to respond to
each new issue of the *Chronicle* with new arrests—arrests of people
suspected by the KGB of publishing or distributing new or past
issues (cf the material on "Case Number 24" in this issue and the
next issue). People faced with the terrible necessity of making
decisions which will affect not only themselves are placed in an
ethical situation the nature of which requires no comment. But to
remain silent would mean to facilitate—even though indirectly and
passively—the use of a "tactic of hostages" which is incompatible
with justice, morality and human dignity. Therefore the *Chronicle* is
resuming publication and will strive to preserve both the principles
and the style of previous issues.

THE DEATH OF YURY GALANSKOV

   On 2 November in the Mordovian camp complex (in institution
ZhKh 385-3) Yury Timofeyevich Galanskov died at the age of 33.
   Yury Galanskov was born in 1939 in Moscow, into a family of

workers. Beginning in 1959 he took part in readings by young poets in Mayakovsky Square. His poems were published in the typescript anthology *Sintaksis*, edited by A. Ginzburg. He was very active in writing on public affairs (expressing a humanistic, social-legal, and pacifist trend) and in 1966 published the anthology *Phoenix-66*.

On 19 January 1967 Yury Galanskov was arrested. At the trial which ensued, in January 1968, he was sentenced to 7 years in strict regime camps (A. Ginzburg, A. Dobrovolsky, and V. Lashkova were convicted at the same trial—see *Chronicle* number 1).

Since the summer of 1968 Galanskov had been serving his sentence in camp 17a of the Mordovian complex. He actively participated in actions of political prisoners for their rights, and took part in hunger strikes.

The serious case of ulcers which had troubled Galanskov even before his arrest made his life in camp enormously more difficult. Medical care was given him only irregularly and was ineffective.

Galanskov's relatives and friends and also his camp-mates appealed repeatedly to the authorities, asking that he be given adequate medical care. In particular, they asked that he be put on a special diet and be given a complete examination at the central hospital of the Ministry of Internal Affairs in Leningrad. These requests were not granted.

In the autumn of 1972, because of his worsening health, Galanskov was sent as a matter of routine to the Dubrovlag hospital compound in the settlement of Barashevo. After an operation he developed peritonitis. As his condition became increasingly critical, the camp administration began to call in physicians, first from the district hospital, then from Saransk, and finally, apparently from Moscow. But it was too late.

At the beginning of November the USSR Ministry of Internal Affairs urgently summoned Galanskov's mother and sister to Mordovia. When they arrived, Yury Galanskov was already dead.

Permission was given to place a cross on his grave and to inscribe his name.

A funeral service was held on 11 November in the Nikolskaya Church in Moscow (on the Preobrazhenka). Several dozen people attended, including those who had been Galanskov's friends both inside and outside of prison. No actions on the part of the KGB were observed.

*   *   *

The *Chronicle* has received the following obituary:

Yury Timofeyevich Galanskov died on 2 November of this year. Our hearts are overflowing with grief and anger. But it is not an ordinary kind of grief or an ordinary kind of anger, since this was not simply a death: it was a death with all the signs of political murder. Yury Galanskov was not assassinated, nor was he thrown out of a window or poisoned. His murder was prepared gradually, step by step. He was killed by constant persecutions, by an unjust verdict, by the slander of provocateurs, by the harshness of the camp regime. And then he died on the operating table under the indifferent knife of a surgeon from the Mordovian Camp Hospital.

Yury Galanskov was a man of firm character, with an original cast of mind, always pre-occupied with new ideas. But perhaps his strongest trait was a heightened awareness of civil conscience. Before his arrest he took part in the pacifist demonstrations, demanded creative freedom for the intelligentsia, and was one of the editors of the Moscow journal *Phoenix*. He inspired many people by his personal example. His courageous behavior during his investigation and trial engaged the attention and sympathy of the most different kinds of people. The letters from intellectuals in defence of Galanskov and his comrades, with hundreds of signatures, are well known. The voice of his civil conscience could be stifled neither by prison bars, nor by the multiple barbed-wire fences of labour camps, nor by the towers manned by sub-machinegunners. In spite of the illness which caused him so much suffering, Yury Galanskov strove for recognition of the rights of political prisoners, for creative and political freedom for inmates and for free citizens. He dedicated himself entirely to this cause. He strove to achieve his aims by means of hunger strikes, appeals, and his own example. And this was terrifying to the inert, thick-skinned and soulless organism of tyranny. For these qualities he was valued by all the prisoners. All those who met him in the camp compounds always responded to his ready sympathy, his kindness and his desire to help everyone in trouble, and they trusted him.

We honour the memory of our friend Yu. T. Galanskov, who remains for us an example of conscience and a sense of duty. We will multiply our ranks and carry on his cause!

We call upon all citizens of Russia and the whole world to honour his memory with a minute of silence. Let this minute become a kind of oath of fidelity to our common hopes and aspirations. It is time to awaken from criminal indifference and realize that only by acting all together can we achieve freedom for all the peoples of Russia alike.

The vivid memory of Yury Galanskov will remain with us forever!

> Political prisoners of the Ural
> and Mordovian camps.

The *Chronicle* has also received the following texts:

Dear Ekaterina Alekseyevna, Timofei Sergeyevich, and Lena!

We well understand that the grief of those who have lost a son and a brother is immeasurable; that no words, even those of the most sincere sympathy, can lessen it. And still we want to tell you that we, Yury's friends, share this profound grief with you. We want to tell you that you can take pride in your son and brother, as sooner or later all Russia will take pride in him. He was one of the few who, even in the hour of most difficult trials, affirm people's faith in the triumph of justice. His whole life is for us an example of struggle for the victory of good over evil. We, Yury's friends, will forever preserve in our hearts the memory of your son and brother as one of those people who should serve as a model. . . .

Ekaterina Alekseyevna, Timofei Sergeyevich and Lena! Allow us once more to express our deepest condolences for your loss.

> Yu. I. Fyodorov, S.A. Malchevsky, M. Ya. Makarenko, Suslensky, N. N. Borozdin-Braun, Shimon Grilyus, Mendelevich, Abankin, M. Sado, L. Lukyanenko, R. Lapp. S. M. Ponomaryov, A. Jastrauskas, I. Cherdyntsev, V. Chamovskikh, Pokrovsky, V. Kolomin, E. S. Prishlyak, O. I. Zaidenfeld (Frolov), Uzlov, Tolstousov, A. K. Chekhovskoi, N. V. Bondar, V. Platonov.

Statement to USSR Procurator-General R. A. Rudenko from V.K. Pavlenkov and G. V. Gavrilov, political prisoners in corrective-labour colony 389/35.

In March of this year a statement was sent to you, signed by seven political prisoners of corrective labour colony 385/17. We, now located in colony 389/35, were among the signatories. The statement protested against the anti-humanitarian conditions established in corrective-labour establishments of the USSR Ministry of Internal Affairs, which transform healthy people into sick ones and can bring the sick to premature death. We protested against the poor and low-grade food, against the lack of special diets for sick prisoners to meet their nutritional requirements, against the prohibition on receiving the needed quantity of food and medicines from home (especially in the case of the sick). We protested against the fact that, for all practical purposes, the legal provision for the early release of seriously-ill prisoners is not applied. We wrote that as a result of this, and in the absence of appropriate medical care, several people who had been sentenced only to a specific term of imprisonment were in fact condemned to gradual death. In the first place we related all the above to our fellow prisoner, Yu. T. Galanskov, who was seriously ill and who was slowly expiring before our eyes. Despite his illness he was receiving neither the necessary diet, nor qualified medical care, nor was he being excused from work. He frequently did not sleep for several nights in a row because of his terrible pain; for several days on end he ate nothing, did not have the necessary medication, and so forth. The colony's administration deprived him of the chance to buy food products in the canteen with his pittance of five rubles per month, and also to receive the single food parcel allowed him each year by law; and by its humiliating and provocative actions it forced him into hunger strikes.

Now that we have learned of Yu. T. Galanskov's death, we cannot but return to the subject of our protests in the above-mentioned statement which we addressed to you—especially as you ignored that statement, and in fact nothing was done about it.

As a result, Yu. T. Galanskov is dead. He has perished behind barbed wire. The Fundamental Principles of USSR Corrective-Labour Legislation stipulate that the execution of punishment must not engender physical suffering in prisoners. But is not poor and low-grade food, which produces illness in healthy people and is directly contra-indicated for the sick, in itself enough to ensure physical suffering? Do not frequent administrative punishments, often arbitrary, contrived, and involving reductions in prisoners' rations (for example, deprivation of canteen privileges or parcels, or confinement in the punishment cells, where one is fed every other day and at a reduced level), have the same effect? Is not the lack of necessary medical care, and often of medicines as well, a state of affairs which inevitably guarantees physical suffering for the sick? And, finally: are not all these conditions enough to ensure the execution, on at least some prisoners, of death sentences which have not been sanctioned by a court? Is not all this a crime before the law, before justice, before humanity?

We do not think that you personally, or any of the individuals invested with full power and responsibility for the maintenance of prisoners in the USSR, deliberately wished the death of Yu. T. Galanskov or of any other prisoner. But the conditions of prisoners' confinement in our country today are such that they produce physical suffering and premature deaths.

For the fact that conditions of precisely this sort have become established, you are personally responsible.

We demand:
1. A special investigation of the circumstances leading to the death of political prisoner of Colony 385/17, Yu. T. Galanskov.
2. An investigation of the reasons why the statement from seven political prisoners of Colony 385/17, who warned in good time of the possible fatal outcome of Yu. T. Galanskov's illness under the existing camp conditions, was not acted on (the reference number given to the statement by your office is 17/485-68), and the punishment of the guilty parties.
3. Changes in the conditions of prisoners' confinement in the corrective-labour establishment of the USSR Ministry of Internal Affairs, so as to make them conform with the humanitarian principles prescribed by law.

20 November 1972

SPRING

by MICHAEL HOGAN

from LETTERS FOR MY SON (Unicorn Press); Cold Mountain Press Post

Card Series; THE AMERICAN PEN

nominated by Harry Smith

Ice has been cracking all day
and some boys on the shore
pretending it is the booming of artillery
lay prone clutching imaginary carbines.
Inside the compound returning birds
peck at bread scraps from the mess hall.
Old cons shiver in cloth jackets
as they cross the naked quadrangle.
They know the inside perimeter is exactly
two thousand and eighty-four steps
and they can walk it five more times
before the steam whistle blows for count.
Above them a tower guard dips his rifle
then raises it again dreamily.
He imagines a speckled trout
coming up shining and raging with life.

(editor's note: this poem won the American P.E.N. award for writing by prisoners.)

ⓕ ⓕ ⓕ

A CHRONICLE OF LOVE

fiction by H.E. FRANCIS

from KANSAS QUARTERLY

nominated by KANSAS QUARTERLY *and Carole Dolph*

T HE CLUB WANDERER IS ALWAYS IN near darkness. Lights burn
from invisible places. A crystal globe revolving over the dance floor
sends out shafts, steady as a light at sea. Against the sunken glow the
band becomes four living shadows. Front spots now and then thrust
them close. During breaks, the juke blinks on for ten minutes,
coiling blue-green-yellow-purple-orange over the faces clustered
around the tables. At the entrance three figures, two women and the
doorman, come stark against the lights whenever the door swings
open. Through an arch, dim lights over the bar glitter—bottles and
glasses, sometimes the flash of eyes or teeth.

The dancers are dark against the lights, silhouettes whose motion the music dictates as if with unseen strings, now leaping and veering, now drifting, swaying, or standing in a quivering freeze—but always moving, moving. The pianist's arms leap, the guitarists sway, the drummer goes frenzied, the vocalist breaks into the flood. Sounds drown over. From all the country around—and all the way from Nashville or Birmingham or even Atlanta, when there is a big-time guest star—the swingers come to hear the country western of the SOUNDS.

The day he was twenty-one, Lawton Wingfield's buddies said, "Field, tonight we're carrying you to a real place. Wow! We'll celebrate this here birthday like it's the *last*. If you don't get you a good drunk and fun and laid all to one time, we been sure miscalculating. . . ." And Field did. Then, come every Friday, he was back at the Wanderer as regular as work or church, a thing not to be omitted without breaking his new rhythm. His whole self came to be attuned to it. Going to the club was how he knew it was the end of work week and the beginning. That's what he told everybody: "Man, when you walk in there, it's the beginning."

(*John Paul Vincent:* When I heard Field's sick in the city, I went; but he wasn't in no room. Mrs. Warner said he didn't hardly stay there a minute after he come from work, got him a shower and changed clothes and gone—she didn't know where—cept she knew he drank, but never said a word to him cause he was good and quiet, paid on the button, and she knew something was bugging him. You all right, Field? she'd say. Right as the day I was born, was all she'd get out of him. Field never was much for talking, after Alice. Don't believe nobody ever heard him say that name, Alice, one time neither, after, like the name died with her too, or her name's just for him, I don't know. Can't be far, Mrs. Warner said, he's got no car. Had a wreck, Field did, and lost it. But you know, she said, I don't think he had no wreck. I think, the way he looks sometimes, I think he let that car go, just let it go, she said. What his friend Hadley said was: he didn't even hear sometimes; and Field told Hadley: I don't know, Had, if it was accident nor not, it just happened like I wasn't there. I seen—But he'd never tell what he seen. That's how come I think he didn't have no accident. I went looking—Field wasn't far: that club one block off, the Wanderer, that's where. Says: Well, John Paul, agrabbing me, and I seen that whole place come up in his eyes like he's not going to make it, like I was something I wasn't or maybe all of Greenville come in with me and surprised him, maybe like it was Alice; but in a minute he's turned on again—gone, way out, sailing like I never seen nobody. And *skinny!* Only I was afraid to say, but after I did: you got to take care now, Field, I said. Hooo, I'm in the best shape I ever been in, not a ounce of fat and all hard's a rock, he says, never was this way on the farm—*feel* that. But his face was like jaundice, no matter what he said; like a ha'nt he was; and I thought, He'll die right here this night, he ain't going nowhere or moving in about a hour, but he's on his pins, high up like a jack, and Je-*sus*, you should of seen that mother! I sure in a hurry changed my mind. And he didn't stop neither. He went at it till the last lick, only I don't know what happened, he all of a sudden went, passed out. We had to carry him home, they got a doctor, he said You bring him around in the morning; but there wasn't no disease nor nothing he could see, but says That boy's so weak he maybe won't get up again if you don't see that he gets to the hospital in the morning. The doctor began to ask about family and all. I told him too, but looked like they'd do him no good here. Only Field came round after—I sat watching him like he was going to fade out—he said You better sleep, hoss—hear? The boys pick me up for work at six. And I slept too—I didn't mean to—and when I come to he was gone. Jesus, who'd of believed it—gone to work and back and that night dancing again! I had to go to Greenville. I had to tell his folks. He couldn't go on too much like that.

Reta: Where are you going, Field? I'd ask him, cause he was already smiling, he was on his way—like doped up or loaded or Jesus-bit. I couldn't think of anything else to say. He looked like traveling, he'd never stop, his eyes were seeing things—he had that look—and I wanted to reach up and jerk his head down and tell him Me me me, look at *me*, but he'd study that globe or the long lights. His eyes followed like they were real and he'd lose them. He made me feel like a *thing*, just nothing. I hated him. I did, I did, I did.

Marylou: Nobody ever danced like Field. I followed him around. I'd sit and watch all night, thinking he'd ask me, but once he picked somebody it was her all the time, he most never let up, held onto her like she's his life, and dance dance dance. When the band took a break, it was the juke, and he'd even bend and bob when he wasn't dancing, aswaying, like he was rubber and couldn't stop. Sometimes it was funny—I wanted to push him like one of them toy clowns with a round bottom.

Reverend Bullard: Lawton used to come to Greenville, to the church—I'd seen him from the rectory window—never when there was service, always Saturday—and stand outside and stare. He'd been there a long time, walk around the grounds, and go back and look at that door, then go away. He never set foot in the church. Perhaps he'd stay fifteen minutes, half an hour. He never looked sad, no—but quiet and natural, a bit at home even. I never went to disturb him.

Wendy: Call me his Tuesday girl. Every Tuesday, like clockwork. And all night. How'd Field ever get to work? Who knows? He'd leave me in bed. I don't think he even knew who I was by then. Sometimes he'd slip and call me Alice. Who cares? He gave me a good time and if I had to be Alice for him to make it that good, okay, so I'm Alice.

Friday night

FIELD: Like it says in the Bible, Alice, I come to a city over five months now, only it ain't like you think. Oh, it's all shining all right, them neons make it so bright you see it miles, yeah, it makes a great big whale of a light in the sky, a mountain you're going to big as a promise, like driving fast to, only when you get there, it come down, you're on it and can't see it anymore, just a couple of miles of neons, and they're pretty, they sure are, like an invite to anything you ever dreamed could be, you know, like the sun at home daytime only this here's here, makes you feel the things are so close you can grab them. Grab what? Well, I had to find out, you gone and all, and came here. It's a stone city, and days, when the neons are gone, it's like they just died quiet come morning, and the city's not even there, not the same one, it's a whole different thing, like it's got a mind of its own and a body too, you know what I mean? And days I get a hankering for green and dirt under my feet, not cement, stone, asphalt and all—makes your feet hurt, cept when you're dancing. I'm dancing all the time now, Alice, like I'm with you and loving dancing the way you did, and got me some prizes even, they're yours, they really are; if it wasn't for you, I'd never of danced anyway, not one time, I don't know—maybe that's a lie, but how do you know? Anyway I'm *telling* you, that's how come you know. *You* taught me— remember? Daddy said no, not to go, he'd give me the farm, always said I'd be him someday and my kids me standing in that same doorway and looking at the view, and I swear to God I can see the view right now bigger than the ceiling and high and wide and so fresh with air, Alice; and Momma she said I'll not have a body to cook for f-you go, son, and that almost broke me up. I couldn't tell them why, why I was going, and you got to hand it to them, they didn't prize it out of me, not even try cept Momma's hangdog look when she wants to get her way, only I still wouldn't tell them, in their hearts they know I guess, I don't know, and I'm getting letters all the time—oh, it ain't but a hour from here, sometimes Daddy comes in to business, I seen him bout a month ago, and he said Son, you looking bad, you better come home, this life ain't doing you no good, but I said Got me a steady job in construction almost five months now, I can't go back on that, and he said Guess you cain't if you feel that way, son. It's that *son* got me. Daddy he don't use it like that all the time, son son son, like he got a hankering to. Well, ain't we all? And he give me all the news, said the Hansons moved to town, mister got too old to keep things going; Whip McCord gone to college—imagine, Whip!— and Bethanne McCune married ole Jimmie Haley—*Jimmie*, what never settled down one minute in his life, and Willa Mae took a job as a librarian in town; seven boys gone to Vietnam; and Wick—you remember how he pestered me to go with him hunt- ing all the same times I was sneaking off with you?—the Viet Cong got him; and all the news, only nothing from your house— that's how come I know Momma and Daddy's sure why I come here without one time saying it; it made me feel better I tell you, Alice, only cept when Daddy went; he said I'll tell Momma we had a long talk; and I give him a linen handkerchief for Momma I bought one time for when she'd go to church, you know when she gets to hacking and one of Daddy's won't do; and then he got in the truck, he said Better be careful, boy, you look mighty bad, I won't tell your momma that; and I almost couldn't see him when he said that, but it don't matter none's long's I can dance, I got to keep dancing, it's the time you're there, Alice, I feel you—you know that—and you know something, Alice—course you do!—you know that ball hangs right smack there in the center of the dance floor, it makes colored lights moving slow, every color, and when it hits, you see faces just one sec, like it's all a dream and you drifting like water's carrying you past everything far far. Last night I sure got going good, you know, I mean that music tore right through me and made my blood sing to it's going like that rhythm abeat and abeat taking me right up there, agoing so my feet's dancing on fire and my arms touching the sky and me like getting longer and longer till my hands near touched that light and it come in my eyes and made me feel all lit up inside and about to bust into it all and—you know what, Alice!—them faces bobbed and bobbed, I got like dizzy and that light white as fire and I seen your face just as clear, it tore me up, and I reached out quick and all that music saying *Alice* and me too *Alice, Alice*, and I must of passed out, I couldn't dance any more, or I fell or something, but my whole heart's to bust I'm so happy cause I seen you, I seen your face.

Six nights a week the band plays. They give the place a soul, slow and fast, always loud, a vibrating voice that trembles everything. All the place keeps moving, the juke instantly merging into their last struck note. One of the three owners is always at the entrance, a smile of welcome. Weekends Jaw sells tickets, fifty cents cover charge, for the whole long night; and Willyjo, the doorman, a kind-faced, ox-broad man not very tall, pounds his fist into his palm rhythmically, and taps, and rolls on heels and toes, arock half the night in a partnerless dance. When the door swings out, the neon freeway pours scorching bright light in. "Hey, Freddie!" What say, Jumbo?" "You're sure lookin' cool, honey." "Man, get a load-a that!" "You'd cream just lookin' at her!" "Which side is up?" They laugh in the warm, near air and cigarette smoke and wafted alcohol. From a side room, especially during band breaks, comes the familiar clack of pool balls. Cries, laughs, jeers fill the room—JoePeteMiriam WaltBickWillaMaeLoisJimmieMurphyAngieRoberta.

Each entry shuts a door. Outside, a hundred rooms vanish. The world recedes into deep and endless dark. The Wanderer holds its own lights, faces, past—familiar. Benn, one of the owners, smiles. "Ready, Will? Say, Gert, another screwdriver here." The bartender, Bob, knows them all inside out and backwards ("You heard

about ole Harry's pullin' a gun on that drummer last night? One
o'clock in the a.m. the cops come, askin' where he headed—"). And
the waitresses, Gert and Eula, are faces constant as drink, despite
the shifting wigs and eyes and lashes and gewgaws and rage of
outfits. And the other constants are there: the half-drunk little
carpetlayer hanging on the end of the bar; the NASA engineer; the
Fayetteville carpenter; the long-haired, dark girl from the
Studebaker place; Alton, the Vietnam vet; Paul, the bootlegger from
New Hope.

Whenever Field looked around they were all there. He breathed
it all in deep. "Hey, Field!" "Hey, Ben. Hey, Eula," he said. "Bud?"
Bob said, bottle and glass ready. "And a double shot of E.T.," Field
said. He relaxed—back, as if at home, a family. Light glowed. The
dark burned.

(Roanna: Met him downtown by Grant's this one Friday morning
and I don't know what but something just stopped him cold when he
saw me like he thought I was somebody—you know, somebody not
me. He near flipped when he came to. Me, Roanna Wilcox, I said. I
know Roanna, he said, looking like he still didn't but looking hard
too, and I put it out for'm to see too. Sure don't look like no country
girl right now, he said. Pure country, I said, you know it—he ought
to, coming from right down my way there by the Piggly-Wiggly
sign—and I touched his arm, quick: You doing all right, Lawton?
And just that quick li'l ole touch did it, he came round, he came right
close like he's going to have me right there against Grant's window,
and I laughed and said Now, Lawton, and quick he said How bout
dancing tomorrow night, it's Sat'dy, and we can go down to the River
Club after and never stop, what say? Why, Lawton, I said. Only he
ain't so dumb; this time he reached out and touched my shoulder
and his hand hard and rough-skinned it just sent shivers down me.
You're from my town, he said, like it was the sweetest thing. And he
made it that way all night too at the club and me thinking every
minute Pretty soon we'll leave, we'll go it somewhere—in the car or
the grass or back of my place, or he got a place, about to die with him
rubbing me like that sometimes, and when it's over, him near
passing out from dancing and drinking, and fell asleep on me and me
on top of him to wake him up and go at it, I couldn't stand it, and
drove back home alone without a thing, Goddamn it.

        *   *   *

Reddick Farr: His daddy was the only one came. Mrs. Warner couldn't say a word to him. I said Field wouldn't have nobody around, a loner he was since he came here, only he didn't seem alone, he had something in his head, I don't know what. His daddy just looked at him. Said How'll I tell his momma? And it Sunday too. Jesus!

Kim: Always did prefer ectomorphs, and he certainly was that. Field was on the construction crew for the new building. He told me how he went dancing at the Club Wanderer. I got the hint and couldn't resist. And he did dance. You're a little out of my class, he said. And you out of my orbit, I said. He laughed, a rather boyish innocent laugh too. There was something terribly moving about him. I wanted to hold him and comfort him, tell him it was all right. And in bed when he was sleeping, I did hold his head, so thin and long his face, with long dark lashes, and long brown hair. But the rest of him was all hard, wiry, all energy—maddening in bed, with a terrible impersonal drive. I felt used, used, with an enormous indifference by him—and I wanted that.)

Saturday night

FIELD: Oh, Alice, I'm telling you this every night, honey, only what can I do, me not wanting to talk to nobody, everybody's you—I can't help it—I'm looking at them, but it's you. Pretty soon I'm dancing up a storm. I know how it is: I try—I say I'm going out with Sue, Alice wouldn't want me to just moon like this; but it's because that—you wouldn't want me to do it—that's why I do it: If you wanted me to it wouldn't mean the same thing, now would it, Alice, honest? It's cause you don't. Maybe that don't make no sense, but it's the onliest way I know. Mornings—not just one time, Alice, but every morning—since you gone I been waking up like I died and come back and it ain't real. First thing, I think The bed's real, I ain't dead, Alice's here; and for a sec I believe it too, I leap out and get in my clothes—it's like back on the farm with Daddy and Momma, and I know if I look out the kitchen window I can see straight out to the sun smack on your bedroom window just the way I could nighttime fore you put your light out, and me watching, like it's the moon right inside your room shining for me—you saying Field, I'm never going to pull the shade down so's you can't stop seeing me—ever. And I ain't—I ain't stopped one second since I seen you in the river. Ohjesusgod, Alice, why why why? Oh, don't, don't answer me, Alice, I can't stand that: I know it's me, I did it, but you got to know: I'm trying, I'll make up for it, I will too, Alice. You won't be ashamed your Field's just gone and forgot with no shame for what he done. Listen here, Alice, I ain't never gonna stop till it's done, and I reckoned with it, and it's right by you, if it takes twenty years—hear? You hear me, Alice? Why don't you answer me? Alice! I been waiting all day for your voice, just one sound since last night, cause I seen your face, Alice, and now I'm waiting for you to say it so I'll know I'm getting there cause I can hear it in my head, I been hearing it day and day and day, like never stopping, only I want to hear it out, I'll know I'm with you, in the same place, I done it, and you forgive me and we'll be together. I work like a dog, Alice, yes—you believe it? ole Field the farmer's son working like a dog in the city! Ain't it a joke? But I got to, I stop one minute and you're there and then I'd of had to leave work and start looking for you, there ain't no way to stop if you get in my head. It's all I can do to keep you back—*Till five* I'd tell me, *Till five.* That's all I could do, even when you was there, say *Till five,* don't think about—I'd not even say your name, but I heard it and I'd work harder, *Till five,* and come five o'clock I'd be in my room and washed and changed, only now I'm not even doing that, I just come straight here to the club and get me that cool beer and a double shot to begin and another cool beer and, oh man, I can say it *Alice,* like free—and you're right there. You come floating up, far—I see you, just like you was, only you're now, in your white dress, all of you so small, and all your legs showing, that little mini, and all your shoulders, I'm smelling your long black hair on me. I want to put my hand right in the mirror and tell you Alice, come dance with me, honey. And you know: I'm already dancing, my heart's dancing thinking about you and you coming with that white dress, and my feet's starting. That ball of light—you see it, Alice—it hits them colors round and round, it goes and goes, and band time it beats with the band, they send the old rhythm right into them lights and pretty soon they're going right into you, like they're touching and warm, and getting warmer, and your blood goes, it begins, it starts abeating, abeating, and your blood beats, abeating; and it's your legs beating, and your toes, and your arms; and it's all of you pretty soon abeating. I got to get up. I got to go get Alice. She's sitting there in the dark. She's at one of them tables. She's all alone waiting for me. She knows I'm coming. I see her eyes, all the light in her eyes, in the dark and holding it for me, yes she is. And I go right to her close, and I feel her hand and take her . . . and quick as anything it's you, Alice, you're right there against me so good it hurts, I'm about to bust, and a minute I shiver like, standing there and swaying, swaying, and I can feel it already going right into you, my hot and my blood like my skin's yours, and you come back into me, and me into you, and you can't tell which, and then moving and swaying like we're all alone, moving round in a circle, standing still and moving; and dipping, dipping, moving and moving; and the lights going round and round till it's like carrying, the music's lifting us and carrying. And I ain't letting you go, Alice, never a time: nothing going to stop us even with you klack-klack-klacking to a fast one and your arms legs and whole body and hair swinging and throwing and flying high and your bubs shaking and hips wiggling and legs leaping, and when I close my eyes feeling you I see you just the same through my eyelids, yes I *do*, that light comes right through, I can feel it—you believe that?—and you, I see you in it, waiting for you to come down, your face, and kiss me, only it don't. I keep thinking it will, I feel me getting longer and longer, I try, I keep reaching only it's like I ain't long enough, but if I got up enough steam and danced harder, I could move, I'd get so light I'd float up on the music, right smack up to you, and I'd feel your face against mine; and I get afraid, Alice: comes a minute—I know it's coming—and it's going to make me want to cry and yell, but I can't he'p it—I think if I open my eyes, I won't see it, but if I do it'll be gone, don't go, Alice! And it's water, everything's water, I'm looking, and there's your face, and all your hair, and the willow branch almost touching it, and a leaf floating by, and you still, looking at me out of the water, and I got to touch your face, Alice, I got to put my hand in the water and touch your face, both of my hands, I can't stand it, I'm reaching and quick my voice's saying *AliceAliceAliceAliceAliceAlice*, my blood's crying it, and all of me beating, and I open my eyes and a minute it's me under, and hands reaching down, but they're mine, going like *mad* like *mad* like *mad* like *mad* and you're there and you going like *mad mad mad mad mad*, your hips and arms and legs and hair and hair and hair hair hair hair hair drum drum drum drum drum woweeeee, we going and leaping leaping and pretty soon close rubbing and sliding, sliding and rubbing, oh baby Alice you going to make me come right here on the floor, slow slow grinding slow slow grinding grinding, and I'm getting there, getting on high, I feel it riding that music, that rhythm coming with a long slow heave, long long long now, and pulling pulling, and I'm getting there slow, slow moving up, up, oh Alice I'm going to, I'm going to, going to touch, right out and reach your face that's coming down to me. And then I'm waking up it's bright light I can't stand, sun, morning sun, and the walls all dirty wallpaper, them flowers like dead and dried in a winter field gone to seed, and dark ribbons straight down the walls, and that light, and them blinds making dark bars on the floor, my eyes're wet from the sun and the night before and I got to get up quick, I wish I was dead, my head's bustin, Jake'll pick me up in a minute. Good thing I'd moved close to the club or I'd be up the creek, only Alice I couldn't stand it, thinking it's the only place I'd get to you, and here I am dancing with you again, I'll never stop, no never till I'm with you 'one minute past eternity,' yes our song: and there I go, it's your face coming up close to the water, only like if I look long I'm under and looking up and you looking down at me, it gets all twisted and I wanted to get out from under the water and to you. Sometimes I want to move my arms only I can't, like the water's holding them down, I want to scream then, only the water's filling my mouth and then quick the water moves and you gone, gone, Alice, and I can't see or yell or touch, thinking I'll never see you again, about to go crazy thinking that, and thinking you're getting even for all them girls I'm dancing with and kissing and screwing, but Alice, you know something: I get dancing and get me going and feel them warm and begin to go, up, high, up up up, and—I don't know how come—but I ain't *here*, I'm floating, oh baby I'm going fast so fast sucked up in a thing so strong I know I'm going to hit, I know it—going to hit and pow explode and go everywhere, smithereens, and then all of a sudden it's you: pow and it breaks like fireworks and then honey it's so quiet and you come so clear, clearest light I even seen, like you're close as that ball turning round in the ceiling and if I reach up I'll touch your long hair and face I love: only somebody's crying, it's my momma—yes, momma—and I say Momma, what's making you cry? like I know only don't, and Poppa's

standing there with his hand on her shoulder and looking at me
like when my dog Wilbur got runned over, and I know: you said to
me It'd get dark forever if I couldn't see you no more, Field; you
said There's no man in this here world for me but you, Field, you
know that, Field; you said I'd not live a day without you if I
thought you believed Andrew Phelps ever come near me cept
that one kiss he snuck and me not knowing he was there, it didn't
mean a thing, I'd of run, I did slap him too; you said Nobody
touched me the month I was at my cousin Willa Mae's, nobody
ever would but you, Field, and the letters are from a boy likes me
but you know I won't look at, I swear it, I'll swear on the Bible, I'll
swear before Reverend Bullard and the whole church, Field; you
said What's in my belly's yours, Field, gonna look like you, you
wait, then you'll be ashamed you ever said a word, you'll take it all
back and love me all your life, you will, just you wait and see. And
oh, Alice, I do, I love you now like never before; never knew I'd
love you so much I couldn't stand even to live without you. I got to
go where you are. I had to find the way, Alice. I come one night
and danced and there you was. You was in my arms, apressing and
agliding, like a miracle come in me, and I knew I couldn't let you
go: when I woke up it wasn't you, but I knew I'd had you for a
minute, maybe a hour, maybe all night, and I'd get you back: so I
come here, I danced, I danced, I kept dancing, I can't now: I'm
getting to you, Alice, I know I am, and I won't stop, never, till I'm
with you—you hear me? And maybe you'll tell me it's not doing
any good, but you just wait till you see this time I mean it, I do, I'll
never stop dancing till I'm in your arms forever and you can't let
me go, I won't let you, only sometimes I can't make it, Alice, you
know I get to falling, I get so weak—me—go ahead, *laugh!* —me,
ole Field, getting so weak he almost can't stand up, but something
pushes me, keeps me going till the last song and then go on like
I'm dancing out the door and in the car and in bed even and
sleeping too, it never stops, the room's still athumping when I
wake up and all day that music's pounding in me when I'm
banging nails and lugging boards. Come five o'clock it gets strong,
stronger every minute, till I'm back in the dark and that light
going round and the band comes *one minute past eternity*; it's like
you, I'm near you, that place; like I lay my head right down in the
dark against your skin, the dark's all warm, and you say Come on,

honey, come onnnnn, Field, we'll dance, honey, and me getting
up feeling you all soft and warm and cool too agin me, and fore I
know it I'm dancing, I'm swinging and swaying and leaping
bouncing and jerking, keeping time, keeping the beat with you
and that music and that hot air touching like it's water and your
face under water, it comes, it's looking at me, oh-jesus it's looking
at me, and if just one time you'd say Field, it's your fault; but you
never did, nobody ever accused me but me, and Momma and
Poppa looking at me so soft and pitying like looking at my own
dog, and Reverend Bullard's soft voice and all them people and
nobody not one accusing, saying a word to me but me me me
me *me*

The neon sign CLUB WANDERER burns around the clock. In
the sun it fades a sickly blue and red, but with nightfall it beckons,
stark and beautiful in the empty sky. With each opening of the door,
some soul loosed from the SOUNDS spills onto the freeway. From
outside, in the night traffic, you would not suspect the seething
rhythm, the collective beat like a heart throbbing deep in the night;
only the parking lot, filled to overflowing, tells you something is
happening close by. During the week it is the lone pool player,
seeking, who comes, and the isolated couple, the vagrant drinker,
the so-called perpetuals; weekends it is the lovers, mates—couple
time, rest and desire, escape and search—commingled with the
usuals. The regulars know that if you go away for days, weeks,
months, even years, and come back, some of them will be there; it is
the place to find them; sit long enough and the missing will walk in,
no longer phantoms from the past, for sooner or later nearly all
return. "How's eveything on the West Coast?" "Hey, man, ain't
seen you since Vegas." "Lauderdale! Too empty. Nothing doing!"
The truckdrivers make the Wanderer known all over the country.
"Wilson struck a hydrant on US 1, off Elizabethtown." "Heard about
Field?" "Heard about Bess Wickham's shooting all the way up to
Dayton." "What's Larry doing now?" "She's making it in New
Orleans, got guts that girl." Inside, they wait—for dates, loan,
two-timer, wife-stealer, thief, friend. Nobody is forgotton. Away
long enough, he comes up in the conversation. "Can't stay away too
long, it's in the blood." They have every confidence. When the
moment comes, the light is burning outside, a stark, beckoning sign.

(*Walt Everst*: I got there too late. His landlady said Field just got took away—to Greenville. Had to turn me around directly and go back home.

Sue: Why was he dancin' that way, for what? I wanted him— yes, I did, me and I went through all that with him, drinking and dancing. My God, I'm sick of dancing; I never want to see a floor in my life, after him. Near killed me with dancing. What for? He'd not answer, he'd look through me, he'd look like I wasn't even there. It'd make me madder'n hell. Sometimes I even hit him and then he'd smile or laugh and grab me, and what could I do then, I wanted him so? I don't go near the Wanderer now. I hate that place, hate it.

Mrs. Wingfield: His daddy stops and stands in the fields. I see him from the kitchen. He stops work and looks, like he's waiting. Only he ain't waiting. He al'ays did. But he cain't now. He keeps lookin' into the ground, and sometimes up. Then he gits mad and works like you never seem him go. But I know he'll sell it. He's waitin' for me to put my foot down and say no. He knows I will too: he cain't stop workin' and sit. He knows that'd kill him sure. Used to be he'd look out there like it'd just go on, somebody else'd come, and somebody else, somebody he knew, and he'd die comf'table knowin' it was one-a his, like he had somethin' to do with it even after he was gone. But seems like to me now he just stops and looks up like he got no place to go.)

Sunday night

FIELD: Alice, you're talking to me, baby, I know you are—there's a sound I never did hear before in that music, like somebody touched the guitars in a way not before, and the piano and the drums and all together they got a extra sound never come before, makes my blood tingle and hum, me all humming, Alice, never hummed like this before; a sound come. What you think of that? A sound—it's taking me to you, I'm riding it, I sure am, Alice, taking me to you like it's your voice in my blood trying to tell me and if I open my mouth it'll come out—I will too, I'll open it—and you'll say it, me talking and you talking like one sound; then I'll know I got you, I'm touching you like that ball of light come to my hand at last, and I'll kiss your face happy out of my mind, blow it, and never leave you, whole hog. Only, Alice sometimes my hand don't do what I tell it, or my legs, I'm dancing in my head, only legs slow or dragging and arms flopping—how come?—I can't fall off now, honey; it's time, been too long; and Momma come last night right in the middle of the night and said Field? You hear me, Field? and I was saying Yes, Momma, only seemed like she'd not hear, saying Field? and my eyes wide open's could be in the pitch black cept for the light over the city. I come to a city, Alice, and Momma's in the city atalking, Field, son, we want you home, you got to come home or there'll be nothing left-a you, Field honey, and then what'll your poppa do, going along with you the way he done so you could try yourself out and then hopefully come home and take over the way he says you're supposed to, ain't no life this city life for a boy's got so much country in him, pure country your daddy says, says How come he's wasting pure country in the city, I'd like to know. Field, honey? And Momma's right there, only my eyes filled with that big dark and I can't touch her; and it's morning and Daddy he's standing there but real, says You going to a hospital, Field, or you ain't living long, and it's the first time I ever seen like a shadow of water in my daddy's eyes, and you know, Daddy he ain't never showing it, but this time ups and shouts at me A hospital, a hospital, you hear me, Lawton Wingfield? And you know, Alice, I had to out and laugh loud's I could to hear my daddy talk thataway, for a minute it was like you caring; and me getting up and putting on my clothes; Alice, I had to hang onto the bureau—you believe that?—and fell, I couldn't he'p it, but had to get out fore they called somebody, I ain't going to no hospital, and it's Sunday and the sun out and burning; everything's so green I think I never seen things before, a tad of grass around the house, but them trees swinging over the houses with wind, like you in it, Alice, it's that good: and Daddy's shouting at me, and me back at him, I couldn't he'p it, Alice, he don't understand, I'll go back home, Daddy, but you let me do it, I'll decide and then pop I'll be there one day on the stoop—okay, Daddy? and him standing there, but I know he's going to do something, I know it. So I got me away, I got to Bill Wamp's place by the church and sat in the fi'ty-six Ford up on blocks, up there on Ninth Street, cause I got this thing to do, my legs are abeat

with it even when they ain't moving, Alice, like dancing in my
head when I ain't dancing, it never stops, I ain't never stopping
cause long's I'm dancing I'm with you, honey, no matter what,
come hell or high water: and your face in the river, the water's
over it, only I feel water, air's all water, touching, only how can I
see your face and it's mine too, I feel the water, only why don't you
let me have it?—you ain't never accused me, only your eyes
looking out of the river at me are worse than anything, Alice; if
only one time you'd say Field, I done forgive you, one time Alice,
I'd maybe sleep a minute and rest and think She's beside me, I
don't worry none; but everywhere I go I'm seeing your face and
eyes in the sky and trees green and the sidewalk and through that
there Ford windshield and working in the cement and on bricks
and in the dark worse, the only thing, like your eyes are that big
white light over the city come down and holding me and never
letting me out, Alice honey, only please please Say it one time:
You done it, Lawton Wingfield, you killed me, so it'll be like I got
down on my knees before Momma and Poppa the first time and
said I did it, I can tell it all now, I did it, I didn't mean to, and to all
my buddies don't know and all the church and all the town and
God even, like as if He didn't know too, Alice; like it's this here
Sunday and I made it to the Sunday afternoon jazz session and
they're all here—like it is, Alice—they are here, every one of
them—and you give me the word, just say it, the word, Alice, and
I can throw me down right in the middle of all that music and
rhythm and pumping and tell it like it was: I killed Alice Falls, my
wife even if we didn't tie the knot yet, and I was wrong playing
around like she wasn't even mine to make her jealous and love me
more and not be able to stand one minute away from me, and
thinking she'll come round when I want her, and she did, she did
it like I told it, and carrying mine and me not knowing a while and
then when she says it, thinking she been cheating the way I'm
doing and wanting to kill her and did—just by walking off and
telling her I'll never see you again, I don't want to see your face,
never want to look at you, hope it's born dead and you gone with
it; and packing my things and telling them I'm going on construction in Huntsville, I'm going there and beginning; beginning, yes,
Alice, and it was the ending; Lonnie he come telling me first thing
I's in a room and making money and thinking Maybe I'll die and
never have to think about her again cause, honest, Alice, I never

thought of anything but you on the walls and in the mirror and in the bed till I'm thinking I can't never sleep in no small box like this room, no box of no kind, without I'm tight in with her and going crazy out of my mind with her. Momma said She's the sweetest thing this world knows, why'd she do a thing like that? and Daddy and Momma and everybody I know at the church and then Field, How come you stayed away? old Bickley says, and me *blind* with you, Alice, ready to die, and couldn't stay away from the Church one day after and that night—you know what, Alice?—I went there—sure you remember—and slept all night right beside you, me near dead too, wishing I was beside both of you, and not knowing, never knowing now, who it'd be, like me or you, a boy or a girl, or what'd it bring with it, maybe it'd have kids and its kids like forever, and it cut off with you in the river and I'm me wanting to know where you done it, how—you jumped off that Runkley bridge way up where we'd go night? or just slip and let yourself not move or fall? maybe you did fall? Jesus, Alice, God help me, it'll drive me crazy you don't tell me or just come down, come down from that light going and no don't tell me, just yell it out It's your fault, Lawton Wingfield, just yell it out, yellllllll, it's in my blood, I can hear it all beating, oh Alice baby, you feel that rhythm, man there never was a band like the SOUNDS, and you dancing like you never danced before tonight, like we never was together thisaway, so close your're ole Field hisself, and that light it's getting so bright almost to blind me but I ain't taking my eyes off it one time, noooooo, Alice, you ain't leaving me tonight, you coming down, you coming close, you going to touch down with that white face and smiling and say Field honey, I love you, Field honey, don't never leave me; and I'm going to touch your face with both my hands, Alice, you so close you'll never get far from Field again, you feeling it now, Alice? that beat like it's your heart, feel it? It's abeat and abeat, uuuuuuuuhhhhhhhhh, man, Alice, it's bout to swell right out of me, it's moving and moving, it's leaping like it's going to bust out and go into this here room, like water, your face, come down, Alice, and kiss me and tell me it's all right, just one time, please, Alice, my heart's to bust if you don't, oh man, listen to that, that sound, that sound like them SOUNDS never made before, never, no, they going to carry me, oh that sound, Alice, it's going to carry me; look at that light, look, I'm looking: it never been so bright; Alice, if I reach I'm going to

touch it, and I'll do it too, Alice, make my arms stretch out I don't
care how long if you'll just one time come closer, say it; I been
trying so hard, Alice, I never in my life tried so hard to do
anything like dancing till I can't no more and every bit of me's
going to you, I can't stop cause if I do, you won't be there; I'm
afraid, Alice, yes I am, I got to tell you that, without you I'd die
and I don't know how, this here's the only way to get to you, Alice,
and be near you and never stop without your're in my arms, oh
Alice you hear that beat, it's going, it's getting there, it's moving
up up up, mannnnnnn, feel it a beat beat beat, my heart's going,
it's so fast, it's making—listen to that, that sound, Alice it's
coming, it's coming yes from down in me, it's in my blood, it's
coming from my heart going to you, Alice; you hear it? yes you do,
you do, I see it, I see your face, it's coming, Alice, jesusgod you do
hear, you coming down, that light's getting there, I getting to it, I
am, Alice, ohjesusgod it's beating beating abeat like never,
abeat-abeat-abeat woweeeeeeeeeee going, I'm going to make I'm
going to come right in my britches, Alice, if you, if you . . . yessss,
bust out into the air, it's going to go right through my skin and into
air and sweat and water and smoke and that light, it's so bright,
and you, Alice, I see you, *Alice!* yes ohmygodjesus, Alice, thank
you, baby, come on, come onnnnnn, we going to make it, we
going to make it together, going to be there, I feel it coming, it's
burning up up up, oh my blood and that heart's beating beating
and this whole room growing and all light and you coming down,
and now, Alice honey, your face, it's so close I can touch if I reach
out with my hands, yes I will, I will, my heart's beating and my
head and all this room, my heart busting out into this whole room,
Alice, Now, now, tell them, *tell* them I done it and I made up for
it, Alice, in the only way I know how, dancing, dancing, and to get
to you, tell them. I'm burning, Alice, and yes I can now I will
touch you; see, honey, my hands, they're moving, my arms,
they're going right up to that light, reaching to touch, I'm going to
touch you, I'm going to touch, I'm going to

🔥 🔥 🔥

PRICKSONG

by MARILYN COFFEY

from APHRA

nominated by APHRA

I am cursed
by a large penis
which I planted in a flower pot
in my living room.
When it grew, like a cactus,
it looked thirsty and,
being kindly at heart,
I allayed its thirst
with water. It sprouted wings.
Now it flies around the house
and sings at me.
Once I tried to shoot it down
but horrified, it shriveled up
into a ball, retracting everything
it had ever said to me. What
could I do? I didn't have the heart
to follow through. Now it tries to get
in bed with me. I am afraid.
It is so big. It looks so thirsty.
It is never satisfied. Last night
when I pushed it back, it cried.

𝄞 𝄞 𝄞

SO MUCH WATER SO CLOSE TO HOME

fiction by RAYMOND CARVER

from SPECTRUM

nominated by SPECTRUM

MY HUSBAND EATS WITH GOOD APPETITE but seems tired, edgy. He chews slowly, arms on the table, and stares at something across the room. He looks at me and looks away again, and wipes his mouth on the napkin. He shrugs, goes on eating. Something has come between us though he would like to believe otherwise.

"What are you staring at me for?" he asks. "What is it?" he says and lays his fork down.

"Was I staring?" I say and shake my head stupidly, stupidly.

The telephone rings. "Don't answer it," he says.

"It might be your mother," I say. "Dean—it might be something about Dean."

"Watch and see," he says.

I pick up the receiver and listen for a minute. He stops eating. I bite my lip and hang up.

"What did I tell you?" he says. He starts to eat again, then throws the napkin onto his plate. "Goddamn it, why can't people mind their own business? Tell me what I did wrong and I'll listen! It's not fair. She was dead, wasn't she? There were other men there besides me. We talked it over and we all decided. We'd only just got there. We'd walked for hours. We couldn't just turn around, we were five miles from the car. It was opening day. What the hell, I don't see anything wrong. No, I don't. And don't look at me that way, do you hear? I won't have you passing judgement on me. Not you."

"You know," I say and shake my head.

"What do I know, Claire? Tell me. Tell me what I know. I don't know anything except one thing; you hadn't better get worked up over this." He gives me what he thinks is a *meaningful* look. "She was dead, dead, dead, do you hear?" he says after a minute. "It's a damn shame, I agree. She was a young girl and it's a shame, and I'm sorry, as sorry as anyone else, but she was dead, Claire, dead. Now let's leave it alone. Please, Claire. Let's leave it alone now."

"That's the point," I say. "She was dead—but don't you see? She needed help."

"I give up," he says and raises his hands. He pushes his chair away from the table, takes his cigarettes and goes out to the patio with a can of beer. He walks back and forth for a minute and then sits in a lawnchair and picks up the paper once more. His name is there on the first page along with the names of his friends, the other men who made the "grisly find."

I close my eyes for a minute and hold onto the drain board. I must not dwell on this any longer. I must get over it; put it out of sight, out of mind, etc., and "go on." I open my eyes. Despite everything, knowing all that may be in store, I rake my arm across the drain board and send the dishes and glasses smashing and scattering across the floor.

He doesn't move. I know he has heard, he raises his head as if listening, but he doesn't move otherwise, doesn't turn around to look. I hate him for that, for not moving. He waits a minute, then draws on his cigarette and leans back in the chair. I pity him for listening, detached, and then settling back and drawing on his cigarette. The wind takes the smoke out of his mouth in a thin stream. Why do I notice that? He can never know how much I pity him for that, for sitting still and listening, and letting the smoke stream out of his mouth . . . .

He planned his fishing trip into the mountains last Sunday, a week before the Memorial Day weekend. He and Gordon Johnson, Mel Dorn, Vern Williams. They play poker, bowl, and fish together. They fish together every spring and early summer, the first two or three months of the season, before family vacations, little league baseball, and visiting relatives can intrude. They are decent men, family men, responsible at their jobs. They have sons and daughters who go to school with our son, Dean. On Friday afternoon these four men left for a three day fishing trip on the Naches River. They parked the car in the mountains and hiked several miles to where they wanted to fish. They carried their bedrolls, food and cooking utensils, their playing cards, their whisky. The first evening at the river, even before they could set up camp, Mel Dorn found the girl floating face down in the river, nude, lodged near the shore against some branches. He called the other men and they all came to look at her. They talked about what to do. One of men—Stuart didn't say which—perhaps it was Vern Williams, he is a heavy-set, easy man who laughs often—one of them thought they should start back to the car at once. The others stirred the sand with their shoes and said they felt inclined to stay. They pleaded fatigue, the late hour, the fact that the girl "wasn't going anywhere." In the end they all decided to stay. They went ahead and set up the camp and built a fire and drank their whisky. They drank a lot of whisky and when the moon came up they talked about the girl. Someone thought they should do something to prevent the body from floating away. Somehow they thought that this might create a problem for them if she floated away during the night. They took flashlights and stumbled down to the river. The wind was up, a cold wind, and waves from the river lapped the sandy bank. One of the men, I don't know who, it might have been Stuart, he could have done it, waded into the water and took the girl by the fingers and pulled her, still face down, closer to shore, into shallow water, and then took a piece of nylon cord and tied it around her wrist and then secured the cord to tree roots, all the while the flashlights of the other men played over the girl's body. Afterwards, they went back to camp and drank more whisky. Then they went to sleep. The next morning, Saturday, they cooked breakfast, drank lots of coffee, more whisky, and then split up to fish, two men upriver, two men down.

That night, after they had cooked their fish and potatoes and had more coffee and whisky, they took their dishes down to the river and washed them a few yards from where the girl lay in the water. They drank again and then they took out their cards and played and drank until they couldn't see the cards any longer. Vern Williams went to sleep but the others told coarse stories and spoke of vulgar or dishonest escapades out of their past, and no one mentioned the girl until Gordon Johnson, who'd forgotten for a minute, commented on the firmness of the trout they'd caught, and the terrible coldness of the river water. They stopped talking then but continued to drink until one of them tripped and fell cursing against the lantern, and then they climbed into their sleeping bags.

The next morning they got up late, drank more whisky, fished a little as they kept drinking whisky, and then, at one o'clock in the afternoon, Sunday, a day earlier than they'd planned, decided to leave. They took down their tents, rolled their sleeping bags, gathered their pans, pots, fish and fishing gear, and hiked out. They didn't look at the girl again before they left. When they reached the car they drove the highway in silence until they came to a telephone. Stuart made the call to the sheriff's office while the others stood around in the hot sun and listened. He gave the man on the other end of the line all of their names—they had nothing to hide, they weren't ashamed of anything—and agreed to wait at the service station until someone could come for more detailed directions and individual statements.

He came home at eleven o'clock that night. I was asleep but woke when I heard him in the kitchen. I found him leaning against the refrigerator drinking a can of beer. He put his heavy arms around me and rubbed his hands up and down my back, the same hands he'd left with two days before, I thought.

In bed he put his hands on me again and then waited, as if thinking of something else. I turned slightly and then moved my legs. Afterwards, I know he stayed awake for a long time, for he was awake when I fell asleep; and later, when I stirred for a minute, opening my eyes at a slight noise, a rustle of sheets, it was almost daylight outside, birds were singing, and he was on his back smoking and looking at the curtained window. Half-asleep I said his name, but he didn't answer. I fell asleep again.

He was up that morning before I could get out of bed, to see if there was anything about it in the paper, I suppose. The telephone began to ring shortly after eight o'clock.

"Go to hell," I heard him shout into the receiver. The telephone rang again a minute later, and I hurried into the kitchen. "I have nothing else to add to what I've already said to the sheriff. That's right!" He slammed down the receiver.

"What is going on?" I said, alarmed.

"Sit down," he said slowly. His fingers scraped, scraped against his stubble of whiskers. "I have to tell you something. Something happened while we were fishing." We sat across from each other at the table, and then he told me.

I drank coffee and stared at him as he spoke. I read the account in the newspaper that he shoved across the table. . . unidentified girl eighteen to twenty-four years of age . . . body three to five days in the water . . . rape a possible motive . . . preliminary results show death by strangulation . . . cuts and bruises on her breasts and pelvic area . . . autopsy . . . rape, pending further investigation.

"You've got to understand," he said. "Don't look at me like that. Be careful now, I mean it. Take it easy, Claire."

"Why didn't you tell me last night?" I asked.

"I just . . . didn't. What do you mean?" he said.

"You know what I mean," I said. I looked at his hands, the broad fingers, knuckles covered with hair, moving, lighting a cigarette now, fingers that had moved over me, into me last night.

He shrugged. "What difference does it make, last night, this morning? You were sleepy, I thought I'd wait until this morning to tell you." He looked out to the patio: a robin flew from the lawn to the picnic table and preened its feathers.

"It isn't true," I said. "You didn't leave her there like that?"

He turned quickly and said, "What'd I do? Listen to me carefully now, once and for all. Nothing happened. I have nothing to be sorry for or feel guilty about. Do you hear me?"

I got up from the table and went to Dean's room. He was awake and in his pajamas, putting together a puzzle. I helped him find his clothes and then went back to the kitchen and put his breakfast on the table. The telephone rang two or three more times and each time Stuart was abrupt while he talked and angry when he hung up. He called Mel Dorn and Gordon Johnson and spoke with them, slowly, seriously and then he opened a beer and smoked a cigarette while Dean ate, asked him about school, his friends, etc., exactly as if nothing had happened.

Dean wanted to know what he'd done while he was gone, and Stuart took some fish out of the freezer to show him.

"I'm taking him to your mother's for the day," I said.

"Sure," Stuart said and looked at Dean who was holding one of the frozen trout. "If you want to and he wants to, that is. You don't have to, you know. There's nothing wrong."

"I'd like to anyway," I said.

"Can I go swimming there?" Dean asked and wiped his fingers on his pants.

"I believe so," I said. "It's a warm day so take your suit, and I'm sure your grandmother will say it's okay."

Stuart lighted another cigarette and looked at us.

Dean and I drove across town to Stuart's mother's. She lives in an apartment building with a pool and a sauna bath. Her name is Catherine Kane. Her name, Kane, is the same as mine, which seems impossible. Years ago, Stuart has told me, she used to be called Candy by her friends. She is a tall, cold woman with white-blonde hair. She gives me the feeling that she is always judging, judging. I explain briefly in a low voice what has happened (she hasn't yet read the newspaper) and promise to pick Dean up that evening. "He brought his swimming suit," I say. "Stuart and I have to talk about some things," I add vaguely. She looks at me steadily from over her glasses. Then she nods and turns to Dean, saying "How are you, my little man?" She stoops and puts her arms around him. She looks at me again as I open the door to leave. She has a way of looking at me without saying anything.

When I returned home Stuart was eating something at the table and drinking beer . . . .

After a time I sweep up the broken dishes and glassware and go outside. Stuart is lying on his back on the grass now, the newspaper and can of beer within reach, staring at the sky. It is breezy but warm out and birds call.

"Stuart, could we go for a drive?" I say. "Anywhere."

He rolls over and looks at me and nods. "We'll pick up some beer," he says. "I hope you're feeling better about this. Try to understand, that's all I ask." He gets to his feet and touches me on the hip as he goes past. "Give me a minute and I'll be ready."

We drive through town without speaking. Before we reach the country he stops at a roadside market for beer. I notice a great stack of papers just inside the door. On the step a fat woman in a print dress holds out a licorice stick to a little girl. In a few minutes we cross Everson Creek and turn into a picnic area a few feet from the water. The creek flows under the bridge and into a large pond a few hundred yards away. There are a dozen or so men and boys scattered around the banks of the pond under the willows, fishing.

So much water so close to home, I think, why did he have to go miles away to fish?

"Why did you have to go there of all places?" I say.

"The Naches? We always go there. Every year, at least once." We sit on a bench in the sun and he opens two cans of beer and gives one to me. "How the hell was I to know anything like that would happen?" He shakes his head and shrugs, as if it had all happened years ago, or to someone else. "Enjoy the afternoon, Claire. Look at this weather."

"They said they were innocent."

"Who? What are you talking about?"

"The Maddox brothers. They killed a girl named Arlene Hubly near the town where I grew up, and then cut off her head and threw her into the Cle Elum River. She and I went to the same high school. It happened when I was a girl."

"What a hell of a thing to be thinking about," he says. "Come on, get off it. You're going to get me riled in a minute. How about it now? Claire?"

I look at the creek. I float toward the pond, eyes open, face down, staring at the rocks and moss on the creek bottom until I am carried into the lake where I am pushed by the breeze. Nothing *will be any different. We will go on and on and on and on. We will go on even now, as if nothing had happened.* I look at him across the picnic table with such intensity that his face drains.

"I don't know what's wrong with you," he says. "I don't—"

I slap him before I realize. I raise my hand, wait a fraction of a second, and then slap his cheek hard. This is crazy, I think as I slap him. We need to lock our fingers together. We need to help one another. This is crazy.

He catches my wrist before I can strike again and raises his own hand. I crouch, waiting, and see something come into his eyes and then dart away. He drops his hand. I drift even faster around and around in the pond.

"Come on, get in the car," he says. "I'm taking you home."

"No, no," I say, pulling back from him.

"Come on," he says, "Goddamn it."

"You're not being fair to me," he says later in the car. Fields and trees and farmhouses fly by outside the window. "You're not being fair. To either one of us. Or to Dean, I might add. Think about Dean for a minute. Think about me. Think about someone else besides yourself for a change."

There is nothing I can say to him now. He tries to concentrate on the road, but he keeps looking into the rearview mirror. Out of the corner of his eye, he looks across the seat to where I sit with my knees doubled under me. The sun blazes against my arm and the side of my face. He opens another beer while he drives, drinks from it, then shoves the can between his legs and lets out breath. He knows. I could laugh in his face. I could weep.

2

Stuart believes he is letting me sleep this morning. But I was awake long before the alarm sounded, thinking, lying on the far side of the bed, away from his hairy legs and his thick, sleeping fingers. He gets Dean off for school, and then he shaves, dresses and leaves for work himself soon after. Twice he looks into the bedroom and clears his throat, but I keep my eyes closed.

In the kitchen I find a note from him signed "Love." I sit in the breakfast nook in the sunlight and drink coffee and make a coffee ring on the note. The telephone has stopped ringing, that is something. No more calls since last night. I look at the paper and turn it this way and that on the table. Then I pull it close and read what it says. That body is still unidentified, unclaimed, apparently unmissed. But for the last twenty-four hours men have been examining it, putting things into it, cutting, weighing, measuring, putting back again, sewing up, looking for the exact cause and moment of death. And the evidence of rape. I'm sure they hope for rape. Rape would make it easier to understand. The paper says she will be taken to Keith & Keith Funeral Home pending arrangements. People are asked to come forward with information, etc.

Two things are certain: 1) people no longer care what happens to other people and, 2) nothing makes any real difference any longer. Look at what has happened. Yet nothing will change for Stuart and me. Really change, I mean. We will grow older, both of us, you can see it in our faces already, in the bathroom mirror, for instance, mornings when we use the bathroom at the same time. And certain things around us will change, become easier or harder, one thing or the other, but nothing will ever really be any different. I believe that. We have made our decisions, our lives have been set in motion, and they will go on and on until they stop. But if that is true, what then? I mean, what if you believe that, but you keep it covered up, until one day something is going to change after all. What then? Meanwhile, the people around you continue to talk and act as if you were the same person as yesterday, or last night, or five minutes before, but you are really undergoing a crisis, your heart feels damaged. . . .

The past is unclear. It is as if there is a film over those early years. I cannot be sure that the things I remember happening really happened to me. There was a girl who had a mother and father—the father ran a small cafe where the mother acted as waitress and cashier—who moved as if in a dream through grade school and high school and then, in a year or two, into secretarial school. Later, much later—what happened to the time in between?—she is in another town working as a receptionist for an electronic parts firm and becomes acquainted with one of the engineers who asks her for a date. Eventually, seeing that's his aim, she lets him seduce her. She had an intuition at the time, an insight about the seduction that later, try as she might, she couldn't recall. After a short while they decide to get married, but already the past, her past, is slipping away. The future is something she can't imagine. She smiles, as if she has a secret, when she thinks about the future. Once, during a particularly violent argument, over what she can't now remember, five years or so after they were married, he tells her that someday this affair (his words: "this affair") will end in violence. She remembers this. She files this away somewhere and begins repeating it aloud from time to time. Sometimes she spends the whole morning on her knees in the sandbox behind the garage playing with Dean and one or two of his friends. But every afternoon at four o'clock her head begins to hurt. She holds her forehead and feels dizzy with the pain. Stuart asks her to see a doctor and she does, secretly pleased at the doctor's solicitous attention. She goes away for a while to a place the doctor recommends. His mother comes out from Ohio in a hurry to care for the child. But she, Claire, Claire spoils everything and returns home in a few weeks. His mother moves out of the house and takes an apartment across town and perches there, as if waiting. One night in bed when they were both near sleep, Claire tells him that she heard some women patients at DeWitt discussing fellatio. She thinks this is something he might like to hear. She smiles in the dark. Stuart is pleased at hearing this. He strokes her arm. Things are going to be okay, he says. From now on everything is going to be different and better for them. He has received a promotion and a substantial raise. They have even bought another car, a station wagon, her car. They're going to live in the here and now. He says he feels able to relax for the first time in years. In the dark, he goes on stroking her arm . . . . He continues to bowl and play cards regularly. He goes fishing with three friends of his.

That evening three things happen: Dean says that the children at school told him that his father found a dead body in the river. He wants to know about it.

Stuart explains quickly, leaving out most of the story, saying only that, yes, he and three other men did find a body while they were fishing.

"What kind of body?" Dean asks. "Was it a girl?"

"Yes, it was a girl. A woman. Then we called the sheriff." Stuart looks at me.

"What'd *he* say?" Dean asks.

"He said he'd take care of it."

"What did it look like? Was it scary?"

"That's enough talk," I say. "Rinse your plate, Dean, and then you're excused."

"But what'd it look like?" he persists. "I want to know."

"You heard me," I say. "Did you hear me, Dean? Dean!" I want to shake him. I want to shake him until he cries.

"Do what your mother says," Stuart tells him quietly. "It was just a body, and that's all there is to tell."

I am clearing the table when Stuart comes up behind and touches my arm. His fingers burn. I start, almost losing a plate.

"What's the matter with you?" he says, dropping his hand. "Tell me, Claire, what is it?"

"You scared me," I say.

"That's what I mean. I should be able to touch you without you jumping out of your skin." He stands in front of me with a little grin, trying to catch my eyes, and then he puts his arm around my waist. With his other hand he takes my free hand and puts it on the front of his pants.

"Please, Stuart." I pull away and he steps back and snaps his fingers.

"Hell with it then," he says. "Be that way if you want. But just remember."

"Remember what?" I say quickly. I look at him and hold my breath.

He shrugs. "Nothing, nothing," he says and cracks his knuckles.

The second thing that happens is that while we are watching television that evening, he in his leather reclining chair, I on the couch with a blanket and magazine, the house quiet except for the television, a voice cuts into the program to say that the murdered girl has been identified. Full details will follow on the eleven o'clock news.

We look at each other. In a few minutes he gets up and says he is going to fix a nightcap. Do I want one?

"No," I say.

"I don't mind drinking alone," he says. "I thought I'd ask."

I can see he is obscurely hurt, and I look away, ashamed and yet angry at the same time.

He stays in the kitchen for a long while, but comes back with his drink when the news begins.

First the announcer repeats the story of the four local fishermen finding the body, then the station shows a high school graduation photograph of the girl, a dark-haired girl with a round face and full, smiling lips, then a film of the girl's parents entering the funeral home to make the identification. Bewildered, sad, they shuffle slowly up the sidewalk to the front steps to where a man in a dark suit stands waiting and holding the door. Then, it seems as if only a second has passed, as if they have merely gone inside the door and turned around and come out again, the same couple is shown leaving the mortuary, the woman in tears, covering her face with a handkerchief, the man stopping long enough to say to a reporter, "It's her, it's Susan. I can't say anything right now. I hope they get the person or persons who did it before it happens again. It's all this violence . . ." He motions feebly at the television camera. Then the man and woman get into an old car and drive away into the late afternoon traffic.

The announcer goes on to say that the girl, Susan Miller, had gotten off work as a cashier in a movie theater in Summit, a town 120 miles north of our town. A green, late model car pulled up in front of the theater and the girl, who according to witnesses looked as if she'd been waiting, went over to the car and got in, leading the authorities to suspect that the driver of the car was a friend, or at least an acquaintance. The authorities would like to talk to the driver of the green car.

Stuart clears his throat then leans back in the chair and sips his drink.

The third thing that happens is that after the news Stuart stretches, yawns, and looks at me. I get up and begin making a bed for myself on the couch.

"What are you doing?" he says, puzzled.

"I'm not sleepy," I say, avoiding his eyes. "I think I'll stay up a while longer and then read something until I fall asleep."

He stares as I spread a sheet over the couch. When I start to go for a pillow, he stands at the bedroom door, blocking the way.

"I'm going to ask you once more," he says. "What the hell do you think you're going to accomplish?"

"I need to be by myself tonight," I say. "I just need to have time to think."

He lets out breath. "I'm thinking you're making a big mistake by doing this. I'm thinking you'd better think again about what you're doing. Claire?"

I can't answer. I don't know what I want to say. I turn and begin to tuck in the edges of the blanket. He stares at me a minute longer and then I see him raise and drop his shoulders. "Suit yourself then. I could give a fuck less what you do," he says and turns and walks down the hall scratching his neck.

This morning I read in the paper that services for Susan Miller are to be held in Chapel of the Pines, Summit, at two o'clock the next afternoon. Also, the police have taken statements from three people who saw her get into the green Chevrolet, but they still have no license number for the car. They are getting warmer, though, the investigation is continuing. I sit for a long while holding the paper, thinking, then I call to make an appointment at the hairdresser's.

I sit under the dryer with a magazine on my lap and let Millie do my nails.

"I'm going to a funeral tomorrow," I say after we have talked a bit about a girl who no longer works there.

Millie looks up at me and then back at my fingers. "I'm sorry to hear that, Mrs. Kane. I'm real sorry."

"It's a young girl's funeral," I say.

"That's the worst kind. My sister died when I was a girl, and I'm still not over it to this day. Who died?" she says after a minute.

"A girl. We weren't all that close, you know, but still."

"Too bad. I'm real sorry. But we'll get you fixed up for it, don't worry. How's that look?"

"That looks . . . fine. Millie, did you ever wish you were somebody else, or else just nobody, nothing, nothing at all?"

She looks at me. "I can't say I ever felt that, no. No, if I was somebody else I'd be afraid I might not like who I was." She holds my fingers and seems to think about something for a minute. "I don't know, I just don't know . . . . Let me have your other hand now, Mrs. Kane."

At eleven o'clock that night I make another bed on the couch and this time Stuart only looks at me, rolls his tongue behind his lips, and goes down the hall to the bedroom. In the night I wake and listen to the wind slamming the gate against the fence. I don't want to be awake, and I lie for a long while with my eyes closed. Finally I get up and go down the hall with my pillow. The light is burning in our bedroom and Stuart is on his back with his mouth open, breathing heavily. I go into Dean's room and get into bed with him. In his sleep he moves over to give me space. I lie there for a minute and then hold him, my face against his hair.

"What is it, mama?" he says.

"Nothing, honey. Go back to sleep. It's nothing, it's all right."

I get up when I hear Stuart's alarm, put on coffee and prepare breakfast while he shaves.

He appears in the kitchen doorway, towel over his bare shoulder, appraising.

"Here's coffee," I say. "Eggs will be ready in a minute."

He nods.

I wake Dean and the three of us have breakfast. Once or twice Stuart looks at me as if he wants to say something, but each time I ask Dean if he wants more milk, more toast, etc.

"I'll call you today," Stuart says as he opens the door.

"I don't think I'll be home today," I say quickly. "I have a lot of things to do today. In fact, I may be late for dinner."

"All right. Sure." He wants to know, he moves his briefcase from one hand to the other. "Maybe we'll go out for dinner tonight? How would you like that?" He keeps looking at me. He's forgotten about the girl already. "Are you . . . all right?"

I move to straighten his tie, then drop my hand. He wants to kiss me goodbye. I move back a step. "Have a nice day then," he says finally. Then he turns and goes down the walk to his car.

I dress carefully. I try on a hat that I haven't worn in several years and look at myself in the mirror. Then I remove the hat, apply a light makeup, and write a note for Dean.

Honey, Mommy has things to do this afternoon, but will be home later. You are to stay in the house or in the back/yard until one of us comes home.

Love

I look at the word "Love" and then I underline it. As I am writing the note I realize I don't know whether back yard is one word or two. I have never considered it before. I think about it and then I draw a line and make two words of it.

I stop for gas and ask directions to Summit. Barry, a forty year old mechanic with a moustache, comes out from the restroom and leans against the front fender while the other man, Lewis, puts the hose into the tank and begins to slowly wash the windshields.

"Summit," Barry says, looking at me and smoothing a finger down each side of his moustache. "There's no best way to get to Summit, Mrs. Kane. It's about a two and a half hour drive each way. Across the mountains. It's quite a drive for a woman. Summit? What's in Summit, Mrs. Kane?"

"I have business," I say, vaguely uneasy. Lewis has gone to wait on another car.

"Ah. Well, if I wasn't all tied up in there"—he gestures with his thumb toward the bay—"I'd offer to drive you to Summit and back again. Road's not all that good. I mean it's good enough, there's just a lot of curves and so on."

"I'll be all right. But thank you." He leans against the fender. I can feel his eyes as I open my purse.

Barry takes the credit card. "Don't drive it at night," he says. "It's not all that good a road, like I say, and while I'd be willing to bet you wouldn't have car trouble with this, I know this, car, you can never be sure about blowouts and things like that. Just to be on the safe side I'd better check these tires." He taps one of the front tires with his shoe. "We'll run it onto the hoist. Won't take long."

"No, no, it's all right. Really, I can't take any more time. The tires look fine to me."

"Only takes a minute," he says. "Be on the safe side."

"I said no. No! They look fine to me. I have to go now. Barry . . ."

"Mrs. Kane?"

"I have to go now."

I sign something. He gives me the receipt, the card, some stamps. I put everything in my purse. "You take it easy," he says. "Be seeing you."

Waiting to pull into the traffic, I look back and see him watching. I close my eyes, then open them. He waves.

I turn at the first light, then turn again and drive until I come to the highway and read the sign: SUMMIT 117 miles. It is ten-thirty and warm.

The highway skirts the edge of town, then passes through farm country, through fields of oats and sugar beets and apple orchards, with here and there a small herd of cattle grazing in open pastures. Then everything changes, the farms become fewer and fewer, more like shacks now than houses, and stands of timber replace the orchards. All at once I'm in the mountains and on the right, far below, I catch glimpses of the Naches River.

In a little while a green pickup truck comes up behind me and stays behind for miles. I keep slowing at the wrong times, hoping he will pass, and then increasing my speed, again at the wrong times. I grip the wheel until my fingers hurt. Then on a long clear stretch he does pass, but he drives along beside for a minute, a crewcut man in a blue workshirt in his early thirties, and we look at each other. Then he waves, toots the horn twice, and pulls ahead of me.

I slow down and find a place, a dirt road off the shoulder, pull over and shut off the ignition. I can hear the river somewhere down below the trees. Ahead of me the dirt road goes into the trees. Then I hear the pickup returning.

I start the engine just as the truck pulls up behind me. I lock the doors and roll up the windows. Perspiration breaks on my face and arms as I put the car in gear, but there is no place to drive.

"You all right?" the man says as he comes up to the car. "Hello. Hello in there." He raps the glass. "Are you okay?" He leans his arms on the door then and brings his face close to the window.

I stare at him and can't find any words.

"After I passed I slowed up some," he says, "but when I didn't see you in the mirror I pulled off and waited a couple of minutes. When you still didn't show I thought I'd better drive back and check. Is everything all right? How come you're locked up in there?"

I shake my head.

"Come on, roll down your window. Hey, are you sure you're okay? Huh? You know it's not good for a woman to be batting around the country by herself." He shakes his head and looks at the highway and then back at me. "Now come on, roll down the window, how about it? We can't talk this way."

"Please, I have to go."

"Open the door, all right?" he says, as if he isn't listening. "At least roll down the window. You're going to smother in there." He looks at my breasts and legs. The skirt has pulled up over my knees. His eyes linger on my legs, but I sit still, afraid to move.

"I want to smother," I say. "I am smothering, can't you see?"

"What in the hell?" he says and moves back from the door. He turns and walks back to his truck. Then, in the side mirror, I watch him returning, and close my eyes.

"You don't want me to follow you toward Summit, or anything? I don't mind. I got some extra time this morning."

I shake my head again.

He hesitates and then shrugs. "Have it your way then," he says.

I wait until he has reached the highway, and then I back out. He shifts gears and pulls away slowly, looking back at me in his rearview mirror. I stop the car on the shoulder and put my head on the wheel.

The casket is closed and covered with floral sprays. The organ begins soon after I take a seat near the back of the chapel. People begin to file in and find chairs, some middle-aged and older people, but most of them in their early twenties or even younger. They are people who look uncomfortable in their suits and ties, sports coats and slacks, their dark dresses and leather gloves. One boy in flared pants and a yellow short-sleeved shirt takes the chair next to mine and begins to bite his lips. A door opens at one side of the chapel and I look up and for a minute the parking lot reminds me of a meadow, but then the sun flashes on car windows. The family enters in a group and moves into a curtained area off to the side. Chairs creak as they settle themselves. In a few minutes a thick, blonde man in a dark suit stands and asks us to bow our heads. He speaks a brief prayer for us, the living, and when he finishes he asks us to pray in silence for the soul of Susan Miller, departed. I close my eyes and remember her picture in the newspaper and on television. I see her leaving the theater and getting into the green Chevrolet. Then I imagine her journey down the river, the nude body hitting rocks, caught at by branches, the body floating and turning, her hair streaming in the water. Then the hands and hair catching in the overhanging branches, holding, until four men come along to stare at her. I can see a man who is drunk (Stuart?) take her by the wrist. Does anyone here know about that? What if these people knew that? I look around at the other faces. There is a connection to be made of these things, the events, these faces, if I can find it. My head aches with the effort to find it.

He talks about Susan Miller's gifts: cheerfulness and beauty, grace and enthusiasm. From behind the closed curtain someone clears his throat, someone else sobs. The organ music begins. The service is over.

Along with the others I file slowly past the casket. Then I move out onto the front steps and into the bright, hot afternoon light. A middle-aged woman who limps as she goes down the stairs ahead of me reaches the sidewalk and looks around, her eyes falling on me. "Well they got him," she says. "If that's any consolation. They arrested him this morning, I heard it on the radio before I came. A guy right here in town. A longhair, you might have guessed." We move a few steps down the hot sidewalk. People are starting cars. I put out my hand and hold on to a parking meter. Sunlight glances off polished hoods and fenders. My head swims. "He's admitted having relations with her that night, but he says he didn't kill her." She snorts. "You know as well as I do. But they'll probably put him on probation and then turn him loose."

"He might not have acted alone," I say. "They'll have to be sure. He might be covering up for someone, a brother, or some friends."

"I have known that child since she was a little girl," the woman goes on, and her lips tremble. "She used to come over and I'd bake cookies for her and let her eat them in front of the T.V." She looks off and begins shaking her head as the tears roll down her cheeks.

3

Stuart sits at the table with a drink in front of him. His eyes are red and for a minute I think he has been crying. He looks at me and doesn't say anything. For a wild instant I feel something has happened to Dean, and my heart turns.

Where is he? I say. Where is Dean?

Outside, he says.

Stuart, I'm so afraid, so afraid, I say, leaning against the door.

What are you afraid of, Claire? Tell me, honey, and maybe I can help. I'd like to help, just try me. That's what husbands are for.

I can't explain, I say. I'm just afraid. I feel like, I feel like, I feel like . . . .

He drains his glass and stands up, not taking his eyes from me. I think I know what you need, honey. Let me play doctor, okay? Just take it easy now. He reaches an arm around my waist and with his other hand begins to unbutton my jacket, then my blouse. First things first, he says, trying to joke.

Not now, please I say.

Not now, please he says, teasing. Please nothing. Then he steps behind me and locks an arm around my waist. One of his hands slips under my brassiere.

Stop, stop, stop, I say. I stamp on his toes.

And then I am lifted up and then falling. I sit on the floor looking up at him and my neck hurts and my skirt is over my knees. He leans down and says, You go to hell then, do you hear, bitch? I hope your cunt drops off before I touch it again. He sobs once and I realize he can't help it, he can't help himself either. I feel a rush of pity for him as he heads for the living room.

He didn't sleep at home last night.

This morning, flowers, red and yellow chrysanthemums. I am drinking coffee when the doorbell rings.

Mrs. Kane? the young man says, holding his box of flowers.

I nod and pull the robe tighter at my throat.

The man who called, he said you'd know. The boy looks at my robe, open at the throat, and touches his cap. He stands with his legs apart, feet firmly planted on the top step, as if asking me to touch him down there. Have a nice day, he says.

A little later the telephone rings and Stuart says, Honey, how are you? I'll be home early, I love you. Did you hear me? I love you, I'm sorry, I'll make it up to you. Goodbye, I have to run now.

I put the flowers into a vase in the center of the dining room table and then I move my things into the extra bedroom.

Last night, around midnight, Stuart breaks the lock on my door. He does it just to show me that he can, I suppose, for he does not do anything when the door springs open except stand there in his underwear looking surprised and foolish while the anger slips from his face. He shuts the door slowly and a few minutes later I hear him in the kitchen opening a tray of ice cubes.

He calls today to tell me that he's asked his mother to come stay with us for a few days. I wait a minute, thinking about this, and then hang up while he is still talking. But in a while I dial his number at work. When he finally comes on the line I say, It doesn't matter, Stuart. Really, I tell you it doesn't matter one way or the other.

I love you, he says.

He says something else and I listen and nod slowly. I feel sleepy. Then I wake up and say, For God's sake Stuart, she was only a child.

𖤐 𖤐 𖤐

LECTURING MY DAUGHTER IN HER FIRST FALL RAIN, 6 OCTOBER 71

by TOM MONTAG

from MAKING HAY AND OTHER POEMS (Pentagram Press)

nominated by Pentagram Press

this then is fall rain.
i spoke of it

in july, telling you
rain has textures,

telling you july
rain drives deep for

dry roots, to fill them,
drives in at warm

angles, softly. i
told you then fall

rain is cold, rough as
wrought-iron, sometimes,

bent as rusted nails.
you were content,

though, to wait, to learn
this rain by touch,

to measure your blue
fingers against

the still-warm places
between rain-drops

on your surprised face.

ALCOHOL AND POETRY: JOHN BERRYMAN AND THE BOOZE TALKING

by LEWIS HYDE

from THE AMERICAN POETRY REVIEW

nominated by Joyce Carol Oates

IN LOOKING AT THE RELATIONSHIP between alcohol and poetry I am working out of two of my own experiences. For more than a year now I have been a counselor with alcoholics in the detoxification ward of a city hospital. I am also a writer and, when I was an undergraduate at the University of Minnesota, I knew John Berryman (briefly, not intimately).

Berryman was alcoholic. It is my belief that his disease is evident in his work, particularly in *The Dream Songs*. His last poems and *Recovery*, his unfinished novel, show that by the time of his suicide in January of 1972 he himself was confronting his illness and had already begun to explore its relationship to the poetry. What I want

71

to do here is to continue that work. I want to try to illuminate what the forces are between poetry and alcohol so we can see them and talk about them.

Alcohol has always played a role in American letters. Those of our writers who have tangled with it include Fitzgerald, Hemingway, Malcolm Lowry, Hart Crane, Jack London and Eugene O'Neill, to name a few. Four of the six Americans who have won the Nobel Prize for literature were alcoholic. About half of our alcoholic writers eventually killed themselves.

This essay begins with a short description of alcoholism and then a longer sketch of the ways in which it is entangled in our culture and spiritual life, the two areas where it bears most heavily on poetry. In the second part of the essay I will turn to Berryman and take a close look at *The Dream Songs*.

I

Most of what we know about alcoholism comes from alcoholics themselves, specifically from Alcoholics Anonymous. It is their experience that an alcoholic is someone who cannot control his drinking once he has started. He cannot pick up just one drink ("one is too many, a thousand's not enough," is the saying). Another way of putting this is to say *if you are alcoholic, you cannot stop drinking on will power*. In this it is like other diseases of the body. It may be hard to believe—and harder for the active alcoholic!—but I have seen enough strong-willed alcoholics to know that good intentions and will power are as useful for recovering from this disease as they are for curing diabetes.

Because of this it seems clear that alcoholism has a biological component. It is common to call this an 'allergy,' that is: alcoholics' bodies react differently to alcohol. Some people may be born with this 'allergy' (it seems to run in families), others may develop it through heavy drinking. Once present in a person, it hooks into his social, mental and spiritual life and it is in these areas that most alcoholics first get hurt. Most have trouble in their family life or with their jobs or end up doing things they don't want to, long before the alcohol destroys their bodies.

Alcoholism cannot be cured. Once a person becomes alcoholic, he can never again drink in safety. However, there is a way to arrest the disease, and that is the program of Alcoholics Anonymous. AA is the 'medicine' and it works. Of those who join a group, get a sponsor, and become active, more than half never drink again and all enjoy some improvement. Those alcoholics who don't manage to find sobriety end up in jail or in mental institutions or dead from cirrhosis, brain damage, suicide or something else related to alcohol.

It is commonly believed that AA is a religious group, but it is more correctly described as a spiritual program. It has no creed. The only requirement for membership is a desire to stop drinking. It does have a series of "12 steps to recovery" and these include the concept of a "higher power." The first three steps read:

We admitted that we're powerless over alcohol—that our lives had become unmanageable.

Came to believe that a Power greater than ourselves could restore us to sanity.

Made a decision to turn our will and lives over to the care of God *as we understood Him.*

They say you can get sober on the First Step alone, but certainly not with the ease of those who find their way to the others. The move from the First to the Second step is a problem for many, but logically it shouldn't be for every active alcoholic already has a higher power at work in his life: the booze.

In AA it is common to refer to alcoholism as a threefold disease: it is physical, mental, and spiritual. This wholistic description was first put together in this country in the 1930s and it led immediately to the first recovered alcoholics and the founding of AA. A key insight—that the disease includes the spirit—came indirectly from Carl Jung. The story is interesting and helps me begin to show how alcoholism is tied up with creative life.

Many alcoholics try psychotherapy of one sort or another to deal with their problems. It notoriously fails. They say that alcoholism is "the siren of the psychiatrists." In 1931 an American alcoholic sought out Jung for treatment. Whatever analytic progress they made did not affect his drinking and Jung told him that his only hope was to become the subject of a spiritual experience, a true conversion.

It was Jung's belief, as he explained in a letter 30 years later, that the "craving for alcohol was the equivalent, on a low level, of the spiritual thirst of our being for wholeness . . . , (for) the union with

God." He included the line from the 42nd Psalm: "As the hart panteth after the water brooks, so panteth my soul after thee, O God." And he concluded his letter: "You see, 'alcohol' in Latin is spiritus, and one uses the same word for the highest religious experience as well as for the most depraving poison. The helpful formula therefore is: *spiritus contra spiritum.*"*

What is a 'spirit' in this broad sense? There are several things to say. First, a spirit is something larger than the self and second, it has the power to change you. It alters your Gestalt, your whole mode of perception and action. Both alcohol and the Holy Ghost can do this. But a spirit does more than give you new eyes: it is the mover. This is the sense of spiritual power when St. Paul says "I have planted, Apollos watered, but God gave the increase." A good spirit does not just change you, it is an agent of growth.

Spiritual thirst is the thirst of the self to feel that it is a part of something larger and, in its positive aspect, it is the thirst to grow, to ripen. The self delights in that as a fish delights in water. Cut off from it, it seeks it again. This is a simple and basic human thirst, comparable to the body's need for salt. It is subtle and cannot be extinguished. Once woken, it is very powerful. An animal who has found salt in the forest will return time and again to the spot. It is the same with a taste of spiritual powers.

The disease of alcoholism includes what they call a "mental obsession" with alcohol and a "physical compulsion" for it. Once we have understood this matter of spiritual thirst, we see that this is like saying that the moon has a "compulsion" to orbit the earth, or a whale has an "obsession" with the ocean. Man is compelled to move with powers greater than himself. The compelling forces may be mysterious, but they are not a problem. The problem is why a person would get hooked up with alcohol—which is a power greater than the ego, but not a benevolent one. I do not know why, though by the end of this essay I will make a few guesses.

All the psychotropic drugs—alcohol, the amphetamines, LSD, mescaline and so forth—could be called spirits in the sense I am using. But I would prefer to call them spirit-helpers, first because they are material spirits and seem to be limited to that level, and second because it now seems clear that they are not actually agents

*All my sources are listed at the end of the essay.

of maturation. They do have power: they can show the novice in a crude way the possibility of a different life. I call it crude because it is big-footed and able to bust through the novice's walls. I say 'show' because a spirit-helper does not give you the new life, it merely points.

The amphetamines, for example, can show you that it is possible for huge amounts of energy to flow through the body and leave you in a state of almost hopeless attentiveness. However, this is not you. It affects you, but you do not own it. Properly used, such a spirit-helper makes a demand: Find the path that leads to the place where you can have this experience without the help. Often the path is long and the things the spirit-helper shows you do not actually become yours for 5 to 10 years. The risk, especially in this civilization and without a guide, is that you will get weary, forgo the 5-year walk, and stay with the material spirit. And when you stay with the material spirit you stay at its level, you do not grow. This is why we speak of their effect as 'getting stoned' or 'intoxicated,' rather than 'inspiration.' 'Inspiration' refers to air spirits such as those which come through meditation, or the Holy Ghost, or the power that rises above a group of people. Air spirits are less crude and they abide. They have power over matter.

Few of these spirits are good or evil of themselves. Their value varies by their use. Alcohol has many uses and all of them change depending on a person's drinking patterns. It is a relaxant and social spirit; it has always been used as a ceremonial spirit; it is a medicinal, a sedative hypnotic and an anaesthetic.

It is also, along with others of the material spirits, a possessing drug: it is addictive. (Withdrawal from alcohol addiction is worse than that from heroin.) As a spirit possesses a person he more and more becomes the spirit itself. In the phrase of AA's First Step—"powerless over alcohol"—is implied the idea that the alcoholic is no longer running his life, the alcohol is. Booze has become his only experience and it makes all of his decisions for him.

If he senses this at all it is as a numbed recognition that he himself is being wiped out. After several years an alcoholic commonly begins to have apocalyptic fears. He stops going out of the house because he is afraid that buildings will fall on him. He won't drive across a bridge because he fears the car will suddenly leap off of it.

This is the self realizing it is being forced out, but so blind with the booze that it can't see the true cause, it can only project its death onto everything in the outer world.

I am saying that as a person becomes alcoholic he turns more and more into the drug and its demands. He is like a fossil leaf that mimics the living but is really stone. For him the drug is no longer a spirit in the sense I have used or, if it is, it's a death spirit, pulling him down into itself. He has an ever-increasing problem knowing what 'he' is doing and what the booze is doing. His selftrust collapses. He doesn't even know if his feelings are his own. This state does not require physical addiction. Long after his last drink, the symptoms of the alcoholic's physical addiction linger and recur— sometimes for years—a phenomenon known as the 'dry-drunk.' The drinker becomes alcohol in a human skin, a parasite dressed up in the body of its host.

These issues—spiritual powers, possession, growth, inspiration —clearly have to do with the life of a creative person. But there is a further thing to say about alcohol that connects it even more closely with poetry. Alcohol is described medically as a sedative hypnotic or an anaesthetic. It progressively relaxes and numbs the different centers of sensation, coordination and control, starting with faculties such as judgment and physical grace and progressing (as with other anaesthetics like ether) down through the voluntary nervous system.

'Anaesthetic' does not just mean a thing that reduces sensation. The word means 'without-aesthetic,' that is, without the ability to sense *creatively*. The aesthetic power, which every human has, is the power which forms meaningful configurations out of all we sense and feel. More than that, it makes configurations which are themselves lively and creative, things which, like art, begin to exist separately from their creator and give meaning and energy back to all of us. If this power were not free and active a human being would die, just as he would die if he lost the power to digest his food.

An anaesthetic is a poet-killer. It is true that some poets have found alcohol a spirit-helper; for some it has broken up static and useless interpretations of the world and allowed them to "see through" and move again. Theodore Roethke appears to be an example. But this doesn't happen for alcoholics. An alcoholic cannot control his drinking and cannot selectively anaesthetize. A poet who has beome wholly possessed by alcohol is no longer a poet, for these powers are mutually exclusive. The opposition of these forces is a hidden war in our civilization. On one level it is a social war, for ours is a civilization enamoured of drugs which deaden the poetry-creature. But for many the fight is personal, it has already entered their bodies and become a corporeal war between the powers of creation and the spirit of alcohol.

To conclude the first part of this essay I want to show some of the ways in which alcohol is involved in our culture and civilization. To look at it from this level I want to turn to some ideas developed by Ivan Illich in his new book about health care, *Medical Nemesis*.

One of Illich's main points is that pain asks a question. Discomfort makes an urgent demand on us to find its cause and resolution. He distinguishes between suffering and feeling pain. The latter is passive but it leads to suffering which is the active process, the art, of moving from dis-ease to ease. It turns out that the idea of a 'pain-killer' is a modern one. This phrase appeared in this country only a century ago. In the Middle Ages it was the belief of doctors that if you killed the pain you killed the patient. To the ancients, pain was only one sign of disharmony. It was nice if it went away during the healing process, but this did not mean that the patient was whole. The idea is that if you get rid of pain before you have answered its questions, you get rid of the self along with it. Wholeness comes only when you have passed *through* pain.

Illich's thesis is that "health care and my ability to remain responsible for my behavior in suffering correlate." Relief of this ability, through the use of drugs to separate pain from the performance of suffering, is a cornerstone of which Illich calls "medical technocracy." He writes:

Pain had formerly given rise to a cultural program whereby individuals could deal with reality, precisely in those situations in which reality was experienced as inimical to the unfolding of their lives. Pain is now being turned into a political issue which gives rise to a snowballing demand on the part of anaesthesia consumers for artifically induced insensibility, unawareness, and even unconsciousness.

A culture in the sense being used here is, by nature, a healing system. Illich speaks of "the health-granting wholeness of culture," and of "medicinal cultures." The native American tribes are a good example: they called their whole system of knowledge and teaching 'the medicine,' not just the things that the shaman might do in an emergency. As a member of the tribe it was your privilege to walk daily inside of the healing air.

A culture faces and interprets pain, deviance and death. It endows them with meaning; it illuminates how they are a part of the whole and thereby makes them tolerable. We do not become trapped in them because the culture continually leads out of pain and death and back into life. Medical civilization reacts in the opposite way: it tries to attack, remove and kill these things. With this the citizen becomes separated from his own healing and interpretive powers and he and the culture begin to pull apart and wither, like plants pulled from the soil until both become dust.

The widespread use of alcohol and other central nervous system anaethetics is directly linked to a decline in culture. The wider their use, the harder it becomes to preserve, renew and invigorate the wisdom that a culture should hold. This then doubles back and escalates. Alcoholism spreads when a culture is dying, just as rickets appears when there is no Vitamin D. It is a sign that the culture has lost its health-granting cohesion.

The native American tribes would again be an example. Here were cultures rich in spiritual life and healing power. The Indian, cut off from the sources of his own spiritual strength by the European tribes, and unwilling to adopt the gods of his oppressors, was left with an empty spiritual space, and too often the spirit of alcohol moved in to fill it. The Europeans were all too happy at this and often shipped the liquor into the dying Indian villages.

Nobody knows what causes alcoholism. It is one of those things, like a war, whose etiology is so complex that attempts to describe it do not yet help us heal. One of the insights of AA was to quit wondering why a person drinks and just work with the situation at hand. In doing this they figured out how to keep an alcoholic sober after he has stopped drinking. Two chapters in the AA "Big Book" describe how the program works. They list typical situations in which alcoholics who have found sobriety begin to drink again. By looking at these, we can do a sort of backwards etiology of the disease. Here are three examples:

"Resentment is the 'number one' offender. It destroys more alcoholics than anything else. . . ."

The alcoholic is "driven by a hundred forms of fear, self-delusion, self-seeking, and self-pity. . . ."

"The alcoholic is an extreme example of self-will run riot."

In summary, AA has found that the following may lead a sober alcoholic back to drinking: resentment, self-centeredness, managing, trying to do everything yourself, and keeping secret the things that hurt you. There are two categories in this list. An alcoholic will drink again (1) if he sets himself up as self-sufficient and (2) if he gets stuck in the mechanisms that defend this autonomy. *Individualism and its defences support the disease of alcoholism.* Just one more example: in this civilization we take personal credit for change and accomplishment. But it is AA's experience that if an alcoholic begins to feel personally responsible for his sobriety, or if he tries to take control of the group, or if he breaks his anonymity, he will probably drink.

Getting sober goes against the grain of our civilization. This grain consists of money and technology. For more than a century these have been our dominant models for security and liveliness. I want to show quickly how these models feed 'individualism' and its false sense of human and higher powers. To begin with we have misperceived the nature of machines. First, we have assumed that they run by themselves, that they can be isolated and self-sustaining. Second, we have thought they were our slaves. But it has turned out that the model of life that includes slavery diminishes humans, regardless of whether those slaves are people or machines. And finally, we have forgotten that mechanical power is only one form of power. It is authentic and important, but limited. In the last 50 years it has become so inflated as to impoverish other forms of power. (These points can also be made about money—we have assumed that money could be left alone to 'work' for us and out of this assumption it has become an autonomous and inflated power.)

But neither money nor machines can create. They shuttle tokens of energy, but they do not transform. A civilization based on them puts people out of touch with their creative powers. There is very little a poet can learn from them. Poems are gifts. The poet works them, but they are not his, either in their source or in their destination. The differences between mechanical & monetary power and creative power are not of themselves a problem, but when the former become inflated and dominant, as they have in this century, they are lethal to poetry.

Hart Crane is an example. He was a poet born into a typically mercantile American family. His father invented the life saver and built up the family candy business. Between the time he left home and the time he killed himself, Crane made endless flesh trips back and forth between his creative energies and his father's designs. There was one horrible hot summer when he ended up in Washington D.C. trying to sell the family sweets. You cannot be a poet without some connection to others—to your group or family or class or nation . . . —but all that was offered to Crane was this thing that kills poets. It is not an exaggeration to say that these forces divided him from his own life energies and contributed to his alcoholism and his death.

The link between alcoholism and technical civilization—and the reasons they are both antithetical to poetry—is their shared misunderstandings about power and powerlessness. It is a misunderstanding which rises out of the inflation of mechanical power and results in the impoverishment of personal power, the isolation of creative energy, the blindness to high powers, the limitation of desire to material objects and a perversion of the will.

In a technological civilization one is deprived of authentic expressions of creative energy because contact with the outer world does not lead to real change (transformation). When this happens it becomes impossible to make judgments on the limits and nature of your personal power. You become stupefied, unable to perceive either higher powers or your own. You have a vague longing to feel creative energy, but no wisdom to guide you. Such a person is a sitting duck for alcoholism.

The disease begins and ends with an empty willfulness. The alcoholic fighting his disease has not authentic contact because nothing changes. The revelation that the alcoholic is powerless over his drinking was one of the founding insights of AA. And the admission of this powerlessness is the First Step in arresting the disease. The paradox is that the admission of powerlessness does not lead to slavery or obliteration, but the opposite. It leads to revaluation of personal power which is human, bounded and authentic.

II

Here is a curious quote from Saul Bellow's introduction to John Berryman's unfinished novel, *Recovery*. It refers to the time when Berryman began *The Dream Songs*:

John had waited a long time for this poet's happiness. He had suffered agonies of delay. Now came the poems. They were killing him. . . . Inspiration contained a death threat. He would, as he wrote the things he had waited and prayed for, fall apart. Drink was a stabilizer. It somewhat reduced the fatal intensity.

What does this mean, "Inspiration contained a death threat"? Bellow is hot on the trail of a half-truth. When one is in-spired, filled with the breath of some other power, many things die. The conscious ego dies, or at least falls back, when the inspiring powers speak. But is this a *threat*? Certainly it is a risk, like any change, but religions and artists have long held that this inspiration is joyful and enlivening, not threatening.

There seem to be two kinds of death: the 'greatful death' that opens outward with release and joy, and the bitter or stone death that tightens down on the self. An alcoholic death is of the second kind. The self collapses, it does not rise. Bellow is right, there was a relationship between this poet's drinking and his inspiration, but he has the structure of it wrong. For an alcoholic, imbibing itself is fatal to inspiration. The poems weren't killing Berryman. Drink was not the "stabilizer" that "reduced the fatal intensity." Alcohol was itself the "death threat."

It is my thesis here that this war, between alcohol and Berryman's creative powers, is at the root of the Dream Songs. I will show how their mood, tone, structure, style and content can be explicated in terms of alcoholism. Further, that Berryman himself (at the time he wrote the poems) was blind to this. His tactics, aesthetics and epistemology were all wrong and by the end of the book booze had almost wholly taken over. He lost the war. The bulk of the Dream Songs were written by the spirit of alcohol, not John Berryman.

Before I unfold a particular example I want to say a few words related to the tone of the Dream Songs. As I outlined above, in the course of getting sober an alcoholic must deal daily with his own anger, self-pity, willfulness and so on. If he doesn't face these, the booze will latch onto them and keep him drinking. As the "Big Book" says, they "may be the dubious luxury of normal men, but for alcoholics these things are poison."

Self-pity is one of the dominant tones in the Dream Songs. To understand it we must first look at pity. William Blake wrote that "Pity divides the soul." Apparently a part of the soul goes out to a person we pity. A corollary to this is that one cannot grow or change and feel pity at the same time, for growth comes when the soul is whole and in motion. This is old wisdom, common in ancient tales. For example in Apuleius' story "Amor and Psyche" (lately revived by Erich Neumann) Psyche, when she has to journey into the underworld, is warned by a tower that pity is not lawful down there. "As thou crossest the sluggish river, a dead man that is floating on the surface will pray thee, raising his rotting hands, to take him into the boat. But be thou not moved with pity for him, for it is not lawful." Another example: among the Suni Indians, a gravedigger is supposed to be immune to pity, for if he pities the newly-dead he will be vulnerable to their cries and they will carry him off.

In pity, when a part of the self goes out to the sufferer, the self is not free to move until the sufferer has been relieved of his hurt. So there are two situations in which pity is dangerous. One is that in which the self is in need of all its faculties to survive, as in Psyche's passage through the underworld. The other is the case in which the sufferer cannot be made whole again, as with the truly dead. It seems that death-energy is so strong that if a person identifies with the dying he will be hopelessly sucked in.

This is why Jesus says "Let the dead bury their dead." When Jesus himself took pity on Mary and her tears over Lazarus, his own soul was torn. (St. John says that he "groaned in the spirit.") The interesting thing is that he could not raise the dead in this condition. Before he could act, he had to first address the Father in order to regain his wholeness. You cannot raise the dead if you have pity on them. It is only done with love and love's wholeness. Pity is directed to the past and present, love is directed toward the future. So Nietzche says "All great love is above pity: for it wants to create what is love!" It wants the future and pity is a stony place in the present.

Self-pity has the same structure, only it works entirely inside a person, he needs no outer object. His own soul is divided, to use Blake's image, and self-pity is the mechanism through which the

division and its stasis are enforced and solidified. The self casts off its
hurt part, sets it up as an object, and broods over it. Resentments
work the same way and to a similar end, the maintenance of the
status quo. In alcoholism they call it 'the poor-me's' and its
metaphysics is "Poor me, poor me, pour me a drink."

In the end, all the dividing emotions—self-pity, pride, resentments, and so on—become servants of the disease of alcoholism.
Like political palliatives, they siphon off healing energy and allow
the sickening agent to stay in power. Their tone and mood are part of
the voice of booze.

Let us look at a poem, one of the early, solid Dream Songs. When
Robert Lowell reviewed the first book of Songs back in 1964 he
chose to print Song 29 in full as "one of the best and most unified." It
reads:

There sat down, once, a thing on Henry's heart
so heavy, if he had a hundred years
& more, & weeping, sleepless, in all them time
Henry could not make good.
Starts again always in Henry's ears
the little cough somewhere, an odour, a chime.

And there is another thing he has in mind
like a grave Sienese face a thousand years
would fail to blur the still profiled reproach of.
                    Ghastly,
with open eyes, he attends, blind.
All the bells say: too late, This is not for tears;
thinking.
But never did Henry, as he thought he did,
end anyone and hacks her body up
and hide the pieces, where they may be found.
He knows: he went over everyone, & nobody's missing.
Often he reckons, in the dawn, them up
Nobody is ever missing.

Though not apparent at first, this poem is deeply connected to
alcohol. The last stanza describes what is known as a 'blackout,' a
phenomenon of heavy drinking in which the drinker goes through
periods of un-remembered activity. In a blackout one is not *passed*

out; he goes to parties, drives home, has conversations and so forth, but afterwards he has no memory of what he has done. The next day he may meet someone on the street who thanks him for the loan and returns money or he may find himself in an airport and call home only to discover he has inexplicably taken a plane halfway across the continent. Berryman gives an example in the novel. The main character is a teacher (so close to Berryman that we needn't maintain the fiction) who reports "my chairman told me one day I had telephoned a girl student at midnight threatening to kill her—no recollection, blacked out." This incident may be the actual basis of the last stanza here. (The misogyny of the Dream Songs would take another essay to unravel. Suffice it to say here that sexual anger and alcoholism are connected through similar misconceptions of human power. As it has been men who "get into power," men have traditionally outnumbered women alcoholics. This will change to the degree that women mistake feminism for a route to centralized power.)

This poem has one other personal allusion in it. When he was a 12-year old boy, Berryman's father killed himself. (It is implied in the novel that his father may also have been alcoholic.) His suicide is the subject of several of the Dream Songs, especially numbers 76 and 384. In fact it lurks throughout the book. William Meredith reports that Berryman once said of the Dream Songs that "the first 384 are about the death of his father . . . and number 385 is about the illegitimate pregnancy of his daughter." This remark is as much truth as wit. I have no doubt Berryman believed it, certainly when he wrote the Songs and perhaps even when he was writing the novel. Though it is intentionally vague in this poem, if you had asked him what the "thing" was that sat down on Henry's heart, he would have said his father's suicide.

Let us return to Song 29. I take this poem to be about anxiety and I should say a few words about this to make it clear why it is not just the mood of the poem, but the subject. Anxiety differs from fear in that it has no object. This means there is no *action* which will resolve the feeling. The sufferer who does not realize this will search his world for problems to attend to in hopes of relieving his anxiety, only to find that nothing will fill its empty stomach. For example, anxiety is a major symptom of withdrawal from alcohol addiction, in which case it has a cause—the sudden absence of the addicting drug—but still no object. There is still nothing to do to resolve the feeling. If the alcoholic in withdrawal begins to drink again, his anxiety may be relieved but not resolved, it is merely postponed with an anaesthetic glow.

Anxiety is a symptom not just of withdrawal, but of active alcoholism and it even plagues sober alcoholics long after their last drink. The mood in this poem is typical of alcoholic anxiety: it is intense, mysterious and desperate. This is not grief and this is not suffering. It is important to make this clear because both Berryman and his critics have seen the mood here as grief or suffering. But both of these differ from anxiety in that they are active and directed toward an end. The grief we feel when someone dies moves toward its own boundary. The mourning song usually lasts three days and its biological point, as it were, is that it leads out of itself. Grief that lasts much longer than a year does so because it has been blocked in some way. It is then pathologic, just as a blockage in the blood system is pathologic. In fairy tales the person who weeps and cannot stop finally turns into a snake, for unabated grief is not human.

Suffering, like grief, is an activity, a labor, and it ends. There are healthy ways to suffer—that is, ways which move with grace from pain to ease. This is not what happens either in the Dream Songs or in this poem.

Now let us look more closely at the content of Song 29. It is one of the strongest of the Dream Songs precisely because its vagueness is true to anxiety. Throughout the Songs the character Henry is bothered and doesn't know why. The cause of his pain is always abstract, "a thing" here; elsewhere "a departure," (1)* "something black somewhere," (92) and so on. Typically an anxious person does not realize this lack of content but projects his mood onto the outer world. Everyone else knows something is being projected because the proportions are all off, as when a dying man begins to worry about his cat. A strength of this poem is that Berryman does not unload his mood directly. However, behind the vagueness there are ghosts.

The first stanza I sense as a description of the recurrent and inescapable memory of his father's suicide. The anxiety is projected backwards. The second stanza has as its main image the "grave Sienese face." The reference is obscure to me but I associate it with art, religion and death ("grave"). It carries Berryman's sense of the future: his hope is that spiritual life and poetry will be the path out of

*Parenthetical numbers refer to the numbered Dream Songs.

his misery, but he fears he won't make it. (That this was in fact the form of his activity can be shown from other poems. In both Songs 73 and 99, for example, he approaches temples but is unable to make any contact. Song 66 has spiritual wisdom as its background but at the end, "Henry grew hot, got laid, felt bad" and is reproached as he is by the Sienese face here.) The middle stanza of Song 29 is future directed and hopeless. It has in it a premonition, certainly the fear, of his own suicide.

Therefore the structure of the poem is the structure of his anxiety: it is felt as inescapable, it is projected backwards (onto the father's suicide) and forwards (onto his own) and he senses himself, in the blackout stanza, as an alienated field of violence between these two deaths.

We can now return to self-pity which I judge to be the final tone of this song and of the book as a whole. The Dream Songs do not move to a resolution. Berryman told Richard Kostelanetz in 1969: "Henry is so troubled and bothered by his many problems that he never actually comes up with solutions, and from that point of view the poem is a failure." The core mood in the poems is anxiety and dread and when they leave that they do not rise out of it but slide sideways into intellectualizing, pride, boredom, talk, obfuscation, self-pity and resentment. This happens so often that these are the dominant tones of the Dream Songs. Here are a few examples of resentment and self-pity:

God's Henry's enemy. (13)
Life, friends, is boring.(14)
Henry hates the world.
What the world to Henry
did will not bear thought.
Feeling no pain,
Henry stabbed his arm and wrote a letter
explaining how bad it had been
in this world. (74)

All this is being scrutinized in the critical literature about Berryman under the fancy handle of "the epistemology of loss." But it's really just an alcoholic poet on his pity-pot. Not having decided if he wants to get well he is reinforcing his disease with a moan. The poems articulate the moods and methods of the alcoholic ego. But as

the "Big Book" says, "when harboring such feelings we shut ourselves off from the sunlight of the Spirit. The insanity of alcohol
returns and we drink again. And with us, to drink is to die." This
means that when approached by an alcoholic with a magnificent
problem, all years a-drip with complication and sorrow, one's response has to be "Yes, but do you want to get sober?" To become
involved in the pain before the disease has been arrested is to help
the man or woman stay sick.

Berryman's father killed himself more than 40 years before these
poems were written. It is a hard judgment, but inescapable, that the
use of the father's death here and elsewhere in the Dream Songs
amounts to self-pity. Certainly there is grief and anger, but in the
end the memory of that death is used as a device in a holding action
of the alcoholic ego. I think Berryman himself saw this before he
died. I presume he is referring to the two books of Dream Songs
(1964 & 1968) when he writes in the novel of his "self-pity, rage,
resentments—a load so great I've spent two well-known volumes
on it."

When making judgments like these the question arises whether
or not Berryman was trapped. If he couldn't resolve his pain for
reasons beyond his control, then his expressions of it are not self-
pity. This is important because this was Berryman's sense of himself.
He identified with the trapped and oppressed: Anne Frank, Bessie
Smith, Victoria Spivey, Job, Jeremiah in the Lamentations and so
on. Can an alcoholic be classified in this group? In one sense yes, he
is trapped: once the booze has possessed him it also baffles his
healing powers so that demanding he simply quit drinking is a bit
like asking a catatonic to snap out of it.

And yet people get sober. AA guarantees a day of sobriety to any
who follow their suggestions. So once the alcoholic, like the early
Christian, has heard the Word, he is no longer trapped; it comes
down to whether or not he wants sobriety. And then the real war
begins. It is when the active alcoholic is presented with the option of
sobering up that he starts to defend his right to drink, to deny he is
having any trouble with alcohol, to attack AA, and to hoard his
resentments and pain.

In the end Berryman's tone leads me to judge he was not trapped.
The blues don't have that tone. They are not songs of self-pity.
Leadbelly or Billie Holiday have more resonance than the Dream
Songs precisely because they were not divided against themselves

by their oppressor (as an alcoholic is) and because the enemy is identified (not vague as in Berryman) and the self is in motion. Likewise the strength of Anne Frank is that her diary is direct, not whiny. Berryman was lost and in pain, but not trapped.

> *and something can (has) been said for sobriety*
> *but very little. (57)*
> *Why drink so, two days running?*
> *two months, O seasons, years, two decades running?*
> *I answer (smiles) my question on the cuff:*
> *Man, I been thirsty. (96)*

This voice is to alcohol what the Uncle Tom is to the racist.

I want to turn now to the structural innovations, the emotional plot, of the Dream Songs. As a person becomes alcoholic he becomes divided inside and typically turns into a con-man. The booze-hustler in him will command all of the self's true virtues to maintain its hold. He has a double voice then: sincerity with a motive. Berryman's device of having his central figure, Henry, be a white man in black face is an accurate imitation of this. Henry has become a con-man and can't figure out why. His mood is accurate to alcoholism: he is anxious, guilt-ridden, secretly proud, baffled and driven.

> *Huffy Henry hid the day*
> *unappeasable Henry sulked. (1)*

As Berryman wrote, Henry has "suffered an irreversible loss." He knows somewhere that he is not responsible for it and yet he can't escape it either. His sidekick in the poems, a black man who calls him Mr. Bones, is exactly like the alcoholic's spouse who keeps saying "You're suffering, you must be guilty." They conspire in keeping each other unhappy.

When Berryman says that the book is a "failure" in terms of finding a solution to Henry's problems, it seems clear that he would have preferred to work with Henry, to exorcise him or at least objectify him and his loss. But this is a disease and not susceptible to such powers. "Will power is nothing. Morals is nothing. Lord, this is illness," he wrote in the novel. That is: when confronted by the will and the ego, alcohol always wins. James Dickey noticed that when a dream Song gets off the ground, Berryman gets it there "through sheer will and guts." Some of the poems do work this way, through will-power, like Song 29. But they are oddly empty, like screams.

The will is a power and a necessary one, but by itself it is neither creative nor healing. But it is Berryman's tool, and this is why I said earlier that he loses his fight with alcohol because his tactics and epistemology are all wrong. Of course it did not help him that these misunderstandings about power and willfulness are everywhere imitated in our civilization.

The original design of the Dream Songs has a resonant tension that is lost as the spirit of alcohol (Henry) takes over. This begins in Book III. Berryman's inspiration in Book IV was to kill Henry off. The poems are written from the grave. My guess is that he hoped to cleanse him through a night journey. It fails. Henry leaves the grave in Song 91 and it is the resurrection of a material spirit: the media invoke Henry to rise, he does and immediately calls for a double rum. The last stanza I judge to be Berryman's horror at this, caught in the gut assumption that if the spirit of alcohol won't die, he'll have to:

A fortnight later, sense a single man
upon the trampled scene at 2 a.m.
insomnia-plagued, with a shovel
digging like mad, Lazarus with a plan
to get his own back, a plan, a stratagem
no newsman will unravel.

Berryman always insisted that Henry was "an imaginary character, not the poet, not me." Everyone has disregarded this as a poet's whim, for the two are so clearly connected. When Berryman goes to Ireland, Henry goes; when Berryman is visited by the BBC, Henry is visited, and so forth. So we have said that Henry is only a thin disguise for Berryman. But the opposite is more accurate: during those years, Henry came out of the book and possessed his creator. Berryman was reduced to a shadow. He hardly appears in Book VII at all. Its flatness and silly pride are nothing but booze talking. Nowhere can you find the passion, insight, erudition and music that mark Berryman's earlier poetry. "He went to pieces./ The pieces sat up & wrote." (331)

As a final part of this look at the Dream Songs I want to say a few words about their style. The innovations are fairly well represented by the last stanza of Song 29. They are mostly syntactical oddities: mixed tenses ("never did Henry . . . hacks") and reordered phrases ("he reckons, in the dawn, them up"). It is a deliberately broken speech which is striking when it fills with music and alternates with direct statement. Songs 29 and 1 are both good examples. The voice is reminiscent of and drawn from several sources: black blues & dialect, baby talk, drunk talk, and the broken syntax of extreme anxiety.

Why was Berryman drawn to these sources? The connection is in power relationships. In a power structure, dialect is the verbal equivalent of the slave's shuffle. It is an assertion of self in an otherwise oppressive situation. It says: "I'll speak your language, but on my own terms." Baby talk works the same way. It is the speech equivalent of the child's pout. Both are signs that there is a distance between real personal power and desired personal power. And yet neither of them is a true confrontation of that distance. They reveal that the imbalance has been neither accepted *nor* rejected, for such would lead to direct speech. When the child pouts he doesn't want his parents to leave. When the slave shuffles he has been baffled into the myth that he has no internal power and his only hope is to cajole a piece of the action out of the master. The cloying voice depends on the audience it hates. It is divided, identifying with a power not its own and hoping to control that power through verbal finesse. This is the style of the con-man.

In a case of real and inescapable oppression, stylized speech might be an assertion of self. But this would be short term; when it becomes a way of life, it is something different. In these poems, written by a grown white male, the voice is a whine. When the child whines he doesn't want the grown-ups to go away and when Berryman writes like this he doesn't want to give up the booze.

The question arises: who is the mean parent/slave driver? At times Berryman thought it must be God himself. He commonly equated Henry with Job, announcing that "God's Henry's enemy." (13) But this won't wash. As before, the tone is the top-off. Job is neither cynical nor ironic. What successfully imitates anxiety in Song 29 deflates into weary irony as it is spread over 385 songs. Irony has only emergency use. Carried over time it is the voice of the trapped who have come to enjoy their cage. This is why it is so tiresome. People who have found a route to power based on their

misery—who don't want to give it up though it would free them—
they become ironic. This sustained complaint is the tone of active
alcoholism.

The stylistic innovations in the Dream Songs are epistemologi-
cally wrong—an alcoholic is not a slave—and this is why they are so
unsatisfying. The style obscures and mystifies, it does not reveal.
Berryman himself knew there was a growing distance between his
style and his self. The question is honesty. The more developed the
style became, the more he was conning himself, reinforcing the
walls of his case. So in *Recovery* when he tries to write out some
self-criticism he reads it over and comments to himself: "No style:
good." This is a remarkable sentence for a poet to write.

His last poems, written at the same time as the novel, move away
from the old style. They were written in a drying-out place where
Berryman had gone for help. Judging from the novel many of his old
ploys were falling away as he attended to his disease and, more
importantly, as he attended to other people and received their
attention. Through other people he began to feel a "personal sense
of God's love," which he had not had since his father's suicide. The
poems from this period still have syntactic twists, now more like an
old nerve tic, but on the whole they are direct and clear, descriptive
and loving:

> *Jack went it was, on Friday, against the word*
> *of the staff & our word . . . violent relief*
> *when Sunday night he & his son, absurd*
> *in ties & jackets, for a visit brief*
> *looked back in, looking good.*

I have shown that the Dream Songs can be explicated in terms of
the disease of alcoholism. We can hear the booze talking. Its moods
are anxiety, guilt and fear. Its tone is a moan that doesn't resolve. Its
themes are unjust pain, resentment, self-pity, pride and a desperate
desire to run the world. It has the con-man's style and the con-
game's plot. It depends for its survival on an arrogance of will,
ascendent and dissociated from the whole. These poems are not a
contribution to culture. They are artifacts of a dying civilization, like
one of those loaves of bread turned to lava at Pompeii.

The way out of self-pity and its related moods is to attend to
something other than the self. This can be either the inner or the

outer world, either dreams and visions which do not come from the self, or other people and nature. The point is that the self begins to heal automatically when it attends to the non-self. Pablo Neruda is a good example of a poet who did this. He had great trust of the interior world and turned to it automatically when he was otherwise isolated. And when I asked him once what made the melancholy of his early work disappear, he spoke immediately of politics. The Spanish Civil War made him change. "That was my great experience," he said. "It was a defeat but I never considered life a defeat after that. I had faith in human things and in human people."

Berryman found neither of these things. I think his trust was broken early in both the inner and the outer worlds and he was never able to regain it despite his desire. He had no politics except patriotism and nostalgia. He refused to read at the first anti-war readings in Minneapolis. He wrote the only monarchist poem (Song 105) to come out of the sixties. And there is no spiritual energy or dream-consciousness at all in the Dream Songs.

This leads to the question of how Berryman was handled by the rest of us. We did not handle him well. Few of his critics faced the death in these poems. Most were snowed, as he was himself, by Berryman's style and brains, as if they thought rhetoric, intellectualizing and references to famous friends were what poetry is all about. At the end Berryman began to see that his fame was built on his sickness. The character in his novel "really thought, off and on for twenty years, that it was his duty to drink, namely to sacrifice himself. He saw the products as worth it." Berryman felt that "the delusion that . . . my art depended on my drinking . . . could not be attacked directly. Too far down."

This is not true. He could have attacked it. But it would not have been easy. He would have had to leave behind a lot of his own work. He would have had to leave his friends who had helped him live off his pain for twenty years. And the civilization itself, which supported all of that, weighs a great deal. *Life* magazine unerringly made the connection between our civilization and disease and went straight to Berryman as their example of the poet from the sixties. They called the piece "Whiskey and Ink, Whiskey and Ink," and there are the typical photographs of the poet with the wind in his beard and a glass in his hand. Berryman bought into the whole thing. Like Hemingway, they got him to play the fool and the salesman the last ten years of his life.

I am not saying that the critics could have cured Berryman of his disease. But we could have provided a less sickening atmosphere. In the future it would be nice if it were a little harder for the poet to come to town drunk and have everyone think that it's great fun. You can't control an alcoholic's drinking any more than he can, but the fewer parasites he has to support the better. No one knows why some alcoholics get sober and others don't. They say in AA that it takes a desire to stop drinking and, after that, the grace of God. Here are Berryman's words on this, with which I will close.

> Is escape . . . too difficult? Evidently, for (1) the walls are strong and I am weak, and (2) *I love my walls* . . . Yet some *have escaped* . . . With an effort we lift our gaze from the walls upward and ask God to take the walls away. We look back down and they have disappeared . . . We turn back upward at once with love to the Person who has made us so happy, and desire to serve Him. Our state of mind is that of a bridegroom, that of a bride. We are married, who have been so lonely heretofore.

SOURCES

Part I.

The AA "Big Book" is properly referred to as *Alcoholics Anonymous* (The General Service Board of Alcoholics Anonymous, New York: 1955). This is available at any AA meeting or by mail ($4.50) from Box 459 Grand Central Station, New York, N.Y. 10017. It is the best place to start reading about alcoholism.

Jung's letter is printed in the AA monthly magazine, "AA Grapevine," November 1974, pp. 30-1.

Ivan Illich's *Medical Nemesis* was just published by Calder & Boyers in England.

Part II.

The Dream Songs were originally published as two volumes: 77 *Dream Songs* (Farrar, Straus and Giroux, New York: 1964) and *His Toy, His Dream, His Rest* (Farrar, Straus and Giroux, New York: 1968).

All quotations by Berryman in prose are taken from *Recovery (A Novel)* (Farrar, Straus and Giroux, New York: 1973). Saul Bellow's remark is from the introduction, p. xii.

Amor and Psyche, The Psychic Development of the Feminine, A Commentary on the Tale of Apuleius, by Erich Neumann (Princeton University Press, New York: 1971), p. 48.

Robert Lowell's review was in *The New York Review of Books*, 28 May 1964, pp. 2-3. James Dickey's was in *The American Scholar*, 34 (Autumn 1965), pp 646f.

The William Meredith quotation is taken from *John Berryman: A Checklist*, compiled by Richard J. Kelly, with a foreword by William Meredith. (The Scarecrow Press, Metuchen, N.J.: 1972), p. xviii.

Berryman's remark to Richard Kostelanetz was made in an interview published in *The Massachusetts Review*, II 2 (Spring 1970), pp. 340-47.

The hospital poems were published in *The American Poetry Review*, Vol. 4, No. 1 (January 1975). The stanza I use is from "5th Tuesday."

HURRY

by OCTAVIO PAZ (translated by Eliot Weinberger)

from CHICAGO REVIEW

nominated by CHICAGO REVIEW

IN SPITE OF MY TORPOR, my puffy eyes, my paunch, my appearance of having just left the cave, I never stop. I'm in a hurry. I've always been in a hurry. Day and night a bee buzzes in my brain. I jump from morning to night, sleep to waking, crowds to solitude, dawn to dusk. It's useless that each of the four seasons offers me its opulent table; useless the canary's morning flourish, the bed lovely as a river in summer, that adolescent and her tear, cut off at the end of autumn. In vain the noon sun and its crystal stem, the green leaves that filter it, the rocks that deny it, the shadows that it sculpts. All of these splendors just speed me up. I'm off and back, cough and hack, I spin in a grin, I stomp, I'm out, I'm in, I snoop, I hear a flute,

I'm deep in my mind, I itch, I opine, malign, I change my suit, I say adieu to what I was, I linger longer in what will be. Nothing stops me. I'm in a hurry, I'm going. Where? I don't know, know nothing —except that I'm not where I should be.

From when I first opened my eyes I've known that my place isn't here where I am, but where I'm not and never have been. Somewhere there's an empty place, and that emptiness will be filled with me and I'll sit in that hole that will senselessly team with me, bubble with me until it turns into a fountain or a geyser. And then my emptiness, the emptiness of the me that I now am, will fill up with itself, full to the brink with being.

I'm in a hurry to be. I run behind myself, behind my place, behind my hole. Who has reserved this place for me? What is my fate's name? Who and what is that which moves me and who and what awaits my arrival to complete itself and to complete me? I don't know. I'm in a hurry. Though I don't move from my chair, though I don't get out of bed. Though I turn and turn in my cage. Nailed by a name, a gesture, a tic, I move and remove. This house, these friends, these countries, these hands, this mouth, these letters that form this image that without warning has come unstuck from I don't know where and has hit me across the chest, these are not my place. Neither this nor that is my place.

All that sustains me and that I sustain sustaining myself is a screen, a wall. My hurry leaps all. This body offers me its body, this sea pulls from its belly seven waves, seven nudes, seven whitecaps, seven smiles. I thank them and hurry off. Yes, the walk has been amusing, the conversation instructive, it's still early, the function isn't over, and in no way do I pretend to know the end. I'm sorry: I'm in a hurry. I'm anxious to get rid of my hurry. I'm in a hurry to go to bed and to get up without saying: goodbye, I'm in a hurry.

THE FLOWERING CACTI

by GENE FOWLER

from FELON'S JOURNAL (Second Coming Press)

nominated by Leonard Randolph and Hugh Fox

Chin tucked into collar.
Red and white eyes rolled up
into steel blue sockets.
Scruffy rooster cackling in my throat.
Unhired, Unhinged.
Derelict with a few poems in print.
Arms folded, back bent,
trying to keep my belly warm.
Squeaking doors in that belly.
Too stubborn to admit
all the poets are dead,
I keep croaking, "Some of us
are only dying."

I WISH YOU WOULDN'T

fiction by WILLIAM GASS

from PARTISAN REVIEW

nominated by Ben Pesta

Mr. HESS SAID, his hat turning slowly between his knees. His wife lay sick in a chair, quite silent. Mr. Hess was leaning forward, his weight on his forearms, hat hanging from the pads of his fingers, carpet across his eyes. Um, he thought. Aah. His wife tipped back in the lounger, rigid as always, her risen feet in a V. Mr. Hess, however, sagged in contrast, his whole weight pressing against his thighs above his knees, brown hat dangling between his trousers. His missus stretched out staring at the ceiling in order not to see, and he couldn't endure that either. The canary, or whatever the hell it was, rattled its beak and then shrieked . . . shrieked and rattled its beak. Hess moved his shoes to stand inside the florals. The venetian blinds were scratched, though you couldn't see the scratches in the shade they threw. Their shadows simply said how crookedly the slats hung. What to do? although the question required no answer, hurrying after itself with furthermore of itself like a second hand. He had sucked the center from that old cliché: *and time lay heavy on his hands.* Dust sank through the light to snow his shoes—the air so thick, the fall so fast—while whatever it was—canary bird, cuckoo—rapped its beak along the bars till Hess remembered boyhood pleasures too . . . with a pang like the smart of a stick. What? what? what to do? Thin tan lines flew parallels inside his suit no matter how he moved, but his wife could barely stretch herself about her bones. Mr. Hess was afraid she had cancer—something, at any rate, lingering and serious. Her skin was a poor color and she was wasted as an ad for famines. Maybe her mind had been affected by the illness, too; that would explain the peculiarities of her behavior. Change of life, he'd heard, often did them funny. He felt that he should get her to a doctor. A doctor—he pendulumed his hat—a doctor, yes, that was his duty. The doctor would report upon her. Smiling gently, rimless-eyed, he'd write her up as dying. Then he'd instruct Mr. Hess in the society of symptoms which his wife's disease had founded. They always turn queer in a case like this, the doctor would say; oh they go strange, sometimes very early. We suspect, the doctor would say—my science does, you understand—that there's a kind of signal of the future in it. Poor things, he'd say, they're done for from the first: an abnormal placenta, don't you see, pressure from a pelvis that's too small, or some slight chemical disturbance, sudden stress, internal turbulence or organ tumble, a quiet slow infection, and it's all over: sizz-z-z-z until the air's out; so don't heavy your head any further with it, Mr. Hess, don't dent your hair, not even by a hat's weight, none of it's your doing, she was born at half eleven in her life . . . chew this bit of candy here to sweeten up your teeth, possess yourself in patience . . . death should follow shortly now, though her soul can only sweep away, not fly, it has so little stamina. You've no young children, I suppose, Hess, have you? and I trust you're well insured. Ha ha, Mr. Hess thought. Ha ha. And he solemnly prayed for his wife's demise. Too weary for hate or even malice, he certainly didn't feel ashamed; foreign, rather, to remorse or any sorrow. She was sick enough to be lots better dead. That was a fact, god's truth. Hess wished her speedy passage o'er the great divide as he wished,

weekends, for green golfing weather. It was reflexive, a wish as mild
and futile as it was heartfelt and desperate, because he'd given up
golf, as he'd given up bowling. Laid to rest, he'd want the shoveling
ceremony, please, run through just once again. The disappearance
of her bier beneath the earth was a constant longing like the thirsty
for another dram. His hat dropped softly to the carpet, quashing an
edge. He slid his right arm forward to recover it. Only a doctor, only
a definite "soon she must die," could give him hope, for his own
heaviness was overcoming him. Every day he hung a little lower on
himself. It grew more difficult to rise in the morning, lift himself
from chairs or slide from cars, even stir at all, accomplish stairs or
carry any trifling action to completion, and the blood which fell out
of his heart was siphoned back painfully. But she would never
submit herself to any sort of physical examination. It was inconceiv-
able. She knew she had a body of extraordinary kind, and that
strange gray oblong organs would be discovered swimming like sea
animals in the plate of the X ray. No . . . he had to be satisfied, since
it was always possible that the doctor might frighten her off from the
brink of her death with a knife or a needle, whereas her present ill
health, hopefully plain, though he only conjectured it, advanced
with a steadiness no one as deeply concerned as he could fail to
appreciate. He would accept the uncertainty. Mr Hess knew no
more of the spirit than his hat did—that is, not directly; and if his
flesh seemed to be sliding slowly from him like thick batter or a
heavy syrup, it did not make his bones more saintly. Nevertheless it
was that realm, mysterious in its work as magnets, and moving
always out of sight and underground like rivers of electricity, which
was the source of his dismay and the cause of his anguish. He did feel
that with ingenious instruments it probably could be seen, in some
way metered or its passage mapped, for this invisible world in which
his wife lived made her weary; the stream she swam in was perhaps
impalpable, but it left her damp; indeed, there were times when
Mr. Hess sensed, somehow, the current flowing, and knew that
sallow as her skin looked, lifeless as she seemed flung down on a
couch or discarded in a chair like emptied clothing, she was lit up
inside and burning brightly like a lamp. Even so, the only lamp he
knew which fit his image of her was the sort which smoked above a
poker table; surely she had no sky inside herself to fall from, no
ceiling fixture, ceiling chain, or wire burning like a worm. She had
her distances, all right, but within was their one direction, and Mr.

Hess could not help but wonder once again exactly why he was sitting where he was; how it had happened to him, so bodily a being, even if he were a bit baggy and had all those habits she disapproved of in her subtle aerial way, never saying a word, just exuding an odor like ripe cheese when he appeared, causing the temperature and light to alter, holding up time so that it seemed he'd been picking his nose forever, or simply sending a sigh through the house like a breeze; how had it happened he should be so fastened to this—this twig, he sometimes thought in those moments when the past seemed as though it had held a promise and he'd once been a blossom, then a fruit, full of juice and flavor; how had it happened to him? prisoners must say that, over and over, he thought, handcuffed, chained, hit, Christ even thought it, as he was hanging there, nailed; but Mr. Hess had no head for searches, he could scarcely find his slippers, answers were out of the question, as his wife said sometimes, no, only these same wonderments circled through him, wooden in their wheeling as a roundabout. I've got to slow down, Mr. Hess thought. He ran along paths in the carpet, in the tan, around the turns of leaves and flowers. She hasn't enough blood in the narrow channels of her flesh to pink a tear, while mine is like sand in a sand-clock, almost wholly in my head—thick, moist, flushed, hot—or in my feet—heavy, old, cold, quiet—awaiting the tipsy-turvy to trickle out, thus I alternate a lot, don't I? she's not the only one whose spirit's like electric current, but alas I've none of the instant capacity of wires. Hang in there, anyhow, Hess. Hang in. But she was having her weirds now, the stiffish kind, and he wished she wouldn't. He could hit her again, of course. He could always do that. Instead he groaned and tried to spin his hat upon his finger. She was ill. She was dying. So he hoped. But she didn't have to tell fortunes. She didn't have to sit in the kitchen with the cards spread out, absorbed by the tale they were telling, bad news for Edgar, when he came home. She didn't have to leave the house to squat on the front step, in the drive, where he would find her making noises like a key-wound engine. Nor did she have to disgrace his needs, throwing up her skirt quite suddenly to leave him thunderstruck. I'll be needing lawyers, if I'm not careful. Not so heavy with the fall of the fists, Hess, hey? he cautioned himself. Not so quick with the kick. When the jury learns what you've been through, Mr. Hess, don't worry, they will give you sympathy; they'll put her beaten body behind bars; they'll hiss when she is carried through the court.

You've heard of the victimless crime, Hess, haven't you? Well, there are crimeless victims, too. You're one of them—one of those. What's a paltry kick compared to the piteous smiles she's inflicted on you, the looks thrown heavenward with such aboriginal skill and cunning with curves they stone down later in your living room the whole naked length of a sofa-soft Sunday afternoon, passing through the shield of the Sunday paper, bruising your eyes; or the little whimpering moues which cower in the corner of her mouth, how about those? the glances which scuttle away like bugs to the baseboard to wait the night, all the tiny gnawing things she keeps about her: frightened knees and elbows, two flabs of breast with timorous nips, disjointed nose, latched eyes? There are laws against that, Mr. Hess, unwritten laws, the laws of common deceny, laws of the spirit and the soul, what she knew best, Hess, didn't she? sure, her silences, for instance, are against the law, silence is against the law, silences are blows, and you can plead self-defense, you plead extenuation, you can argue quite agreeably that you were driven to extremes, out of reason as out of town, by all those occasions when she struck you with inwardness—oh—witholding is wicked, refusing to respond, that's malice, Hess, you have every excuse, don't worry your warts, and when the jury hears how you have borne yourself these long weary dreadful, ladensomely heavy years, they'll set you free to cheers and to the sound of bells, though it'll help your case if you don't have young children, Mr. Hess, you haven't have you? that's best. Ha ha, Mr. Hess thought. Ha Ha. Please to observe, Mr. Hess, now, that she isn't dead. She's having one of her little nervous spells, a little dab of the dizzies, so she's resting, that's all, she's merely unmoving, stiff and staring, eyes wide as a picture window, watching god knows what going on on the screen of the ceiling, some soap opera of the soul, a few new developments in the Grand Design, I shouldn't wonder—ha, Mr. Hess, hey? ha—no, it's just another quietly ordinary sagamuffin Sunday in the Hess household, and you're no stranger to it, sweat it out the same as always, lean on the your knees till your thighs dent, you know how it goes, you know the routine—oh my goodness, what's to be done, Hess, what's to be done? His urine fell out of him as out of a nozzleless hose, while she was forever listening . . . listening . . . in constantly alert and continuously expectant receivership, so to speak, like a line of ears for early warning, *Pamphila*. Faugh. What's done is done; then done, it's done, and then it's done. So why wait any

longer? when every act is over and we're filing out. Anyway . . . my
wife, to picture paths and patterns in resting rocks, deep tides of
feeling, vast programs of action . . . well, she became positively
seismographic, and registered dirt in hugh mud-bond hunks
roundly wibble-slob-wobbling like a dancer's tum. Wait? Thin ass
on a fat chance. Run? She said she heard his grass and claimed it was
up to no good and had ungracious plans. What could he do but close
his hands? She's pick up stray transmissions even in the splash of his
pee, the hum of motors, the surreptitious click of switches. Everything which entered the house, whether from above or below
ground, entered her . . . entered without knocking: the wind, of
course, and the rustle of leaves, sunfall as noisy as Niagara, day-mist
and light spatter, they were welcome as Holy Water because she
sensed the presence of the Sacred Word in bird whistle, rain
plop—noises natural and noises not—squirrel chatter, pipe rattle,
buzz, bloom, shadow; she parsed them all as easily as he read Dick
and Jane—St. Francis couldn't hold a sparrow to her—and she had
for each of this world's blurts a warm greeting, not for him, though,
just for the holing of moles and earth-eating worms, just for the
paths, traps, and caches of beetles and spiders, for ants, wasps,
cicadas—veterans as jovial in their cosy halls of relaxation as members of the American Legion. She'd have an immediate sympathy for
the growth of roots, too, Hess was prepared to bet, their efforts, the
energy, life's task, how it was . . . like fingers struggling into gloves.
It was a contradiction he couldn't countenance or fathom, because
for all her foreknowledge, he still had to yoo-hoo when he came
round a corner, and without that cheerful next door warning, or the
boop-boop-boop of a rubber horn he'd filched from the handlebars
of a neighbor tike's bike—ha, oh lord, ha ha, ha ha—she'd startle
like a sparkler, burn with indignation briefly, and darken on the
wire. Otherwise she was stoical. She was patient. Rapt, she waited
for erosion, rust, chip, flake, craze, settle, since slowness didn't faze
her, accumulations of the gradual, the thick that gets there bit by bit
the way fog sags in a hollow, little reiterations, all the overtold
anecdotes of the actual, same upon same, she said, were satisfying,
though her face did not betray her pleasure, if, in fact, she felt some,
giving away only what a dial would, so he sometimes knew where his
wife was tuned without any sense for the source or substance of the
signal, and because she was a stranger to class and its consequent
snobbery, she listened equally to gravel scatter or the incontinent

wetting of basement walls. The further within she went, the more numerous the noises, an orchestra hot for its A couldn't compete for cacophany, and they delivered her news as diverse as the dailies. To tap drip, naturally, she bowed like a rod; to knuckle pop and cloth scrape, she was a wand . . . how do you stand it, Hess often said, with so much going on, if it's as you say, and there are vibrations in ethers as yet unimagined, sounds exceeding sound even in the customary shoe squeak and silk slither, or from drapes, morose and heavy, hanging in a skin of dust, there comes the prolonged metal shudder of a gong? Of course, it's only me who has the wonder, and who am I—so dull, so down; but I think it's remarkable that you should be responsive to the low moan of cushions; if you ask me, it's even suspicious how warmly you are washed by every slow hydraulic sigh released by grease racks, barber chairs and door stops; strange that you are passionately moved—image—by the yearn of warping boards, the tireless cries of wood rot, thin as thread and exquisitely tangled, but perhaps it's that sadistic element in you which appreciates broken slats and tacks like teeth, screws, nails, staples with their twin penetration like the drilled wounds of eyes, the elongating pains of picture wire, the screams of burning bulbs, and although in your overburdened state it may be kind of you to regret the steady dampening of salt on humid days, still, one need not be a queen and have a palace to enjoy the sweet granular silence of sugar in its crock. Voices: they were everywhere around her like gnats. In snowfall, frost. He had his hat. To rise? to doff one final time? good day, Madame—good-by, surprise— . . . to leave? He could do that. Run under it out of the rain. How many of his dreams had flight and freedom in them? Ham and eggs, Pie and cheese. Muff and sniff. She'd hear the Southern slurs of melting custard and be . . . entranced. He had his hat. He could do that. But noises he made deliberately to set her off, stomps around the room or weights he placed on the floor to make it groan, soda he shook and swallowed, screws he gave an extra turn to, fists he left printed in the air, the pounding he gave the coverlet, or conversely the squeaks he silenced with sewing machine oil, the jars he swaddled in socks, the lids he glued or the many things he simply removed in the trunk of their car to cast on the dump or drop in a lake or bury: none of these acts moved her because, he said, under torture matter could be made to say anything. Mud, mold, matter—what one called it didn't count—but it had neither courage, nor loyalty, nor conscience. In her husband's police chief state matter would moisten its tongue for its own ass, and she didn't believe that right, she refused absolutely to consider it, matter alone meant nothing, a calf or slime, she said, not an object of thought, of piety or speech; it was a convenient carrier at best, a carton for cats, and so she thought of it the way typhoid must have thought of Mary, no more, not even as a necessary ambience or elevation or so much as a stand for music, pediment for a statue or tower with an aerial, though that was closer, and what was he, then, in his dense maleness, a series of surfaces like a stack of plates, what was he with his bowling and his beer and his business—charging the living for their life and paying off only when death was a winner—what was he with his busy pencil and greedy teeth, in the flesh of his flesh, but the purest muck, individuation driven to the point of indifference, asafetida not energy, sheer dumb disagreeable stuff, unworked, unrealized, raw, foolish in its lean teeter, its oils, wows, and ouches, as an Evereadied dolly, yet with a prick which led him on his little trot through life like a leash held at the loop end in the Pope's fist? Butterflies leave laces in the air like a courtier's cuffs, she said. Faugh. Easy to say such, harder to prove so. Still, in order not to shit, she would refuse to eat—intolerable the sounds of devoured food: unfeathered, fried, carved, bitten, chewed—therefore why was his pissing so productive? How about a belch, he'd asked her, much message in that? How about a fart? What can you read in a sneeze or the ooze of sweat, the collar of water on the toilet pipe—ha—what do you say?—what about the petulent whine and then the frightened whinny of laboring machines? leap of light from a mirror? unkinking cock? but she would smile her sad peacemaker's smile at his coarseness, face him with a calm forbearing palm, explain that only the plainest idea could be contained in such a short intemperate sound as a sneeze, bereft of feeling and every fineness, say how often there'd be but blunt sense in the sharpest signal, because you never can tell about such things, Edgar, you must know that by now, surely you do, you do, surely, and though paint slides from a brush sometimes in a way that's purely meditative, never mind, I have heard hush! in the batter of hammers, the clatter of cans, and please in the rasp of a file. I know every letter of the law, Hess said: L . . .A . . . —and I know of the awe in it, was her reply. It helped her to hit her, Hess knew that. Surely he knew that. Who had his hat? She hadn't his hat. He had his hat. She wanted hitting in the worst way, although her surrender to his will was like another conquest of China. Still, what did it matter whether she was out from a blow or lost in her dizzy mind's movies, since she could easily have dreams during dinner, trances during a doze? There was no place or moment she was willing to occupy the way Hess took over his air and hours—fully, heavily, persistently—so he was unable to feel there were any outlines to her—no weights, no volumes, no shifts—she was never anywhere. His wife might undergo visions while steaming a crease in his office trousers, plume out a chimney and disappear, receive visitations washing dishes, her thin hands gloved in suds as delicate as underclothes, or entertain omens and other astral submissions as though they were coffees set out in kitchens, as though one's daughter or less likely one's son had come home from a party and wanted to talk and you had perhaps pie and a bit of cheese to go along with the midnight signs and ciphers, the symbols and the codes, while you listened numbly dumbly to the life you'd passed by years ago like some display in a window turntabled once again—turntabled—ha—ha ha—and your daughter or less likely your son awkwardly dancing to it as if it were a new tune and not a revival routinely fiddled by Old Bones and his Big Band. Ha, Mr. Hess thought. Ha ha, Articles in attics: so much for her visions. Voices spoke to him too, spoke to Hess, nicknouned the Hessian by his mates—ha—ha ha—they spoke to him from out of the past as hers did out of the walls, because—it was true—what has gone before goes before like a hound, peeing a path, and damn if the old days didn't dump on her, she was no different for all her fancies, because Hess knew from his own bitter history, hers too, that when today caught up with yesterday they would call it tomorrow. Visions, she said. Voices. Faugh. He had cause: cause like cotton is the cause of wounds, Blah. He knew. He had grounds. But his eyes did not step from the carpet where they were confined by stems and leaves to little curlicues. There was no need to look. Even if the room changed around him , it would be the same to his shoulders. I have cause, good cause, for what I do. My god, I've grounds, grounds like this floor here, concrete covered with fur, and beneath that earth forever and the few pipes we shit through. Listen, Father I have cause. I do what I have to, always with cause, good cause, and only when I have to, only with cause. I've *grounds*. That's why I wait/wait till I have to/to do what I have to . . . do. I wait while the years pile up and cause after cause comes like snow in a storm, so that now I may have too

many, grounds too great like a park around a puddle, because they
get suspicious if you have too many, they suspect that if you have
too many, you haven't any, and oh god, Father, I have many—
many, many—still .

.
.
.

: not too many, just enough, although they may
say what are these causes which never effect? what is the mass
which never moves? but I have many—many, many, many—and
who can blame me if I run past complaint now as if it were a STOP
I hadn't seen? Visions. Indeed. Faugh. Blah. Visions of what,
though? Never of gods and goddesses, never any angels, scarcely
a cupid, not a single streak of light like the sperm of a star to pierce
some window to where she was sitting, not Fate or a Fury or a
vampirish mouse with a flat furry face like Bela Lugosi . . . no-
bodies, every one, not a name among them, not an old demon
even, out of work or with an odd hour off and able to visit. No.
Faugh. Nooooh-bodies. The walls stood up around him, tan as a
turkey, and the ceiling smirched along overhead as though in a day it
might rain. It must be tiring to stay that stiff, he thought, for she
wasn't dead, that would be restful, the stiffness, the silence, of
death. This was tense, this as a bellow, a hugh howl which steadily
grew and now contained the room which contained them. Father,
she's all right. I mean, she's sick, and her soul is like a Cape Cod
shingle, but she's all right. Never could detect a pulse. That's
normal. Arm like a dry vine climbing her trunk. Normal. Chest as
still as a stove top. Fire's out. Sick, then. Normal. She's all right.
Voices, she said Messages. All right, messages: blah, what were
they? what did they come to? sniffles and yipes from *Little Orphan
Annie*, whining about lost dogs, weeping because there were boys
away in the war, anxieties about men: boorish insensitive husbands
like himself, brutal brothers, inconstant companions, faithless
friends, lying lovers—bitching, bemoaning—nothing that came out
of the great gentle richness and happiness of life, nothing about the
sweet thunder of the pins or the excitement of a homer, the comforting closure of a jaw in a bun—so—so much for the spiritual telegraph, for ESP, because only diseases sent messages of any length
and complexity—moment by moment readings, hourly bulletins,
daily summaries, weekly releases—every sickness seemed to be
somehow a triumph of the spirit, especially stopped-up sinuses, and
migraines, like static on the radio, headaches so electric they halo'd

your hair, and it completely flummoxed Mr. Hess who held his own
head and groaned, even whimpered, while his missus felt giddy,
had a spell of dizziness, or fell softly to the floor in a faint the way
clothes slide sometimes from a hanger. Then there were discharges,
menstrual moans, and the whites like a fog of sound. Mr. Hess hated
to think about the others and couldn't—didn't dare—ask, nevertheless what he gathered was that the ethereal world his wife loved was
nothing but the loathsomely oozy body done into jiggles and jogs
like the huff and puff of someone running. The books he consulted
agreed in substance, though seldom in detail: it was a school of the
dance, vibrations in vapors or ripples around rocks; it was streaks in
cloth, they said; it was speeding clocks; it was clouds in chambers,
ozone after lightning; it was wow, ow, ouch; it was apples on vacation
from their cores. And the things in nature which proved most mute
were therefore most sound, were in equipoise and balance like the
billiard before its score, so equal and so uniform it was impossible to
guess where a lean might come from or what tilt it might topple
toward. Scrape, scratch, rasp: it was this inefficiency, this illness,
this grumble in the works, which caused the uproar—indigestion,
for instance, arthritis, epilespy, ulcer—so that Hess felt sometimes
that if the world would fall silent, she would be silenced. The hope
led him to let his watch stop, although she said it kept on keeping
time, and this was yet another reason why he double-washered taps,
over oiled hinges, smothered the sharpener, and carried things out
of the house tightly wrapped. He had long since ceased to smoke
because Ella complained of the foggy swowl in every draw, the ploan
like a stormhorn in every puff. Now he went to the garage to grind
his teeth. If you're all so big about the Spirit, Ella, he said, why are
you all so physical, hey? why so gut and head sick, so eager to hear
the earth? and why are you each so ugly: you're either flat-faced or
fat, thin-haired or moppy, lime-lipped, gum-gray, the teeth spilled
in your mouth like a damp pan of beans, not elegant, not opulent,
not delicated, not shy, no ma'am, rather wart-, wen-, and liver-
spotted, vein-roped, yeah, albino-eyed, allergic, snivel-nerved and
pukey, with tits loose and shriveled as emptied balloons, man-oh-
man, or melted and sloping, uddery, why? drunk on disapproval,
are you? and is every pain a blessing like a boy scout's badge for
merit? proud—I guess so—vain as if you were a Beauty, spoiled in
the same way as a Jewish Princess, still I wonder how you came to be
so fuckless if so female, hey? so juiceless, dry as oatmeal overboiled,

oh even your stout ones like Madame Betz have dustbowls standing in their bellies, even in July when every skin is slithery, cunts closed and lying buried in their sweaty secret hair like clams in silt, hey? and you have the gall to despise me for guzzling beer at the ballpark and playing with my toes. It was the only time Ella had ever raised her fist against him, and hadn't he fetched her a good one, but there's really no use talking to her, Father, to hammer some sense, because she won't listen to me. She hears muscles jumping in my jaw; she will hear a hair gray, milli-inch by milli-inch; she covers her ears when the belly rumbles; she listens to my face flush and moistens her brow with a cloth; frequently she sings along: she hears all this, each secret part and public parcel, but she won't pay any mind to *me*. Father, Mr. Hess said seriously, I have cause to believe she's committed adultery with a drainpipe. Well she raised her fist that solitary time and said something overgrand and stucco like a thirties theatre. It was really rather remarkable, come to consider it, how she seemed to gather the pieces together, various panels of her clothing, a collar, a pocket, a sleeve, each moving as separately as ants yet together like clasp and tie, too, all soft and bony at the same time, the way a scarecrow would grow if it grew, and mouth open- ing, wider than when a muffin entered or a triangle of toast, and the muscles tensing along the length of her neck, the veins enlarged, quite blue, and the cry coming slowly out atop her tongue, in scraps, in flecks, the way she'd risen from the floor—Ayeeeeee—"shall" the only word which seemed to have a stop to it, curling up at the end like a pair of skies—beeeeeeeeeeeeeeeeeeee—monsters in the movies wailed like that at the threat and showing of the Cross— freeeeeeeeeeeeeeeeeeeeeeeeeeeeeee—ha—ha ha—I shall be free. Not of me, he'd answered automatically; not of me, he'd said, with a depth of seriousness no dipstick was notched sufficiently to mea- sure; not of me, he'd said, shouting, and he fetched her a second and a better one. What are you at the cards for, if you can hear so much? horoscoping, number-noising, syllable counting, peering at the leaves, or skittering out to consult that bubble-reading Madame Betz, all gyp, by god, no gypsy, just to show off to the competition? and didn't she call you a copy-cunt right in the pleasure of my hearing? and then didn't I have to rough her up? how well you get along, you mystical ladies, pretending to concerns so delicate they can't be seen but only seen through like a pair of seductive panties. Well, none of that's real, you hear me? I'll tell you what's real. I am.

I AM REAL. And she had smiled at him from the floor, smiled a smile which spread like syrup, so full of slow sweet pity for him he could have killed her—well—and he did give her a stern toe on account of it and his foot felt as if it were entering a basket of laundry. The idea that his missus had been chaffing for something like the same thing that he, Hess—knicknacked the penholder by his playmates—had, was . . . infuriating, it was . . . humiliating, it was . . . intolerable. Well, no, Father, truth to tell, it's hardly been a successful union, a kind of side-by-side life, you might say, as close and on our own, each one of us, as two plants in the same row, stealing substance from one another, water and air and all the rest, what's near, what's by, that's all, yet meeting, I suppose, once in a while, like leaves meet in a pile, for breakfast or in bed—ha—ha ha—never touching except, like I've said, when I reach out and whack her, and not even then, she sees to that, I think she knows days in advance—yes siree, no mistake—why sometimes the bruise will be there, yellow and green like a young banana, before the day before the blow. The rug rolled. Goal or threat. Perhaps a promise. Designs slid out of the rim of his eye. Something to aim at: a telepathic bull's-eye. I don't .
.
.
.
.
: know. The shriek of the bird left silence foaming behind it like a boat's wake and Mr. Hess thought of the boats he had seen in the showroom, turning slowly around and gleaming on their cradles like the girls he had ogled on the stage, paint too perfect for a world of logs and oil, and promising more escape than a plane. So. Well. Who had his hat? Mr. Hess thought he would apologize first for being so faithless—no—he wouldn't put it like that—for being so irregular in attendance, whatever it was, but it didn't matter because he hadn't come about himself, he'd say, but about his wife, Ella, who was in dreadful danger, he felt, he'd say, danger of conspiring, was it? with the Devil. She was a goddamned witch, that's what she was . . . a witch. She said sometimes her real name was Pamphila, Father, and I looked it up at the library, with a little help in the library, and it's the name of a witch—who would believe—? She said it with a small smile—true—a small smile, but in the bathroom one day he'd overheard her singing in her thin thin seldom songful singing voice: *I Conjure and Confirm upon you,*

something like, *ye holy Angels*, though she never encountered any, what pretensions, what a liar, *and by the name Cados, Cados, Cados, Eschereie, Eschereie, Hatim, Ya, strong founder of the worlds*, it filled his feet with immobility to hear her, *Cantine, Jaym, Janie, Auie, Calbot, Sabbac, Berisay, Alnaym*, noises she accompanied by clapping, *and by the name Adonay, who created Fishes, and creeping things in the waters, and Birds upon the face of the earth, and by the names of the angels serving in the sixth host*, better she'd been masturbating, Father, when I barged in, *before Paster*, she sang, *a holy Angel, and a great Prince*, and she said she was only trying out a conjuration of Thursday that she'd got from Madame Betz, and which amused her . . . amused her! *by all the names aforesaid, I conjure three, Sachiel, a great Angel, who art the chief ruler of Thursday, that for me thou labor*, Father listen to that—my god! Thursday—and he'd lowered his fist like a flag at tas. A witch. A ghoul. Ha, never put a broomstick between those thighs, though, no sir, no siree, she'd ride nothing so phallic as that; she traveled in her mind, rode another wind; and he'd tell the Father how it was, and that although she was spiritual to the point of lily-wilting, she wasn't spiritual in the churchly chichi sort of way, on the contrary, she was the only cunt he ever knew to wear galoshes, the kind that buckle, that swallow your shoe, and he, Hess, who sold insurance and knew about investments in a modest, even humble fashion—money, Father, is my métier—knew she put great stock in all those lives she planned to lead beyond the grave, took great store from them, took . . . tock . . . Who had his hat? He had his hat. The feather and the felt. Then run for fun—he could do that. Who would be missed, the missus or himself? The label and the lining: silk. There was a sign above the hooks which always warned him to watch his coat, and Hess would watch so wrathfully, on celebration Sundays, sometimes, when they went out, he could have swallowed worms and felt well fed, been none the wiser for a wedge of mud. No, no, he'd have proud pie and royal cheese. And take a poster boat to distant cities, see famous landmarks done in strident inks, shape a shy smile of gratitude for the frank solicitations of dark and unintelligible tongues. Then outdoors, what? leafy trees, new green, a breeze. Play catch as catch can there. Watch. She might have been the hook itself he'd hung his hat from, her nose in the band above the brim. Outdoors, what? not the rush and the roar of a wind but the light lift, the almost imperceptible touch, of elevating air. For if Ella looks before, I after, if I left who would replace me? the present has already gone, though in a way it lay around his wrist still, keeping tabs, perhaps more perfectly now it had no need to tick continually and mill its hands or waste its face in darkness. Go. Though catch would come after. Either. It's just that, well, he, Hess, her husband, was worried about her chances since she lately seemed so sick and was this minute stiffer than most corpses, open and empty-eyed, and he had noticed recently, that is, in the few moments previous to his present speaking, several brief breaks in her oh-so-shallow breathing, ominous interruptions of the ceiling reading, and little lapses in reception which caused her silence to fall short of itself, toward another silence, like a broken arc, and now her pauses had a puff and stutter to them like that bird of hers when it was angry, and he thought she might be about to Kick the Habit and Cross over, or whatever one did. Li .

ve. Die. He couldn't settle his heart about it, couldn't get his guts to decide. The Universal Insurance Company of North America presents to Mr. Edgar Hess this Electronically Prepared Personal Proposal of . . . The blue folder contained no certificate, no diploma, no golden seal, no ribbon like a panting tongue, but a promise of protection: the Estate Builder, Economatic Life. Reality broke in like a burglar and stole his dreams before he could etch his name. He would raise the hue and cry. He would never be out of work. His desk was littered with electronically prepared proposals. His appointment book was black. His tie was parched, his throat was dry. Hey there, stop—stop wife, stop life. Ha ha. Hess wondered just who had his hat. The rug rose, wetting his knees. Perhaps you might sprinkle her with something, Father, water and oil, to snuff her evil out and sail her off to heaven like a paper airplane. They were blue folders with a red stripe, in soft tabbed paper, privacy assured. The last business was his business, UNICONA's deep concern, he always said, and his clients would nod submission, extend their hands, shake like canisters of ice. Now this moment she might. . . she might go Hence, cut from his face like a whisker, and Hess wondered whether it might have been otherwise, whether their life together had been so totally enformulated that they couldn't help rubbing wrongly together and consequently being in a

constant state of mutual exasperation like the sawing legs and so the laughing screams of the cicada—an ill mix from the first, bad match, poor pair, punk job, odd lot, and so forth, a complete and perfect botch; but if she were oil, then he was water, and if she lay quietly in a skirt of colorful irridescence, he fell slowly into darkness and into the depths of himself, beyond all light, beyond the last fish, stonily to stony bottom, or perhaps beyond that, bottomlessly un .
.
.
.
 der

. . . no, he didn't th .
.
.
.
: ink so; he thought rather that they might have made it with a little counseling—right—maybe that's all it would have taken—sure—just some authority figure to tell her to V her legs and buck a bit, to come down out of the cumulus and clown around a little, a lot of ladies like to go to the games, scream for the team, lap up a beer, some bowl, and—my gosh—many will respond to a nibble or a twiddle even, consequently square up, Missus Hess, therefore straighten around, don't endeavor to be exceptional, to see camels in clouds or become what we call cipher silly, what do you say? that's zero, the cipher, zerrr-oh, the cold, the O in obliteration. I've known several like you in my time and practice who sought clues to the future in the daily crossword, games of that kind—the X in eccentric is a cancellation, remember—how did they fare? well, they went up, then down, across, or desperately took diagonals like last-minute shoppers at Lazarus's, in the Christmas rush to Macy's or Marshall Field's, but black blocks cut them off eventually, hemmed them in on every hand like smudges on a diner's napkin—Ella, Ella— backed into byways, uneasy always, and there to remain as cats are caught at the hairs' ends of alleys, illumined by doglight— Ella, Ella, Missus, Madame—or compelled to live on a letter like K—what a coffin—so content yourself, ma'am, run for calm like a carrot, resign, accept . . . and Hess felt he could have been content, the conviction had grown on him—indeed was a callus—for what had he asked for? honey in the comb? had it been much? . . .so much? perhaps if he gave her a book of some kind, one which explained marriage and contained diagrams and pictures, anatomy

and arrows, though she never had much interest in words laid to rest like that: in so many glassy-eyed rows like results of a gunning. What he wanted was calm, calm was quiet, the stillness of a world which spoke about as often as an onion. Chewing on a hard roll, for instance, the sweet work of the teeth, the thought, sufficiently contained itself. Yes. He felt he could have been content. Ella, however . . . She was never joked, never saw the funny side of life; when was the last time they'd had a good ho ho together? no, she was always, what? grim? serious at any rate, intense, pitched past every la ti do they'd so far found a line for, prim. Pris .

sy. Cold. Patronizing. She gave him the length of her nose, not a hair—not a fart—from her quim. Ha. Ha ha. Flightly. Notional. Picky. Poky too. Thin. A shoe stirred everslightly beneath the level of the rug. Was it his? Step on a slat, make your mother fat. Five, six, pull your pricks. Why did he remember that? His memory was mostly reluctance. And then she was always so sickly. Sickness in a skinny woman is particularly . . . . Splaugh. What would happen? malutrition? cancer? kidney failure, then? Cold. Consider it: ummmmmm. What could he do? Die. Live. I just don't know. Head-strong but bowelweak. Ran in the family. Distant. Cold .. Hearthard but tummytender. Normal, then. Cold. While I only wanted . . . . What was it, I once wanted? honey in the comb? Still, I wish, Mr. Hess said . . . . Anyhow, Ella, really, I wish you wou .

🔥 🔥 🔥

THE DOG

fiction by AVROM REYZEN

(translated by Joachim Neugroschel)

from *ANTAEUS*

nominated by Harry Smith

NO ONE KNEW WHERE HE CAME FROM. One bright summer
morning, the men in the old synagogue noticed a newcomer in the
gang of kids. He was about fifteen, in rags and tatters, with unkempt
hair under his cap and scratches all over his face.

"A new duck!" said Khone, who had caught sight of him upon
coming early to prayers, and he ogled him wryly: "Who are you?"

"My parents' child!" the kid retorted sarcastically, scratching
himself all over.

"Ugh!" said Khone, spitting on the ground and heading for his
pew.

The kids accepted him without giving him any trouble at first. But when they started hazing him, he straightway knocked them down. Getsl, the barley-woman's son, earnestly exclaimed:

"You're pretty tough, all right!"

"Like a soldier!" agreed Fayvl-Kulye.

The others came over to take a close and respectful look at the newcomer.

"Ya ain't from aroun' here, are ya?" asked Getsl.

"Nope!" he replied in a dry, standoffish tone.

"Where ya from?"

"Kletsk."

"A bunch of robbers!" someone threw in.

"They're more honest than the people around here," the newcomer angrily snapped back.

"Ya got any folks?" asked someone else.

"Nope!"

"Whatta ya gonna do here?"

"I'm gonna stand my ground!" he answered proudly, like a grownup; winking his eye.

That was all the kids could get out of him at first.

Later on, after weeks, when he got to know Getsl a bit better and had taken a few drags on Getsl's cigarette, the kid began to tell them his story:

"I walked here . . . ."

"All the way from Kletsk?" the gang was startled.

"It was nothing," he boasted. "Gimme another drag, Getsl," and he held out his hand.

Getsl, not trusting the cigarette out of his own hand, put it in the kid's mouth himself; the newcomer puffed with all his might.

"Some drag!" Getsl made a face. "You've smoked up the whole cigarette."

"So what! When I get cigarettes, I'll share 'em with you. I ain't selfish."

"Ain't no one more generous than beggars!" someone joked.

"I'll tell ya why I ran away," the newcomer continued his biography: "When my ol' man died—"

"Ya got a mother?" someone interrupted.

"I already told ya I don't . . . . She died when she had me. When my ol' man died, this neighbor, a shoemaker, took me up and says to me:

"'Okay, Hatskl . . . it's over—'"

"Your name's Hatskl?" they interrupted.

"Hatskl," he answered quietly, as though embarrassed by his name.

"'It's over,' says the shoemaker to me, 'No more loafin'. Time you grew up. I'm gonna take ya in, and you're gonna become a shoemaker . . .' But I didn' wanna, goddammit! Who wants to sit around a whole day banging nails! It would kill me. Why work? I says to myself. It's best to live free. As for eating . . . ? I wouldn't mind workin' just a li'l bit: say, four hours a day—."

"Four hours a day is still too much," Getsl broke in. "An hour a day's enough. I help my ma grind the barley one hour a day. That's all I'm up to."

"But the shoemaker wanted me to sit and work all day long. Whenever I goofed off a li'l he'd beat my ass. It really pissed me. Like, I don't mind if the guys in town mess aroun' with me. I sock them, they sock me, we're even. But I couldn't hit the shoemaker back, he was as skinny as a greyhound, I could have knocked him out with my li'l finger. Whenever he'd lay his skinny fist on me, I felt like puking . . . . But it never hurt."

"I woulda let him have it straight in the kisser, and so hard he wouldna had the strength to hit anyone," said Getsl scornfully.

"I did something much better. I ripped off a coupla boots from him and ran away."

"Where're the boots?"

"Sold. I got two rubles for them," Hatskl boasted.

"But ya ain' got no passport."

"I don' need no passport. I come from around here. This is where my ol' man useta get his passport."

"Ya got any relatives here?"

"Relatives?" he shrugged. "Maybe, only I don't know 'em."

"Fuck relatives!" Getsl cursed. "My ma's got relatives here, and they won' even let her in the house."

"They must be rich."

"Very rich," Getsl was all worked up. "One of them, Yankl Hatshes, must be worth about ten thousands rubles. He lends money on interest."

"A relative like that is good to rip off!" said Hatskl with a smirk.

"He can go to hell!" replied Getsl with a wave of his hand.

*   *   *

When the guys got better acquainted, they found out that Hatskl was a thoroughgoing prankster. They particularly enjoyed his barking like a dog.

"Hatskl, whey don'tcha bark a li'l?" Getsl would ask him.

"Bow-wow-wow!" Hatskl would start barking, and the guys would split their sides laughing.

"Just like a dog!" they praised him.

"Back in Kletsk, I scared everybody at night." Hatskl said laughing. "This rich guy. Leybe Wolfs, got so scared he fell over when I started barking at him one night."

"Punks," the guys laughed.

"Bow-wow-wow!" Hatskl showed how he had barked.

And the guys came up with a nickname for him: "The Dog." Gradually, his real name was forgotten, and "Dog" became his normal, natural handle.

And he didn't mind at all. On the contrary, he even liked the fact that the name set him apart from everyone else, from all the people he didn't much care for. It kept him from having any contact with any other human beings, except for his buddies, the gang of kids. The name put him at liberty to run around, to go hungry, and to sleep wherever he could. If the beadle threw him out of the anteroom of the synagogue, he could spend the night on the porch of the women's section, just like a dog. And at times, barking, he would actually forget he was human. He would play his canine role with a vengeance, deeply, viciously, murderously, as though he were about to tear someone to shreds.

Once Getsl called him over to his mother's place:

"Hey Dog, wanna earn some money?"

"Yeah!" replied the Dog lukewarmly.

"Come over and help us turn the stones for the barley, and Ma'll give ya five kopeks.

The Dog hesitated and finally started out. On the way, he barked: "Bow-wow-wow!"

"You're goin' to work. Whatcha barkin' for?" asked Getsl.

"Don' feel like going," the Dog said lazily.

"You're a real dog!" Getsl reproved him. "You'll starve to death, like a dog."

"Better than workin' . . . . Bow-wow!"

Entering Getsl's home, the Dog shot a scornful look at the huge stick attached to two flour-covered stones, and he started scratching himself.

"So this is your fine feathered friend . . .," the barley-woman grimaced, "A respectable man if ever I saw one!"

"Bow-wow!" barked the Dog, laughing wildly.

"None a your crazy tricks now," snapped the widow. "If you wanna help turn the stones, then fine. If not, goodbye!"

The Dog began turning the stones, every so often barking to himself.

"What's sa matter? Does he have a dybbuk or somethin'!" The barley-woman was frightened. "All he does is bark."

"Bow-wow!" the Dog burst into angry barking. "I'm sick of turning, gimme my money."

"You think you can earn five kopels that quickly! You dog!" snapped Getsl's mother. "Ya gotta turn for a whole day!"

"Over your dead body!" yelled the Dog, running off without his money.

"It's better to be a dog than to turn the stones for a whole day," he spit as he walked along, and started barking. . . .

*   *   *

And thus the Dog spent the homeless years in the town, running around the synagogue yard, sometimes in the streets, and sometimes in the open countryside. Out there, he felt better than anywhere else; he would do his canine tricks, walking on his hands, and barking and barking. . . . He felt as though he were a real, free dog out there and as though the whole world were his. But whenever he got really hungry, he would angrily look around the vast, open meadow and see there was nothing here but grass, and he would start to bark, and, standing up erect, he would run back to town and go looking for food. . . .

*   *   *

"Ain'tcha ever gonna stop?" Getsl once asked when the Dog had burst out barking.

"Never!" yelled the Dog. "When I bark, I forget all my troubles. . . . You think I don't mind goin' aroun' in rags, like I was crazy. . . .? Uhn-uhn! Sometimes I feel like tearing the whole world to pieces, and that's when I get a hankering to bark, you see?"

"Then go ta hell, you Dog!" Getsl cursed. "As long as you keep barking, you'll never have anything. People won't take you in their home."

"Fuck them, and fuck their home! I need them like a hole in the head!"

"You'll die like a dog! You'll see," Getsl was trying to scare him.

"Make no difference whether you're dog or a human!" the Dog philosophized. "I like dogs better'n people. Fuck people!" he spit out.

One day, in the synagogue yard, Getsl came over to the Dog, and, laughing, said to him:

"You know what, Dog, tomorrow they're poisoning all the stray dogs."

"Drop dead!" the Dog replied.

"I swear it's true!" Getsl assured him.

"What're they poisoning'em for?" the Dog asked earnestly.

"Why not!" answered Getsl, "It's the law, ownerless dogs 've gotta be poisoned. . . ."

"Who cares if they run around?" the Dog asked.

"We don't need them."

The Dog started thinking. Finally, he asked:

"How do they poison them?"

"They chop up hamburgers and put poison inside. When they throw the meat to them, they grab it and eat it up."

"Real hamburgers?" the Dog interrupted.

"Sure 'nuff. Real, delicious hamburgers. If you like, you can taste one. You probably never ate a hamburger like that in your entire life."

"Go fuck yaself!" the Dog yelled, and turned pale.

"They're gonna give you one of those hamburgers, you're a dog too, ya know!" Getsl laughed.

Instead of answering, the Dog socked Gestl and ran off.

Night came on. It was cold and dark in the anteroom of the synagogue, where the Dog was spending the night. He was lying with open eyes, thinking. He was in turmoil over the news that Getsl had brought him that day. He was frightened.

"Why am I scared?" He tried to calm himself. "I'm not a real dog, no one's gonna throw me a poisoned hamburger."

But it didn't help. He felt that in the morning he would get up hungry, unable to hold himself back, and, along with all the hungry dogs, he would pick up a hamburger and gulp it down, poison and all.

"Bow-wow!" he started barking.

But now he was frightened by his own bark. He had to stop being a dog, he decided. "It's better to be human. . . ."

"But how do you start livin' like a human being?" he wondered. "I'm so ragged, I'm so cut off, I never talked to people. I hate them and they hate me.

"Fuck them!" he cursed, and started barking again.

The sleepless night made him even hungrier the next day. He had never been so hungry in all his life.

"They're throwing hamburgers to the dogs today," kept flashing through his mind all morning.

And barking furiously, he ran off to the marketplace. . . .

(1902)

🔥 🔥 🔥

SCIENCE AND THE COMPULSIVE PROGRAMMER

by JOSEPH WEIZENBAUM

from *PARTISAN REVIEW*

nominated by William Phillips

T HERE IS A DISTINCTION between machines whose ultimate function is to transduce energy or deliver power, and abstract machines, i.e., machines that exist only as ideas. The laws which the former embody must be a subset of the laws that govern the real world. The laws that govern the behavior of abstract machines are not necessarily so constrained. One may, for example, design an abstract machine whose internal signals are propagated among its components at speeds greater than the speed of light in clear violation of physical law. The fact that such a machine cannot actually be built does not prohibit the exploration of its behavior. It can be thought about and even simulated on a computer. (Indeed, the Education

Research Center at M.I.T. has made computer generated films that place their viewers in the position of observers of a world in which vehicles travel at physically impossible speeds.) The human imagination must be capable of transcending the limitations of physical law if it is to be able to conceive such law at all.

The computer is, of course, a physically embodied machine and, as such, cannot violate natural law. But it is not completely characterized by its manifest interaction with the real world. Electrons flow through it, its tapes move, and its lights blink, all in strict obedience to physical law, to be sure, and the courses of its internal rivers of electrons are determined by openings and closings of gates, again by physical events. But the game the computer plays out is regulated by systems of ideas whose range is bounded only by the limitations of the human imagination. The physically determined bounds, on the electronic and mechanical events internal to the computer, have no significance whatever with respect to that game, no more, that is, than it matters how tightly a chess player grips his bishops or how rapidly he moves it over the board.

A computer running under control of a stored program is thus detached from the real world in the same way as is every abstract game. The chess board, the thirty-two chessmen, and the rules of chess constitute a world entirely separate from every other world. So does a computer system together with its operating manual. The chess player who has made a bad move cannot explain his error away by pointing to some external empirical fact that he could not have known but that, had he known it, would have led him to make a better move. Neither may a programmer whose program behaves differently than he intended it to look for the fault anywhere but in the game he has himself created. He may have misread the computer system's manuals, or otherwise misunderstood his computing environment—just as a novice chess player may misread the rules with respect to, say, castling—but no datum existing in the world outside the computer system he is using can be at all relevant to the behavior of the world he has created. A computer's failure to behave exactly as its programmer intends cannot even be attributable solely to some limitation unique to the computer. In effect, every general purpose computer is a kind of universal machine that can in principle do what any other general purpose computer can do. In this important sense, a specific general purpose computer has no limitations unique to it. The computer then is a playing field on which one may play out any game one can imagine: one may create worlds in which there is no gravity, or in which two bodies attract each other, not by Newton's inverse square law, but by an inverse cube (or nth power) law, or in which time dances forward and backward in obedience to a choreography as simple or complex as one wills; one can create societies in whose economies prices rise as goods become plentiful and fall as they become scarce, and in which homosexual unions alone produce offspring. In short, one can singlehandedly write and produce plays in a theater that admits of no limitations. And, what is most important, one need know only what can be inferred directly from one's computer system manual, or constructed by one's own imagination.

An engineer is inextricably impacted in the material world. His creativity is confined by its laws; finally, he may do only what may lawfully be done. But he is doomed to exercise his trade in a Kafkaesque castle from which there is, even in principle, no escape. For he cannot know the whole plan that determines what rooms there are in the world, and how what doors between them may be opened. When, therefore, a device an engineer has designed doesn't work, he cannot always know, or tell by his own reasoning alone, whether he is in an antechamber to success and only his blunders keep him from opening its doors, or whether he has wandered into a closet from which there is no exit. Then he must appeal to others, his teachers, his colleagues, his books, to tell him, or at least to hint at, a formula that will compel the insouciant attendant (nature) to lead him out and on.

The computer programmer, however, is a creator of universes for which he alone is the lawgiver. So, of course, is the designer of any game. But universes of virtually unlimited complexity can be created in the form of computer programs. Moreover, and this is a crucial point, systems so formulated and elaborated act out their programmed scripts. They compliantly obey their laws and vividly exhibit their obedient behavior. No playwright, no stage director, no emperor however powerful, has ever exercised such absolute authority to arrange a stage or a field of battle and to command such unswervingly dutiful actors or troops.

One would have to be astonished if Lord Acton's observation that power corrupts were not to apply in an environment in which omnipotence is so easily achievable. It does apply. And the form in which the corruption evoked by the computer programmer's omnipotence manifests itself is instructive in a domain far larger than that related only directly to the computer. To understand it, we will have to take a look at a mental disorder that, while actually very old, appears to have been transformed by the computer into a new genus: the compulsion to program.

Wherever computer centers have become established, that is to say, in countless places in the United States as well as in virtually all other industrial regions of the world, bright young men of disheveled appearance, often with sunken glowing eyes, can be seen sitting at computer consoles, their arms tensed and waiting to fire their fingers, already poised to strike, at the buttons and keys on which their attention seems to be riveted as is a gambler's on the rolling dice. When not so transfixed, they often sit at tables strewn with computer print-outs over which they pore like possessed students of a cabalistic text. They work until they nearly drop, twenty, thirty hours at a time. Their food, if they can arrange it, is brought to them; coffee, Cokes, sandwiches. If possible, they sleep on cots near the computer—but only a few hours—then back to the console or the print-outs. Their rumpled clothes, their unwashed and unshaven faces, and their uncombed hair all testify to their obliviousness to their bodies and to the world in which they move. They exist, at least when so engaged, only through and for the computer. These are computer bums, compulsive programmers. They are an international phenomenon.

How may the compulsive programmer be distinguished from a merely dedicated, hard working professional programmer? First, by the fact that the ordinary professional programmer addresses himself to the problem to be solved while the compulsive programmer sees it mainly as an opportunity to interact with the computer. The ordinary computer programmer will usually discuss both his substantive as well as his technical programming problem with others. He will generally do lengthy preparatory work, such as writing and flow diagramming, before beginning work with the computer itself. His sessions with the computer may be comparatively short. He may even let others do the actual console work. He develops his program slowly and systematically. When something doesn't work, he frames careful hypotheses to account for the malfunction and designs crucial experiments to test them. Again, he may leave the actual running of the computer to others. He is able, while waiting for results from the computer, to attend to other aspects of his work such as documenting what he has already done. When he has finally composed the program he set out to produce, he is able to complete a sensible description of it and to turn his attention to other things. The professional regards programming as a means toward an end, not as an end in itself. His satisfaction comes from having solved a substantive problem, not from having bent a computer to his will.

The compulsive programmer is usually a superb technician, moreover one who knows every detail of the computer he works on, its peripheral equipment, the computer's operating system, etc. He is often tolerated around computer centers because of his knowledge of the system and because he can write small subsystem programs quickly, that is, in one or two sessions of, say, twenty hours each. After a time, the center may in fact be using a number of his systems. But because the compulsive programmer is essentially impossible to motivate to do anything but programming, he will almost never document his programs once he stops working on them. A center may therefore come to depend on him to teach the use of and to maintain the systems he wrote—and whose structure only he, if anyone, understands. His position is rather like that of a bank employee who doesn't do much for the bank but is kept on because only he knows the combination to the safe. His main interest is, in any case, not in small subsystems but in very large, very ambitious supersystems. In most cases the systems he undertakes to build, and on which he works feverishly for perhaps a month or two or three, have very grandiose but extremely imprecisely stated goals. Some examples of these ambitions are: new computer languages to faciliate man-machine communication; a general system that can be taught to play any board game; a system to make it easier for computer experts to write super-systems. (This last is a favorite.) It is characteristic of many of such projects that the programmer can, for a long time, continue in the conviction that they demand no knowledge apart from knowledge about computers, programming, etc. And that knowledge he, of course, commands in abundance. Indeed, the point at which such work is often abandoned is precisely when it ceases to be purely incestuous: when programming would have to be interrupted in order that knowledge from outside the computer world may be aquired.

Unlike the professional, the compulsive programmer cannot attend to other tasks, not even to tasks closely related to his program, while not actually operating the computer. He can barely tolerate

being away from the machine. But when he is forced by circumstances to be separated from it nevertheless, he has his computer print-outs with him. He studies them, he talks about them to
anyone who will listen, though no one can understand. Indeed,
while in the grip of his compulsion, he can talk of nothing but his
program. But the only time he is, so to say, happy is when he is at the
computer console. Then he will not converse with anyone but the
computer. We will soon see what they converse about.

The compulsive programmer spends all the time he can working
on one of his big projects. "Working" is not the word he uses, it is
rather "hacking." To hack is, according to the dictionary, "to cut
irregularly, without skill or definite purpose; to mangle by or as if by
repeated strokes of a cutting instrument." We have already said that
the compulsive programmer, or hacker, as he calls himself, is usually a superb technician. It seems, therefore, that he is not "without
skill," as the definition would have it. But the definition fits in a
deeper sense than the sense that is related merely to technique; the
hacker cannot set before himself a clearly defined goal together with
a plan for achieving it, for he has only technique, not knowledge. He
has nothing he can analyze or synthesize; in short, he has nothing to
form theories about. His skill is, therefore, aimless, even disembodied. It is simply not connected with anything other than the
instrument on which it may be exercised. His skill is like that of a
monastic copyist who, though illiterate, is a first-rate calligrapher.
Thus his grandiose projects must necessarily have the quality of
illusions, indeed of illusions of grandeur. He will construct the one
grand system in which soon, all other experts will write their systems. (It has to be said that not all hackers are pathologically compulsive programmers. Indeed, were it not for the, in its own terms,
often highly creative labor of people who proudly claim the title
"hacker," few of today's sophisticated computer time-sharing systems, computer language translators, computer graphics systems,
etc., would exist.)

Programming systems can, of course, be built without plan and in
the absence of any knowledge, let alone understanding, of the deep
structural issues involved, just as houses, cities, systems of dams,
and national economic policies can be so hacked together. As a
system so constructed begins to get large, however, it also becomes
increasingly unstable. When one of its subfunctions fails in an
unanticipated way, it may be repaired so as to make the manifest

trouble disappear. But since there is no general theory of the whole system, the system itself can be only a more or less chaotic aggregate of subsystems whose influence on one another's behavior is discoverable only piecemeal and by experiment. The hacker spends part of his time at the console piling new subsystems into the structure he has already built—he calls them "new features"—and the rest of his time in attempts to account for the way in which substructures already in place misbehave. That is what he and the computer converse about.

The psychological situation, in which the compulsive programmer finds himself while so engaged, is strongly determined by two apparently opposing facts: first, he knows that he can make the computer do anything he wants it to do, and second, the computer constantly displays undeniable evidence of his failures to him. It reproaches him. There is no escaping this bind. The engineer can resign himself to the truth that there are some things he doesn't know; but the programmer moves in a world entirely of his own making. The computer challenges his power, not his knowledge.

Indeed, the compulsive programmer's excitement rises to its highest, most feverish pitch when he is on the trail of a most recalcitrant error, when everything ought to work but the computer nevertheless reproaches him by misbehaving in a number of mysterious, apparently unrelated ways. It is then that the system the programmer has himself created gives every evidence of having taken on a life of its own and, certainly, of having slipped from his control. This too is the point at which the idea that the computer can be "made to do anything" becomes most relevant, and most soundly based in reality. For, under such circumstance, the misbehaving artifact is, in fact, the programmer's own creation. Its very misbehavior can, as we have already said, be the consequence only of what the programmer himself has done. And what he has done he can presumably come to understand, to undo, and to redo to better serve his purpose. Accordingly, his mood and his activity become frenzied when he believes he has finally discovered the source of the trouble. Should his time at the console be nearly up at that moment, he will take enormous risks with his program, making substantial changes, one after another, in minutes or even seconds, without so much as recording what he is doing, always pleading for just another minute. He can, under such circumstances, rapidly, and virtually irretrievably, destroy weeks and weeks of his own work. Should he, however, find a deeply embedded error, one that actually does account for much of the program's behavior, his joy is unbounded. It is a thrill to see a hitherto moribund program suddenly come back to life; there is no other way to say it. When some deep error has been found and repaired, many different portions of the program that until then gave nothing but incomprehensible outputs, suddenly behave smoothly and deliver precisely the intended results. There is reason for the diagnostician to be pleased and, if the error was really deep inside the system, even proud.

But the compulsive programmer's pride and elation are very brief. His success consists of having shown the computer who its master is. And having demonstrated that he can make it do this much, he immediately sets out to make it do even more. Thus the entire cycle begins again. He begins to "improve" his system, say, by making it run faster, or by adding "new features" to it, or by improving the ease with which data can be entered into it and gotten out of it. The act of modifying the then existing program invariably causes some of its substructures to collapse; they constitute, after all, an amorphous collection of processes whose interactions with one another are virtually fortuitous. His apparently devoted efforts to enhance and promote his own creation are really an assault on it, an assault whose only consequence can be to renew his struggle with the computer. Should he be prevented from so sabotaging his own work, say by administrative decision, he will become visibly depressed, he will sulk, display no interest in anything around him, etc. Only a new opportunity to compute can restore his spirit.

It must be emphasized that the portrait we have drawn is instantly recognizable at computing installations all over the world. It represents a far less ambiguous psychopathology than, say, do the milder forms of schizophrenia or paranoia. At the same time, it represents an extremely developed form of a disorder that afflicts much of our society.

How are we to understand this compulsion? We must first recognize that it is a compulsion. Normally, wishes for satisfaction lead to behaviors that have a texture of discrimination and spontaneity. The fulfillment of such wishes leads to pleasure. The compulsive programmer is driven; there is little spontaneity in how he behaves, and he finds no pleasure in the fulfillment of his nominal wishes. He seeks reassurance from the computer, not pleasure. The closest parallel we can find to this sort of psychopathology is in the relentless, pleasureless drive for reassurance that characterizes the life of the compulsive gambler.

The compulsive gambler is also to be sharply distinguished from the professional gambler. The latter is, in an important sense, not a gambler at all. We may leave aside the cheater and the professional confidence man, of whom, certainly, neither are gamblers. The so-called professional gambler is really an applied statistician, and perhaps an applied psychologist as well. His income depends in almost no way on luck alone. He knows applied probability theory and uses it to calculate odds and then to play those odds in such combinations and aggregates that his income over a period of, say, a year is predictable by him to nearly a mathematical certainty. That is not gambling. Then there are people who gamble but who are neither professional nor compulsive gamblers. To the compulsive gambler, gambling, the game, is everything. Even winning is less important than playing. He is, so to say, happy only when he is at the gambling table.

Anyone who has ever worked in a computer center, or a gambling casino that closes its doors at night, will recognize the scene described by Dostoevski, himself a passionate gambler, in *The Gambler*.

> By eleven o'clock, there remain at the roulette table only those desperate players, the real gamblers, for whom there exists but the roulette table . . . who know nothing of what is going on around them and take no interest in any matters outside the roulette saloon, but only play and play from morning till night, and would gladly play all round the clock if it were permitted. These people are always annoyed when midnight comes, and they must go home, because the roulette bank is closed. And when the chief croupier, about 12 o'clock, just before the close calls out, "the last three turns, gentlemen!" these men are ready to stake all they have in their pockets on those last three turns, and it is certain that it is just then that these people lose most.

Dostoevski might as well have been describing a computer room.

The medical literature on compulsive gambling concerns itself mainly with the psychogenesis of that compulsion, and then almost entirely from a psychoanalytic perspective. It is, however, not necessary to recapitulate the psychoanalytic argument here, nor would such a detour serve our present purpose. It is enough to say here that psychoanalysts, beginning with Freud, saw megalomania and fantasies of omnipotence as principal ingredients in the psychic life of the compulsive gambler. We have to neither accept nor reject pyschoanalytic accounts of the origins of such fantasies—e.g., that they are rooted in unresolved Oedipal conflicts leading to wishes to overpower the father that in turn lead to unconscious motivations to fail—in order to join the psychoanalysts, and novelists like Dostoevski, in seeing the central role megalomaniac fantasies of omnipotence play in compulsive gambling.

The gambler, as the psychoanalyst Edmund Bergler states in *The Psychology of Gambling*, has three principal convictions: first, he is subjectively certain that he will win; second, he has an unbounded faith in his own cleverness; third, he knows that life itself is nothing but a gamble.

What grounds can there possibly be for knowing that one will win a game of pure chance? To know that the roll of a pair of dice or the turn of a card is a purely chance event is to know that nothing one does can possibly effect the outcome. There precisely is the rub! The compulsive gambler believes himself to be in control of a magical world to which only few men are given entrance. "He believes," writes Bergler, "fate has singled him out . . . and communicates with him by means of small signs indicating approval or reproach." The gambler is the scientist of this magical world. He is the interpreter of the signs Fate communicates to him just as the scientist in the real world is an interpreter of the signs nature communicates to everyone who cares to become sensitive to them. And, like the natural scientist, the compulsive gambler always has a tentative hypothesis that accounts for almost all the signs he has so far observed, that, in other words, constitutes a very nearly complete picture of those aspects of the universe of interest to him. The test of the adequacy of both the scientist's and the magician's view of the world is its power to predict and, under suitably arranged conditions, to control. Hence, according to Bergler, the compulsive gambler sees himself as "not the victim, but the executive arm of unpredictable chance."

What an outsider regards as the gambler's superstitions are in fact manifestations of the gambler's hypothetical reconstruction of the world Fate has, bit by bit, revealed to him. Experience has taught him, say, that in order to win he must touch a hunchback on the day of play, carry a rabbit's foot in his left pocket, not sit at the gaming table with his legs crossed, and so on. This sort of knowledge is to him what, say, the knowledge of the mathematics of airflow over wings may be to an aircraft designer.

Because the gambler's superstitions are effectively irrelevant to the motions of dice and the orderings of cards, and so on, his hypotheses are very often empirically falsified. Each falsifying experience, however, contains certain elements that can be integrated with the main lines of his hypothetical framework and so save its overall structure. Losing, therefore, doesn't mean that carrying a rabbit's foot, for example, is wrong or irrelevant but only that some crucial ingredient for success has so far been overlooked. Perhaps the last time the gambler did win, a blond young lady stood behind his chair. Ah! So that's it: Touch a hunchback, carry a rabbit's foot, don't cross legs, and have a blond young lady stand behind the chair. When that doesn't work, he calculates that that particular combination works only on Thursday, and so on and on and on. Bits and pieces of explanation are added on, some are removed, and the entire structure becomes more and more complicated. Eventually, the gambler really does command a conceptual framework that rivals a body of scientific knowledge, at least in its complexity and intricacy. He is an expert in a richly complicated world open only to the relatively small group of initiates who have, through their own hard work and risk taking, learned its mysterious lore and language.

The magical world inhabited by the compulsive gambler is no different in principle than that in which others, equally driven by grandiose fantasies, attempt to realize their dreams of power. Astrology, for example, has constructed an enormously complex conceptual framework, a system of theories and hypotheses which allegedly permit the cognizant to control events. To know, for example, that the conjunction of certain stars on a particular date bodes ill for a particular venture, but that some other conjunction on some other date bodes well for it, and then to undertake that venture on the favored date, that is to attempt to control events.

But the hypotheses of astrology, too, are routinely falsified by events. How then does astrology, and how do other such magical systems, remain at all a force in the minds of men? Exactly as do the hypotheses of the compulsive gambler. First, any contradiction between experience and one magical notion is explained by reference to other magical notions. Thus the entire structure of the magical system of beliefs is supported by its very circularity. This way of protecting the system against assaults upon it that come from reality is especially effective if objections are always met one at a time. For then, the very demonstration that an apparently anomalous fact can be incorporated in the system serves to validate the system. The gambler may, for example, appeal to the fact that he didn't tie his shoelace, as he knew he should have, to account for his "bad luck" on a particular day. That sort of explanation is formally equivalent to the complusive programmer's assumption that his program's misbehavior is caused by a merely technical programming error.

A second way the conceptual frameworks of gamblers and programmers are protected is by cyclical elaboration. The gambler who suddenly realizes that certain of his tricks work only on Thursday simply incorporates this new "insight" into his already existing framework of superstitions, thus, in effect, adding an epicycle to its structure. The programmer is free to convert every new embarrassment into a special case, to be handled by a specially constructed *ad hoc* subprogram and thus incorporated into his overall system. The possibility of this kind of unbounded epicycle elaborations of their systems provides both programmers and gamblers with an inexhaustible reserve of subsidiary explanations for even the gravest difficulties.

Finally, the conceptual stability of a magical or of a programming system may be protected by denying, as Michael Polanyi writes in *Personal Knowledge*, "to any rival conception the ground in which it might take root. Experiences with support (the rival conception) may be adduced only one by one. But a new conception. . . which could take the place of (the one held), can be established only by a whole series of relevant instances, and such evidence cannot accumulate in the minds of (gamblers or programmers) if each of them is disregarded in its turn for lack of the concept which would lend significance to it." The gambler constantly defies the laws of probability. But he refuses to recognize the operational significance of these laws. He can, therefore, not permit them to become a kernel of a realistic insight. A particular program may be foundering on deep structural, mathematical, or linguistic difficulties about which relevant theories exist. But the compulsive programmer meets most manifestations of trouble with still more programming tricks and thus, like the gambler, refuses to permit them to nucleate relevant theories in his mind. Compulsive programmers are notorious for not reading the literature of the substantive fields in which they are nominally working.

These three mechanisms, called by Polanyi, circularity, self-expansion, and suppressed nucleation, constitute the main defensive armamentarium of the true adherent of magical systems of thought, and particularly of the compulsive programmer.

Psychiatric literature informs us that his pathology deeply involves fantasies of omnipotence. The conviction that one is all-powerful is, however, one that cannot rest, it must constantly be verified by tests. The test of power is control. The test of absolute power is certain and absolute control. When dealing with the compulsive programmer, we are therefore also dealing with his need to control and his need for certainty.

The passion for certainty is, of course, also one of the great cornerstones of science, philosophy, and religion. And the quest for control is inherent in all technology. Indeed, the reason we are so interested in the compulsive programmer is that we see no discontinuity between his pathological motives and behavior and those of the modern scientist and technologist generally. The compulsive programmer is merely the proverbial mad scientist who has been given a theater, the computer, in which it is possible for him to, and in which he does, play out his fantasies.

The gambler, as we have already said, is subjectively certain that he will win. So is the compulsive programmer; only he, having created his own world on a universal machine, has some foundation in reality for his certainty. Scientists, with some exceptions, share the same faith. What science has not done, it has not yet done. The questions science has not answered, it has not yet answered. Second, the gambler has an unbounded faith in his cleverness. Well?! Third, the gambler knows that life itself is nothing but a gamble. The compulsive programmer is convinced that life is nothing but a program running on an enormous computer and that therefore every aspect of life can ultimately be explained in exclusively scientific terms. Indeed as Polanyi correctly points out, the stability of scientific beliefs is defended by the same devices that protect magical belief systems: "Any contradiction between a particular scientific notion and the facts of experience will be explained by another scientific notion; there is a ready reserve of possible scientific hypotheses available to explain any conceivable event . . . within science itself, the stability of theories against experience is maintained by epicycle reserves which suppress alternative conceptions in the germ."

Hence we can take out a continuum. At one of its extremes stand scientists and technologists who much resemble the compulsive programmer. At the other extreme are scientists, humanists, philosophers, artists, and religionists who seek understanding as whole persons and from all possible perspectives. The affairs of the world appear to be in the hands of technicians whose psychic constitutions approximate those of the former to a dangerous degree. Meanwhile, the voices that speak the wisdom of the latter seem to be growing ever fainter.

There is a well known joke that may help clarify the point: One dark night a policeman comes upon a drunk. The man is on his knees, obviously searching for something under a lamppost. He tells the officer that he is looking for his keys which he says he lost "over there," pointing out into the darkness. The policeman asks him why, if he lost the keys over there, is he looking for them under the streetlight. The drunk answers, "because the light is so much better here." That is the way science proceeds too. It is important to recognize this fact. It is irrelevant and useless to blame science for it. Indeed, what is sought can be found only where there is illumination. Sometimes one even finds a new source of light in the circle within which one is searching. Two things matter: the size of the circle of light that is the universe of one's inquiry, and the spirit of one's inquiry. The latter must include an acute awareness that there is an outer darkness, and that there are sources of illumination of which one as yet knows very little.

Science can proceed in no other way but to simplify reality. The first step in its process of simplification is abstraction. And this means leaving out of account all those empirical data which do not fit the particular conceptual framework within which science at the moment happens to be working, which, in other words, are not illuminated by the light of the particular lamps under which science happens to be looking for keys. Aldous Huxley remarked on this matter in *Science, Liberty and Peace*, with considerable clarity:

Pragmatically (scientists) are justified in acting in this odd and extremely arbitrary way; for by concentrating exclusively on the measurable aspects of such elements of experience as can be explained in terms of a causal system they have been able to achieve a great and ever increasing control over the energies of nature. But power is not the same thing as insight and, as a representation of reality, the scientific picture of the world is inadequate, for the simple reason that science does not even profess to deal with experience as a whole, but only with certain aspects of it in certain contexts. All this is quite clearly understood by the more philosophically minded men of science. But unfortunately some scientists, many technicians, and most consumers of gadgets have lacked the time and the inclination to examine the philosophical foundations and background of the sciences. Consequently they tend to accept the world picture implicit in the theories of science as a complete and exhaustive account of reality: they tend to regard those aspects of experience which scientists leave out of account, because they are incompetent to deal with them, as being somehow less real than the aspects which science has arbitrarily chosen to abstract from out of the infinitely rich totality of given facts.

One of the most explicit articulations of the way science deliberately and consciously plans to distort reality and then goes on to accept that distortion as a "complete and exhaustive" account is the computer scientist Herbert A. Simon's own statement of his fundamental theoretical orientation in his book *The Sciences of the Artificial*.

An ant, viewed as a behaving system, is quite simple. The apparent complexity of its behavior over time is largely a reflection of the complexity of the environment in which it finds itself.

. . . the truth or falsity of (this) hypothesis should be independent of whether ants, viewed more microscopically, are simple or complex systems. At the level of cells or molecules, ants are demonstrably complex; but these microscopic details of the inner environment may be largely irrelevant to the ant's behavior in relation to the outer environment. That is why an automaton, though completely different at the microscopic level, might nevertheless simulate the ant's gross behavior.

. . . I should like to explore this hypothesis, but with the word 'man' substituted for 'ant'.

A man, viewed as a behaving system, is quite simple. The apparent complexity of his behavior over time is largely a reflection of the complexity of the environment in which he finds himself.

. . . I myself believe that the hypothesis holds even for the whole
man.

With a single stroke of the pen, by simply substituting 'man' or
'ant' the presumed irrelevancy of the microscopic details of the ant's
inner environment to its behavior has been elevated to the irrelevancy of the whole man's inner environment to his behavior!

Simon, who is by the way one of America's most prestigious
scientists, also provides us with an exceptionally clear and explicit
description of how, and how thoroughly, the scientist prevents
himself from crossing the boundary between the circle of light cast
by his own presuppositions and the darknesss beyond. In discussing
how he went about testing the theses that underly his hypothesis,
i.e., that man is quite simple, etc., he writes:

> . . . I have surveyed some of the evidence from a range of human
> performances, particularly those that have been studied in the
> psychological laboratory.

> The behavior of human subjects in solving cryptarithmetic problems,
> in attaining concepts, in memorizing, in holding information in
> short-term memory, in processing visual stimuli, and in performing
> tasks that use natural languages provides strong support . . .

> . . . generalizations about human thinking . . . are emerging from
> the experimental evidence. They are simple things, just as our
> hypothesis led us to expect. Moreover, though the picture will
> continue to be enlarged and clarified, we should not expect it to
> become essentially more complex. Only human pride argues that the
> apparent intricacies of our path stem from a quite different source
> than the intricacy of the ant's path.

The hypothesis to be tested is, in part, that the inner environment of
the whole man is irrelevant to his behavior. One might suppose that
in order to test it, evidence that had the potential of falsifying it
would be sought. One might, for example, study man's behavior in
the face of grief or of a profound religious experience. But these
examples do not easily lend themselves to the methods for the study
of human subjects developed in psychological laboratories. Nor are
they likely to lead to the simple things an experimenter's hypotheses
lead him to expect. They lie in the darkness in which the theorist, in

fact, has lost his keys; but the light is so much better under the lamppost he himself has erected.

There is thus no chance whatever that Simon's hypothesis will be falsified in his or his colleagues' minds. The circle of light that determines and delimits his range of vision simply does not illuminate any areas in which questions of, say, values or of subjectivity can possibly arise. Questions of that kind, being, as they must be, entirely outside his universe of discourse, can therefore not serve to lead him out of the conceptual framework which, like all other magical explanatory systems, has a ready reserve of possible hypotheses available to explain any conceivable event.

Almost the entire enterprise that is modern science and technology is afflicted with the drunkard's search syndrome, and with the myopic vision which is its direct result. But, as Huxley, too, pointed out, this myopia cannot sustain itself without being nourished by experiences of success. Science and technology are sustained by their translations into power and control. To the extent that computers and computation may be counted as part of science and technology, they feed at the same table. The extreme phenomenon of the compulsive programmer teaches us that computers have the power to sustain megalomaniac fantasies. But the power of the computer is merely an extreme instance of that same power inherent in all other self-validating systems of thought. Perhaps we are beginning to understand that the abstract systems, the games computer people can generate in their infinite freedom from the constraints that delimit the dreams of workers in the real world may fail catastrophically when their rules are applied in earnest. We must learn that the same danger is inherent in other magical systems that are equally detached from authentic human experience—particularly in those sciences that insist they can capture *the whole man* in their abstract skeletal framework.

🔥 🔥 🔥

LYNDA VAN CATS

fiction by ALEXANDER THEROUX

from ANTAEUS

nominated by Gordon Lish and Ben Pesta

One morning, it was the Middle Ages.

The sun shone down on the foundling home at the end of Duck's-foot Lane in the quiet little dorp of Sleutel in the Netherlands. The year was 1307 (by Pope Hilarius's corrected calendar, of course).

Master Snickup, a tiny ward there—wearing the black and red uniform of the home—gleefully played punchball against the cobbled wall beneath a yew tree near the town weigh-house.

It was a feastday: the Pardon of St. They. Cattle were blessed. Children processed. You heard litanies.

"Wat is Uw naam?" asked a new little orphan girl who suddenly appeared at his side, smiling, plum-cheeked, and wearing a chaste wimple. Her beauty put to shame the roses of Paestum.

Lynda—for this was the name of the flax-haired *frokin*—immediately stole Master Snickup's heart quite away.

The two children, thereafter, spent day after day playing games of noughts-and-crosses, stickjaw, stitch away tailor, egg-in-cap, ducking mummy, backy-o, all the winkles.

And skip-rope, when they frisked and jumped to the jingle

> *"Do you love me,*
> *Or do you not?*
> *You told me once,*
> *But I forgot."*

Happily, Master Snickup even did her chores for her, cups, dipping tallow, and decoaling the squinches; he did the washpots, as well. She played the dulcimer.

A decade passed, just like that.

Lynda, who'd bloomed into indescribable loveliness, now drew smiles from each and all. There is no potential for permanence, Master Snickup told his heart, without a fear of threat.

And so they were betrothed one day at the shrine of St. Puttock of Erpingham and swapped gifts: he gave her two white pigeons and received at her hands a wonderful blue cloak.

Now there lived on the verge of the village, at that time, one of the richest burghers in all Gelderland—the ill-living Mijnheer van Cats, an unctuous cheesegobbling fat pants who smoked a clay pipe and wanted sons. He owned the black windmill.

But who'd be his wife? A purse of 2,000 gulden was put up.

In vain did the merchants of the guild offer their daughters, a group of off-sorts who had pointed noses and pointed caps.

"Knapweed!" "Hake!" "Twisses!" screeched van Cats, and hurled other unprintable names at them. Modest pious folk covered their eyes.

One winter dusk, it so turned out, the orphans were all given special dispensation to go to the Haymarket to watch the "illuminations." Mijnheer van Cats, in attendance, sat up on the balustrade of the guildhall, whereupon his gaze fell—fatefully—upon Lynda. That little boompjes, thought he, will soon be mine.

An ouch of heavy gold was hers the day following; his was a sealed envelope—which he slit open with his pipestem. What could be the decision?

"Yaw, yaw," guffawed the fat Dutchman.

A record of the wedding can be found to this day as a small entry in the old chronicle of Nuewenburgensis.

You will do, as the diverb has it, what you are.

Master Snickup—disedged with grief—took up scrip and staff and, wearing only his blue cloak, set out to pick his way across nearer Europe. He sought the antipodes.

Hither was yon, yon hither.

Mountains were climbed, mazes thrid. He crossed a sea that had no motion on the ship *"What is Pseudonymry?"* and came to a desert where he said penances and fed on caper buds, dormice, lentils. Still he pilgrimaged,

Reading the footprints of geese in the air,

To reach eventually the Black Sea where, living alone on an uncharted shale island, he chastised himself with thongs and subsisted only on air and dew. Rain fell on his blue cloak, which he sucked, supplying himself with vitamin B12.

Swallows sang upon his wrists.

"Sero te amavi," whispered Master Snickup, and he prayed constantly with perfectly folded hands, a shape best fitted for that motion. Small furious devils hated that—

And visited him in a variety of shapes and torments: six-fingered Anaks, freexes, nasicornous beetles, chain-shaking kobolds, Saüba ants, red-eyed swads, sorcerers who could disconnect their legs and flap about like bats, and pin-headed Hippopodes, with reversed feet, who leapt instead of walked.

Master Snickup fell ill. But who could help? For ships in sight there were none.

The town of Sleutel, meanwhile, rang with news. Lynda van Cats was delivered of a son. "A witty child! Can it swear? The father's dearling! Give it two plums!" boasted its sire, butterballing it with his gouty feet.

But hear of more. Mijnheer van Cats, now fattened on perfidy itself, had turned syphilitic and even more hateful than before. He sang curses against his wife in the taproom, and roiling and hissing, streeled home. He locked her nights in the black windmill. He chased her through town slashing her with timothies.

Sadism and farce are always inexplicably linked.

The orphanage, in the meantime, closed down—without so much as two coppers snapped together to prevent it, despite the bulging wallets of all the soap-boilers, razor-makers, brewers, and guilder-grubbing rentiers that lived nearby. O events! God could not believe man could be so cruel!

Winter settled hard over the Black Sea. The soul of Master Snickup now grew pure—a hagiographical commonplace—as his body grew diseased. He never washed his bed save with tears. The tattered blue cloak had become infested with worms and rotifers,

Which also battened on his holy flesh.

It snew. And on that desolate shale island, since fabled, Master Snickup one day actually looked into the heart of silence, rose, and—with a tweaking-and-shake of finger and thumb toward the sky—died. Rats performed the exequies.

The moon, suddenly, was o'ercast blood-red in an eclipse. Thunder rumbled. Boding?

Ill.

A rat flea, black in wing and hackle, flittered out of the shred of blue cloak and flew inland—as if carried along by destiny—toward the Crimean trading port of Kaffa. The infamous date was 1346.

Stinks were soon smelt—in malt, barrels of sprats, chimney flues. Physicians lost patients in spates.

"Plague! Plague!" bellowed the chief magistrate, running swiftly in circles, his fauces black, streaks of jet vivid along his nose and wicks—and dropped dead as a stone. Fires were lighted. The harbor was sealed.

But it was too late. Ships, laden with produce, had already set sail in the pestiferous winds and headed out along the trades to Constantinople, to Cyprus, to Sardinia, to Avignon. and points beyond—

Sleutel, among them: a town that, recently, had expanded and grown to the clink of gold in the guilds, the crackle of flames in the tile-kilns, and the mercantile sermons in the new protestant kirks.

There was even entertainment.

The town brothel—formerly the orphanage—represented the major holding of a certain Mijnheer van Cats who now lived alone with his son, a dissolute half-wit seen once a year moping into town to paint its shutters and to touch up the wooden sign out front that read: *De Valk Gravin.*

It became famous. Merchant sailors, visiting in droves, always wept with laughter at the idle boast of its madam, that she had once been the village beauty.

Or was Time, indeed, the archsatirist?

For the place was run by an ooidal-shaped sow, with chin hairs, a venomous breath, and grit-colored hair, who always carried a ladle and trounced her girls. They called her "Mother Spatula."

The legacies passed on by the sailors were worse than the legacies they received. It began with "the sweats."

The town of Sleutel was soon aflame with flews, black spots, boils, pink eye, and the stinking wind that broadcast one to another. Lost souls screamed aloud to be crimped with knives like codfish.

A whole Arabian pharmacy could do no good.

Nothing could stop the contagion, neither chanters nor flagellants. The townsfolk spun into dancing fits, cat-concerts, and fell to biting each other and frying jews. Men castrated themselves and flung their severed genitals into the hopeless sky to placate an angry God.

"The Black Death" struck, and struck, and struck. Bodies fell like the leaves of Vallombrosa. It beggared rhetoric: recorded only by historians as the worst disaster that had ever visited the world.

Mijnheer van Cats, having stared upon his son's flapping black tongue and drooling insanity, waddled up high into the black windmill, took off his clogs, and—pinching his nose—stepped past the revolving vanes and cowardly made his quietus.

They went to their accounts impenitent.

Mother Spatula ran into her dank room, made mouths in a glass—and shrieked! Horrified at the tell-tale nosebleed, her drazels held to her lips a little statue of St. Roch the Plague Saint; but she went deaf as a beetle to their pleas, curled up into a fork and died, notwithstanding the fact that to her black feet—in order to draw the vapors from her head—they had applied two dead pigeons.

She didn't seem to attach a good deal of importance to them before she went.

VARIATIONS ON *THE MOUND OF CORPSES IN THE SNOW*

by STEPHEN BERG

from CHICAGO REVIEW

nominated by H. L. Van Brunt

For Bill Arrowsmith

Sleet blows through the city,
gray. An old Jew's black skull-cap's
flecked with snow. He looks
into the sky. Nothing. Flakes
spin into his mouth and eyes.
For two years

I've been reading
an Israeli poem about God's silence in evil,
about a child
watching Nazis murder his father in the snow
then fling him on a mound of corpses.
First they made him undress

but he left his underpants and socks on.
When the officer saw this
he walked up behind him and rammed
the butt of his rifle between the shoulders
of the boy's father, who coughed and fell down.

The officer smoked.
"The snow on both sides of my father's face
was melting, reddening,
because of the blood
that came out of his mouth, from his burst lungs."
Like prayers spilled into the earth.

I keep trying to find out why we do these things
and hear my mother scream "Your father
used to pinch me at parties whenever I spoke
or he'd disappear and shack-up with his secretary.
After he died I found eight hundred-dollar
checks he wrote to a woman nobody knew!"

At Arrowsmith's the goats, the boulders
strewn over the hillside across from the studio,
his wife's chickens in the barn and the vegetables
she grew, sheep cropping grass, melted into
the son, the father, all of us.
The rocks lay down, the Jew

was a rock, the rock was his back,
his face was in the grass so deep I couldn't
even see his ears. When Bill and I talked this week
he said the first snow had blinded
everything except the crests of the rocks,
which the wind blew clean.

One morning last summer when I drove to see him
we stood very close to each other, watching the air clear.
It was like being with my father again.
A mist like fine snow hung over the valley, then thinned off.
The rocks appeared, scarred humps
clawed out of the ground by retreating ice. Oh

that shy man who had stood naked only in front of his wife! And
    God? Listen—
"When the night fell the stars
glittered, the pile of corpses
lay in the field,
and snow came down out of the night
with soft, cruel abundance."

PEACE IN THE NEAR EAST

by GERALD STERN

from AMERICAN POETRY REVIEW

nominated by AMERICAN POETRY REVIEW

While I have been flooding myself with black coffee
and moving slowly from pajamas to underwear to blue corduroys
my birds have been carrying twigs and paper and leaves and straw
back and forth between the box elders and the maples.
—They are building the Aswan Dam out there;
they are pulling heavy wheelbarrows up the hillsides;
they are dragging away old temples stone by stone;
they are wiping the sweat from their black bodies.

Ah, soon, soon they will be sitting down
like rich Mamelukes in their summer palaces on the Nile,
greeting the Arabian ambassador on the right,
greeting the Russian ambassador on the left,
and finally even the Jew himself, a guest
in his own garden, a holder of strange credentials,
one who is permitted to go through the carrots
only with special consent, one who is scolded
if he gets too close to the raspberry bushes,
one who looks with loving eyes at the water
and the light canoes that float down to the locks
for the meeting of princes in their little rubber tents—
by the picnic tables and the pump and the neat pile of gravel and the
    naked sycamores;
by the cement spillway that carries a ton of water a minute
under the old generating plant;
by the sandy beach down below where the fishermen sit
on their canvas stools feeding worms to the river—
worm after worm to the starving river,
in exchange for the silver life in their tin buckets,
in exchange for silence.

NOTHING VERY MUCH HAS HAPPENED HERE

by RHODA SCHWARTZ

from WORD-SMITH

nominated by PUSHCART PRESS

The black spool of hair is wound
on top of your head, loosening
in wisps about your face.
The sky at dusk is the color
of columbine as you croon songs,
spooning heavy cream
into the soup
and cutting
wheels of black bread.
Your hands move faster than birds
to catch the falling crumbs.
The fire is lit in the stove, the lace
curtains are drawn.
We will wait for him together.
Great-grandmother, tell me, do I have your eyes,
your bones?
Why are you so hard? My softness
did not come from you.
In sleep, I step
into holes. I can't find my way out of sleep.
Your hair is black forever. I have found white
in mine and I'm afraid.
No one will sit with me when I am old.

I'm listening like the wind at your
elbow. I whisper your name. The cold has placed its hand
on my shoulders and shadows fill the pleats in your skirts.
The stories you tell me about my father and the Tsar
are not for children. Where do you get off filling my head
with such sadness?
But now, we are alone with the music, and Russia,
wide and long at night, is waiting outside in the darkness.

A LIBERAL'S AUSCHWITZ

by CYNTHIA OZICK

from CONFRONTATION

nominated by CONFRONTATION

THE LIBERAL IS A HUMANIST—which is to say, he is an anthropomorphic idolator: his god is called *humanity*.

And because he is a humanist, the liberal is also an egalitarian—which is to say, he is a leveler: like death. He speaks, of course, only about life, which he conceives of perhaps as a kept lawn, every blade equal to every other. Only grass can respond to the mower like that: green grass, which masks death.

The liberal asserts the unity of humankind. He means by this only the universalism of biology. Shakespeare, nowadays praised often for Shylock's plea to be counted among the mammals—"Hath not a Jew eyes? Hath not a Jew hands, organs, dimensions, senses, affec-

tions, passions?"—is famously liberal for granting the Jew entrance
into the animal kingdom: biological equality. But biology is God's
miracle, and ought not to be called into service by humanists and
liberals, who are notoriously indifferent to the dust of the cosmos,
and other divine sweepings.

What makes a human being, after all, is not the biological sweepings, not eyes, organs, dimensions, senses, not even affections and
passions (dogs and cats have those), but an ingenious communal
invention no other creatures know: civilization. Not the mechanical
village of organ and instinct, which characterizes the ants and the
bees, but a willed organization of conduct wherein is implicit not
simply pulse, but *idea*.

Biology levels. Ideas differentiate. Ideas differentiate because
every idea, and every civilization which expresses it, is situated in
history, and history—unlike organs, dimensions, senses, etc.—is
singular.

To say that all humanity is one is a biological statement, interesting enough to gynecologists (who can see that every normal human
female has a uterus) and dentists (who can see that every normal
human mouth has molars) and other such technicians; but there is no
philosophical value in it. Shylock's ventriloquist can perceive no
civilization, no culture, no history, no *idea*, in his Shylock; which is
what Shakespeare means when he concedes that a Jew hath organs.
Shylock's argument against his pariah status—it shocks, it offends, it
leaves out the human element by putting in only the mammalian:
why then is it always called "moving"?—could be made, in the same
words, for any member of any pariah group anywhere. This, we are
told, is its literary glory: it is "universal."

Now if being a Jew is being only what is universal, then a Jew is no
more than his organs—no more than the dust of "dust unto dust"—
and then what matter cremation? An idea, a culture, a *meaning*,
transcends and outlives the pot of organs that fleetingly contains it.
But what if the pot made of organs is seen to be empty? To Shakespeare, the Jew was such an empty pot. The Jew as culture-bearing
creature was invisible to Shakespeare, who, with his good liberal
conscience, could perceive only the pariah made of organs. And,
having perceived the pariah, he could perceive him as victim only
after having overwhelmingly perceived him as victimizer.

But it is not enough to be able to perceive the victim in the pariah.
It is not even enough to want to spare the pariah-victim—though

the intent to spare separates the Hitlers from the non-Hitlers, a saving if gross distinction. If the pariah—down with these vaguenesses! I am speaking of Jews—if the Jew is ground into the metaphorical dust of "humanity," or of "victim," if he is viewed only as the emblematic "other," if he is viewed only as an archetype of the eternal oppressed, if he is not seen as covenanted to an on-going principle, if he is not seen as the transmitter of a blazingly distinctive culture, if he is imagined only as a vessel no different from Esau's pot of red vittles, or if he is symbolically turned into "mankind"—but here I stop, having stumbled on Shylock's plea again.

Whoever thinks it necessary to declare the Jews members of "mankind" is not quite sure of the very proposition he finds it necessary to declare; and, like Shakespeare, he can end by confusing the victim with the victimizer.

"Mankind," "humanity," "universal"—these are among the most dangerous words in the language. In the name of not-killing, in the name of wanting-to-spare, they can erase, wipe out, be unsparing. The liberal—to whose refined heart and lips these ferocious words come glibly—does what he damns.

An illustration.

The novelist William Styron goes to Auschwitz on a visit. He sees what you and I would see, hath he not eyes?—evidences of the Nazi program of Jew-killing. He feels what you and I would feel, hath he not passion?—horror. But then he observes something else, and this observation aspires beyond his organs, dimensions, senses, etc., to the premises of his civilization. Auschwitz, he observes, is not only anti-Jewish, it is "anti-human": it is of course imperative to observe this, because to assert that Auschwitz is "merely" anti-Jewish would in effect raise doubts as to whether it is truly anti-human. Mr. Styron—let us surmise unwittingly: his heritage and Shakespeare's are the same—has gone to school to Shylock.

So now Mr. Styron has seen the cooled ovens of Auschwitz, and afterward he writes about it on the Op Ed page (June 25, 1974) of *The New York Times*. Sadly and eloquently he reminds us that the "dark and mysterious discord" of anti-Semitism is not rooted wholly in Christian theology.

The despairs of history savagely confirm his view. This unending fouling of many civilizations is both post-Christian and pre-Christian; it is non-Christian, as in the Koran; it is also "socialist," as in the Soviet Union, Communist China, the American New Left, and the writings of Marx himself. Amalek is born and reborn, and we do not know why.

But to recognize that the human heart as a whole is infected is not to erase or diminish what happened concretely, in an actual moment: specifically *who* did specifically *what* to specifically *whom*. Christianity does not stand responsible all alone in the world; nevertheless it stands responsible. The Inquisition was the known fruit of concrete Christian power. That thirteenth-century Pope (his name was Innocent) who ordered Jews to wear the yellow badge was not innocent of its Nazi reissue seven hundred years later. Oppression has a chronology, murder has a place. If we make an abstraction out of human wickedness—as when Mr. Stryon wants to call the Auschwitz impulse "anti-human" and "anti-life" rather than "narrowly" anti-Semitic—we will soon forget that every wickedness has had a habitation and a name.

The two and a half million Jews murdered at Auschwitz were murdered, Mr. Styron recalls for us, in the company of a million Christian Slavs. This is an important reminder: every soul swallowed up by that martyrdom ought to be remembered for and in its specificity, with all its heritage and characteristics intact—the Jew for being a Jew, the Slav for being a Slav, the gypsy for being a gypsy. And the murderers too, in their chronology and place, ought to be remembered precisely for and in *their* specificity: the Nazis for being Germans; at Babi Yar the Nazi-helpers for being Ukrainians; at Maalot the terrorists for being Palestinians. The point *is* the specificity—if we are to remain minimally honorable we must not muddle our daily perceptions and our historical memories by falling into the perils of poesy, which somehow always finds the word "humanity" more palatable than "Jew."

The enterprise at Auschwitz was organized, clearly and absolutely, to wipe out the Jews of Europe. The Jews were not an *instance* of Nazi slaughter; they were the purpose and whole reason for it. Like any successful factory in roaring production, the German death-factory produced useful by-products: the elimination of numbers of Slavs and most gypsies. We can speculate, as Mr. Styron does, on what might have happened to other peoples deemed inferior to the Nazis "had Hitler won the war"; indeed there might have been other genocides, and of Christians; but we know of a certainty, we are not fortunate enough to be only speculating about, what befell the Jews of Europe.

Auschwitz as a "threat to humanity" seems to Mr. Styron its "ultimate depravity," even more horrible than "its most terrible single handiwork," the death of entire populations of Jews; it is as if what did not happen appears to him more horrendous than what did happen. And though it may be metaphorically true that "humanity" was threatened and "life" itself denied, it was Jews who did most of that vast dying, it was the historic life of the Jewish people in Europe which was brought to an end.

Jews are no metaphors—not for poets, not for novelists, not for theologians, not for murderers, and never for anti-Semites. Mr. Styron's children, he tells us, have a Jewish mother. Had they been born into Nazi Germany, their fate would not have been designed according to those universalist words, "humanity" and "life," which blur over everything real. The Nuremberg Laws did not blur anything over, and Mr. Styron's children would have come, not by virtue of their "humanity" but through their Jewish mother, to join the other Jews in that so terrible, and so unmetaphorical, a place.

One cannot take, as Mr. Styron suggests, too "narrow" a view of that evil; the idea of its "ecumenical nature" is air and chimera. It is an idea that lessens the pain of right seeing. There are some things—like birth, and agony, and justice, and death—which come each in its eachness, felt by one body at a time, narrowed to the utmost singularity. "Humanity" did not suffer the consequences of the Nuremberg race laws; Jews in their uniqueness, gypsies in theirs, did. The more narrowly we look into the perplexing lens of Auschwitz, the more painful will the perception be. Perception of what? Of that deep and mysterious disorder, that dark and vindictive discord, blandly called anti-Semitism.

Blurring eases. Specificity pains. We have no right to seek a message of ease in Auschwitz, and it is moral ease to slide from the particular to the abstract. We have no right, in the nourishing name of "life," in the perilously ennobling name of "humanity," to divest the Jews of Europe of their specifically Jewish martyrdom. The Soviets have already done that at Babi Yar—only "Soviet citizens" perished there, not Jews. It breaks the heart to see an American novelist, the father of Jewish children, compassionate perceiver, go down that cold road.

FIVE BLACK POETS: HISTORY, CONSCIOUSNESS, LOVE AND HARSHNESS

by EUGENE B. REDMOND

from PARNASSUS: POETRY IN REVIEW

nominated by Ishmael Reed

Lyn. *Singing Sadness Happy*. Broadside Press 1972. 32 pp. $1.50 (paper).

Habte Wolde. *Enough To Die For*. Broadside Press 1972. 46 pp. $1.50 (paper).

Clarence Major. *The Cotton Club*. Broadside Press 1972. 22 pp. $1.25 (paper).

Ai. *Cruelty*. Houghton Mifflin Company 1973. 46 pp. $4.95.

Jay Wright. *The Homecoming Singer*. Corinth 1971. 96 pp. $3.00 (paper).

The whole sky caught. The thick sea heaved like petrol.
The past hissed in a cinder.
They heard the century breaking in half.
Then, towards the daybreak, rain
sprinkled the cinders. Clouds
steamed from the broken axle-tree.

(Derek Walcott, *Another Life*)

Three men and two women challenge life through distinctly different voices. It is, of course, *the challenge* to which we all are drawn (and sometimes quartered)—*the challenge* to conquer (and thus self-destruct) or live in harmony with the things of this world.

To such an either/or fury Lyn addresses herself in *Singing Sadness Happy*. Hers is a personal voice—almost a plea at times—but she emerges as part of a recognizable tradition in recent Black Poetry, one which views the poet as a director-general of the people's thoughts and actions. She is a Broadside Poet, and, as such, joins several dozen Black writers, mostly young poets, who have been published by Dudley Randall's Detroit-based company. Lyn's thematic, if not linguistic, influences are Don L. Lee (the biggest name at Broadside, though not the ablest talent there or in Chicago! See Sterling Plumpp or Carolyn Rodgers or Ethridge Knight), Nikki Giovanni, Sonia Sanchez, Imamu Amiri Baraka, and others identified with the Black Arts Movement of the Sixties. Randall opened for business in 1966 and has published almost 100 poets (some of whom are available on tape), nearly the same number of single poems—in the Broadside Series—and several Broadside Posters. While there is some controversy over his approach to selecting and promoting poets, Randall has been and remains one of the most important influences on, and promoters of, contemporary Black Poetry.

On the back of her book Lyn confesses that she believes "words are a means to the end of self-determination and self-definition." After having "lived in two worlds, unevenly spaced, dangerously close to madness," she feels writing poetry "has been a means of spanning the spread between the two." That Lyn came of age during the era of civil rights and nonviolent protest demonstrations is evident in her poetry. "The Final Indignity" recalls the bruises, cuts, and insults that only Demerol could defy; so

> i vowed never
> again to
> be nonviolent (????)

Why the marring question marks? Many a young Black poet, caught in the vise of a seemingly inflexible language, resorts to typographical graffiti—with little satisfaction. (Ossie Davis has said, "The English Language is my enemy." But Robert Hayden, Gwendolyn

Brooks, and Julia Fields do quite well in spite of it!) Yet Lyn
continues to win fights. *Singing Sadness Happy* is about overcoming
one long, hard battle—the right to be Black, woman, and loved. As
the heroine in her own poetic narrative ("Homecoming—Mass.
General Hospital"), she lies in the hospital recovering from another
"nonviolent" demonstration, and sees

> papa smiling deep inside
> cause below the carefully
> manipulated fear
> he knew i won the
> fight

In many ways, *Singing Sadness Happy* is a eulogy for the civil rights
movement and the lives given to it. The faith, the hope, the belief
that spurred the NAACP, the Urban League, and Martin Luther
King are spat on by those who respond violently to peaceful protest.
This element, coupled with rising nationalist/Pan-Africanist feelings
and activities among U.S. Blacks, helped lay the basis for a new
militant or defiant brand of Black poetry. Black poets of the late
Sixties (Baraka, Lee, Crouch, Touré, Sanchez, Knight, and others)
seized upon the deaths of political and cultural luminaries to hammer home messages about Black Power, Black unity, and to gal-
vanize Blacks around certain specific or general political issues.
Implicit in most of the new poetry was a rejection of Dr. King's
brand of battle—which was seen by many as a continual "turning of
the other cheek." Hence, Lyn tells us:

> i buried nonviolence
> before it had the chance
> to bury me!

In "Replacing Faith," she announces that

> i have replaced my faith
> with conviction

after telling us the gun now sits where "the bible used to." But one
wants to ask if this is *really* true; and, if it is, why announce it? Some
of her efforts sprawl on the pages, and others get off to good starts

only to wind up unresolved. "Loving" has merit of statement and purpose, but not of poetry: "Revolutions must be made of love, people . . . not hate." or:

As we talk the words of the revolution,
   and reiterate the duties we feel to the rebellion
  why don't we turn our heads around and look at the person
      beside us?

We share Lyn's sentiments, but sentiments and "commitments" (same poem) don't themselves make poetry. Another poetry-less item is found in "Dare to Struggle—Dare to Win":

     each day
     grow a little Blacker
     each day
     grow a little stronger
     each day
     grow a little hipper
        to the steps they
     plan for me to take.

In the same poem, Lyn constantly refers to "they" and "their"—a kind of Black code for "enemy," "whitey," or "the man"—but it is time Black poets refuted such a simplistic philosophical and linguistic rationale for the Black predicament in the world. There are countless more-interesting ways to show that one grows a "little hipper" each day.

Despite the faults, however, Lyn continually surprises the reader. She knows ("Define Revolution") that "nothing human is all nice" and that sometimes in our revolutionary "rush"

     . . . to the battle we step
     on someone, sometwo, somethree.

In "A Love Word" (a fine treatment of a Blues motif) she finds that it is

> hard to write *love*
> poems
> when you've been
> writing *lack* of love
> poems for so
> long.

There are also poetic gifts and trinkets in other pieces. "To Harriet Tubman: A Plea" leans as heavily on typography as it does on language for success:

> TAKE MY HAND
>   AND LEAD
> ME TO THE PROMISED
> LAND.
>   THEY TOOK MY
>   MAN AWAY
> AND I CAN'T
> FIGHT ANYMORE.
>
> ALONE.

"Ecology Home-Style" streams a series of images to tell a story now very familiar to Black urban poetry:

> sterile radiators
>   steamless clankings
>
> sent roaches
>   scurrying away
>
> from a bread crumb
>   on a warped wooded floor. . . .

The harsh world of Black ghetto life is again portrayed in "Junkie Lost/Junkie Found":

they found
    billy
squashed in a   corner
    cold

. . .

    crouched under
an umbrella
    6 broken spokes
dripping rain
    down his face
melting into his
    own tears
    laughing. . . .

"Abbreviation" is part of a series of poems describing the loneliness, need, and various changes experienced by a woman whose man is imprisoned. Although many contemporary poets confuse readers with designed grammatical and spelling violations, Lyn is convincing and clear in her experimental poem:

    my lfe hs bn
    abrev's since yr
    bust

    a collection
    of I's

        no we's to
        they's

    or you's

    a series of
    hlf read bks
    and worse
        hlf written

    poems

wds with no
ooo's or
    aaahhh's

all hrd
ttt's

    and
    vvv's

no uuuu's
    with meeee's

or heeee's with
    sheeeee's

    jst me and
    they

singular with
no apostrophe S

the aahhh is
    aahhhlone
cause the
    uuuuuuu is
gone.

Finally, "Precarious" is her *"warning to lovers without their loves"*:

i will do
nothin.

because anything
will remind me
of him.

After the flood of Black Pride/Black Power poetry of the Sixties
and early Seventies, Habte Wolde does not present evidence
Enough to Die For. Like Lyn's, his is a poetry of consciousness-

building. But, unlike, Lyn, he is not able to pull it off as well—or even convincingly. Wolde's attempts, in fact his being published, are further indication of what one Black critic recently called "the crisis in Black Poetry." For how many good and superior writers have been unable to get in print! *Enough to Die For* contains all the familiar themes and clichés that even high-school students are hip to nowadays. Neither are those robotlike polemics presented uniquely or arrestingly. Many of the poems take their cues from the first one in the book, "For the Sisters." The fact that Wolde quotes from a Nina Simone song does not make what follows poetry:

> TRUTH KNOWLEDGE
> LOVE UNDERSTANDING
> UNITY AND ONENESS
>
> ALL BLACK
> FOR ALL
> BLACK PEOPLE
>
> PLEASE COME TOGETHER
> BEFORE IT'S TOO LATE

In his efforts to salute the Black woman, Wolde writes a poem like "Blackwoman You is What You is" which stagnates in lines like:

> BEAUTY AND GRACE
> absolute magnetism
> and perpetual motion . . .

Ending the poem, he notes that "you can reach beyond the stars sister" to become:

> BLACK
> BLACK
> BLACK
> ALL BLACK.

Maybe this poet equates using the *word* Black (and its numerous synonyms) with the actual architectonics of good *Black* poetry and a sustaining force, he could learn from a master like Senghor ("Black Woman"):

> Naked woman, dark woman
> Oil that no breath ruffles, calm oil on the athlete's
> flanks, on the flanks of the Princes of Mali
> Gazelle limbed in Paradise, pearls are stars on the
> night of your skin
> Delights of the mind, the glinting of red gold against
> your watered skin
> Under the shadow of your hair, my care is lightened by
> the neighbouring suns of your eyes. . . .

But who can knock a Black man for taking a name given him by the Ethiopian Orthodox Church? For being proud of his African heritage? For saluting Black women in at least half a dozen of these "poems"? For chiding fakes and charlatans and revolutionary pimps? For even managing (here and there) to write an effective line or stanza? In "Preception [word?] of the Blackwoman" he notes

> The nation flowing from her womb
> rising in the valley of her thighs
> set into motion by the rhythm of her hips
> being fed into oneness by the nectar of her breast
> and tied into a nation
> by the bonds of her arms

Here a potentially good piece is marred by the intrusion of the word "nation' and confusing imagery like "valley of her thighs." The same poem contains one of the best lines in the book, though one might quarrel with its simple, self-indulgent solution to a complex and history-lodged situation: "build sister on the back that we provide. . . ." Except for the vertical arrangement of words, there is little other evidence that Wolde is a poet. Here, of course, things get somewhat ticklish because there is an insidious anti-intellectual movement in some quarters which implies that Blacks do not think very deeply and are capable of digesting only the "Last Poets" syndrome of poetry. Unfortunately, Black and other readers have been given an overdose of this kind of thinking. And much of the artistically sound poetry has taken a back seat to acoustics and punchline rhetoric. While oral and political topics rightly pervade the work of many Black poets, such expressions are often best made by the Malcolm X's, the Stokely Carmichaels, the Dr. Kings, and the Rap Browns. Serious Black writers need to keep in mind that the word *art* is not silent in the phrase "Black Art." Black poets cannot risk passing to a rising Black readership (and others who share their visions) the assumption that writing "Afro-American" poetry is any easier than writing Chinese, French, Japanese, African, or Chicano poetry.

Such thinking would give Leadbelly and Moms Mabley reasons for pause—let alone Joe Gonçalves or Alice Walker. So many other *poets* do so well what Wolde is attempting. So many who refuse to strip Blacks of their humanity; who, in the words of Lance Jeffers, "pour these lives into this horn." They must be heard; they will be heard. They know the Black Experience is an aggregate one and, in its totality, is *Enough to Die For*.

In 1927, Duke Ellington's band opened at Harlem's famed Cotton Club. One wonders if Clarence Major's book does not warrant a brief introduction to this significant period in Black history. A biographical note says Major's writings have appeared in over 125 publications; he is also an editor (*The New Black Poetry*), a critic ("Open Letters," regular column in *The American Poetry Review*), a novelist (*No, All-Night Visitors*), and a recognized pathfinder in the New Black Literature. In *Interviews with Black Writers* he recants statements made about Black writers in "a Black Criterion" (*The Journal of Black Poetry*, 1967). In that article (reprinted in *Black Voices*, 1968, and *Nommo*, 1972), Major outlined a rather monolithic position for Black writers. He now believes Black writers should select any subject matter or technique that is amenable to them. His current stand indicates important growth.

Major himself has been in the forefront of experimental poetry and prose. In prose he fits "loosely" into a category with William Melvin Kelley and Ishmael Reed. But his influences and antecedents in poetry are not so easy to identify. He is usually very competent as a writer, and he has written better poetry than *The Cotton Club* (see *Swallow the Lake* and *Symptoms and Madness*), which is economic almost to the point of emaciation. His subject matter is "vital," as Gwendolyn Brooks might put it. Few Black

poets today, excepting Robert Hayden and Jay Wright, are working
well with history. Of the attempts being made, too many are laden
with forced "integration." Major, however, is aware of the need to
preserve and present a Black past. In the title poem he tells us to

> . . . honor
> the institutions, the
> idea of duke. tho a person,
> human through his own
> nights. sleeping late,
> being slow at home. knew
> & remembered jungle nights.
> recorded harlem on
> the open wings of a
> bluebird.

Major conducts narrative tours of Harlem and urban Black America,
primarily during the first two or three decades of the Twentieth
Century. He looks at Lenox Avenue ("In the Crowd on Lenox Ave &
135th Street"), Black participation in World War I ("1919"), white
inhibitions at the dawn of the Freudian Age ("Ladies Day: 1902"),
the Great Depression ("1930: Hardtimes"), and the joys and agonies
of Black entertainers ("Black Theatre"/1928 Blues). Then there is a
tapestry-of-a-poem (one of the best in the book: "Madman of the
Uncharmed Debris of the South Side") in which Major employs
obscure references, a suggestion of the supernatural, tidbits of
history, and other erudite meanderings. The poem contains a
Gwendowlyn Brooks-like economy which is where any resemblance
between these two poets stops. Major says that he and the "madman"

> met inside a dust-filled lyre
> shop, he
> scared shit out of me, miss. his edges
> his loose shingles.

Frustrated writer, teacher, drunkard, and genius, the madman
squanders his life and leaves "no records":

> only the student he knocked up
> and married will have
> memory of his last years
> he threw up
> she told me,   on his manuscripts &
> joined a funeral
> procession, never
> came back

Many of the themes that recur in the literature and conversation about these times (the mulatto, violence against Blacks, the creation and development of jazz and blues, etc.) occupy space here. In "Black Theatre," for example, Major notes that:

> then all those light
> skinned chicks up there
> really was white.

The language in these poems is direct, sometimes almost unpoetic—reminiscent of the "listings" of Michael S. Harper—and maybe there is a move afoot to dispense with metaphor and simply be sparse. Too, one has some trouble identifying the personae. The speaker seems, alternately, to be an unlettered street denizen or itinerant observer. At other times he appears to be the poet himself, divided between two or more people in a dialogue. Major keeps it unclear until near the end of the book when he breaks through nicely with "importers":

> bring to the relics carted by whites
> from a functional lie. of
> life: dramatize the skin the cover a
> thousand wooden heads, their horns
> the eyes: evil enough

> to protect, even this far, away. the
> chase manhattan national bank to say
> nothing of its function. an irony in
> any world.

Last, the fine but unsettling poem that closes out the book ("Personal and Sexual freedom") would certainly not be taken with coffee at the offices of *Ms* or *Encore*. After an undecorated look at the pros and cons of Women's Liberation, he tells the women to remember that in " . . . sailing/keep your helm up." We want to replace "helm" with "hem" or "hymn" or even "him"—to make the double *entendre* work. Major has written well in the past and, being young, will write well again. His history work is important but he has not worked out the most effective way to present his ideas. We await *The Syncopated Cakewalk*.

Pictures of Ai (on the cover of *Cruelty* and in *The American Poetry Review*) show her as having African blood; but little about her poetry suggests that she is conscious of it in any political or cultural sense. The poet's self-view *vs*. world-view has preoccupied more than just a few Black American poets in this century. Countee Cullen wanted to be known simply as a "poet," not a "Negro poet." Fifty years later Robert Hayden issued the same demand. Curiously, Cullen and Hayden are most intense when writing about (or out of) their Blackness. However, Ai cannot be fitted into either the Cullen/Hayden universe or the current Don L. Lee-imposed portrait: that a Black poet *must* always write *consciously* out of his Black predicament. Nevertheless, *Cruelty* does follow the ways of English and American Poetry—including the self-denigrating, woe-is-me morbidity that prevails in much confessional verse. Ai's voice, though, is firmer—notwithstanding the oppressive repetition—and distinct. Here is a "Forty-Three-Year-Old Woman, Masturbating":

> I want to kill this female hand—
> its four centipede fingers;
> the thumb, cricket, that lags behind,
> digging its nail into me, until I move my legs apart;
> the palm, the body of a tarantula,
> that sinks down over my clitoris,
> as the fingers inch into my vagina—
> but each time, after it happens,
> the fingers, moist and flaccid, crawl up to my mouth,
> my grasshopper tongue, darting out, licks them
> and I am grateful for a small taste of anything.

Indeed, each character, each speaker seems almost to be "grateful" for whatever is received—grateful or ungrateful, for such is the fate of those trapped in *Cruelty*. In reading Ai, one is reminded of Claude McKay's lines about being born out of clime and place because Ai, just past twenty-five years old, seems to write in what a colleague called "an old voice." But one wants to ask if it is possible in poetry, a form so closely identified with the individual and the "voice."

"Twenty-Year Marriage" leaves a wife disillusioned and frustrated:

> I'll pull, you push, we'll tear each other in half,
> Come on baby, lay me down on my back.
> Pretend you don't owe me a thing
> and maybe we'll roll out of here,
> leaving the past stacked up behind us;
> old newspapers nobody's ever got to read again.

In "Abortion" the husband comes home to find the "fetus wrapped in wax paper" and tells his wife:

> Woman, loving you no matter what you do,
> what can I say, except that I've heard
> the poor have no children, just small people
> and there is room only for one man in this house.

"The Estranged" is gore-filled, a mixture of items drawn from the recipe of a meal being cooked and the anatomy of a woman. The narrator avows that her "monthly blood, mixed with water":

> will be a blanket of gravy to cover you
> from one icy night to the next.

"The Tenant Farmer" watches his "woman" slip from life to death via hunger. "Each day she bites another notch in her thumb" and the farmer has to "pretend relief is coming." Finally in an italicized chant that enumerates the essentials of an agrarian diet, the farmer eulogizes his woman:

> *roll on home to Jesus,*
> *it's too late now you're dead.*

"Starvation" holds a similar tragedy. Hunger, and its accompanying traumas, is handled with precision and understatement:

> The white oak frame of the house shakes
> when I slam the door and stand on the porch, fanning
> myself with a piece of cardboard
> cut in the shape of a ham.

The same depressive weight is found in "Prostitute," "Young Farm Woman Alone," and in a "Tired Old Whore" going her last few rounds at forty-five when her "breath's short":

> But wait, I need a little help, help me, sweet thing.
> Pull down your pants,
> I like to see what I'm getting now,
> before it gets into me.

The tapestry of *Cruelty* also includes the "Hangman" (whose opening lines are reminiscent of Jean Toomer's "Harvest Song"), "The Corpse Hauler's Elegy," "The Hitchhiker," a "Deserter," and "Indecision."

The different, yet merging, portraits of *Cruelty* often make us put old photographs in new frames as in "The Suicide"; but there is also pointlessness (as in "The Cripple") and corny tacked-on endings ("Child Beater"). Cruelty often comes on the heels of high-heartedness and temporary optimism; and sometimes through a male voice—making you stop and rethink what you've just read against the beautiful face you've seen on the cover of the book. The hard-woman theme and Women's Liberation sentiment trickle through such pieces as "Woman," "The Rivals," and "Woman to Man":

> For a while, I'll let it make you strong,
> make your heart lion,
> then I'll take it back.

The accolades and superlatives attending the publication of Ai's poetry are deserved. Though void of the music and dazzling rhythms found in Jayne Cortez, Ai's poetry aims at the vital parts of the personality and sensibility. Cruelty—stripped bare of all pre-

tention and prettiness—is examined "to the bone." Even the victims of Ai's cruelties become offenders. It is a virulent cycle in which
neither the outcast nor the unspoiled escapes the Sado-masochistic
vampire of life. Brilliantly Ai lays the unpleasantries—utter truths
in most instances—before our eyes. And so much of Ai is unre-
quited; so much, like Toomer's "Karintha" (*Cane*), cut down before
the race has hardly begun. Yet, like the defiant and arrogant Karintha, Ai tells you "Before You Leave":

> I'm a mare. Every nail's head
> in my hooves wears your face,
> but not even you, wolf, can bring me down.

For Ai, titles are important. In fact most of the poems make little
contextual sense unless the titles are read and remembered. Occasionally, the reader must return to the title, after losing the theme,
in order to refocus on the poem. Again, it is clear that Ai is a product
of, and contributor to, the contemporary mood of American poetry.
And if *Cruelty* is her authentic voice, she has found it at a remarkable
early age. Her poetry reflects a complex and far-reaching intelligence. But it does not seem too much of an intrusion to suggest that
she take a closer look—beyond Charles Simic, Diane Wakoski,
Sylvia Plath, and Robert Lowell—at Jayne Cortez, Julia Fields,
Robert Hayden, and Margaret Walker.

Variety is not an ingredient of Ai's poetry but it might help: about
halfway through the book, you have to ask yourself if you've read
some of the pieces before. And always, especially for this reader,
there was the question: What would be the impact of import or Ai's
work if—given both her innate intelligence and sound
scholarship—she were to tap the African strain in her complex
genealogy? Only a fraction of ethnic writers (Yerby, Motley) have
successfully side-stepped this fundamental question.

Erudition in any other poet's hands might be self-defeating and
incomprehensible. But Jay Wright, as *The Homecoming Singer*,
makes scholarship—esoteric and out-of-the-way places and
names—come alive with excitement. Wright is a world-traveler
who, on any given day, might drop you a note from Scotland,
Chapultepec, or New England. His seriousness of thought is only
equaled by his seriousness of tone and subject. A former theology
student, Wright's religious training (home and school) shows up

frequently in his work—but here is no Brother Antoninus or beat
poet posing as savior or guru. Wright has thought hard and long
about what he calls "the rhythm of perception," and in his brilliant
introduction to Henry Dumas' *Poetry for My People* (1970) and in
Play Ebony Play Ivory (1974), he outlined concerns of Black Poetry
that had not been explored up to the time of his writing. Yet
Wright's is a poetry of contemplation and as such will not be as
widely read or known (in the short-run) as that of Don L. Lee or
Nikki Giovanni.

There is an authentic ring to Wright's Black-nestled work, but his
Blackness does not scream babbling slogans and ideologies. In
"Wednesday Night Prayer Meeting" his voice is controlled, his
emotions free, his portraits exact:

> Outside, the pagan kids
> scramble in the darkness,
> kissing each other with a sly humility,
> or urinating boldly against trees.
> The older people linger
> in the freshly lit light, . . .

Nor does Wright overlook the strange contradictions inherent in
the Black Christian:

> . . . innocent of the insoluble
> mysteries of being black
> and sinned against, black
> and sinning in the compliant cities.

And finally, the fate-handlers in their relaxed libraries—a Jesuit?:

> What do the young know
> about some corpulent theologian,
> sitting under his lamp,
> his clammy face wet,
> his stomach trying to give up
> the taste of a moderate wine,
> kissing God away with a labored
> toss of his pen?

Combining scholarship, autobiography, and manipulated soul, Wright continues to examine bones and slices of Black life in such poems as "The Baptism":

> They came,
> naked under white robes,
> their hair pressed down in stocking caps,
> hesitating,
> and looking into the eyes
> of women who had been familiar
> a moment ago,
> of men who had been laughable
> as they shuffled to the church,
> a little dim in the eye,
> a whiff of Sen-Sen on their breaths.

These "slices" are also found in "The End of an Ethnic Dream" and "The Man From Chi":

> for this is the City
> and love is a dangerous thing
> get you there singing Stagolee
> and looking for a woman who dips snuff
> at night when the moon is out
> he'll show it a piece of silver.

The Homecoming Singer sees his life via "A Month in the Country," "The Neighborhood House," "An Invitation to Madison County," "First Principles," "Collection Time," "Variation on a Theme by LeRoi Jones," "My Mother Dances on the Jut of God's Good Hip," "The Desert Revival," and "The Regeneration" (a deeply mythical and moving piece). Especially rich in Black folk material is "Night Walk," where

> These streets wake up at night
> with tongues and eyes to spear you

and

> It is there in the language
> & you are you if you are recognized
> & you are recognized if you can rap

because

> The old man was right
> > Death is the language of these streets
> > though death will never own them/
> > When it is all done
> > so much of your life
> > is how & what you speak/
> > if you go away
> > you carry the speech in your bones/
> Nothing is invented here/ in you
> > > you come to that
> > even though the streets cluck their triumph
> > > & you sit in the dawn
> > with the old man piercing your tongue.

Wright is equally adept in poetizing history ("Crispus Attucks," "W.E.B. DuBois at Harvard," "Origins," "Death as History"—a brilliant and terrifying allegory) and his extensive and provocative travels ("Jálapeña Gypsies," "*Bosques de Chapultepec*," "Morning Leaving Calle Gigantes," "Chapultepec Castle"). Allegorical, picturesque, and consummately strong, *The Homecoming Singer* is the kind of bedtime reading that takes the place of fiction or predose article perusal. Wright has the narrative sense and technique and the ability to maintain poetic precision even throughout his lengthier projects. At the book's benediction, he tells us that he is "Beginning Again," an appropriate notice served by an Afro-American poet genuinely immersed in his and the world's tradition and predicament:

> An aching prodigal,
> who would make miracles
> to understand the simple given.

Jay Wright refuses to skim the top of Black humanity. Ai's poetry is searchingly intellectual (though sometimes the "mash" is evident) even if she is not semantically Black. Though Clarence Major's form often places distance between his reader and the poem's meaning, it is clear that he is thematically and linguistically at home. Habte Wolde rarely affords the reader an opportunity to interpret the complex codes of the human heart and mind—since he is so busy strangling or distorting them. On the other hand, Lyn possesses both the hope and the curse of Black poetry. For she has genuine gifts—which must be nurtured and developed. She has already surpassed some of her models of the 1960's. She must now read more challenging, more growth-oriented poetry and general literature.

Whether Black poets subscribe to James Weldon Johnson's vision of them (as dismissers of dialect and creators of new dimensions in a blend of Black tongues) or Sterling Brown's rebuff—break the "mold" whites have placed on Black speech and restate the experience through real folk idioms and symbols—it is clear that the challenges today are no less demanding than they were on the last generation of poets. To be sure, there is strength in the argument that Black writing travels cyclically rather than chronologically. This is so because, while focuses and priorities shift, the "problems" of Blacks have remained essentially the same: i.e., grappling with the numberless daily horrors caused by not being seen as complete humans in a white world. With radical differences, most Black poets express their disdain and hatred for a system which pays lip-service to their humanity. As humans, and as men and women, these poets personally feel the sting of racism like the masses of their brothers and sisters of color. It remains to be seen, then, whether—given the limited number of options—Black poetry can "rise" above the situations of those who write it.

On the other hand, as Lorraine Hansberry pointed out, one does not (since there is a complete duality) go around twenty-four hours a day thinking that he/she is Black. It is during those "other" hours that one loves, makes babies, eats, works, sleeps, studies, laughs, drinks, toasts, plays, performs, cries, and dies. And it is of these pits, these rises, these crests, that Black poets must sing. It is out of these ecstasies, exigencies, and splendors that the poets must carve reaffirmations. Consciously or unconsciously, the symbols, as Johnson said, must come from within rather than from without. But these symbols can express anything and everything since Black humanity is no more nor less than white, yellow, or brown humanity. And since Blackness can, like Whitman, contain "multitudes."

POPOCATÉPETL

translated from the Aztec by FRANK M. CHAPMAN

from THE SPELL OF THE HUNGRY WOLF: AZTEC VISIONS

(Sunstone Press)

nominated by Sunstone Press

The Smoking Mountain breathes
His darkness into the sky:
His darkness heavy in the air:
It rises and goes.
It goes away.
All we have:
These flowers,
This gold:
All these things will go.
Like smoke in the sky
they go away.
Our lives will rise and go,
will go away.
All that is left
Of us at last
Is the scroll,
The little painted people
Made of red ink,
Of black ink.

🔥 🔥 🔥

THE DEATH OF SUN

by WILLIAM EASTLAKE

from THE FAR SIDE OF THE STORM (San Marcos Press)

nominated by Leonard Randolph

THE BIRD SUN WAS NAMED Sun by the Indians because each day their final eagle circled this part of the reservation like the clock of sun. Sun, a grave and golden eagle-stream of light, sailed without movement as though propelled by some eternity, to orbit, to circumnavigate this moon of earth, to alight upon his aerie from which he had risen, and so Sun would sit with the same God dignity and decorous finality with which he had emerged—then once more without seeming volition ride the crest of an updraft above Indian Country on six-foot wings to settle again on his throne aerie in awful splendor, serene—regal and doomed. I have risen.

"Man, Fyodor Dostoevski said," the white teacher Mary-Forge said, "without a sure idea of himself and the purpose of his life cannot live and would sooner destroy himself than remain on earth."

"Who was Dostoevski?" the Navajo Indian Jesus Saves said.

"An Indian."

"What kind?"

"With that comment he could have been a Navajo," Mary-Forge said.

"No way," Jesus Saves said.

"Why, no way could Dostoevski be an Indian?"

"I didn't say Dostoevski couldn't be an Indian, I said he couldn't be a Navajo."

"Why is a Navajo different?"

"We are, that's all," Jesus Saves said. "In the words of Soren Kierkegaard—"

"Who was Soren Kierkegaard?"

"Another Russian," Jesus Saves said.

"Kierkegaard was a Dane."

"No, that was Hamlet," Jesus Saves said. "Remember?"

"You're peeved, Jesus Saves."

"No, I'm bugged," Jesus Saves said, "by people who start sentences with 'man.'"

"Dostoevski was accounting for the high suicide rate among Navajos. Since the white man invaded Navajo country the Navajo sees no hope or purpose to life."

"Then why didn't Dostoevski say that?"

"Because he never heard of the Navajo."

"Then I never heard of Dostoevski," Bull Who Looks Up said. "Two can play at this game."

"That's right," Jesus Saves said, sure of himself now and with purpose.

"What is the purpose of your life, Jesus Saves?"

"To get out of this school," Jesus Saves said.

Jesus Saves was named after a sign-board erected by the Albuquerque First National Savings & Loan.

All of Mary-Forge's students were Navajos. When Mary-Forge was not ranching she was running this free school that taught the Indians about themselves and their country—Indian country.

"What has Dostoevski got to do with Indian country?"

"I'm getting to that," Mary-Forge said.

"Will you hurry up?"

"No," Mary-Forge said.

"Is that any way for a teacher to speak to a poor Indian?"

"Sigmund Freud," the Medicine Man said, "said—more in anguish I believe than in criticism—'What does the Indian want? My God, what does the Indian want?'"

"He said that about women."

"If he had lived longer, he would have said it about Indians."

"True."

"Why?"

"Because it sounds good, it sounds profound, it tends to make you take off and beat the hell out of the Indians."

"After we have finished off the women."

"The women were finished off a long time ago," the Medicine Man said.

"But like the Indians they can make a comeback."

"Who knows," the Medicine Man said, "we both may be a dying race."

"Who knows?"

"We both may have reached the point of no return, who knows?"

"If we don't want to find out, what the hell are we doing in school?"

"Who knows?"

"I know," Mary-Forge said, "I know all about the eagle."

"Tell us, Mary-Forge, all about the eagle."

"The eagle is being killed off."

"We know that, what do we do?"

"We get out of this school and find the people who are killing the eagle."

"Then?"

"Who knows?" Mary-Forge said.

Mary-Forge was a young woman—she was the youngest white woman the Navajos had ever seen. She was not a young girl, there are millions of young girls in America. In America young white girls suddenly become defeated women. A young white woman sure of herself and with a purpose in life such as Mary-Forge was unknown to the American Indian.

Mary-Forge had large wide-apart almond-shaped eyes, high full cheekbones, cocky let-us-all-give-thanks tipsy breasts, and good brains. The white American man is frightened by her brain. The

Indians found it nice. They loved it. They tried to help Mary-Forge. Mary-Forge tried to help the Indians. They were both cripples. Both surrounded by the white reservation.

High on her right cheekbone Mary-Forge had a jagged two-inch scar caused by a stomping she got from high-heeled cowboy boots belonging to a sheep rancher from the Twin Slash Heart Ranch on the floor of the High Point Bar in Gallup.

Mary-Forge did not abruptly think of eagles in the little red schoolhouse filled with Indians. A helicopter had just flown over. The helicopter came to kill eagles. The only time the Indians ever saw or felt a helicopter on the red reservation was when the white ranchers came to kill eagles. Eagles killed sheep, they said, and several cases have been known, they said, where white babies have been plucked from playpens and dropped in the ocean, they said.

You could hear plain the whack-whack-whack of the huge rotor blades of the copter in the red schoolhouse. The yellow and blue copter was being flown by a flat-faced doctor-serious white rancher named Ira Osmun, who believed in conservation through predator control. Eagles were fine birds, but the sheep must be protected. Babies, too.

"Mr. Osmun," Wilson Drago, the shotgun-bearing sado-child-appearing co-pilot asked, "have the eagles got any white babies lately?"

"No."

"Then?"

"Because we are exercising predator control."

"When was the last white baby snatched by eagles and dropped into the ocean?"

"Not eagles, Drago, eagle, it only takes one. As long as there is one eagle there is the possibility of your losing your child."

"I haven't any child."

"If you did."

"But I haven't."

"Someone does."

"No one in the area does."

"If they did, there would be the possibility of their losing them."

"No one can say nay to that," Wilson Drago said. "When was the last time a child was snatched?"

"It must have been a long time ago."

"Before living memory?"

"Yes, even then, Drago, I believe the stories to be apocryphal."

"What's that mean?"

"Lies."

"Then why are we shooting the eagles?"

"Because city people don't care about sheep. City people care about babies. You tell the people in Albuquerque that their babies have an outside chance, any chance that their baby will be snatched up and the possibility that it will be dropped in the ocean, kerplunk, and they will let you kill eagles."

"How far is the ocean?"

"People don't care how far the ocean is, they care about their babies."

"True."

"It's that simple."

"When was the last lamb that was snatched up?"

"Yesterday."

"That's serious."

"You better believe it, Drago."

"Why are we hovering over this red hogan?"

"Because before we kill an eagle we got to make sure what Mary-Forge is up to."

"What was she up to last time you heard?"

"Shooting down helicopters."

"All by herself?"

"It only takes one shot."

"You know, I bet that's right."

"You better believe it, Drago."

"Is this where she lives?"

"No—this is the little red schoolhouse she uses to get the Indians to attack the whites."

"What happened to your other co-pilots?"

"They got scared and quit."

"The last one?"

"Scared and quit."

"Just because of one woman?"

"Yes. You're not scared of a woman, are you, Drago?"

"No, I mean yes."

"Which is it, yes or no?"

"Yes," Wilson Drago said.

Below in the red hogan that was shaped like a beehive with a hole on top for the smoke to come out the Indians and Mary-Forge were getting ready to die on the spot.

"I'm not getting ready to die on the spot," Bull Who Looks Up said.

"You want to save the eagles, don't you?" Mary-Forge said.

"Let me think about that," Jesus Saves said.

"Pass me the gun," Mary-Forge said.

Now, from above in the copter the hogan looked like a gun turret, a small fort defending the perimeter of Indian Country.

"Mary-Forge is an interesting problem," Ira Osmun said— shouted above the whack-whack-whack of the rotors.

"Every woman is."

"But every woman doesn't end up living with the Indians, with the eagles."

"What causes that?"

"We believe the Indians and the eagles become their surrogate children."

"What?"

"That they become a substitute for life."

"Oh? Why do you hate me?"

"What?"

"Why do you use such big words?"

"I'm sorry, Drago. Do you see any eagles?"

"No, but I see a gun."

"Where?"

"Coming out of the top of the hogan."

"Let Mary-Forge fire first."

"Why?"

"To establish a point of law. Then it's not between her eagles and my sheep."

"It becomes your ass or hers."

"Yes."

"But it could be my life."

"I've considered that, Drago."

"Thank you. Thank you very much," Wilson Drago said.

Sun, the golden eagle that was very carefully watching the two white animals that lived in the giant bird that went "Whack-whack-whack," was ready.

Today would be the day of death for Sun. His mate had been killed two days before. Without her the eaglets in the woven of yucca high basket nest would die. Today would be the day of death for Sun because without a sure idea of himself, without purpose in life, an eagle would sooner destroy himself than remain on earth. The last day of Sun.

"Because," Mary-Forge said, and taking the weapon and jerking in a shell, "because I know, even though the Indians and us and the eagle, even though we have no chance ever, we can go through the motions of courage, compassion, and concern. Because we are Sun and men, too. Hello, Sun."

"Stop talking and aim carefully."

"Did I say something?"

"You made a speech."

"I'm sorry," Mary-Forge said.

"Aim carefully."

Mary-Forge was standing on the wide shoulders of an Indian named When Someone Dies He Is Remembered. All the other Indians who belonged in the little red schoolhouse stood around and below her in the dim and alive dust watching Mary-Forge revolve like a gun turret with her lever-operated Marlin .30-30 pointing out of the smoke hatch high up on the slow turning and hard shoulders of When Someone Dies He Is Remembered.

"Why don't you shoot?" More Turquoise said. He almost whispered it as though the great noise of the copter did not exist.

"The thing keeps bobbling," Mary-Forge shouted down to the Indians.

Looking through the gunsights she had to go up and down up and down to try and get a shot. She did not want to hit the cowboys. It would be good enough to hit the engine or the rotor blades. Why not hit the cowboys? Because there are always more cowboys. There are not many eagles left on the planet earth, there are several million cowboys. There are more cowboys than there are Indians. That's for sure. But what is important now is that if we give one eagle for one cowboy soon all the eagles will have disappeared from the earth and cowboys will be standing in your bed. No, the helicopter is scarce. They will not give one helicopter for one eagle. A helicopter cost too much money. How much? A quarter million dollars, I bet. Hit them where their heart is. Hit them in their helicopter.

But it danced. Now Mary-Forge noticed that although it was dancing it was going up and down with a rhythm. The thing to do is to wait until it hits bottom and then follow it up. She did and fired off a shot.

"Good girl," the Medicine Man said.

"That was close," Ira Osmun said to his shotgun, Wilson Drago. "Now that we know where Mary-Forge is we can chase the eagle."

Ira Osmun allowed the chopper to spurt up and away to tilt off at a weird angle so that it clawed its way sideways like a crab that flew, a piece of junk, of tin and chrome and gaudy paint, alien and obscene in the perfect pure blue New Mexican sky, an intruder in the path of the sun. Now the chopper clawed its way to the aerie of Sun.

The eagle had watched it all happen. Sun had watched it happen many times now. Two days ago when they killed his mate was the last time. Sun looked down at his golden eagle chicks. The eaglets were absolute white, they would remain white and vulnerable for several months until the new feathers. But there was no more time. Sun watched the huge man junk bird clawing its way down the long valley that led to Mount Taylor. His home, his home and above all the homes of the Indians.

Like the Indians the ancestors of Sun had one time roamed a virgin continent abloom with the glory of life, alive with fresh flashing streams, a smogless sky all the world a sweet poem of life where all was beginning. Nothing ever ended. Now it was all ending. The eagle, Sun, did not prepare to defend himself. He would not defend himself. There was nothing now to defend. The last hour of Sun.

"Catch me," Mary-Forge shouted from the top of the hogan and jumped. When she was caught by More Turquoise she continued to shout as the noise of the chopper was still there. "They've taken off for Mount Taylor to kill Sun. We've got to get on our horses and get our ass over there."

"Why?"

"To save Sun," Mary-Forge shouted. "Sun is the last eagle left in the county."

"But this is not a movie," the Medicine Man said. "We don't have to get on horses and gallop across the prairie. We can get in my pickup and drive there—quietly."

"On the road it will take two hours," Mary-Forge said. "And we'll need horses when we get there to follow the chopper."

"What would Dostoevski say about this?" the Medicine Man said.

"To hell with Dostoevski," Mary-Forge said.

Outside they slammed the saddles on the amazed Indian ponies, then threw themselves on and fled down the canyon a stream of dust and light a commingling of vivid flash and twirl so when they disappeared into the cottonwoods you held your breath until the phantoms, the abrupt magic of motion appeared again on the Cabrillo draw.

"Come on now, baby," Mary-Forge whispered to her horse Poco Mas. "What I said about Dostoevski I didn't mean. Poor Dostoevski. I meant seconds count. We didn't have time for a philosophical discussion. Come on now, baby, move good. Be good to me, baby, move good. Move good, baby. Move good. You can take that fence, baby. Take him! Good boy, baby. Good boy, Poco. Good boy. I'm sure the Medicine Man understands that when there are so few left, so few left Poco that there is not time for niceties. You'd think an Indian would understand that, wouldn't you? Still the Medicine Man is a strange Indian. A Freudian Medicine Man. But Bull Who Looks Up understands, look at him go. He's pulling ahead of us are you going to let him get away with that Poco?" Poco did not let the horse of Bull Who Looks Up stay ahead but passed him quickly, with Mary-Forge swinging her gun high and Bull Who Looks Up gesturing with his gun at the tin bird that crabbed across the sky.

"You see, Drago," Ira Osmun shouted to Wilson Drago, "we are the villains of the piece."

"What?"

"The bad guys."

"It's pretty hard to think of yourself as the bad guy, Mr. Osmun."

"Well, we are."

"Who are the good guys?"

"Mary-Forge."

"Screw me."

"No, she wouldn't do that because you're a bad guy. Because you kill eagles. People who never saw an eagle, never will see an eagle, want eagles all over the place. Except the poor. The poor want sheep to eat. Did you ever hear of a poor person complaining about the lack of eagles? They have got an outfit of rich gentlemen called the Sierra Club. They egg on Indian-lovers like Mary-Forge to kill ranchers."

"Why?"

"They have nothing else to do."

"You think Mary-Forge actually has sex with the Indians?"

"Why else would she be on the reservation?"

"I never thought about that."

"Think about it."

"I guess you're right."

"Drago, what do you think about?"

"I don't think about eagles."

"What do you think about?"

"Ordinarily?"

"Yes."

"Like when I'm drinking?"

"Yes."

"Religion."

"Good, Drago, I like to hear you say that. Good. What religion?"

"They are all good. I guess Billy Graham is the best."

"Yes, if you're stupid."

"What?"

"Nothing, Drago. Keep your eye peeled for the eagle."

"You said I was stupid."

"I may have said the Sierra Club was stupid."

"Did you?"

"No, how could you be stupid and be that rich?"

"Why are they queer for eagles then?"

"They are for anything that is getting scarce. Indians, eagles, anything. Mary-Forge is against natural evolution, too."

"What's natural evolution mean?"

"When something is finished it's finished, forget it. We got a new evolution, the machine, this copter, a new bird."

"That makes sense."

"Remember we don't want to kill eagles."

"We have to."

"That's right."

The eagle that had to be killed, Sun, perched like an eagle on his aerie throne. A king, a keeper of one hundred square miles of Indian country, an arbiter, a jury and judge, a shadow clock that had measured time for two thousand years in slow shadow-circle and so now the earth, the Indians, the place, would be without reckoning, certainly without the serene majesty of Sun, without, and this is what is our epitaph and harbinger, without the gold of silence the long lonely shadow beneath silent wing replaced now by the whack-whack-whack of tin, proceeding with crablike crippled crawl—the sweet song of man in awkward crazy metallic and cockeyed pounce, approached Sun.

Sun looked down on the eaglets in the nest. The thing to do would be to glide away from the whack-bird away from the nest. To fight it out somewhere else. If he could tangle himself in the wings of the whack-bird, that would be the end of the whack-bird. The end of Sun. Sun jumped off his aerie without movement not abrupt or even preemptory but as though the reel of film had cut and then proceeded to a different scene. The bird Sun, the eagle, the great golden glider moving across the wilds of purple mesa in airfed steady no-beat, in hushed deadly amaze, seemed in funeral stateliness, mounting upward on invisible winds toward the other sun.

"If he climbs, we will climb with him, Drago. He is bound to run out of updrafts."

Wilson Drago slid open the door on his side and shifted the Harrington & Richardson pump gun into the ready position.

"How high will this thing climb, sir?"

"Ten thousand feet."

"The bird can climb higher than that."

"Yet he has to come down, Drago."

"How much fuel we got?"

"Fifty gallons."

"What are we consuming?"

"A gallon a minute."

"Shall I try a shot?"

"Yes."

Sun was spiraling upward in tight circles on a good rising current of air when the pellets of lead hit him. They hit like a gentle rain that gave him a quick lift. Sun was out of range. Both the copter and Sun were spiraling upward. The copter was gaining.

"Shall I try another shot?"

"Yes."

This time the lead pellets slammed into Sun like a hard rain and shoved him upward and crazy tilted him as a great ship will yaw in a sudden gust. Sun was still out of range.

Now the upward current of air ceased, collapsed under Sun abruptly and the copter closed the distance until Ira Osmun and Wilson Drago were alongside and looking into small yellow eyes as the great sailing ship of Sun coasted downward into deep sky.

"Shall I try a shot?"

"Yes."

Wilson Drago raised the Harrington & Richardson shotgun and pumped in a shell with a solid slam. He could almost touch Sun with the muzzle. The swift vessel of Sun sailed on as though expecting to take the broadside from the 12-gauge gun that would send him to the bottom—to the floor of earth.

"Now, Drago."

But the gliding ship of bird had already disappeared—folded its huge wing of sail and shot downward, down down down downward until just before earth it unleashed its enormous sail of wing and glided over the surface of earth—Indian Country. Down came the copter in quick chase.

There stood the Indians all in a row.

"Don't fire men," Mary-Forge shouted, "until Sun has passed."

As Sun sailed toward the Indians the shadow of Sun came first, shading each Indian separately. Now came the swifting Sun and each mounted Indian raised his gun in salute. Again separately and in the order which Sun arrived and passed, now the Indians leveled their guns to kill the whack-bird.

"Oh, this is great, Drago," Ira Osmun shouted, "the Indians want to fight."

"What's great about that?"

"It's natural to fight Indians."

"It is?"

"Yes."

"Well I'll be."

"My grandfather would be proud of us now."

"Did he fight Indians?"

"He sure did. It's only a small part of the time the whites have been that they haven't fought Indians."

"Fighting has been hard on the Indians."

"That may well be, Drago, but it's natural."

"Why?"

"Because people naturally have a fear of strangers. It's called xenophobia. When you don't go along with nature you get into trouble. You suppress your natural instincts and that is dangerous. That's what's wrong with this country."

"It is? I wondered about that."

"There's nothing wrong with shooting Indians."

"I wondered about that."

"It's natural."

"No, Mr. Osmun there is something wrong."

"What's that?"

"Look. The Indians are shooting back."

Ira Osmun twisted the copter up and away. "Get out the rifle. We'll take care of the Indians."

"What about the eagle?"

"We've first got to take care of the Indians who are shooting at us and that girl who is shooting at us."

"Is she crazy?"

"Why else would she have intercourse with the Indians?"

"You mean screwing them?"

"Yes."

"She could have all sorts of reasons. We don't even know that she is screwing them. Maybe we are screwing the Indians."

"Drago, we discussed this before and decided that Mary-Forge was."

"What if she is?"

"Drago, you can't make up your mind about anything. You're being neurotic. When you don't understand why you do something you're being neurotic."

"I am?"

"Yes, get out the rifle."

"I still think it's her business if she is queer for Indians and eagles."

"But not if she shoots at us when she's doing it, that's neurotic."

"You're right there, Mr. Osmun."

"Get out the rifle."

"O.K."

"You know, Drago, people, particularly people who love the

Indians are suppressing a need to kill them. It's called a love-hate relationship."

"It is? You can stop talking now, Mr. Osmun, I said I'd get the rifle."

Below the helicopter that circled in the brilliant, eye-hurting New Mexican day, Mary-Forge told the Indians that the copter would be back, that the ranchers would not fight the eagle while being fired on by Indians. "The ranchers will not make the same mistake Custer did."

"What was that?"

"Fight on two fronts. Custer attacked the Sioux before he finished off Sitting Bull. We are the Sioux."

"We are? That's nice," the Navajo Bull Who Looks Up said. "When do we get out of this class?"

"We never do," Jesus Saves said.

"Get your ass behind the rocks!" the teacher Mary-Forge shouted. "Here they come!"

The copter flew over and sprayed the rocks with M-16 automatic rifle fire.

"That should teach the teacher that we outgun them, Drago," Ira Osmun said. "Now we can get the eagle!"

The golden eagle called Sun spiraled upward again, its wings steady, wild, sure, in the glorious rapt quietude of the blue, blue, blue New Mexico morning, a golden eagle against the blue, a kind of heliograph, and a flashing jewel in the perfect and New Mexico sea of sky. The gold eagle, recapitulent, lost then found as it twirled steady and upward in the shattered light, followed by the tin bird.

Sun knew that he must gain height. All the power of maneuver lay in getting above the tin bird. He knew, too, and from experience that the tin bird could only go a certain height. He knew, too, and from experience that air current he rode up could collapse at once and without warning. He knew, too, and from experience of several battles now with the bird of tin that the enemy was quick and could spit things out that could pain then kill. All this he knew from experience. But the tin bird was learning, too.

The tin bird jerked upward after the golden eagle. The golden eagle, Sun, wandered upward as though searching and lost. A last and final tryst in the list of Indian Country because now always until now, until now no one killed everything that moved. You always had a chance. Now there was no chance. Soon there would be no Sun.

*   *   *

"Remember, Drago, I've got to stay away from him or above him—he can take us with him. The last time when we got his mate he almost took us with him; I just barely got away when he attacked the rotors—when the rotor goes, we go, Drago—we fall like a rock, smash like a glass. They will pick you up in a dustpan."

"Who?"

"Those Indians down there."

"Mr. Osmun, I don't want to play this game."

"You want to save the sheep, don't you?"

"No."

"Why not?"

"I don't have any sheep to save."

"You don't have any sheep, you don't have any children. But you have pride."

"I don't know."

"Then fire when I tell you to and you'll get some."

"I don't know."

"Eagles and Indians at one time controlled this whole country, Drago, you couldn't put out a baby or a lamb in my grandfather's time without an Indian or an eagle would grab it. Now we got progress. Civilization. That means a man is free to go about his business."

"It does?"

"Yes, now that we got them on those ropes we can't let them go, Drago."

"We can't?"

"No, that would be letting civilized people down. It would be letting my grandfather down. What would I say to him?"

"Are you going to see your grandfather?"

"No, he's dead. We'll be dead, too, Drago, if you don't shoot. That eagle will put us down there so those Indians will pick us up with a dustpan. You don't want that, do you?"

"I don't know."

"You better find out right smart or I'll throw you out of this whack-bird myself."

"Would you?"

"Someone's got to live, Drago. The eagle doesn't want to live."

"Why do you say that?"

"He knew we were after him. He knew we would get him, he

could have left the country. He could have flown north to Canada. He would be protected there."

"Maybe he thinks this is his country."

"No, this is civilized country. Will you shoot the eagle?"

"No."

"I like the eagle and the Indians as well as the next man, Drago, but we have to take sides. It's either my sheep or them. Whose side are you on, Drago?"

"I guess I'm on theirs."

The helicopter was much lighter now without Drago in it. The copter handled much better and was able to gain on the eagle.

Ira Osmun continued to talk to Wilson Drago as though he were still there. Wilson Drago was one of Ira Osmun's sheepherders and should have taken a more active interest in sheep.

"The way I see it, Drago, if you wouldn't defend me, the eagle would have brought us both down. It was only a small push I gave you, almost a touch as you were leaning out. By lightening the plane you made a small contribution to civilization."

"We all do what we can, Drago, and you have contributed your bit. If there is anything I can't stand, it's an enemy among my sheep."

The copter continued to follow the eagle up but now more lightsome and quick with more alacrity and interest in the chase.

The Indians on the ground were amazed to see the white man come down. Another dropout. "Poor old Wilson Drago. We knew him well. Another man who couldn't take progress—civilization. Many times has Drago shot at us while we were stealing his sheep. We thought anyone might be a dropout but not Wilson Drago. It shows you how tough it's getting on the white reservation. They're killing each other. Soon there will be nothing left but Indians."

"Good morning, Indian."

"Good morning, Indian."

"Isn't it a beautiful day? Do you notice there is nothing left but us Indians?"

"And one eagle."

The Indians were making all these strange observations over what remained of the body of the world's leading sheepherder, Wilson Drago.

"He created quite a splash."

"And I never thought he would make it."

"The last time I saw him drunk in Gallup I thought he was coming apart, but this is a surprise."

"I knew he had it in him, but I never expected it to come out all at once."

"I can't find his scalp. What do you suppose he did with it? Did he hide it?"

"The other white man got it."

"I bet he did."

"They don't care about Indians anymore."

"No, when they drop in on you they don't bring their scalp."

"Please, please," Mary-Forge said, "the man is dead."

"Man? Man? I don't see any man, just a lot of blood and shit."

"Well, there is a man, or was a man."

"Well, there's nothing now," Bull Who Looks Up said, "not even a goddamn scalp."

"Well, Drago's in the white man's heaven," More Turquoise said. "On streets of gold tending his flock."

"And shooting eagles."

"Drago's going higher and higher to the white man's heaven, much higher than his what do you call it—"

"Helicopter."

"—can go," Jesus Saves said.

"I don't like all this sacrilege," Mary-Forge said. "Remember I am a Christian."

"What?"

"I was brought up in the Christian tradition."

"Now you're hedging," When Someone Dies He Is Remembered said.

Ah, these Indians, Mary-Forge thought, how did I get involved? And she said aloud, "Once upon a time I was young and innocent."

"Print that!" Bull Who Looks Up said.

"We better get higher up the mountain," Mary-Forge shouted at the Indians, "so when Osmun closes on the eagle we can get a better shot."

"O.K., Teacher."

"There's only one white guy left," she said.

"I find that encouraging if true," More Turquoise said.

"Load your rifles and pull your horses after you," Mary-Forge said.

"My Country 'Tis of Theee,'" Ira Osmun hummed as he swirled the copter in pursuit of the eagle. You didn't die in vain, Drago. That is, you were not vain you were a very modest chap. We can climb much higher without you Drago. I am going to get the last eagle this time, Drago. I think he's reached the top of his climb.

Sun watched the tin whack-bird come up. The tin bird came up whack-whack-whack, its wings never flapping just turning in a big circle. What did it eat? How did it mate? Where did it come from? From across the huge water on a strong wind. The evil wind. Sun circled seeing that he must get higher, the tin bird was coming up quicker today. Sun could see the people he always saw below. The people who lived in his country, filing up the mountain. They seemed to be wanting to get closer to him now.

Ira Osmun felt then saw all the Indians in the world firing at him from below. How are you going to knock down an eagle when all the Indians in the world are firing at you from Mount Taylor? It was Mary-Forge who put them up to it, for sure. An Indian would not have the nerve to shoot at a white man. You don't have to drop down and kill all the Indians. They—the people in the East—who have no sheep would call that a massacre. Indians are very popular at the moment. If you simply knock off Mary-Forge, that would do the trick. Women are not very popular at the moment. Why? Because they have a conspiracy against men. You didn't know that? It's true, Drago. The woman used to be happy to be on the bottom. Now she wants to be on the top.

No?

Did you say something, Drago?

I thought I heard someone say something. I must have been hit. My mind must be wandering. What was I saying? It's part of the conspiracy. What's that mean? Something. I must have been hit.

What was I doing? Oh yes, I was going to get Mary-Forge—the girl who is queer for Indians and eagles. The eagle can wait.

And Ira Osmun put the copter in full throttle, then cradled the M-16 automatic rifle in his left arm with the muzzle pointing out the door. With his right hand he placed the copter in a swift power glide down.

Sun saw the obscene tin bird go into its dive down. Now would be a chance to get it while the tin bird was busy hunting its prey on the ground. Sun took one more final look over the aerie nest to check the birds. The eaglets were doing fine. Drawing the enemy away from the nest had been successful. The eaglets craned their necks at the familiar shape before Sun folded his great span of wings and shot down on top of the tin bird.

Mary-Forge mounted on Poco Mas saw the tin bird coming, the M-16 quicking out nicks of flame. She could not get the Indians to take cover. The Indians had placed their horses behind the protection of the boulders and were all standing out in the open and were blasting away at the zooming-in copter. Mary-Forge was still shouting at the Indians, but they would not take cover. They have seen too many god-damn movies, Mary-Forge thought, they have read too many books. They are stupid, stupid, stupid, dumb, dumb, dumb Indians. How stupid and how dumb can you get? They want to save the eagle. Standing exposed naked to the machine gun. The stupid Indians. Mary-Forge raised her rifle at the zooming-in copter in a follow-me gesture, then took off in a straight line, the horse pounding, and the flame-nicking copter followed, so did Sun. So now there were three.

The tin bird was alive in flame all at once, something had hit the fuel tank and all of everything exploded in fire, the rotors of the tin bird were still turning and fanning the flame so that it was not only a streaking meteor across Indian Country but at once a boil of fire that shot downward from the terrific draft laying a torch of flame across the desert so that the mesquite and sagebrush became a steady line of flame ending where the tin whack-bird hit into the rocks and went silent in a grand tower of fire.

"It was Sun that did it," More Turquoise said.

The death of Sun.

All of the Indians and Mary-Forge were standing around the dying fire of the big whack-bird in the smoke that shrouded the death of Sun.

"When an eagle," the Medicine Man said, "—when a true bird has no hope—"

"Yes?"

"When the eagle is no more," the Medicine Man said.

"Yes?"

"Then we are no more."

"Yes," every person shrouded in smoke said.

Look up there. It was within three months when Someone Dies He Is Remembered remembered that an eagle named Star by the Medicine Man sailed in one beginning night to reclaim the country of Sun. Now Star's wide shadow passed over the dead tin whack-bird then he, the great eagle Star, settled on his throne-aerie in awful and mimic splendor, and again admonitory, serene—regal and doomed?

THE SPRING

by H. L. VAN BRUNT

from INDIAN TERRITORY (The Smith press)

nominated by Pushcart Press

The sky wore clouds
the way the marshal
wore his hat.
He kept telling us that
we'd like it there.
Movies twice a week,
and school
right on the premises.
His eyes were hidden as the sun.
The highway ran through the trees like a trail.

My sisters always liked the spring.
They built their dollhouse there.
The black
water spilled
into the creek
by its own weight.
We sat on the leaves like Indians,
tossing pebbles at the waterbugs.

They sat us down in a room like a shed.
The woman urging us to eat
was big as a house, or a hall, or the world
that placed us there. But in our eyes
she disappeared.

* * *

I hardly write to my sisters now.
They remind me of the matron
that slapped us till we ate.

Only the one who died has eyes
the color of the spring,
and arms loose as leaves.

"TAKE ME BACK TO TULSA"

by DAVID RAY

from CHARITON REVIEW

nominated by CHARITON REVIEW

I am taken back to Tulsa
and taken to a banquet in my honor
in a fine hotel with gilded mirrors
and red velvet drapes, where darky waiters
light the candles by our steaks.
All this, and oil rich families
regarding lobster as nothing special,
must have been here, just like this,
when I was small, two miles away,
tears on my face, looking toward
these stone buildings, floodlit
all the rainbow colors.
No one brought me in to eat, then.
No one asked me how I felt.
The pillows of the bed were damp all night.
The floodlights changed their colors
till the dawn and even then, the mind
looked back, to sleeping on the floor
down at the farmer's market,
wood planks, tin roof,
waiting for light when Dad would sell
the melons we had grown
(he'd beaten me for hoeing some
instead of weeds.)
Visiting Sundays when no one came,

no mother's steps beyond the beds
of flowers, in no-comment sun
that melted tar until it ran.
And rich folks were escorted through
like tourists, with adolescent girls
staring at us while we washed like Jews
(a dozen of us naked in a shower)
and in the distance, day and night
we heard the tom-tom dancing of mad Indians
who hugged the hills and crouched in valleys.

IS DON JUAN ALIVE
AND WELL?

by ARNOLD J. MANDELL M.D.

from THE ONTARIO REVIEW

nominated by THE ONTARIO REVIEW

THAT TIME OF LIFE has arrived in which I engage in internal exploration in efforts to feel anew and perceive anew. My need to be one of the boys has waned enough for me to move in my own direction and dare to say new things. My internal life has gained dimensions. My mind is less rattled now by anxious monitoring of the opinions of others, less chagrined about living in an unorthodox body, and less embarrassed at its inclinations to claim attention. It is free to roam, to envision, to think in broad and beautiful sweeps.

This freedom was hard won, and only gradually realized, after repeated quick dashes into the open and partial withdrawal. I espoused the metaphysics of exercise, the exhaustion, the pain, and the sweat of physical well being. Then came hypnosis, safe, conscientious surrender of control, initially with another, trusted and more positive in outlook than I. At first it was a show. The hypnotist set it up as if only highly intelligent individuals were really good subjects—the set was for me to be competent at everything, even this. "It's just a matter of concentration." My mind, I found, was very willing to risk the surrender and be freed into a foggy field of spontaneous thoughts and images—all involuntary—flowing to reach new places. I was euphoric about my capacity to escape the box lined with sharp points that usually jabbed into me from any side I tried to relax against. The incessant voices of neglected responsibilities, the criticisms of others, the humiliation of failures could turn into the hum of pre-euphoric swell, not always, but more and more with practice.

And then my research on moods led me to study the structure and function of classes of drugs that modify neurotransmission in the brain, the methoxy amphetamines and indole alkaloids. The technician in me focused on the brain chemistry and behavior of rats. The clinician in me demanded a personal chemical trial. The agents I tried took me to or through the humming and light flight of ideas and visions predictably and easily, as if a magnifying glass were enlarging the part of the mind that I usually turn off because it doesn't have anything to do with taking care of business—the stuff my father wound my spring tight about when I was little. Once experienced, this other part of the brain colors the rest of life. The intensity of niggardly details begins to lose its bite. The ruminator leaves the bed of nails for a couch of feathers. It was scary. I reached out for stories about others who had made the trip. The outcomes were as varied as the people: artistically creative scientists, leading academic administrators, and tattered masochists.

The Castaneda* experience was the most telling. It drives this writing. Games with Don Juan that left Castaneda either sophisticatedly sad or cynically rich were somehow familiar to me. I mused. I knew that dialogue: "Learning by unlearning. Settling for all instead of one. Paradox as symmetry; symmetry as sterility; truth as fraud; fraud as complexity; complexity as truth." But from where? My first thoughts went to my father. Was this his form of rhetoric? No, just the reverse. Always resolve the cadence, even if it is

*Carlos Castaneda, an anthropologist, has published four books about his purported apprenticeship with the mysterious Yaqui sorcerer Don Juan. The most recent was *Tales of Power* (1974).

fallacious. Never finish on a dominant seventh. Chopin as a child had to go to the piano in the middle of the night to play the major chord, to resolve the dominant seventh that his teacher had played at the end of that day's lesson. My father never left that kind of ambiguity.

Was it my analyst? Kind, wise, moneyed, he would do his best. The best that was possible, rather than the absolute, was the theme of his analyses. A tic in the hand or arm could be turned into straightening one's tie. A person with a compulsion to jump up and down was led to discovering his life goal as a cheerleader. No, my analyst was a benign human engineer who saw strengths behind every hopeless quirk; he was no Don Juan. Who, then?

The insight came by accident as I was preparing a lecture about psychiatric diagnosis. It's difficult being a teacher of high priests in a religion in which one's own belief systems are in flux. One way around such a challenge is to tell it as history. Much of psychiatric ritual and practice is the result of historical evolution, and this is often the best way to present the material, much better than assuming a theoretical position and defending it. So I try to present diagnostic schemes *and* cite attacks on the concept of psychiatric diagnosis itself. In preparation for this particular lecture I picked up Harold Garfinkel's book *Ethnomethodology* and reread the chapter on his observation of the UCLA Psychiatric Clinic. Suddenly I knew who my own Don Juan had been.

My mind was forced back to a time in my life that I had forgotten, although it was only eleven years ago, back to an early torturous struggle with the growth of my mind and the collapse of axioms. Prior to the exercise, the hypnosis, and the chemical trials I had sought to purify my intellect. The rite of purification requires passionate adherence to a logical system in order to learn to defend it effectively. It requires a guide, a free and respected adversary, a catechist whose zeal is spurred by the psychic pain of the novice. The interaction is emotionally charged by the threat of humiliation. A little boy with a small wee wee is being watched by a laughing boy; the laughter forces him to stand a long time in front of the urinal because his upset is inhibiting his urinary stream. I struggled to purify my intellect against such an adversary for a year. I couldn't take it. I quit.

Oh, I thought I understood. I wrote a few crazy papers bearing ritual tribute, and then retreated to lick my wounds in the laboratory. The pain was too great, and I looked too foolish to myself. Now that I think about it I was confronted by my own cowardice. For the first time my highly contrived image of professional boldness had been questioned. I peddled psychiatric borscht as far as he was concerned. I would pipe up with some eloquent parafreudian pap and expect an admiring glance. I got silence or a question directed at a definition or an assumption. Not a *why*, a *what*. A *why* is always a legitimate question. That is, it really can't be waved off. On the other hand, a *what* is really unfriendly. A dyadic foolish discussion is not foolish; figure and ground relate. A monologist and a sniper, *that's* foolish.

His office was down the hall from my laboratory. I remember walking past his open door and seeing him sitting rigidly upright, in perfect typing posture. He wrote all day and into the night. Piles of typescript were produced, but little was submitted for publication. He was a powerful and revolutionary leader in academic sociology, and his influence had been felt via the grape vine, bits of unpublished material, and the experience of dialogue with him. When I saw him in his office I would wave and hurry on. The couple of his manuscripts that I had read had eluded my comprehension. He knew I had read them. I didn't know what to say about them except, "Help!" In those days I wasn't able to say that out loud.

One day I looked up from my desk and saw that he had stepped into the doorway. He smiled and said (as though making light social conversation), "Oh, I see—this is a place which those about you would call a laboratory." That stunned me. He seemed correct. In that instant he removed this place from which I had been viewing my work to a vantage point some distance away. I became a worker ant, a beaver building a dam, a fish going upstream, a cat in heat, a cuckoo laying her egg in someone else's nest. He was watching me and characterizing me, and, worse yet, inviting me to do the same, right in the midst of my slavish efforts to climb the pyramid of academic psychiatry! It was like asking an aspiring cardinal to write an anthropological history of the Vatican. He couldn't because he believes in what he is and does, or he wouldn't because it would hurt business. Garfinkel's remark started a struggle within me that lasted almost a year. I went through a period of insane feelings and thoughts which have left indelible colors on my perception of psychiatry and the other social and behavior sciences.

I once heard two women who were high on acid have a long

conversation of great intensity. They exchanged phrases, mutually refined meanings, and consensually validated assumptions. It was a true blending of empathic souls. Only when I came closer did I realize that they were out of contact and did not know that they were talking about entirely different subjects. One was talking about the professional problems of women; the other was discussing a woman's feelings toward her children. Phrase after phrase of adjective and adverb was agreed and expanded upon, like musical phrases at a jam session. The exchange was present, important, and satisfying in spite of the incongruences of the substance. They were unaware of being in Wonderland. Both terminated the discussion with obvious feelings of having communicated.

Harold Garfinkel led me to a model of such transactions from the standpoint of the everyday theorist—the one who makes sense out of the information with which he is presented. He placed an advertisement in the university student newspaper, announcing that an expert on strategies to achieve admission to medical school would be on campus to answer questions from pre-medical students on a certain day. Many eager students showed up. They were led individually to the experimental chamber where each was told that he would be allowed ten questions, which would be out of view behind a wall and would answer each question. The students were asked to summarize the advice they received and indicate whether they would return for another session if they were given the opportunity. A majority of them wrote cogent and interesting essays and indicated their eagerness to return for another session. Of course, the *yeses* and *noes* were randomly arranged on lists for the respondent behind the wall—the shill. Garfinkel compared the students to social scientists researching and analyzing human behavior, and making sense out of it.

The implications of this and similar experiments bothered me mightily during the hours I conducted psychotherapy. My students would want my secrets, and the things I *knew* about human behavior in general and psychiatric patients in particular. For that year, all I knew for certain was that almost any explanation would suffice in the desperately ambiguous field of human behavior and social interac-.tion. But my explanations began to sound like patriotic speeches in favor of a republic that had existed a century before, quaint and friendly, like folk dancing. If only I could have laughed at the hollow sound of it all. Truman Capote in *A Buyer of Dreams* describes the despair of people who have sold their dreams to a mysterious purchaser. They became empty. The ethnomethodological exercise empties. How, then, to do business? Can one really sell any empty package—no matter how pretty the wrapping—no matter how eager the buyer? Of course you must get to the other side of this great dissolve, or wither spiritually and intellectually. The one fringe benefit is a peculiar slackening of pressure from the conscience—"I didn't learn any new lessons today because there aren't any lessons. There aren't any lessons at all."

The myths about Harold Garfinkel are many, and, if not true, certainly consistent with the man I knew. He went to Harvard Law School and asked them, "What is evidence? What is a decision?" They wanted him away. He went to a psychiatric clinic and asked them, "What is a patient?" They arranged an administrative shuffle. He went to a suicide prevention center and asked them, "What is a suicide attempt? Why do you talk like that?" Even Durkheimian answers were to him just so much evidence of previous academic exploitation and conditioned response.

His piercing eyes intent upon contact, nevertheless reflected the universal pain of Jewish social scientists. "Why don't people like me?" came the ethnic cry through the same eyes that burned your frontal lobes if you got too close. His tortured logic, with its apparently defrocked scientific statements, bounced down halls of tilted walls, ricocheting in an infinite regress of contradictions: "Social science is manufactured not discovered." All social science research is a projection of the internal processes of the observer." "These things cannot be known." And yet they are to be sought! A suitable definition must be found. The labored sentences must contain enough qualifying clauses to be immune to the assaults of the approach itself. Such intense dyadic contacts gradually led to belief—partly out of brief glimpses of consistence, partly out of my despair. Orwell knew men would love Big Brother when the pain was intense enough. God, how excited I would be when I left him, and what rage would emerge when the internal auditory replay turned up emptiness! Foolish. I felt flim-flammed, and went to my desk to plot my counterattack.

Upon its presentation those intense brown eyes either would indicate that this domain of discourse was meaningless or stare vaguely until he was ready to push against another as yet untried belief. And the big promise? The big promise was mastery, understanding and perhaps even power over everyday social problems. Yes, the potential for power was implicit. With this neo-nihilism, like Archimedes I would find the power point, the center of truth, and no more be buffeted by biological and historical probabilities. I felt as if I were caught between Rama Krishna and Adolph Hitler.

I was young and full of ambivalence about the theory and practice of psychiatry and my own new identity as a psychiatrist. I discovered Freud as a prophet and a hustler all in the same afternoon. I reached to the edges of my imaginings and experienced the confusion of the schizophrenic, the reality of the depressive, and the judgment of the psychopath. Psychoanalytic ego psychology brought the theory from grunts to words. Sophists would play with these constructs like French conversation at lunch. I had no blood pressure cuff, no knowledge of stitches to invert a wound, or of the layers of fascia covering the abdomen. I did have that feeling of superiority that psychiatrists often hide behind smiles during their own emotional emergencies. I clutched that for insulation while Harold Garfinkel asked about the validity of psychiatric diagnoses. Were we the new social police? What, and why, was I teaching students for my salary? What was I giving my patients for my fees? What were the assumptions and rationales of my existence?

I always went to him with a sticky feeling under my breast bone from the last meeting, and left him with the kind of headache that drove our ancestors to wield rocks and sticks. I'd burn for days. I'd plan the assault: casual—within a formal context—a reference, an unpublished piece of his that I would want to see. Then I would grab last time's issue: By the lapels. And he would laugh and say that I didn't understand, that perhaps I couldn't understand. He would be quiet. Then he would start, and it would run past like knitted ropes and tangled wires. I was desperate to find even one loose end so I could begin to unravel this grotesque tapestry. I got nowhere. Was I part of the performance, or simply the rehearsal piano? His associates studied the function of conversation; he examined the process of examining and the examiner, the one who seeks intellectual (and perhaps spiritual) evolution. He ran a seller's market; he had already learned these insane truths. He was privy to the mysteries by dint of his ability to destroy available models (comforting companions of ambiguous work) without anxiety. He had the sophistication of the agnostic, and a full professorship in a field where all the other giants started or were disciples of systematic schools. The only imaginable result of doubting the methodology and deductions of a questioner is the sound of one hand clapping. Graduate students heard he was tough, and, challenged by this, they often smashed their careers against the barrier reef of his logic. He qualified their every assertion as valid only by definition. He wove yards of methodological theory around mere straws of data. After all, data are only those pieces of phenomenology that fit our predetermined set.

Like all of us, he wanted to be in a place safe from death. All the professional ethnomethodological sophistication notwithstanding, he increasingly needed whatever protection from oblivion he could earn with a trenchant phrase or intellectual coup. The students should join and argue. I once thought that silence would kill him, that the critical counterpuncher would wither without a target. But when I sat silent he would play his typewriter. And the phrases were upside down, funny, backward approaches to common situations, new ways of seeing things, new ways of naming them, and then watching them disappear. The awakening in him of the fear of death was the only hope of getting behind those piston-like jabs, and no one would touch it. He would appear suddenly to be a very important scientist, suffering. His peers arranged conferences where many came to stare and to honor him by listening quietly.

"If a man has no friend is he sick?" His questions seemed naive. They had an almost ingenuous expectancy. "Tell me a story," he would say. How often the pedant in me was stimulated, and came forward.

"The schizoid defense against intimacy is but one of many. Some practitioners feel this one is most revealing of an isolated childhood and the absence of early images for later use in developing real intimacy." I sat back proudly like a young adolescent who has performed his catechism perfectly.

"What is meant by intimacy?"

I would elaborate on the spot, like a new monk defining sin and salvation. "The absence of defenses in a relationship is intimacy."

"What is a defense?"

"Defenses are techniques to avoid natural interpersonal and intrapersonal trends in relating."

"Now, aren't you really deciding for the patient what and how he is to talk in order for you to find him acceptable?" He knew how to get to a pseudoegalitarian. He was correct. That is, I think he was correct.

"God damn it, Harold, you play 'May I ?' games with your graduate students. You're a gatekeeper. You're shaping behavior. We're all shaping behavior."

"But in intimacy, as you call it, who reaches beyond their fences?" No amount of *ad hominen* or profanity deterred him from the attack once enough of my flank was exposed. "You define intimacy as good. You then produce that behavior in your patient, or define some old behavior in this new way. You negotiate the differences, and then charge him money for the right to surrender to an expert. You've constructed a social ritual which has within it the delusion of honest talking and listening. You create a dyadic dysjunction only to take credit for its resolution. You use the resolution as a goal. The goal is an artificial construct used to justify the transaction, and the money seals the bargain. The patient will make sense out of whatever you do. You will make sense out of whatever you do. You will make sense out of whatever he does. Both of you will go home satisfied!"

By then, my head, which liked to have private and personal black masses with the classical theories of psychiatry, felt found out. Worse, out-rebelled, forced to defend the *status quo* in order to preserve my hopes of changing it. I saw why those institutions where values were established by definition eventually threw him out. I would have liked to throw him out too, but I wanted to learn to do what he did. He could destroy anything with those questions. "Come back when you've thought that through," he would adjourn the audience. He would turn back to his typewriter, and I would walk back to my laboratory. I'd look at some neurochemical data to ease the gnawing frustration. I'd go home and read his new explication of Parsons. It was more difficult to understand than Parsons. There was the confidence of the executioner in all his writings; all heads must fall to his skill with the axe.

I wonder how a graduate student could produce a thesis to satisfy him? The instructions would have to read: "Build a systematic analysis of a social circumstance from the point of view that no systematic analysis of any social circumstance is possible. You have four to six years to finish it. Your funds will run out; your children won't eat very well; your wife will be frightened and contemptuous; you will suffer headaches and insomnia. I shall reject your attempts using ethnomethodological techniques. There will be no turning back. Keep trying. We will talk and talk and talk. We will get excited together. Then you will leave empty-handed to sit for hours with your excitement and agitation. You'll rebuild the system. This will happen again and again. You will think you are using only straight data. But data is never straight, because fields are words. Words are only meaningful by definition. It will, therefore, be easy for me to rip up the last effort and the next effort." People say that Harold Garfinkel is crazy; they say it with reverence. If the student can eat the heart of that master he truly will be brave and strong. But the master is eating the hearts of the students.

Imagine a solution. If all the reality of social science is manufactured, and the struggle is to make it real somehow in spite of that, then why not fabricate it all? Why not use the thesis as a probe? Let the thesis test the capacity of *his* system to perceive reality. Outgarfinkel Garfinkel! Then prolonged, detailed field work won't lead to the desperate, painful defense of the validity of your observations. When the laughing time comes you can laugh too. You will have outreached any accusation that you manufactured data by interpretation. Of *course* it's manufactured. All we do is configure our personal inventories in the form of ethnographies anyway. This one will be totally a projection of the mind. A fake ethnography that achieves continuity and a sense of reality would certainly display your capacity to understand and manipulate the analytic tools of your trade, without seriously threatening the posture of sophisticated nihilism.

It has to be the only way to work with this scrambler of tenets. The data for the struggle between student and master are already in. Even the choice of the drug door will fit. Drugs tilt the present. They give oldness new appearances. They fly you over the top and through with analytic counterpoint. Surprise and discovery can be felt in old places—the places you were all along. Or were you? Don Juan probably could have existed inside a cactus, or in a test tube in Switzerland. His words, like chemicals, can be picked up by your brain and recreate seeing and establish the premise that reality is manufactured.

Carlos Castaneda finally earned a Ph.D. at UCLA from Harold Garfinkel. . . Ethnomethodology insists that social science reality is generated not discovered. . . There is no Yaqui language or culture in Castaneda's ethnography . . . The use of three families of hallucinogenic drugs is not consistent with what we know about Yaqui culture . . . Reporters from *Time* Magazine can't find Don Juan.

NUMBER SEVENTEEN

by GEORGE MATTINGLY

from THE LIVES OF THE POETS (Blue Wind Press)

nominated by Richard Morris

One day I took the bus across the San Francisco Bay to
visit my friend Jack Marshall. I rang his buzzer and he
yelled for me to come in. As I was walking down the
hall to his room in the old victorian, a little Mexican
girl grabbed my arm and, smiling with a billion little
teeth, said to me, "Your freend heeze gonna be reech."

Jack was in the bathroom, shaving with a tennis shoe.
"Hi man," he said, "I just found out I don't need a razor
any more; I can just shave with my tennis shoes." He was
using the regular $8.95 Sears Cushion Sole tennis shoe.
I tried it, and it worked perfectly, even on my sideburns
and those hard-to-get whiskers under the nose.

A few months later, in a special ceremony on nationwide
television, live from the White House, President Ford
presented Jack Marshall with a solid gold tennis shoe.
When the cameras came on, Jack was playing frisbee with
Dan Rather out in back of the White House Rose Garden.

Among other things, President Ford said that Jack proved
that American Transcendentalism was still alive and well.

𝅒 𝅒 𝅒

THE HUMAN TABLE

a fable by MARVIN COHEN

from FABLES AT LIFE'S EXPENSE (Latitudes Press)

nominated by Nona Balakian and LATITUDES PRESS

S OMETIMES I USE MY LAP as a human table. This is necessary when tea is served on a saucer but nothing else, with the cup fitted in the saucer, but precariously heaped to the top with tea. (Fulfilling the what-for in the design of the cup.)

The saucer is a kind of junior table for the cup. (The cup is a kind of primary table for the tea. But can a vessel be a table for what it contains? Or is that too much of a contradiction? I'm not eligible to answer this question, having never been either tea, cup, or saucer, or any combination of those three, in any order whatever. So I'm unqualified to speak on the matter, or on any other matter, except on the matter touching what I am, it being my being a human person, which is all I was ever destined to be, and all I ever managed to realize.)

Back to the pre-digression, and then to travel straight from it. The saucer, it was written, is a kind of junior table for the cup (which itself is a kind of primary table for the tea contained in it). But the saucer is unstable unless set somewhere; while the cup of tea is also unstable so long as its own table (the saucer) is. That's where my lap comes in, as a reserve stability agent (or, as said before, human table). If the tea isn't served on a real furniture table (generally of wood material, including "legs" that usually number four) then the human lap is pressed into service, and is fabricated to be improvised as a sort of artificial table. (But since when is the human body "artificial"? Certainly I wear no artificial limbs, they're my own. In fact, they're as natural as nature can be, since nature made them. *I* surely didn't make them. I—all of me—*was* made. That's what being natural consists in. So I'm a *natural* table, not an artificial one. These distinctions are not hair-splitting. They're *essential* distinctions. We'd be lost, without them.)

To go back to the substance that preceded the latest digression (determined not to be waylaid into still another tempting digression, and thus be seduced from the narrow narrative path which, taken straitly, would lead logically somewhere by virtue of itself or else virtually falter in its own purpose, end, and aim, meanly demeaning thereby its own means, by which is meant . . .)

So in the absence of a real manufactured table, I sit forward on the upholstered armchair, and rest on my lap the saucer-held, tea-filled cup. My torso tilted stiff; my upper legs absolutely horizontal, parallel to the floor and the ceiling, from pelvis to knees; my lower legs vertical, from knees to feet. Obviously (it goes without saying) my knees are bent. Bending is done by knees thousands of times before the total death of the whole person for whom the knees serve as parts. Much hinges on this function of the knees. But enough on that subject, whose obviousness is usually beneath the mentioning would derive, as a physically mentalized act. Sometimes knees are above the head. It often happens to ladies who are being ravished in bed. Such indecent behavior, so as to be unobserved, is done in retired private quarters. Romantic images by the participants euphemize the sordid deed. The function of fantasy is often to exalt.

To go back behind this latest digression and recover the rather rambling theme. To recapitulate, before, in despair, I capitulate altogether.

The tea is in the cup. (Still somehow hot, just poured from that procelain teapot where it was brewed in recently boiling water.) The cup is on the saucer. The saucer is on my lap, for want of a real table. My lap is on my upper legs and loins, which, in turn, are on the armchair. The armchair is on the rug. The rug is on the floor. Is the floor the final, all-containing table—the "table-of-contents" to begin and end the whole book? No, the floor is on something. That something is on something else. And that something else is on the earth. But where is the earth on? What table holds the orbiting earth? Magnetic space? And what's the table for that?

All will slip off the table, when the tablecloth is pulled. When the body dies, the table is turned on physical life, for the individual lodged within. Is there a tablet of laws on such a turned table? This is a tale or fable, insecurely set upon a table. All that's "on" is precarious. We use the term "based on". On what, ultimately, does all rest? The discourse on tables comes to perch upon metaphysics. Metaphysics is perched upon a set of premises.

On what, ultimately, is all laid? I'd like to lay my weary mind to rest. I'd like to allay my tedium; to lay a lady; to get laid.

The table is laid, for tea. The tea stuff is laden on it, consisting of saucer, cup, and tea, and little silver spoon. The table is my own lap. My lap may commit a lapse, if unsteadily it lets the tea stuff slip off. I drink the tea while it's hot. Tea is over. I stop my lap by standing up from the chair, ending the improvised "table". The empty cup, the saucer, the spoon, spill off by my act of standing, for the table is taken away from under them, and they don't even have a leg to stand on, so they fall on the floor, or on the rug. This was a lapse in decorum. I kneed my lap, strait. Straightened, it was a lapse. The hostess bends down to retrieve the fallen service. I bend down to retrieve the hostess; to resume my service. Tea is over. We fornicate on the rug, through rips in our body where the clothes are worn through. A fitting ending to a tea. A table to uphold it all. A table to grunt, and bear the weight.

I couldn't bear the wait, from tea to that. My hostess bears my weight, weighted down with my wait. We bear the bearing instruments, unartificial. We make nature, after tea was made. For that we're made.

Our laps are pressed into service, but not for tea. We don't kneed laps for tea-posture now. Our knees are freed. We weigh down heavy. We wear out the human race, as the table groans with our pounding. O Table, can you bear us? And bear too, on you successively from superficials deep down, the rug, the floor, the earth that spins, and the spin that spaces off? What's at the bottom, of this table business?

I now put a ceiling on my flawed talk of floors, and box the room in, with hinged doors. The tableau is based on what table? O Table of rectitude, uphold us!

I COME HOME LATE AT NIGHT

by PATRICK WORTH GRAY

from BLUE CLOUD QUARTERLY

nominated by BLUE CLOUD QUARTERLY

I come home late at night
And my little girl hides
Under her bed, screaming,
And my wife is wearing her Harassed Look
And what did I expect after a month
On the road? I sit down at the littered
Kitchen table as the voice of my wife
Carps on and stare into the muddy
Depths of my instant coffee.
Then the dregs dissolve,
Shift, reform, and I
Am a little boy, screaming
Under my daughter's bed
As my father and I, fuddled
With brandy, push our glasses
Up on our forehead and let
The words of our wife and mother
Wash over our bowed-down back.
I go to my daughter's room
And begin to beat on her drum
A slow and muffled rhythm

And chant a Nowata death-song
My father taught me. She creeps out
And beats the drum and then
My wife is there, singing
Low, her arms about us,
And we are singing, drumming, crying,
Together again for a time.

AT DAWN IN WINTER

by JOHN GLOWNEY

from ANAESTHESIA REVIEW

nominated by Len Fulton

The light brought a single bug
clicking against the bulb,
while we hooked a cable
to the front legs of the calf,
blood pouring over our hands,
the cow growling in labor,
the calf out and fighting
and dead already before dawn.
You go to the house and I start milking,
the earth rising up in the drab light
and meeting the grey snowflakes.
The barndoor open,
the day coming in under the cows' bellies
sun sifted through the brushlines
into thin rays.
I come in after chores and find you asleep, at last,
a pod of warmth on the couch.
I brush your eyelids, the color of butter
under hair fallen over your face.
Is it too much to ask of you,
to wear the earth
as a shirt, to make your buttons
of cowhide, to midwife a wheatfield,
to sing the dirt sorrow?
Here, this is me,
a tinker for barnyards,
a farm-fixer.
I peddle farming from door to door,

I give away handfuls of soil to housewives,
kernels of corn to dirtymouthed kids.
Late in the day we walk
on brittle, flattened cornstalks.
I watch you run for hot coffee
across the field to the house.
The land tears away from me on all sides
and slides off the horizons:

only the woodlot fences hold the earth
from falling apart.

FATHER OF THE BRIDE

fiction by JACK PULASKI

from GODDARD JOURNAL

nominated by GODDARD JOURNAL

C YCLOPES AND FIRE ENGINES, land lords, time payments—why not, anything, any contract, falling sickness, history, the works. I saw her dance in the City College lounge and shortly thereafter, for the first time in my life, accepted the terms of the given world. Her mother, Maria, worried about "el damage." Votive candles were lit so that the earth would swallow me up. And as if the Church weren't enough, Maria had collected from the living room chair several strands of my hair and brought them to Dona Consuelo the Bruja.

Not everyone considered Dona Consuelo a witch, she was also a pharmacist, mid-wife, advisor, intermediary for Father, Son, and Holy Ghost, the Mother of God, cherubim and seraphim, Beelzebub, Lucifer himself, and she raised pigeons on the side. Most of her trade was in errant husbands. I had seen her many times, standing in the doorway of her Botanica, large, pale, eyes transparent, her orange hair a petrified riot, the whole human huge and permanent as any creature preserved by a taxidermist. She stood between two windows. In one window a Pieta, the Madonna white as milk and as enormous as King Kong, and dead Jesus, limp, gorgeous, no bigger than a puppy, dead on Mary's lap. On the floor, standing in the plaster of paris folds of Mary's gown, a platoon of identical copper colored saints, the tin haloes affixed to their heads on lollipop sticks reaching no higher than Mary's knee. Above Mary's head a cloud made of absorbent cotton, and a cardboard sun and beneath the cardboard sun a clothesline wrapped in purple crepe paper from which hung a batallion of three dimensional Jesus faces in gold colored frames, weeping, bleeding, sweating, or winking, depending on how the light hit them. The window to Consuelo's left housed a large dead snake in a jar of formaldehyde, paws and claws of various creatures, a stuffed owl, and a live parrot in a cage, shelves with jars of different colored powders, the three monkeys in brass, hear, speak, and see no evil, white unlit candles, dolls in taffeta gowns and tuxedos with porcelain faces and terrified eyes, flanked by long thin pins,—at the center a phallic shaped candle burned, and all this surrounded by a fungus like vegetation, growing from jars, pots, glasses and tubes, creeping over the brass monkeys, the dolls, the stuffed animals, slithering up the sweating window.

From that time on my temperature has always been three degrees above normal; red welts grew on the palms of my hands, I slipped on some yellow powder sprinkled in front of my door and sprained my ankle. Worse than the delirium and fever, the hair on my face grew more profusely than ever, I had always had a heavy beard but now the bristles of hair climbed over my cheekbones up under my eyes. What with the hair swarming over my face, my red palms and the limp from my sprained ankle I looked like a sick ape. I did retain a pleasant singing voice and a predilection for lofty subjects. Of a quiet two A.M. in the streets, with Margarita at my side, I would sing, "Here In My Heart I'm Alone and So Lonely," screaming to split two octaves, my approach to lofty subjects was pretty much the same.

Margarita said our only hope was to talk to her father. She knew he would not like me, he had reluctantly agreed to let her attend City College, but he was, she said, a renegade Catholic, a freethinker, and neither religion nor magic had an effect on him, moreover, he was head of the household and his word was law. She advised that I tell him that my intentions were serious and that we should be married at once. On top of all this Margarita said she could not come to my apartment anymore because she had eleven uncles and twenty-three cousins in the neighborhood on her mother's side, and she feared for my safety. I must, she said, must, talk to her father right away.

The fever and the screaming were not all mine, I can tell, it is a hot day for everyone. Limping, I chase after him, with a gait like Quasimodo after being airborne on those bells. If I can get him to stand still for a moment I'll explain that great feeling pulls one into these funny shapes, he should understand, after all he's a Latino. As I lift my feet, the asphalt makes a peeling sound from the soles of my shoes. I gulp air, and charge across the street, dodging the fire engines. Carlos laughs, "Yeah, fire belongs to the Fire Department." I can see his smiling face through beads of sweat, beyond: a pink stoop, domino players hunched on milk boxes, drinking beer in brown paper bags,—above, on the firescape, Buddha in an undershirt, lacquered in dreaming sweat, eyes squinted, puffing a cigar.

"I am a foreigner and you are foreign to me." says Carlos.

"I want to marry your daughter."

"Oh yeah," he says cocking his head and placing a finger under my heart, "I may marry her myself boy . . . what you think of that?"

He plunges on ahead of me. Stunned, I stand there, his hand waves good-bye, and the elegantly thin body in the white suit turns, the brown gnomic head turns, the tips of the moustachio pointing up the gleeful eyes. I chase after him, — past pushcarts and babylonian vendors in their bewildered hair, holding hysterical dominion over the ass end of the cornucopia, bobby-pins, canteloupes, pots, crockery, plaster saints, halivah, and mops; people, windows, a havoc of tongues, the little man in the white suit disappears beyond me.

Lost behind the haggard mother, her children bounce off my thighs, fall in front of their mother's feet, I set one little boy upright, but he doesn't acknowledge me, and bawls, "Momma, I want a balloon. Red I want."

The mother clutches the bag of groceries to her chest, her pregnant

belly precedes her trudging feet, and her children surround her—
she is the Czar's palace and they the people chant,
"We wanna balloon, we wanna balloon!"
Her head perched above the brown grocery bag screams,
"What ya want me to do, pull it outta my cunt?"
Her hands let go the bag of groceries, egg yolks and lentils drip from
the children's heads and her fists bloody them. One little boy
negotiates from between my legs,
"It don't have to be red."

"Foist class grade A bananas!" the man hawks, placing the
bananas on the scale, his eyes weighing me as Carlos says, "Yeah
him, Ralph . . . he wants to marry my daughter."
They look at each other and stroke their mustaches. The fruit vendor
hands me a banana. I peel it and take a bite. "What you study at the
collitch?" the vendor asks, winking at Carlos.
Trying to swallow and answer, the piece of banana goes down my
throat whole, I gag, see the hair growing on my knuckles, "Literature and philosophy." I answer through the mashed banana in my
mouth.
The fruit vendor twirls his mustache, and blinks his eyes on and off
waving his arms; Carlos claps and shouts, "Filosofia!" — a diva
hitting the supreme ecstatic note.
"Tell me," Carlos says, "Do you know about the force of reason and
the reason of force?"
I think about it, I want to conjure an answer, I remember my
boyhood nemesis, Hot Dog Jaskobaskitz.
"Look at him, just look at him," Ralph says, "he's got his head up
God's ass, dreaming."
"Gentlemen, I think I understand the question. If I am not a
sufficient predator, how can I be a lover? I understand, I was
educated young, not far from here, Hot Dog Jaskobaskitz looked
into my eye, and saw I was not capable of murder and taught me
humility. But Hot Dog was fried in the electric chair, and me, — I'm
ready to accept God's world, because of his creation, your daughter,
Carlos."
The pigeons on the window sills beat an ovation with their wings, I
sing, good morning lord of the universe, and my ears hear my mouth
bark,
"Hot Dog . . . Hot Dog."
"I think he's hungry," says Ralph, and hands me another banana.

The Lord and Love may have my heart, but the witch has dominion
over my tongue, I can't seem to make any sense to these gentlemen.
I struggle to utter her name, the word "Hot Dog" in my mouth.
"Gur . . . gur . . . gurita"
Carlos puts his hand in front of my face, palm out like a traffic cop,
"Never mind," he says, "I go for a drink."

   Carlos discovers me at his side, his eyes following a variety of
things that delight him.
"You know what I say to my wife offenly? I says, 'Me cago en la agua
bendita, me cago en la Virgen Maria, me cago en Dios' I say this
offenly . . . I shit on the Holy Water, I shit on the Virgin May, I shit
on God."
He doubles up with laughter slapping his pencil like thighs, the
white trousers ballooned and flapping in the breeze like sails. "My
wife Maria, she is very upset because I say this too offenly. She says
to me, 'Carlos when you die and have to face God, what will you do
then?' . . . I answer her, that I at least, will know God when I meet
him, because my shit will be all over him."

   Yes, and when Margarita was to take Communion she vomited up
the Host. The wafer heaved from her tongue to the roof of her
mouth, locked behind her teeth until the flood split her lips. The
priest got out of the way. If it weren't for Consuelo's herbs and
incantations Margarita would have never received Holy Communion.
"You say something?"
"I was about to . . ."
"Ah boy, I'm thirsty."

   Carlos opens the door to the bar, swims forward, a species of
marine life in the deep frosted blue of the saloon. I enter, the
furnace of the street licks at my back, the freezing air rushes over my
face and chest, the skin on the front of me contracts and shivers, my
teeth chatter. Carlos pirouettes in front of the bar and sings, "Ron
Barilito por favor," raising two brown fingers under the bartender's
nose. The bartender is huge and silent. Above his head, a series of
signs, like the tiers of a crown, the letters rendered in ice cubes,

AIR CONDITIONED FOR OUR PATRON'S COMFORT.
BE COOL BROTHER, IF YOU'RE GAY STAY AWAY.
DON'T LET YOUR ALLIGATOR MOUTH OVERLOAD
YOUR CANARY ASS.

The bartender's nose has no bone in it. His eyebrows are stitched with old scars. His face has a kind of benign and bored ferocity that is purely professional. He assays Carlos' two fingers under his nose, and Carlos, —is the little guy a trouble maker, or a crazy angel from the street, a pure soul of delight flying above the prescribed level of decorum. He serves the two glasses of rum and waits.

"Muchas gracias, my friend," says Carlos.

The juke box is playing something that is all percussion, the bongos flare the street's heat, a burning bush at the bottom of an ocean. All the men in this bar are excessively polite to one another. A young man, acne still blooming on his cheeks, a straight razor, sheathed, protruding from his back pocket, squeezes by an older man, (the two are careful not to touch), the older man is coming from the toilet, the young man headed for it, there is a lump under the left side of the older man's cotton jacket, the lump is shaped like a pistol. The two pass each other on tip toe, nod courteously and exchange a grave and audible, "Con su permiso."

There is one woman at the bar, escorted. She is very handsome. None of the men in the bar look at her. I glimpse at her out of the corner of my eye, her lips form the phrase, "Rocky darling" at Rocky darling's ear.

Carlos clinks his glass against mine, his head bent forward to catch the spray of the neon waterfall, it is flanked on one side by the warm amber glow of the whiskey bottles, and on the other, a glossy autographed photo of Ray Robinson mutilating Carmine Basilio's mutilated face. The photo is signed, "With affectionate regard, Sugar Ray."

The rum begins to do its work. I feel extravagant, foolish. The histories I exchanged with his daughter in the dark pile up behind my teeth. I know that on the avenue we just left, she walked, (on her way to Saint Theresa's and Communion, as blind as Santa Lucia who brought her eyes on a plate to God), past this bar, silent in her holy uterine deeps. I know that with the first budding of her breasts, he stood above her, gently touching one young bosom, she feigned sleep, terrified, waiting for her mother to call her father away, to bed. I know that during the first forty days of her life she lies with her father under mosquito netting, in a sleep deeper than either had known with Maria, — breathing his cocoa pigment into her skin. Maria would enter with swollen breasts to nurse her daughter, and find the infant girl of his identical color curled under his male armpit, diminutive foot stuck in the hollow of hair —as if the child had issued from that place.

"Carlos, I am not a stranger." He is tapping an answering rhythm to the juke box and praying to the waterfall, chanting and laughing, "I shit on the Holy Water, offenly I shit on it." Pausing in the cool dark, the rum washes over my tongue the rest of what I would say and a wave of heat rolls in from the door. On the other side of the window people trudge by, their mouths gasping like fishes in their death throes. Again the street's weather is beyond the closed door, the refrigerated air frosts the quiet, (except for the bongos of Mongo Santamaria pounding from the juke box). The man that has entered is enormous. His size ransacks space, his every movement a carnage of air. He resembles both the late heavyweight champion of the world, Charles Sonny Liston (except for the tracks of razor scars that run from cheek to neck) and the mammoth genie that issued from Aladdin's lamp—the genie that caved in the sultan's wall with a sneeze. His face wears a scowl that seems to be a compromise with rage, and his amazed eyes have found mine staring, — his eyes force mine to the floor. I hear a chorus of voices sing uncertainly, "Hello Sonny" and wonder—the ghost of Sonny returned from jails, Detroits and Roman bondage? The bartender serves him, his neck unabashedly assuming the posture of supplicant.
"Carlos . . ." I whisper into Carlos' ear, "do you see what's going on here?"
"What? . . . what?" he says bounding on his stool as pert as a bird.
I whisper into his ear, "That guy over there with the scars on his face . . ."
"This ugly fellow?" Carlos shrills sweetly, "Don't worry about him, worry about the one who gave him the scars. You don't see no scars on my face do you?"

I can't see Sonny's eyes, they are obscured by the back of Carlos' head. But Sonny's ears protrude, turning purple, like Moses' horns roasting in hell. In the long silence of a minute Sonny's ears withdraw beyond sight, the door opens, and buckets of the street's heat consume the ghost of Sonny, the door closes, and in the chilled instant of sudden quiet the bartender serves Carlos one on the house. Carlos drinks the rum, chewing the ice cubes with relish, his fingers probe the bottom of the glass and he dabs the damp remains of the drink behind his ears, and pats my head.

"Boy," he says, "I'm going to marry her myself," jumps from his stool, and dances towards the street. I know that pat on the head wasn't a benediction, it could not have been meant kindly. I'm lost and losing and my feet carry me back to the chase. People in the street move slowly, sucking on a filthy rag of air, and I'm running. Carlos sails down the street, his white suit ballooned with the air his blasphemous bones exude. Shylock, Fagan, Moses, Bugsy Siegel! Brethren of the heavenly host, I'll make a deal, sign now or later, only help! help! I scream at the white sail of Carlos' back, "Carlos, your daughter's ass put my ass in the world—I planted the future in her womb!" He stops. He doesn't turn around. A crowd gathers, I'm screaming at the top of my lungs, the only epithet he can hear, "Grandpa," I scream, "Grandpa!" Across the street some children have gotten hold of a monkey wrench and they are opening a fire hydrant. The two kids turn the wrench at the top of the hydrant, the thing looks like a phallus that has sprung a leak in its side. The drooling rivulet of water widens into a perfect cylinder, getting wider and longer. People around me, exhausted and hot as they are, run as if they are about to be machine gunned. The two kids at the hydrant look like soldiers, their faces intent, ruthless, each of them is on the end of a thick plank, which they have placed under the trunk of water, and they are lifting it up, up, like some enormous world war one artillery piece, the great barrel of water points skyward. Over the roofs of cars, growing, it crosses the gutter, one story up, above my head, adjacent to a firescape, a great pillar about to crash. Storekeepers roll up their awnings, close their doors, the windows of cars are rolled shut, people flee the street and bunches of kids in underwear appear on firescapes for watering. The force of the water creates a wind and newspapers and tin cans float in the air. Rushing streams gurgle along the curb, carrying bottle caps, sticks, condoms, and gobs of spit to sewers which are now gorgeous eddies of swirling water. Dark hallways burst hordes of kids, the street is filled with children. Carlos and I are face to face underwater. Drenched and frozen, stiff as statues under this Niagara, I don't move, but my skin shivers as though it wants to crawl off my body. Carlos' lips turn blue, his thin mustache wears a string of water beads that pop as his mouth trembles, "Salom, salomm, salommbumbitch."

"I love your daughter, grandpa."

"Boy don't be foolish, careful how you address me, besides I am already a grandfather, and I've had children by more women than

you will know in your next three lifetimes. You have a name?"
"Jake is my name."
"Jake," he says, "Jacobo, a Jacobo . . . salommbumbitch, a Jacob.
My daughter and a Jacob. It is a catastrophe that comes from living
in a fucking cosmopolitan place, Jacob. Shit. Me cago en la Auga
Bendita, my cago en . . ."

Starting with water, Carlos is shitting on the angelic orders, he is
working his way through a pantheon of Catholic saints, he shits on
Mary's erstwhile husband Joseph, he calls him a cuckold and an ass,
he says heaven rotates on the horns growing from Joseph's head.

Me, I make note of the fact that there is too much water to shit on,
and scheme, if Margarita and I are to have a future we must get
together and make a bastard. Cyclopes and fire engines . . .

NOW I AM MARRIED

fiction by MARY GORDON

from THE VIRGINIA QUARTERLY REVIEW

nominated anonymously

I AM THE SECOND WIFE, which means that, for the most part, I am
spoken *to*. This is the first visit of my marriage and I am introduced
around, to everyone's slight embarrassment. There is an unspoken
agreement among people not to mention *her*, except in some clear
context where my advantage is obvious. It would be generous of me
to say that I wish it were otherwise, but I appreciate the genteel
silences, and, even more, the slurs upon her which I recognize to be
just. I cannot attempt to be fair to her: justice is not the issue. I have
married, and this is an act of irrational and unjust loyalty. I married
for this: for the pleasure of one-sidedness, the thrill of the bias, the
luxury of saying, "But he is my husband, you see," and thereby
putting to an end whatever discussion involves us.

My husband is English and we are staying in the house of his family. We do not make love here as we do at my mother's. She thinks sex is wicked, which is, of course, highly aphrodisiac, but here it is considered merely in bad taste. And as I lie, looking at the slope of my husband's beautiful shoulder, I think perhaps they are right. They seem to need much less sleep than I do, to be able to move more quickly, to keep their commitments with less fuss. I wish I found the English more passionate; surely there is nothing so boring as the reinforcement of a stereotype. But it is helpful to be considered Southern here; I am not afraid to go out on the street as I am in Paris or Rome, because all the beautiful women make me want to stay under the sharp linen of my hotel. No, here I feel somehow to have a great deal of color, which has, after all, to do with sex. The young girls I can see already turning into lumpish women in rain-coats with cigarettes drooping from their lips. This, of course, makes it much easier. Even my sister-in-law's beauty is so different that it cannot really hurt me; it is the ease of centuries of her race's history that gave it to her, and to this I cannot hope to aspire.

Yesterday we went to a charity bazaar. One of the games entailed scooping marbles up with a plastic spoon and putting them through the hole of an overturned flower pot. My sister-in-law went first. Her technique was to take each marble, one at a time, and put it through the hole. Each one went neatly in. When it was my turn, I perceived the vanity of her discretion and my strategy was to take as many marbles as I could on the spoon and shovel them into the hole as quickly as possible. A great number of the marbles scattered on the lawn; but quite a few went into the hole, and, because I had lifted so many, my score was twelve; my sister-in-law's five. But both of us were pleased with our own performance, and appreciative of the rival technique.

I am very happy here. Yesterday in the market I found an eggplant: a rare and definite miracle for this part of the world. Today for dinner I made *ratatouille*. This morning I took my sister-in-law's basket and went out, married, to the market. I don't think that marriage has changed me, but for the first time, the salespeople appreciated, rather than resented, the time I took in choosing only the most heartwarming tomatoes, the most earnest and forthright meat. I was no longer a fussy bachelorette who cooked only some-times and at her whim. I was a young matron in stockings and high heels. My selections, to them, had something to do with the history

they were used to. They were important; they were not for myself. I
had wanted to write this morning, but I had the responsibility of
dinner, served at one. I do not say this in complaint. I was quite
purely happy in my basket and my ring, in the approval of the
shopkeepers and the pedestrians. I am never so happy writing. It is
not that the housewife's tasks are in themselves repugnant: many of
them involve good smells and colors, satisfying shapes, and the
achievement of dexterity. They kill because they are not final. They
must be redone although they have just been finished. And so I am
doing this rather than polishing the beautiful Jacobean furniture
with the sweet-smelling lavendar wax. I am doing this because I am
dying, so that I will not die.

Marjorie

"Bring her in for a cup of coffee," I said to him. I saw you on the
street and you were so happy looking. Not me and my husband.
Dead fifteen years and a bloodier hypocrite never walked. I pretended I was sorry when he died, but believe me I was delighted.
He was a real pervert, all those public school boys won't do anything
for you till they're beaten, don't let them tell you anything about the
French, my dear.

I was just in France. I was kind of like an *au pair* girl to this
Communist bloke, only he was a millionaire. Well, they had a great
house with a river behind it and every day I'd meet the mayor of the
town there, both of us throwing our bottles from the night before
into the river. They had men go round with nets to gather up the
bottles and sell them. They know how to live there. The stores are all
empty here. Not that I'm much of a cook. We start our sherry here as
soon as we get up. Your coffee all right? Have a biscuit. I'll have one
too. I shouldn't . . . look at me around the middle. I'm getting to
look quite middle-aged, but there's some life in me yet, I think,
don't you?

Look at your husband sitting there with his blue eyes just as
handsome. Fancied him once myself, but he hadn't time for me.
Keep an eye on him, dear, he's got young girls in front of him all day.
Oh, I don't envy you that job. They must chase him all the time,
dear, don't they. Cheer up, a little jealousy puts spice in a marriage,
don't you think?

Well, there's a real witch hunt out for me in this building. I've taken in all the boys around town that've got nowhere to go. Just motherly. All of them on drugs, sleeping out every night. Well, my policy is not to chivvy and badger them. Tried marijuana myself once but I didn't get anything out of it because I didn't smoke it properly. But they all have a home here and I do them heaps more good than some virginal social worker with a poker you know where. Of course the old ladies around here don't like it. Mrs. Peters won't forgive me since I was so drunk that night and I broke into her house and started dancing with her. A poor gormless girl she's got for a daughter, afraid of her own shadow. Starts to shake if you as much as say good morning to her. Thirty-five, she is, if she's a day. Pious, that one. I've seen her chatting up the vicar every evening. You know what *she* needs. My husband was a parson. He was plagued with old maids. I'd 'uv been delighted if he'd rolled one down in my own bedroom just so's he'd leave me alone. Bloody great pervert, he was. And sanctimonious! My God. He looked like a stained glass window to the outsiders. And all the old biddies in the town following him around calling him father. Not me. I'd like to tell you what I called him.

Anyway, all the old bitches here think they can get me thrown out, but they're very much mistaken. This building happens to be owned by the Church of England, of which my husband happened to be a pillar. My pension comes from there, you know. Well, my dear, of course they can't throw one of the windows of the clergy out on her sanctified arse, so I'm really quite safe for the moment.

That's why I wouldn't get married again. I wouldn't give up that bloody pension for the life of me. I'll see they pay it to me till I die, the bloody hypocrites. "Yes, Mrs. Pierce, if you'd conduct your life in a manner suitable to a woman of your position." Bugger'em, I say. They're all dust, same as me.

No, I'm quitting Charlie. I've been with him five years but I must say the rigamarole is becoming trying. His wife sits home with their dachshunds, Wallace and Willoughby, their names are—did you ever hear anything so ridiculous—Wallace—and occasionally she'll ring up and say, "Is Charlie Waring there?" and I'll say, "Who? You must have the wrong number." Five years. It's getting ridiculous.

I think I'll take myself down to the marriage bureau. Thirty quid it costs for a year, and they supply you with names till you're satisfied. Of course, at my age what d'ye have left? And I'd want somebody respectable, you know, not just anybody. Of course you meet men in pubs, but never the right sort, are they? My dear, you wouldn't believe what I come home with some nights, I'm that hard up.

Anyway, Lucinda's sixteen and she's already on her second abortion. How she gets that way I don't know. She simply walked out of school. Told one of the teachers off when she told her to take off her makeup. She said to her, "My mother doesn't pay you to shout at me." Dried-up old bitches those teachers were. Of course, in point of fact, it's not me or her that's paying, it's the Church, but just the same, I see her point. They'll never want her more than they want her now, right. Isn't it true, they won't let us near a man till we're practically too old to enjoy one. Well, I've got her a Dutch cap now, though I don't suppose she'll use it. I never did. That's why I've got five offsprings. I'm sure I don't know what to do with them. Anyway, she's working part-time answering telephones for some lawyer and I'm sure he's got her flat on her back on his leather couch half the time. Smashing looking Indian chap. But it's pocket money for her. And we don't get along badly, the way some do. I give her her own way and if she gets into trouble we sort it out somehow. I suppose she'll get married in a year or so, only I hope it's not a fool or a hypocrite. Bloody little fool I was at her age. My dear, on my wedding night I didn't know what went where or why. Don't ask how I was so stupid. Of course my mother was a parson's wife too and I think she thought if she said the word sex the congregation would burn her house down. Dead right she *was*.

Well, you certainly are an improvement over the other one he was married to. My dear, she thought she could run everyone's life for them. Knew me a week and she came over one morning and said, uninvited, "Marjorie, you should get up earlier. Why don't you watch the educational programs on the telly." "Bugger off," I said and she never came near me again.

Well, I have to go off and see one of my old ladies. This one keeps me in clothes, so I've got to be attentive. Let me tell you, if you could see how respectable I am in front of her, my dear, you wouldn't believe. Well, I take her cashmere sweaters and hope the constable won't see me on the way out. One visit keeps Lucinda and me in clothes for a year. I don't care, it cheers her up, the poor old bugger. Hope someone'll be as good to me when I'm that age. But I'll probably be a cross old drunk, and I bloody well won't have any spare Dior gowns in my closet, that's sure.

You don't mind if I give your husband a kiss goodbye. Lovely. Oh, perhaps I'll just take another one. Fancied him myself at one time. Well, you're the lucky one, aren't you? Come over again, perhaps you could come for a meal, though what I could cook nowadays I'm sure I don't know. I don't suppose that would set well with the family. Can't say that I blame them, they have to live here. Well, slip in some time on the QT and I'll dig you out some tea. Make it afternoon, though, dears, I don't like mornings, though I'm ever so glad of your company.

Doris

I don't go anywhere by myself now. Three weeks ago I got a car but I took it back. I was so lonely driving. That was the worst. I think I'm afraid of everybody and everything now. I'm always afraid there's men walking behind me. I won't even go to post a letter in the evening. I was always afraid of the dark. My mother knew I was afraid of the dark so she made me sleep with the light off. She said if I kept on being afraid of the dark God wouldn't love me.

Of course, it's all so different now George is gone. People are like things, d'ye know what I mean? They're very nice, of course, and they do care for me and call, but it's all I don't know, shallow like. Of course, I do prefer the company of men. Not that I run down my own sex, but men are gentler, somehow, don't you think. The first month after George was gone all I could think about was who could I marry now. But now I look back on it I shudder, d'ye know what I mean. George bein' so sick and all that we didn't have a physical relationship for many years. And men like to be naughty. Sometimes, though, I do enjoy a man's companionship. After George lost his leg he said, "I can't give you much in the way of the physical, Mother." But we were terribly close, really. Talked about everything. He would insist on having his chair here by the door so's he could see everybody coming in. I used to kid him a lot about it. Winter and summer, never come close to the fire. He'd sit right there by the door, winter and summer. And Gwen would sit on the settee at night and never go out. I used to say to her, "Gwen, you must go out. Go to the cinema." But she was afraid, like, to leave her father. Even though I was here. She was afraid if she went out he'd be gone when she got back.

Of course, it was very hard on the children. It'll take them years to sort it out, I suppose. Perhaps they'll never sort it out. Gwen went down to eight stone. Bonnie she looked, but I was worried. Then she got these knots-like in her back and she stopped going to work altogether. Said she couldn't face the tubes anymore. She hated it; bein' smothered-like, she said, it was terrifying. But I think she wanted to be home with Daddy so we let her come home.

Colin has a lovely job now. Got a hundred blokes under him. But they're afraid he'll go back to university and quit so they don't pay him properly. He almost took a degree in logic but he broke down after two years. You should see his papers. Lovely marks on 'em. His professors said if he sat right down he'd come away with a first. But he got too involved, if you know what I mean. Forgot there was a world around him.

He's had a lot of lovely girls, and I guess he's had his fling, but I don't think he'll ever marry. After George died he said, "I don't know how to put it, Mum, but I'm just not that interested in sex." Once a few years ago he came out to the breakfast table. He was white as a ghost, I was worried. He said he felt a kind of calling. He was terrified, he said; he was sure God was calling him to his service. Well, George held his tongue and so did I. He asked Colin what it felt like and Colin said, "Don't ask me to describe it, Dad." He had a lot of sleepless nights and we called the vicar and he took him to the place where the young men go for the priesthood and Colin said that he liked it, but when the time came he never did go.

Him and his father were great pals. Colin of course was studying Western philosophy and he was very keen on it and George just as keen on the Eastern. Oh, they would argue and George would say, "Just read this chapter of the book I'm reading" and Colin would say, "I'm not interested, Dad." Then after George died he took all his books away with him to Bristol. I said, "I thought you weren't interested." He said, "I really always was, Mum."

Lynnie's going to be a mother in September. I'm not really keen on being a grandmother. I'm interested in my daughter; she's an adult. I'm not interested in babies. I've never seen anyone like her for being cheerful, though. That girl cannot be made miserable, not even for an hour. I'm sure it'll be a girl, the way she holds her back when she walks, straightlike. I suppose I'll be interested in it when it's born.

George had a kind of miraculous effect on people, though. One time our vicar asked him to address a group of young people. Four hundred of them there was, packed the house with chairs, they did.

And up on the stage one big armchair for George. One night I made them all mugs of tea, there must have been fifteen of them here on the floor. Half of them admitted they were on drugs. Purple hearts, goofballs, whatever they call them nowadays. And when they left here they said they were all right off them now.

Of course, he had this good friend, the bachelor vicar, Arthur. Like a father to him George was. A very intelligent man, but a terrible lot of problems. Spent all his time here, he did. He'd stay here till two o'clock on Sunday morning and then go home and write his sermons. Said George all but wrote his sermons for him. Once he told me he was jealous of George having me and me having George. Said it was the one thing he could never have. And him a wealthy man. His father had a big engineering firm in Dorset and a great house. Three degrees he has, too. But I think he's really like they say, neurotic. He *cannot* express his feelings. Me and George we told each other everything. We kept no secrets. Not Arthur, though. He's taken me out to dinner twice since George died, but I like plain food, d'ye know what I mean, and he took me out to this Japanese restaurant with Geisha girls and God knows what. Well, they gave me so much I sent half of it back and they said was there something Madame didn't like and I about died of shame. I think old Arthur's knocking but I'm not at home to him. Of course he's a wonderful priest, the kids in the youth group love him. He cried during the whole funeral service. I was so mortified. And he will not mention George's name. He says he can't forgive God for taking George.

I used to feel that way but I don't any more. When George was in so much pain-like, I'd go to the Communion rail and shake my fist at Christ on the Cross and say, "What d'ye know about suffering? You only suffered one day. My George has suffered years." I don't feel that way now. I think there's a reason for it, all that pain, even. George died without one drug in his body, he had that much courage.

Well, I guess I'll be getting you a bath. It's good you've come. You'll never regret the man you've married. George thought the world of him. We've only water enough for one bath. So one takes it tonight and one tomorrow. George and I used to bathe in the same water, but I think we were different from most.

I feel like I've known you all my life. I knew you'd be like this from the letters. Old friends they were, my man and yours. You're not like the first wife. She was a hard one, that one. Ice in her veins.

Perhaps I'll come and visit you in America. I have a job now at the hospital and three weeks holiday in July. Perhaps I'll come out to visit you. But what would I do the two of you out working. I hate to impose, you know. We used to have friends, widows they were and we'd invite them over and they'd say, "Oh, no thanks, we'd be odd man out." I never knew what they meant but now I know. Look at me talking. I can't even go to Epping by myself, and Lynnie made the trip when she was eight. Perhaps if you found out all the details for me. Wouldn't it be something!

It's good having someone in the house at night. I usually sleep with all the lights on, I'm that frightened on my own. I think I'm getting better with the job and all. But sometimes I'm very empty-like, and cold.

Elizabeth

I like living here on my own. Dear lord, who else could I live with? Like old Miss Bates, she lived with another teacher, for, oh, twenty years it must have been. They bought a dear little house in the Cotswolds to live in for their retirement. Lived there a year and up pops some cousin who'd been wooing Miss Campbell for forty years and off they go and get married. Well, Amelia Bates was furious and she wouldn't speak to Miss Campbell and they'd been like sisters for twenty years. Well, poor Miss Campbell died six months later and there's Amelia Bates on her own in that vast house full of regrets and sorrow.

Here's a picture of me in Algeria in 1923. Oh, I had a beautiful ride over on the ship, it took three days. Some people took a trip just to drink all the way, people are foolish. The first night I lay in my cabin and the ship was creaking so badly I was sure it was the end of me. I went up top and the waves were crashing around the deck and they said, "You'd better go down below, Miss," and that's where I met Mr. Saunders. Don't let the others in the family act so proud to you. When I found out that Ethel had cut you, ooh, I was angry. I wrote her a very cross letter. Her mum and dad were separated for years and he was living with a half-caste woman in India and afraid to even write his wife a letter. Of course, he should have left her and stayed with that other woman but he didn't have that much courage. He's been miserable ever since. Poor old Lawrence, he's a decent old boy but terrified to death of Millie. You know she was just a governess for his family when he fell in love with her. She was good-looking, though, the best looking of all of us. Well, poor old Lawrence when he came to Mt. Olympus (that was the name of my father's house, dear. It fulfilled the ambitions of a lifetime for him) well, when he came to Mt. Olympus to meet the family he came down with malaria and was sick in bed for a month. Had to have his meals brought up to him and his sheets changed three times a day. Well, after that there was no getting out of it, he was quite bound. Not that he thought of getting out of it then. People simply didn't in those days, and that's why so many of them were so unhappy. I'm sure things are much better now, in some ways, but nobody seems much happier anyway, do they?

Here is a picture of the family I worked for in India. Now even I had my mild scandal I suppose. It wasn't so mild to father. Millie came home from India and told dear father a great tale. Father wrote to Mr. Saunders and demanded that I be sent home. Then he wrote to me and said I must come back upon my honour as his daughter and an Englishwoman. We simply didn't answer the letters. Mr. Saunders hid them in a parcel in his desk drawer and I simply threw mine in the fire. Then Mr. Saunders took the family back to England and I went back to Mt. Olympus. Father told me I must take a new name and tell everyone I was married, that I was the widow of an officer. I refused; I told him no one knew but him and Millie. Then we never spoke of it.

I started a kindergarten then for the children in the town. Here is the picture of the first class and here's one of your husband as a baby. Wasn't he golden? Then mother got sick and I had to give it up. Nobody took it on after that, it was a pity, really. I regretted that.

Here's a picture of cousin Norman. Doesn't he look a bounder? Wrote bad checks and settled in Canada. He's a millionaire today.

I'm giving you these spoons as a wedding gift. They belonged to my grandmother's grandmother. I think it's nice to have a few old things. It makes you feel connected, somehow, don't you think?

I only hope my mind holds out on me. I love to read and I wouldn't care if I were bedridden as long as my mind was all right. Mother was all right for some time and then when she was in her seventies she just snapped. She didn't recognize anybody in the family and one night she came at Father with a knife and said he was trying to kill her. We had to put her in the hospital then. It was supposed to be the best one in England but it was awful. There were twenty women in a room not this size and in the evenings you could hear them all weeping and talking to themselves. It would have driven me quite mad and I was sane. Then she said the nurses were all disguising themselves to confuse her, and they were tyring to poison her. And then she said they wouldn't let her wash, and she was dirty and smelt ill. Well, we finally took her back home and father wouldn't let anyone see her. I gave up my position (I was working for that woman who writes those trashy novels that sell so well. And her daughter was an absolute hellcat) and came home. She'd call me every few minutes and say, "Elizabeth, what will we do if anyone comes? There isn't a speck of food in the house." And I would tell her no one would be coming. Then she'd say, "Elizabeth, what will we do if anyone comes, the house is so dirty." And it would go on like that. Sometimes she wouldn't eat for days, and sometimes she would stuff herself till she was quite ill. She died of a stomach obstruction in the end, but that was years later. Every night father would go in to her and say goodnight and kiss her and she was hurting us all. But sometimes she would just be her old self and joke with us after supper and play the piano and sing or read—she loved the Brontës—and we'd think she was getting better, perhaps. But the next morning she'd be looking out the window again, not talking to anyone.

I can't go near anyone who has any kind of mental trouble. When my friend Miss Edwards was so ill in that way she wrote and begged me to come and the family wrote and I simply couldn't. I get very frightened of those sorts of things. I suppose I shouldn't.

Here is a caricature my brother drew of the warden, and here is one of the bald curate and the fat parson who rode a bicycle. He was talented, our Dick, but of course he had a family to support and that awful wife of his put everything on her back that he earned. And here is one of our father turning his nose up at some Indian chap who was trying to sell him a rug he didn't fancy.

Here I am in Malta and here's one of me in Paris. Wasn't I gay then? When the Germans took over Paris, I wept and wept. I didn't want to go on. Have you been to Paris, dear? Beautiful city, isn't it? You feel anything could happen there. It wouldn't matter where you'd been or what you'd done, you could begin all over, no regrets or sorrows.

Here is a picture of your husband's mother, wasn't she beautiful.

Turn your head like that, you look rather like her when you put your face that way. She would have loved you, dear, and she was a beautiful soul. She used to laugh and laugh, even during the war when we'd have to stay in the shelter over night and we were terrified we wouldn't see the sunlight ever again. She'd tell us gay stories and make us laugh. She had a little bird, she used to call it Albert as a joke. She let him fly out all about the house on his own. And she taught the creature to say funny things; it was so amusing. She would be very happy for you, dear; she loved to see people happy.

I don't suppose I'll do any more traveling. I remember when I went to France last summer I said "Elizabeth, this is your last voyage," and I felt so queer. But I have this house and my garden and Leonard's wife Rosemary and I go out every week and do meals-on-wheels—we take food around to the shut-ins, dear. I suppose they'll be doing that for me some day, but not for a while, I don't think. I like to be active and work in the garden. These awful pillow roses have taken over everything and I haven't the heart to prune them. And then, when people come, it's so lovely, isn't it, I wish they could stay forever.

Susan

It's good to have company. Sometimes I feel as though I haven't had a day off in three years since Maria was born. Geoffrey doesn't seem to want to be weaned; he's seven months. I suppose he will when he's ready. It's the only thing that quietens him. I'm beginning to feel very tired. And now Maria wants everything from a bottle, she wants to be a baby too. I suppose they'll stop when they're ready.

My days are very ordered, though. I remember when I was single and I lived in London I'd think what will I do with myself now? And then I'd just go out and walk down the street and I'd look in the windows at the china and the materials and then I'd stop somewhere and have a cup of tea and go home and read something. It's so difficult, isn't it, to remember what that kind of loneliness was like when you're with people constantly. It's like hunger or cold. But now my time is all mapped out for me. I give everyone breakfast and then I do the washing up and we go for a walk and it's time for lunch. It goes on like that. It's better now. When we lived in the high-rise building I felt terribly alone. There would be other push-chairs in front of other doors and occasionally I'd hear a baby crying in the hall but I wouldn't know whose it was and when I opened the door there was never anybody in the corridor, only the queer yellow light. And I hated the air in that building. It tasted so false in my mouth and we couldn't open up any of the windows. It was beautiful at nights and I would hold the baby by the window and say, "moon," and "star," and sometimes when they were both asleep Frederick and I would stand by the window and look out over the city at all the lights. The car horns were muted like voices at the ocean; it was very nice. I liked it then. But I did feel terribly lonely.

Sometimes I go up to the attic and I look at the piles of my research in egg cartons but I don't even take it out. I suppose I should want to someday. I suppose I should get back to my Russian. But it all hangs around me like a cloud and I feel Maria tugging at me, pulling at my dress like a wave and I think how much more real it all is now, feeding and clothing, and nurturing and warming and I think of words like "research" and "report" and even "learning" and "understanding" next to those words and they seem so high, so far away, it's a struggle to remember what they mean.

I love marriage, though, the idea of it. I believe in it in a very traditional way. My friends from graduate school come over and they say I'm worn out and tired and I'm making a martyr of myself. I should make Frederick do some of the work. But it's the form of it I love and the repetition: certain tasks are his, some are mine. That's what these young people are all looking for, form, but it's a dirty word to them. I suppose I'm not that old, I'm thirty-two, that's young, I suppose, but I like feeling older. I wish I were fifty. I like not having a moment to myself, it's soothing and my life is warm and sweet like porridge. Before Geoffrey was born sometimes I'd spend the whole day and Maria was the only one I would talk to. She was two then and Frederick would come home and he was so terribly tired and I was too. We scarcely said a word to each other except "how's the baby today" or "your shirt got lost at the cleaner's." It was the happiest time of my life. She wanted to know everything, and sometimes we'd spend whole mornings doing things like taking the vacuum cleaner apart or boiling water or walking up and down stairs. Then Frederick would come home and he'd want to talk about Talleyrand or something and I couldn't possibly explain to him how perfectly happy I was all day, taking everything out of my sewing basket and showing it to Maria, he would have thought I was stark, staring mad.

But I love that: sleeping next to someone you haven't spoken to all day and then making love in the dark with our pajamas on and even then going to sleep not having spoken. It soothes me, like wet sand. We couldn't have that without marriage, I mean marriage in the old way, with the woman doing everything.

Here's something for your lunch. I cook such odd things now, sausages for the children, tins of soup, sandwiches. But I always make this stew for us. I just boil up a hambone with lentils and carrots. I suppose you're a very good cook. I used to be but now I don't like that kind of thing.

The babies have broken nearly all the china, so we use everything plastic now. Do you think it's terribly ugly? I do miss that, nice thin china and glassware, I miss it more than books and the cinema. And the furniture's terribly shabby now. We'll wait until they're grown to replace it.

Don't worry about what people say. When I married Frederick even his mum wouldn't come and people would run down his first wife, thinking they were doing me a favor, and all the time they were making it worse because I'd think if she was so bloody awful why did he marry her and then I thought if he loved her and she's so dreadful and he loves me I must be dreadful too. And I kept going around in circles and hating Frederick and myself and some poor woman whom I used to think of as a perfectly harmless remote monster. I could scarcely get out of bed in the morning, and people thought they were being kind. You must simply shore up all your courage to be silent. That's what I have done and sometimes I am so silent I like myself a great deal, no, more than that, I admire myself and that's what I've always longed for.

You shouldn't listen to me either, I'm probably half mad talking to babies all day. Only there's something sort of enormous and grey and cold about marriage. It's wonderful isn't it, being part of it? Or don't you feel that way.

Gillian

My mother had this thing about beauty, it was really very Edwardian the way she approached it. She had this absolutely tiny private income and my father took off the absolute second I was born and we hardly ever had any money and my mother kept moving around saying these incredible things like "it'll be better in the next town" and "when our ship comes in" and things like that you expect to read in some awful trashy novel.

But she was a beautiful woman and she taught me these oddly valuable things, about scent and clothes and makeup. I'm trying to be kinder to her now I'm forty. I suppose one gets some kind of perspective on things, but what I really remember is being terribly, terribly insecure all the time and frightened about money and resentful of other girls who wore smart clothes and went off to university when they weren't as smart as I was. My mother used to dress me in the most outlandish outfits as a child, velvet and lace, and what not. I hated it in school. I was forever leaving schools and starting in new ones and I was perpetually embarrassed.

Well, when I married for the first time I was determined to marry someone terribly stable and serviceable. As soon as I could I bought these incredibly severe clothes, they just about had buttons on them and I married Richard. I was eighteen. I suppose it is all too predictable to be really interesting—and we lived in this fanatically utilitarian apartment, everything was white and silver and I couldn't imagine why I felt cold all the time. Suddenly I found myself using words like beauty and truth, et cetera, and I went out and got a job so we could buy a really super house. I spent all my time looking at wallpaper and going to auctions and the house really was beautiful. Then I met Seymour and he was so funny and lugubrious—I just adored it. Here was this Jewish man taking me to little cabarets. The first time we went out he said to me, 'You know, Gillian, girl singers are very important,' and I hadn't the faintest idea what he was talking about. Here was this quite famous psychologist who bought a copy of Variety—that American show-people's paper—every day, but it was very odd, the first time I met him I thought how marvelous he'd be to live with.

And then, of course I did a terribly unstable thing, I suppose. Shades of my mother only more so I divorced Richard and married Seymour. He gave all his money to his wife and I let Richard keep everything of mine and we started out without a penny. We slept in the car in our clothes, but we were terribly happy. So I got a job and we got another lovely house, only this was a really cheerful one, a very motherly home. Then I went back to school. I suppose it's hard for you to understand how important it would be for me: doing something on my own with my mind and speaking up and having people listen. I'd had too much sitting on the sidelines pushing the silver pheasant down the damask cloth and cradling the salt cellar while the men spoke to each other. So I told Seymour I simply had to go back to college and he agreed with me for a while in theory but when the time came he said to me "what about the house." But I was very firm and I simply told him, "the house will simply be a bit less beautiful for a while." Then he understood how important it was to me, and he stood right behind me. We didn't do much entertaining for a while, but I did very well, really, everyone was surprised. I guess everyone else was much less smart than I expected.

Then I took a job teaching high school and it was a disaster, really. There were all these perfectly nice people who wanted to grow up and repair bicycles and I was supposed to talk about Julius Caesar and the subjunctive. It was all too absurd, really. I simply cared about the books too much to do it. I suppose to be a really good high school teacher you have not to care about the books so. Well, one day I simply didn't go back. I suppose it was awful, but there were plenty of people who wanted the job. I didn't feel too badly about it. Going in like that every day was making me so ill.

Now I've gone back to writing. I don't know if I'm any good. I don't suppose it matters, really. It's a serious thing, and that's important. I see everyone off in the morning and I go up to my study—the window looks out on a locust tree—and I write the whole day. The hardest thing is closing the door on Seymour and the children—but I do. I close the door on being a wife. I close the door on my house and all the demands. I suppose art demands selfishness and perhaps I'm not a great artist so perhaps it's all ridiculous and pitiable, but in the end it isn't even important whether I'm great or not—I'm after something, myself, I suppose, isn't that terribly commonplace. Only the soul, whatever that is, whatever we call it now—gets so flung about one is always in danger of losing it, of letting it slip away unless one is really terribly careful and jealous. And so it is important really and the only answer is, whatever the outside connections, that one must simply do it.

*   *   *

Who is right, and who is wrong? For years, I have waited for a sign, a sentence, periodic and complete. Now I begin to know there is a loneliness even in this love. I begin to think of death, of solids. My friend, who is my age, is already a widow. She says that no one will talk to her about it. Everyone thinks she is tainted. They are frightened by her contact with dead flesh, as if it clung to her visibly. I should prepare for a staunch widowhood. I begin to wish for my own death, because I am happy now and vulnerable to contagion. A friend of mine who has three children tells a story about a colleague of his, a New England spinster. She noted that he had been out sick four times that winter; she had been healthy throughout. "But that is because I have a wife and three children," he said, "and I am open to contagion."

There is something satisfying about marriage at this time. It is the satisfaction of a dying civilization: one perfects the form, knowing it has the thrill of doom upon it. There is a craftsmanship here; I am conscious of a kind of labor. It is harder than art and more dangerous. Last night was very hot. I didn't want to wake my husband so I moved into the spare bedroom where I could thrash, guiltlessly. I fell asleep and then heard him wake, stir, and feel for me. I ran to the door of our bedroom. "You gave me a fright. I reached for you and the bed was empty," he said. Now I know I am not invisible. Things matter. My feet impress a solid earth now. I am full of power.

The most difficult thing is my tremendous pride. To admit that there are some things I do not know is like a degrading illness. My husband tries to teach me how to use a hoe, a machete. I do not learn easily. I throw the tools at his feet and in anger I weep and kick. He knows something I do not; can I forgive him? He is tearing down a wall; he is building a fireplace. I am upstairs in the bedroom, reading, dizzy with resentment. I come down and say, "I'm going away for a few days. Until you finish this." Then I cry and confess: I do not want to go away, but I hate it that he is demolishing and building and that I am reading. It is not enough that I have made a custard and a beautiful parsley sauce for the fish. He hands me a hammer, a chisel, a saw. I am clumsy and ill with my own incapacity. When he tries to show me how to hold the saw correctly, I hit him, hard, between the shoulder blades. I have never hit another person like this; I am an only child. So he becomes the brother I was meant to hit. I make him angry. He says I should have married someone with no skills, no achievements. What I want, he says, is unlimited power. He is right. I love him because he is powerful, because he will let me have only my fair share. Stop, he says, for I ask too much of everything. Take more, there is more here for you, I tell him, for he is used to deprivation. We are learning to be kind to one another, like milky siblings.

Two people in a house, what else is it? I love his shoes, his shirts. I want to embrace his knees and tell him "You are the most splendid person I have ever known." Yet I miss my friends, the solitude of my own apartment with its plangent neuroses, the coffee cups where mold grew familiarly, the little grocery store on the corner with the charge account in my name only.

But I feel my muscles flex, grow harder, grow supple with intimacy. We are very close; I know every curve of his body; he can call to mind in a moment the pattern of my veins. He is my husband, I say, slowly, swallowing a new, exotic food. Does this mean everything or nothing? I stand with him in an ancient relationship, in a ruined age, listening beyond my understanding to the warning voices, to the promise of my own substantial heart.

GRANDPARENTS

by HOWARD ZIMMON

from RANDOM (Seamark Press)

nominated by Paul Engle

the corner of the curtain
falls back
as soon as I get off the bus

the door opens
before the bell rings

my grandmother
asks what took so long
I say I walked across
the street
as fast as I could.

we sit
at the kitchen table
and all afternoon
she brings me
everything I can remember
out of the breadbox.

we play cassino
and drink tea
with strawberry preserves.

the old butcher
makes his weekend
delivery and they
banter in a language
I barely understand.

this time I
learn where we
are from:

Brchon, Bessarabia and
Kamenets-Podolsk
in the Ukraine
and this is where
the boat first landed
in Chelsea, Mass.

(take the subway south
change at Maverick
take the streetcar
down Central Ave)

at 5:30 pm
my grandfather
walks in
through
the back door
his face grimy
from sorting
wool all day
(50 yrs now)
takes his gray
cap off his
bald head
smiles and says
'huh, look
who's here.'

He takes
a long hot bath
comes out steaming
wrapped in two
white bath towels
my grandmother
rubs and dries
his back

then he sits down
at the table
sweeps some crumbs
onto his palm
pours himself one
shot of whiskey
looks at me
pours me one
and says
'so'

𝕚 𝕚 𝕚

THE MOTHER-IN-LAW

a tale by ED SANDERS

from CENTER

nominated by CENTER *and Ben Pesta*

WHEN SHE MARRIED THE DIRTY BEATNIK, the calamity of it spiralled upward and outward through the extant family tree. That a girl of impeccable family, destined to marry well and wealthily, beautiful, conversant in three languages, with 9 years of piano study behind her, should stoop to wed a mumbling, shabby poetry-writing person with an unknown family from an unknown place, perhaps Nebraska, was a profound shock that sent the parents into a numbed period of consulting the police, lawyers, private investigators and laws involving insane asylums.

As for the beat poet, he didn't care. The parents were just another couple of notches on the stick of squares. This was his attitude: they do not exist. And if they try to exist, I will travel with their daughter, my love, where they do not. And this was the message he once bothered to convey, after which there was no message from the accused beatnik to the parents, only silence.

The bazooka-spews of hostility, however, began years before the wedding. They met in a cafe on MacDougal Street in late summer of 1959. He was more or less the resident balladeer at the coffee house and was busily occupied that summer, organizing a series of Sunday afternoon poetry readings at the cafe attended by the finest talents of beatdom.

The day they met she was dressed Being & Nothingness ballerina beat. Her long blonde tresses were pulled back into a bun, and there were wonderful golden bangs in front. She wore black dancer's stockings and black high heel spikes with those stylish spear-toes. Her brown leather vest, with laces up the sides, was the rage of Bleecker Street, worn over a tight black turtle neck with no brassiere, the ultimate of boldness in 1959.

Her eyes were Nefertiti'd with great Juliette Greco streaks of kohl and lots of green eye shadow. No one would have ever, she was anxiously certain, thought *she* was a tourist from Queens. She *knew* she looked like an authentic Villager.

They sat and talked for eight hours that first mesmerizing day. They agreed to meet after school the next day. And then the next. And the next.

Well, to dress the way she did was one thing, her parents reasoned. After all, it was New York and not some whistle stop. But to begin to— to— hang around with and god knows what else with, a filthnik in Greenwich Village, well, that was unacceptable to parents, grandparents, uncles, aunts, and cousins in the sprawllands of Flushing, N.Y. They banded together, the family, to ban the nascent love. She was 17 and her 18th birthday was only two months away so they had to move fast.

They wrote, they phoned, they sent telegrams to the beatnik, to his parents, to the school. They hired investigators. But all threats passed right through the young lovers' consciousness into the tunnel of chaos. The parents tried to insist that she transfer to an out-of-town school, a classic technique of parents who dislike the loves of their son or daughter. Fuck you, she countered, I'll just not go to school.

They ran away the Christmas vacation of '59. They tried to check into the all-male derelict hotel on Bleecker Street and were laughed out of the lobby. They stayed up all night in a Times Square movie house watching *The Blob* and *I Married a Man From Outer Space*, over and over. The parents called the police on New Years Eve with a missing person report but the officer asked them, "How old is she?" —followed by "Does your daughter have a boy friend?" Since she had just turned 18, there was nothing to be done.

They prowled the "beat scene"—frankly starve-eyed, looking for a rational salvation. They wandered together, living that famous line of Auden's *September 1, 1939* with every lust-speckled muscle, along the trampled via of face-the-terror. There was no poetry reading, no art show, no film, no ritual of abandoned filth, no concert in an obscure loft, no lecture, no event of sufficiently rebellious nature, that they ever missed. They spent countless afternoons scoring splendid data in the 4th Avenue bookstores—those 20 or so dusty stores of used tomes from 9th to 14th Streets. What a paradise.

Their main problem was no place to plank. His landlord at the 11th Street rooming house would not allow guests of any gender up to his pitiful closet, and he could scarcely afford the rent plus deposit for lights, to get his own pad. The parks of N.Y. were their boudoir. They planked in them all. They were the only ones who had ever made love under the street light in the midpoint of the arching stone bridge near the Central Park Zoo, according to the policeman who broke up their coupling at a most urgent pre-spew critical moment.

They tried it lying up against the little jungle gym park in Washington Square Park after the park was closed. They planked on the cinder riding track near 72nd Street on the West Side of Central Park and were interrupted by police horses—again at a critical moment. They planked sports-car style on a bench at 72nd on the *East* side of the park (the same night as the cinder-track interruption).

They loved to make it in Inwood Park. One New Years Eve they climbed high in the rocks, above the Columbia University boat basin at the north edge of Inwood, and were lean/lying on a steep icy incline between huge boulders—when, right in the middle, they began to slide, were unable to break it, but still kept planking, and her buttocks were treated to 15 feet of thrillies down the twiggie glaciation.

That incident was absolutely the last straw. They sold everything they could lay their hands on, and hocked and borrowed, and with the loot rented a small pad on East Third Street and Avenue B, which caused a further useless shriek from the parents.

When he dared to drop out of school for a semester, the hatred of her family nearly got him in trouble with the Feds. The father learned of the drop-out and wrote a letter to the F.B.I. sternly complaining that a scurrilous draft-dodging beatnik, who had missed a charge of statutory rape by only two months, should be flouting the law by not attending college while still enjoying an exemption from the draft. Why did the F.B.I. hesitate for even one minute—the father raged—to arrest this communist beatnik churl? Or why was he not forced immediately to join the army?

The letter did stir some attention directed against the beatnik on the part of the F.B.I. They visited the lower east side pad of the young lovers who luckily were not home. The procedure of the F.B.I. in those ways was standard when they found a person not at home. They slid a 3x5 index card under the door, bearing the following thrill-producing message: they wrote at the top the full legal name of the "subject" with whom they deigned to babble, under which they wrote, "Please contact Special Agent Edward Barnes, Federal Bureau of Investigation". Under that was the F.B.I. phone number and the agent's extension.

The poet, of course, had not known that the father had sent in the letter. Eery Police State fears crowded his mind. The pot in the pad was flushed immediately. Was it some sort of crackdown on beat poets? Absurd. He had signed a petition urging clemency for Caryl Chessman—maybe that was the reason for the visit. Whatever the reason, he was haunted by the phantom sound of handcuffs and the soundtrack of the F.B.I. radio show.

He telephoned the Agency and they asked him to bop up to the F.B.I. office on East 67th on a little matter regarding his draft status. Uh-oh. Uh-oh and terror. He was interviewed in a cavernous room full of desks and agents. They informed him they were not out to "get" him or anything but that once requested from the chain of command above, the agents were required to file a report. He assured them that he was going to be back in class the very next semester, and carefully attempted to paint a picture of his future father-in-law as a trembly-fingered nut.

Because of her father's letter to the Feds, the couple felt it reasonable to assume that the father had written to the N.Y. police also, perhaps a letter about drugs. For the next several years they hid their grass in carefully prepared stashes. They used, for instance, the hang-the-bag-of-pot-out-the-window-on-a-string-hanging-above-the-toilet stash. It was boring to have to take such precautions, but it was very common at that time. The couple knew one fellow who had a dog trained as a living stash of grass-gobble, should the fuzz raid. In fact, during the beat era, one of the considerations when deciding whether or not to take an apartment was the presence of built-in stashes such as crevices, shaftways, etc.; or how long the door would hold up in a dope-raid.

The next crisis occurred when they got married, at which time the family considered putting her, or him, or both, into a nuthatch. An uncle in the family was a doctor. There was a lot of phone pressure on the uncle to look into committing the beatnik, "to save Marie," the mother cried, tears dripping on the receiver. In response to this the beatnik sent the message, You'll never take us alive, into the family tree and things grew quieter.

Children eased the hatred. For his part, the poet wrote and was silent. Faced with a total cut-off from seeing their grandchildren, the parents began to soften up. They could all walk down vomit alley, was the poet's attitude after the years of warfare. If they got on his back, he decided that he would snarl or glower and say nothing whatsoever. A sneering, glowering beatnik dressed in weird rags was a match for many a middle-class mom visiting the slums for a peep at a grandchild.

So the years of poverty roamed past, roach-ridden, garbage-strewn, happy with rodents. Sometimes they were reduced to using tee shirts for diapers, unable to afford the disposables. Once they seized the teeshirt of a visiting National Book Award poet, right off his back, just days after receiving the Award, to use as a diaper. On occasion, they gathered their first editions of poetry and novels and sold them to rare book dealers. He was always getting writers to sign their books. At poetry readings at the 92nd Street Y, he usually managed to hang out back stage grabbing the 'graphs, man. A *signed* first edition, ahhh, that was a pleasure.

In rare desperation, he joined the line of humans at the Third Avenue Blood Bank to get his arm sucked for the ten dollar pint. Ten dollars: 1.98 for Chux disposables, 4 packages of spaghetti 70ᶜ, 1 box spinach egg noodles 35ᶜ, 1 lb. ricotta cheese 69ᶜ, sugar, potatoes, gallon milk, eggs, 3 marshmallow cookies at Gem Spa, two cans beer, one cola—and they had a bare three dollars remaining. That meant tomorrow was another partial day of schemes—but schemes interspersed with hours of mimeographed treason, learnèd chit-chat, at Tompkins Square Park, four distinct hallucinations, numerous strolls in the direction of the Fourth Avenue bookstores, and f r e e d o m.

As the years went by, there began to occur the phenomenon of the shopping bag. That is, when the mother-in-law made her occasional quick Saturday or Sunday afternoon visits to the squalid, enemy pad, she bore shopping bags of largesse. Often she would pick stuff from her own pantry, wild "bohemian" substances like ungobbled tins of palm hearts, Streits brand chocolate-covered matzohs, pickled watermelon rinds or partial boxes of kasha. But the shopping bags also contained staples such as diapers and milk and sugar. The mother-in-law apparently never threw anything away. One of her thrills was to present to the grandchildren baby clothes that the mother, her daughter, had worn at the same age. Ditto for toys and dolls that had belonged to the mother 20 years previous.

Occasionally the mother-in-law would show up in the middle of a political meeting, say for the planning of a demonstration, and some of America's most notorious radicals, men and women on whom the government spent millions bugging, harassing, auditing and burglarizing, would shift apart in silence as the mother-in-law walked through with the bundles of choff. The father-in-law was the last to soften and remained rather intransigent in his hatred of the "beatnik punk with no excuses". Once he even injected green vegetable dye into an unopened gallon of milk brought to the hovel on a shopping bag Sunday. They opened the milk later. There is nothing quite like pouring a glass of fresh milk and viewing green fungus juice from Mars coming out of the spout. But gradually even the father-in-law began to calm down and to tolerate the marriage.

There was no hovel, no geodesic summer dome in the woods within driving range, no junkie-ridden tenement so forboding as to prevent the m-i-l, carrying 35 pounds of raw produce, clothes, notebook paper, vitamins, magazines, in 2 or 3 Care Packages as the couple called them, from climbing up however many flights of steps it took.

In the summer of 1964, the couple and children spent several months in the woods off a logging trail in the Catskill hills near Phoenicia, New York. They were living in an old striped party-tent from somebody's Long Island estate, above which were second story sleeping quarters in a clear plastic-roofed treehouse. They lived in fond desolation for several weeks until one Sunday afternoon they heard "skwonch! skwonch! skwonch!"—approaching footsteps in the twigs and dry growth, as toward the tent, laden with protein and cheer, walked the mother-in-law.

As the years passed, they were not surprised to learn that the phenomenon of the mother-in-law as the Demeter of Bohemia, was widespread. Wherever writers and artists banded together to struggle, they were present. All hail the mother-in-law.

𝕭 𝕭 𝕭

THE MONSTER

fiction by RONALD SUKENICK

from IOWA REVIEW and 98.6, (Fiction Collective)

nominated by Pushcart Press

T HIS IS THEIR FIRST MONEY CRISIS . Ron feels they ought to have a
meeting about it but one of their rules is that they don't have any
meetings. It's not a rule exactly it's just not the way they do things.
So what they do is they get George and drive over to the River
Queen. The River Queen people are allied with The Planet Krypton
in their mutual difficulties with the Earthmen. The difference is that
while The Planet Krypton is always getting victimized The River
Queen mostly comes out on top because they have a lot of money
and the reason why they have money is that they're big dealers
which is why they have difficulties with the Earthmen to begin with.
The River Queen people live on a big old ferry hulk docked in a

lagoon on the river near a colony of houseboats. George knows their bosslady through Altair and Betelgeuse who deal with her. This is important because to the River Queen folks there are only two kinds of people. Friends and fuzz. The bosslady is a local character named Fatima who is supposed to have made a fortune in flesh some years back. She still deals a little in flesh on the side but mainly now it's dope. When you work for Fatty as everyone calls her you can pick up your pay in flesh dope or cash take your choice. Fatty sweeps out to meet them in a long dress a red bandanna and lots of big gold jewelry. An Everest of flesh double chins double elbows every joint doubled and dimpled with quivering fat when she hugs George hello he actually disappears for a while. Fatty is hospitable passing around some dope as they talk about work they're always working on their boat over there and you can usually pick up something to do. But two things make the boys nervous one is the presence of Fatty's enormous Great Dane Prawn with which she is said to copulate and it is true that it has a funny look on its face for a dog even though she's a nice lady. Oh well her friends always say to one another that's her trip. The dog trip. Nice Prawnie give momma a kiss. The other thing that makes them nervous is two bikers with eyes like pickled onions who keep staring at them. Paul remembers seeing them before.

It turns out the only thing Fatty has is some carpentry work for George so he tells Ron and Paul to go on back and he'll hitch home tonight. When George in fact doesn't come back that night they figure he's stayed over at the River Queen. Next morning George stumbles into the settlement head crusted with blood eyes discolored one arm hanging limp. Still spitting blood he tells them all he remembers about getting a ride that drops him off at the other side of the nearby woods about getting around three fourths of the way through the woods about suddenly noticing an enormous footprint in the path and then another about five feet on and a third after another five feet a sudden rushing in the dark underbrush and that's all he knows. He thinks it was a human footprint. He's missing one of his front teeth. The money Fatty paid him he still has. When they go back of course the footprints aren't there.

That night Paul hears the motorcycles cruising in the hills. Or is that something he makes up. Or is there some other noise or not so much a noise as the feeling of a noise that he calls motorcycles because he can't call it anything else.

*   *   *

Feather comes often now to Al's tent to make love. She still lives with Dave. Al and Dave are developing a kind of intimate camaraderie Dave dark and bony Al blond and thick. The three of them together are quite charming. Sly jocular arm in arm. Generating a lot of energy. Just being around them makes everybody horny.

Feather has a sudden urge to hurry on with her big tapestry. She's been working on designs ever since the beginning of the settlement and now decides to start weaving even though nothing's been completely worked out. She sets up her loom in the area of the nearly completed house that will be her studio. The manycolored yarns are scattered in hanks about the loom. She's using ten different yarns for this piece and it's going to be enormous in fact she has no idea where it will end it's completely openended. This is because she feels completely openended due to her feverish sexual relations with Al and Dave. How does it feel to be making love with two people? It feels feverishly pleasant but a little unreal that is in her calmer moments Feather feels that it can't last though in other moments she wishes that it would. Well maybe it will after all in an eccentric time who can say what aberration or mutation will suddenly become the livable norm. All these feelings and the need to make them coherent not to mention the sudden access of erotic energy are behind Feather's impulse to plunge ahead with her tapestry. She has all these feelings in her body and all these ideas about them in her head and she wants to bring the two together in the nonobjective patterns of her weaving but as the tapestry begins to take shape yarn after yarn she finds that the actual work gives her a tremendous pain in the neck. Of course it gives her a pain in the neck the neck is what's in between the head and the body.

Dave feels so changed by his new relation with Feather that he too changes his name. His new name is Goose. It has to do with this new feeling of risk he has in trusting Feather with Al so much. It's like he's really sticking his neck out but the more it sticks out the further he flies. What's so new to Goose is that oddly he's never had so much confidence in a woman before nor such sweetness in a relation with a man. When the guys kid him about his new name he barely notices he feels so nice.

*   *   *

George comes running out of the woods saying he's seen another footprint like the ones he saw before he got slugged but when they go back with him to see it it isn't there. Very strange.

Every now and then somebody in the area sees something black and huge sliding through the air. Something way up perfectly still sliding through the air black and so big it's impossible that it's alive yet it is. The ancient Condors live in the mountains to the east the biggest birds in the world bigger than their South American brothers there are possibly fifty of them left in these mountains and on the earth. Someone who has just seen one of these birds will grab you with pale face and glowing eyes without knowing exactly what he wants to say so what he says is I saw a Condor. What he really wants to say is something like I just saw a vision of universal death and eternal life but of course he doesn't believe in those things as tangible realities. If he doesn't know about Condors and the apparition came at dusk with the light not so good he might make something up to relieve himself Jeez I just saw this big damn thing floating through the sky it looked like a man with wings only bigger some kind of flying giant. There are wonders here. The brown snowpeaked mountains ancient empty shimmering with dreams through blankets of heathaze. Shapes materialize out of the misty pines in the morning and evening and at night with the surf throbbing and the breeze in the pines it's hard to distinguish what you hear from what you make up. The way Paul makes up motorcycles at night if in fact he's making that up. He feels a need to make things up to fill the emptiness to fill it with themselves their dreams and their nightmares the fantastic shape of their house.

For a long time Joan wanted to have a baby but she doesn't any more. Ralph and Joan are the only couple in the settlement who are legally married. She still has the same feeling of love for Ralph as always but lately she has a lot of other feelings. She feels she wants to do her work she wants to give her time to her work not to a baby and she doesn't want to give a baby her body or her whole attention or her independence. She feels the strength of the physical bond with her husband the sheer physical bond of his touch and the touch of his body in bed every night but she knows it's a bond she's going to break. She doesn't think about it and she hasn't thought about it but it's something that she knows. Just the way she knows without thinking about it that since moving to the country her capacities have in some way increased that she's capable of things she wouldn't even have thought about before that she has new energies at her disposal not so much a new feeling of this or that as that she simply feels more. And needs more to meet what she feels. For one thing she finds she has time for everything takes an interest in everything going on around her and gets an awful lot done so that when she thinks back on her day she wonders how she had time for all she did. It's not a matter of efficiency as when she worked in an office but a kind of absorption in everything around her. And she works better than she ever has before wherever she goes she finds materials for her mirrors and constructions odds and ends of wood rusty metal bits of glass stones broken shells things of no value that she immediately puts to use in her pieces. This is why when Paul comes on her making a pie of apples picked from their trees he finds her crying. What's wrong?

Nothing it's just that I haven't thought of making this for years. So?

It's the only recipe my mother taught me. Don't you think it's pathetic how little your parents can teach you? An immense sky watery grey. On the horizon a mountainous black thunderhead spits lightning at the wheatfields. The house is painted white. The first floor is hidden beneath the surface of the wheat but the second story and peaked roof the silo can be seen from fifty miles away. The father comes in big heavyfisted too tired to speak no words to say what he feels too numb to feel very much all this in Paul's head. Did you live on a farm he asks.

Yes is suddenly all she feels like saying about it.

Ralph is driving down the highway in The Log Cabin thinking about potatoes when he sees someone wearing the intergalactic embroidery of The Planet Krypton hitching on the shoulder. The Log Cabin is what they call their truck since Al and Goose rebuilt it to look like a rolling lob cabin including a chimney connected to the stove they use for cooking when they're away from the settlement. Besides the kitchen there's a family room and a bunk room in the attic so anyway Ralph pulls over and picks her up it's Cassiopeia whom he recognizes because Paul brought her to the settlement once. Cassiopeia looks kind of beat and depressed. Where've you been to Ralph asks her. Over at The River Queen she says.

What do you want with The River Queen Ralph doesn't dig The
River Queen people much. They're too watery for him too fluxy
maybe it's because Ralph is an agronomist or used to be now he does
the vegetable garden and the fruit trees. Besides that they're okay
with him except he thinks a lot of them are sex creeps and they tend
to make him feel a little creepy. Like the way conversation turns
indifferent and flat once they figure you don't want to get it on with
them one way or another. And then he doesn't put down astrology
Fatty is a ninth degree black belt astrologer they don't wipe their
noses over there without consulting the stars and he's really kind of
fond of Fatty you can't not like Fatty he just gets weary of the refrain
What sign are you? What sign are you? If you really want to know I
ran away from Krypton says Cassiopeia. How come?

Because Altair and Betelgeuse had a fight over me.

You don't mean they're jealous.

No we don't get jealous I don't know where their heads are at.

So how come you're going back.

I don't know Fatty talked me into turning a trick. It made me
homesick.

Ralph goes back to thinking about potatoes. The reason Ralph is
thinking about potatoes is that potatoes make him feel calm. Together. Rooted. And now he finds Cassiopeia disturbing. Her presence to him is like water rising behind a dam. Or a boulder on the
edge of a cliff. An immense instability. Her slim body as she sits
loosely on the seat next to him emanates blue throbs of sexuality that
repel him and attract him while at the same time he feels her on the
verge of some kind of emotional flood that could sweep the ground
from under his feet. And Ralph is right when Cassiopeia goes into
high tide there's no stopping her no containing her no directing her
nothing to do but hold on or get swept away.

Evelyn doesn't want anything to do with it. Screw it. If Ron's
going to start with his comic shtick she's had it she's been there
before. Okay she has no sense of humor she doesn't want a sense of
humor. She's only a nurse she doesn't need a sense of humor. She
feels the whole bit is based on some kind of evasion and she thinks
it's loathsome. Already she feels Ron moving out of contact. Turning
hard. Besides she knows what it leads to for Ron after the Borscht
Circuit comes the sex trip if he's into a sex trip let him go over to The
River Queen not screw up her relations with Helen who she likes.

This is what Evelyn thinks but actually there's more to it than that. Evelyn sees everything in terms of Ron but that's only part of the picture. Ron is only venting what everybody feels everybody is off balance waves of irritation are sweeping through the settlement. The relation among Feather Goose and Tom Al has changed his name to Tom is making everybody horny and dissatisfied. There's been so much fucking going on around this place that nobody can get his work done any more and instead of satisfying them it just makes everybody hornier. A new beat a new rhythm is starting and nobody knows yet how they're going to answer it nobody knows what kind of music it will make.

Helen rides into the clearing on her stallion Lawrence. Helen makes money working as a part-time groom on neighboring ranches but that's not why she keeps a horse. Helen has a horse at the settlement because she's always had a horse and she works as a groom because she's always worked as a groom. Even during her brief marriage. Just as mailmen are now women so also brides are grooms she muses amused again with the local cowboys' reaction to her horning in on their work. Nothing like a horny cowboy for the old male cock and bull. They can't make up their minds whether to be nostalgic for the old wrangler or look to the possiblity of getting laid so they tend to lapse into dull shitkicking hostility. Well like anything else it solves some problems and raises others that's the way Helen thinks about it. With George it works out all right he and Helen meet like the king and queen of two different countries allied but completely independent. Though George can ride he isn't interested in the feel of a live animal between his legs George rides the most powerful bike they build the new Mitsubishi 1300 souped up chopped down and all set to go to town. George is fascinated with the power of machines and that's all right with Helen who thinks that women are far more tuned in to animals anyway. She gets down in front of The Monster and hitches Lawrence to one of Joan's metal sculptures Ron is helping Tom and Goose finish up the plumbing. I think she's just about ready to take us in says Ron gesturing at The Monster.

I think of it as he.

Shehe then but I feel like we're about to move in to a furnished womb speaking of wombs. He puts his arm around her Ron likes to kid her this way she assumes it's kidding Helen doesn't understand

Ron at all but she likes him. How about coming out into the woods with me.

You know I can't do that Ron this is my family Helen is an orphan and it's true that she thinks of the settlement as her family. You're my brother.

What about incest.

I've tried that.

How is it.

It's nice but it leads to complications.

Ron wants to know more but he can tell that Helen is in her egg. He can tell by the absorbed expression on her face and the way her eyes seem to look out at nothing. Going Into the Egg is what they do to solve the problem of privacy in the settlement with a lot of people living in close contact. Imagine you're surrounded by a large transparent egg imagine it with great intensity and if you imagine it hard enough it becomes real. Try it it works.

They decide to have a ritual basketball game maybe that'll clear the air. How is a ritual basketball game different from a regular basketball game it isn't. It's just that they decide to call a basketball game a ritual basketball game when they feel they need one and that in fact makes it different. The men decide to call one when they feel there's something to be cleared up among them even though they don't know what it is especially when they don't know what it is. They go back to the half court they have behind the house and they choose sides by chance by coin toss. Then they just attend carefully to what happens in the game with a kind of split consciousness half in the game and half out of it like simultaneous instant replay then later on each man tries to put it back together in his head what they see with what they do. It makes for a rather intense and stately game the way people move when they're carrying too much to hold on to. The sides are Tom Goose and George against Ralph Ron and Paul. Twenty-four wins Tom passes in to George he drives it to the keyhole fakes a jump shot and passes off to Goose under the backboard instead of shooting he dribbles under the basket tosses the ball high to the opposite side of the court which is completely empty except for Tom who appears under the ball out of nowhere and takes it for an easy lay up. George passes the ball in from midcourt Ron steals it passes to Ralph who passes back to Ron who dribbles once takes a high arching two-handed set shot on the run that can't possibly hit it swishes right in to a scattering of stunned obscenities. George is easily both the tallest and the best player among them but he sees Tom and Goose working so well together he just passes off to them feinting and holding the ball over his head in the keyhole till he sees a possible play. As soon as Tom or Goose gets the ball they lock into psychic contact with one another as they triangulate on the basket with impossible blind passes and unpredictable fastbreaking rhythms they make three consecutive baskets this way before their opponents can figure out what's happened. Then Ron gets hold of the ball again and without hesitation scores with another long high running set to general amazement. Everybody's amazed but Ron Ron knows he's in to a run that's what he calls it. When Ron is in to a run he can't do anything wrong it's this extraordinary thing that happens to him sometimes it can happen when he's playing ball or poker or betting on horses or when he's performing or writing even in social situations he doesn't know what it is or why it comes but he knows when it's happening it's a kind of power. Ron knows it but the others don't not until he gets his hands on the ball and makes another one of those long sets almost without looking then Ralph and Paul start feeding him the ball every chance next time he gets it it's a long hook shot then a push shot from the corner then another long set he can't miss George starts charging him so he can't get off any more long ones he passed under him to Ralph who sends it back to Ron for an impossible left-handed hook shot next time it's a fastbreaking lay up meanwhile Tom and Goose still working beautifully together keep their side in the game. The score is eighteen-ten Ron gets off another hook shot while falling down George slaps himself on the forehead so hard he almost knocks himself out. Next time he gets the ball he fakes to Goose past Paul guarding him and goes up against Ron jumps for the lay up getting Ron in the chin with his shoulder Ron is down. They stop the play but Ron is only dazed next time George gets the ball he does the same thing getting Ron under the eye with his elbow missing the shot Ralph gets it off the board and dribbles to halfcourt the game goes on. But now there's this thing between Ron and George where Ron is angry and concentrating on George's drive in competition instead of being absorbed by the circle of the basket and it spoils his run when Ron makes a shot he knows it's not going to go in and it doesn't go in or if it goes in it rims around the basket and by some negative magic pops out again. George is getting every rebound off the backboard and now instead of making plays takes every shot himself hitting one after another and the score is even at twenty. But then something happens with Paul Paul is guarding George and he starts reading his mind sensing every move George makes an instant before he makes it so George starts feeding the ball to Tom and Goose but now they fumble around like a couple of clowns kicking the ball away or passing to Ron by mistake and nobody can make a basket. Everybody's taking shots they know won't hit making flashy pointless passes dribbling listlessly suddenly no one cares about the game there's no more fun in it. Ralph grabs the ball slams it against the ground starts peeling his clothes off yelling Time for a swim the others yelling stripping run after him down to the riverbank and naked leap madly into the water.

In the late afternoon after he's done with his work George often gets his board and goes surfing. If you ask George why he likes surfing so much he gets a thoughtful look on his face strokes his blond beard squints gazing into emptiness and after a while says Guess I just like it.

Here's what the women think about Feather having two lovers. Helen's seen everything she doesn't think about it. Besides she's done that Helen's done everything she knows how it is. Evelyn has her feet on the ground she thinks it's silly. She can't see it. Joan is curious. She disapproves. She wonders what it's like. She's jealous. It turns her on.

Here's one of Evelyn's exercises. First hold your finger in front of your nose and keep your eyes focussed on it. Then move your head from side to side keeping your eyes focussed on it. Then close your eyes while you move your head from side to side keeping your eyes focussed on it. Then take your finger away with your eyes closed while you move your head from side to side keeping your eyes focussed on it. Now open your eyes with the finger away while you move your head from side to side keeping your eyes focussed on it. Even though it isn't there. Or is it?

*   *   *

Hey says Ralph.

Hey is for horses says Joan.

Meaning what.

Meaning you know what my name is glares Joan. Ralph gazes back at her as if she were some kind of lunatic.

Don't look at me as if I'm a lunatic says Joan. I just wanted to know if you want to go for a walk says Ralph. It's plain to Ralph that Joan's got something against him lately but he can't find out what. At the same time she's become more and more demanding but he can't figure out what it is she wants. But this is precisely where Joan is at she feels like she has a grudge against Ralph but at bottom she doesn't really know for what nor does she know what it is she wants from him. Or even whether it's something he can give her. Ralph hopes that moving from the cramped sometimes irritating confines of the tent into the house will help the situation but it won't. One look at Joan's sullen face and he can't help withdrawing into silent anger himself. When Feather comes over to the front of their tent where they're sitting on the ground these are the vibes she picks up the dead look on Joan's face and the stubborn hunched posture of Ralph's shoulders. Ordinarily Ralph is shaped pretty much like a potato anyway but when he's feeling good he radiates a kind of earthy warmth and Joan can be as mobile as a poplar blowing in the wind. Without saying anything she sits down between them and grabs each by the hand. Joan and Ralph incapable of any flow of feeling between one another respond to Feather Ralph with a guarded greeting Joan with a smile. This is what Tom and Goose call Making the Sun Come Out she says.

How's the tapestry coming asks Ralph.

I think it's lovely but it's the hardest thing I've ever done. That's why I came over here I have just a terrible pain in my neck from working on it. Do you think one of you could rub it a little?

Sure says Joan Feather lies down her face in Joan's lap Joan suddenly all good nature massaging and smiling Here? More to the side? Ralph goes over to the vegetable garden.

Ron is weeding along the row of celery. How's it going asks Ralph.

Noi voh hunza schnecken.

What's that Chinese?

It's a patois. I learned it in Mexico. There's a small area on the coast of Yucatan in the jungle where an alien tribe speaks a language no one understands some people say they don't understand it themselves. These people are dark but not Indian no one knows where they came from or when they got there. The local natives call them Turks. They work as itinerant merchants and they run restaurants. They're also famous for being good dentists. The Indians hate them because they're rich but they're also afraid of them because of their language which is like a secret code and which they believe has magical properties. The Turks know this and play it to the hilt. It's entirely possible that they just use this gibberish to impress the Indians and that actually their only real language is Spanish they're real smart. When they start jabbering at one another you don't know whether they're laying a curse on you or saying let's cut his balls off or just please pass the salt. Anyway I picked up a few phrases when I was there. Vash znagel p'tooi.

What's that mean?

I don't know.

They work down the row together. In his previous life Ralph managed to crossbreed celery with endive producing that very white variety of celery with the extralarge heart that you're now just beginning to see in your supermarket. Ralph calls it potato celery. That's the kind of celery they grow in their garden. It's because of potato celery that Ralph is able to contribute a small income to the settlement. Do you know that celery originally comes from Iceland says Ralph.

Really.

Yeah. It was brought from there to Europe. By the Vikings.

The broadtail are running and George and Paul tack out of the cove on *The Wave. The Wave* is the white sloop George brought along from his previous life. The sea is calm except for a gentle swell sky blue light wind blowing off the coast. George handles the tiller and mainsheet Paul the jib outside the cove they set a course downwind and take their clothes off. Paul basks on the foredeck given up to the slapslush of the bow cutting water the bob and heel of the boat the radiance of the sun on his body. They're out after broadtail and the whales are migrating along the coast. If they see a spout George will drop everything to chase it it's the kind of thing George likes to do. Paul worries a little about getting too close to one of those monsters there are stories of small boats being wrecked.

George doesn't worry he never worries he just does Paul looks back at George his blue eyes sweeping the seascape. George has sky in his head thinks Paul.

It's not animals. Animals don't break windows and set fires. Or even slash tents. Every time it happens George looks carefully for footprints he never finds any. Once he goes off into the woods with his hunting rifle. Paul dreams motorcycle noise. Ralph is for building a fence but they can't decide.

They're ready to move into The Monster the way they do it is for a whole day everyone fasts and goes into his egg. The tents are down and everything is set for the potlatch which they hold that evening in the patio under the redwood around the fire. Everyone stays in his egg until they all join hands in the larger egg of the Big O. Ralph has a sense of imminence of new birth of a change beyond his doing. After all that's why you create a monster to do things you can't do. Isn't it? And then it does them to you. The omming and the energy go around when the egg is complete full of feeling and life then they break it. They break it with Evelyn's exercise Imagine a rose in front of your nose. Close your eyes keeping the rose in front of your nose. With your eyes closed see the color of the rose in front of your nose. With your eyes closed seeing its color smell the rose in front of your nose. Smelling the rose and seeing its color open your eyes and look at the rose in front of your nose. Take it in your left hand and pass it to your left taking in your right hand the one from the right holding the rose in front of your nose. Smell the smell and see the color of the rose in front of your nose. Smelling its smell and seeing its color make believe it isn't there the rose in front of your nose. Making believe it isn't there watch it disappear as you unimagine the rose in front of your nose. And now it isn't there what isn't there the rose in front of your nose.

To the accompaniment of Goose on the guitar Ron sings an interpretation of his song Famished crowbars rape the lute then they begin the ritual meal of venison stew baked squam wheat berry bread tomatoes cress and homemade peach icecream washed down with the sacral asparagus wine. And as they eat George begins to tell a story a story he knows from the local Indians some of them still live in the woods. It seems that in the time of the animals before men were created a god called Flows-with-the-streaming-clouds was lonely and wanted somebody to talk to. So he created animals who could talk and these animals were something like bears and something like men. They could talk but not through their mouths through their navels they used their mouths for other things like eating and fighting and reproduction. Also they couldn't talk about the kinds of things we talk about because their voices weren't connected with their brains they were connected with their bodies and instead of coming through the windpipe came through the intestines. So they could only talk about what they felt they couldn't talk about what they thought. It's not that they didn't have heads on their shoulders they did but they used them for other things besides thinking like seeing hearing smelling tasting and butting. What they didn't have was necks. But then they didn't need them because they didn't have any voice box. It's not as if they were stupid they weren't stupid just different. Now these Sasquatch as the Indians call them were very happy. Their words were growls squeaks farts gargles clicks and chuckles and they were always jabbering to one another. They were something like bears who have just learned how to play the piano. The only trouble was they couldn't learn how to talk to the gods and this made Flows-with-the-streaming-clouds very angry. So he sent the Condors after them and the Condors carried them off by their navels and shook them till their guts ripped and their heads were nearly torn from their bodies and when the Condors were through with them their voices came out their mouths and they were men. And that's why men have necks because after the Condors they needed something to keep their heads connected with their bodies. But though men were now able to learn the speech of the gods they always remembered the pain that gift caused them and they weren't happy. And so it turned out that the the gods didn't want to talk to them anyway because it was such a down. So Flows-with-the-steaming-clouds ended up as lonely as he was to begin with. And the Indians say there are still some Sasquatch left still hiding from the Condors and sometimes they come out at night but that they're very bitter after all that's happened.

Anthropologists consider this a very old myth that may actually represent an unknown stage in the evolution from animal to human that's why they like to dig around here. Some inconceivably subhuman but superanimal species preceding Pithecanthropus Erectus that might in fact have lived at the same time as the Condors which are very ancient. Some species intelligent enough to be free but too dumb to be unhappy.

The Missing Lunk says Ron.

There's an awful lot of energy flowing through the potlatch this time Ralph wonders if anybody else can feel it. Unstable energy roiling around making Ralph think of thunderclouds. Feather sitting between him and Joan catches both their hands and starts Making the Sun Come Out though it seems to come out mostly between her and Joan smiling at one another. Ralph starts thinking about potatoes. Ron gets up. Though this settlement was originally my idea as you know I've long since stopped being its creator he says. Instead we all invent it as we live it. And in very real ways it begins to invent us in return. And now as we move into this big poppamomma that we've made I feel a change of heart coming on.

For better or for worse asks Evelyn.

I don't know but a change. And I want to say that whatever happens from now on there isn't anybody here who I don't like I won't use the word love because it's too crapped up there isn't one of you motherfuckers or fathersuckers who I don't like a lot. And because I feel this change coming on in myself especially what I want to destroy in this potlatch is my name for a name that's more appropriate to the way I feel. And the way I feel is cloudy so from now on that's my name. Cloud. Thank you brothers and sisters.

And then everybody starts changing names. Evelyn changes to Eucalyptus because Cloud's changes make her feel heavy and left behind. Paul becomes Wind because he wants to change. Joan changes to Valley because she needs a mask. Helen becomes Dawn because she feels like a new kind of person. George changes to Lance and Ralph stays Ralph because he feels stubborn. Then Tom Goose and Feather change to Branch Bud and Blossom.

When Cassiopeia wanders into the settlement she can't find any signs of activity though it's well toward noon so she drifts on into The Monster. Half nude bodies are strewn on mats and mattresses on the floor on pieces of furniture in pairs and larger clumps. Under the redwood in the patio Valley and Blossom are hugging and kissing. Bud and Branch are off at the creek for a dip. Far out says Cassiopeia Valley jumps up.

That's cool says Cassiopeia. What's going on here.

We had a potlatch last night says Blossom.

That musta bin some potlatch.

What happened was we all became brothers and sisters. How are things at Krypton.

It's not Krypton any more they changed the name.

To what.

Golgotha they've all become jesus creeps. Last night Betelegeuse converted he was the last holdout. Him and me. We've all been fighting about it for weeks.

So where does that leave you.

Out.

Where will you go.

I was thinking of heading over to The River Queen.

You don't think you'll go back.

Krypton's had it man. It's a dead planet. Jesus kills.

Nobody can be very exact about the potlatch it's all that asparagus wine. Everyone remembers having a pile. A pile is when they all crawl together in a heap on the floor everybody hugging everybody else this is nothing new. What's new is this time everybody is naked and everybody is supposed to keep his eyes closed. After that everyone's version gets a little murky. A big pulsing pile of naked loving flesh everybody can agree on that. A lot of giggling. A lot of affection. Suddenly quiet and a serious mood. Then for some people it was sexy for some just affectionate a lot of people say it was all anonymous but who knows who really kept his eyes closed and who was peeking. Two people were holding my tits one was a girl says Dawn. I was hugging a naked man I can't get over that says Wind. I know I fucked somebody says Blossom. It's like being babies says Eucalyptus. It made me feel so happy says Bud. They try to reconstruct it but it's like trying to reconstruct a snowstorm. The wind was in the eucalyptus. A branch was growing in the valley. A lance nipped a blossom in the bud and rosy-fingered dawn burned through the clouds. And some time during the night a high wind swept through the valley and wandered sighing into the pines.

🔥 🔥 🔥

(untitled poem)

by LAURA PERSHIN

from THE LANSING STAR (Cosmic Information Agency)

nominated by Cosmic Information Agency

My grandfather died in a nursing home
where two new friends lay on beds beside him.
One only spoke in dirty words,
the other just smiled and nodded his head.

The three of them peed into tubes,
had bed sores on their asses
that smelled bad,
the same plastic water containers
and hands, a transparent blue,
lying cool next to steel bars of beds.

Once they were fishermen
on different docks
wore red wool hats
talked about tackle
shoulders damp from waves
that smacked the edges of piers.
They sliced eggs out of momma trout
tossing them into the lake.

Once they were fishermen
Once they were lovers
Fingers moving lightly
Over soft bodies.

They drank too much wine
on the sabbath.
Stuffed themselves with schmultz,
it hardened and cracked in their veins
like clay
but it tasted so good.

Once they took trains
women beside them big breasted skinny ankled
wide hipped for bearing nice jewish boys
who became lawyers married nice jewish girls
who watched their hearts begin to fail
sudden loss of muscular control
mouth twisting too much to one side
never returning to its place on the face.

One only said the words "shit hell damn ass bitch
oi vey"
The other never spoke.
My grandfather talked.
Something about the window turning black
Crashing into the room at night.

SILENCE

by MICHAEL HOGAN

from LETTERS FOR MY SON (Unicorn Press)

nominated by Unicorn Press

We walked by there several times
never noticing the grass turning brown
or the yellowing lace curtains;
never hearing her fingernails
rattling against a window pane.
She must have dried her clothes
in the upstairs bathroom
because we never heard the snap
of sheets in the autumn wind.
The house was always quiet
and the ambulance
rolled up without a sound.

LATE TRACK

by JANE BAILEY

from MONTANA GOTHIC

nominated by Hugh Fox

His art rarely surfaced,
maybe a phrase now and then
in letters.
Sly, he sank behind
an intricate
network of beer cans, bad jokes.
A bit sick.
In good spirits, so to speak.
—No need for a doctor.
  Certainly
  no clean mint green
  hospital.
Coughed up his red life
at home.
In triumph.
His ashes, the bits of bone
his wife and children cast
into the Missouri,
as he directed.
Some, he felt,
might reach the sea.

FUNERAL

by CLARENCE MAJOR

from THE SYNCOPATED CAKEWALK (Barlenmir House)

nominated by Barlenmir House

American Airlines to Chicago. Mae is here grinning,
the same cheeks I grew up touching. And her cool,
beautiful movements. The moving staircase and,
"Man, whata you got in *that bag?*"

And Nebraska and Missouri. Maybe next we go
to Topeka or down to Mexicali and San Diego.

But my stepfather dies. And they have his face
propped up in the casket. Powdered,
he is neatly tucked in a suit.
There is this quiet hysterical laughter we all share.

Later, the young folks from everywhere, Kentucky,
Tennessee, South Carolina, Virginia, gather in
the front, and the old, from Mississippi,
North Carolina, Oklahoma, Arkansas, sip hard liquor
in the kitchen.

Mother has fried chicken and mashed potatoes
spread out. And a dude is talking about Wichita Falls
last summer, some fifty year old white chick
who fell in love with him. *Daddy daddy.*

Now morning again. Here we are in Alabama
watching the body descend into the earth
at a grave site near a bright park. Mother's face
does not know what expression it should hold.

As we drive back I hold the airline tickets and Mae.

BLACK MONEY

by TESS GALLAGHER

from STEPPING OUTSIDE (The Penumbra Press)

nominated by Paul Engle

His lungs heaving all day in a sulphur mist,
then dusk, the lunch pail torn from him
before he reaches the house, his children
a cloud of swallows about him.
At the stove in the tumbled rooms, the wife,
her back the wall he fights most, and she
with no weapon but silence
and to keep him from the bed.

In their sleep the mill hums and turns
at the edge of water. Blue smoke
swells the night and they drift
from the graves they have made for each other,
float out from the open-mouthed sleep
of their children, past banks and businesses,
the used car lots, liquor store, the swings in the park.

The mill burns on, now a burst of cinders,
now whistles screaming down the bay, saws jagged
in half light. Then like a whip
the sun across the bed, windows high with mountains
and the sleepers fallen to pillows
as gulls fall, tilting
against their shadows on the log booms.
Again the trucks shudder the wood framed houses
passing to the mill. My father
snorts, splashes in the bathroom,
throws open our doors to cowboy music

on the radio, hearts are cheating,
somebody is alone, there's blood in Tulsa.
Out the back yard the night-shift men rattle
the gravel in the alley going home.
My father fits goggles to his head.

From his pocket he takes anything metal,
the pearl-handled jack knife, a ring of keys,
and for us, black money shoveled
from the sulphur pyramids heaped in the distance
like yellow gold. Coffee bottle tucked in his armpit
he swaggers past the chicken coop,
a pack of cards at his breast.
In a fan of light beyond him
the Kino Maru pulls out for Seattle,
some black star climbing
the deep globe of his eye.

STEELMILL BLUES

by STEVE PACKARD

from LIBERATION

nominated by LIBERATION

I had worked off and on in factories all my life, but never as a radical organizer. Even as I began to contemplate the possibility, I doubted whether the left and I knew what kind of leadership to offer.

But in the cold Chicago February of 1971, I was in bad political shape for making choices. Our emotional-total-revolutionary-collective had been clobbered by police pressure, factional fights, sex conflict, purges, right-wing raids on our offices, left-wing raids too, and at last the group disintegrated. That shock was followed briefly, mercifully briefly, by an attempt to forge a half-dozen of us into some kind of urban guerrilla cell. The most extreme among us

*turned out to be an agent. I left him with his bombing plans—feeling
naked and wrong with no collective around me—but with my dedi-
cation intact.*

*It was about this time I felt the Marxist-Leninist arguments win-
ning out inside me. A leader of what I had always called a "sect
group" began visiting me, recruiting me. Matt and I spent hours
debating whether the Dictatorship of the Proletariat really would
fulfill my ideals. The fact that I was broke—and those working-
class-organizing-jobs had company paychecks attached—finally
won me over. What follows are some thoughts and journal notes
about the next six months.*

Matt calls. Bad connection. But he's ecstatic and using every
available ounce of movement-heavy charm to make my mind up for
me—fast. There's a place in Gary where he and I and another guy
can all be hired if we go tomorrow.

"Gary?" I say. "Isn't that a long ways off?"

"Sure it is!" he jumps aggressively back at me through the buzzing
clicking phone. "It'll take more than an hour, maybe an hour and a
half each way. But it's the perfect organizer's job. And really, how far
is it? Some middle-class executive would go that far for a little
money."

I really need a job. And a new direction. Basically my reaction is:
thrilled.

Early next morning Matt and John pick me up in an old Chevy.
Matt's eyes are shining and excited, like this job is going to be one of
life's great blessings, the pure smile of a kid's birthday party, or a
fisherman setting first boot into the trout stream on his one-week
vacation.

As soon as the first round of joking and small talk breaks, I ask
Matt where he's taking us. He wouldn't tell me yesterday because
the phones are tapped and it would be too easy for the secret
listeners to warn capitalism that we are coming. (Members of the
collective have been fired recently following visits to their com-
panies by F.B.I. agents.) After many mysterious hints, Matt finally
pauses meaningfully and then says, "Gary Works!"

Well. I don't know what "Gary Works" is. I would like to ask him,
but I would clearly be telling him I am some total idiot. So I must
carry on the conversation and listen for clues. Slowly I figure out we

are going to the Gary Works of United States Steel Corporation, the biggest steel plant in the country.

Matt says the Gary Works is a beautiful place to be, anytime. About half the workers are black, the union is worthless, and the basic wage is at least a third less than in most other basic industry. Basic industry is the place to be, and steel is the best of it.

Matt gives us his analysis of the situation we're getting into. "Now in this plant, they have a strike coming up. They'll hire anything white that's strong enough to walk in the door. Most predictions are that the strike is going to be a long one, which means a heightened political situation between now and August (when the contract runs out) and a potentially explosive situation during the strike." You two guys are going to be surprised when you go to work in the mill," he continues. "You'll see that Negroes do have the hardest and dirtiest jobs. But they have a tremendous amount of power, because the mill stops without them. And without steel the whole country stops. And the Negroes know it."

Matt invented the term "white skin privilege" and has been pushing the idea of "black leadership" for years, so his use of the word "Negro" obviously signals some change in strategy. I ask, "Do blacks play a leading role in the rank-and-file caucuses that fight the unions?"

Matt's smile fades. "Look Steve," he says, "we are going to have to give you some political education. I think that there's a lot in the collective's politics that you could learn from. We've come a long ways since the old New-Left. I don't use the word 'black' anymore. On the job, most of the Negroes, including the most responsible and conscious ones, call themselves 'Negroes.' It's only the extreme and undisciplined types who have a big thing about calling themselves 'black'—them, and of course, all the white radicals.

"And we have to have a real talk about rank-and-file caucuses too. They're not the way to organize anything. Let me just say that 'rank-and-file caucuses' are an illusion. They always say they are fighting the union. But I. W. Able's bunch was a rank-and-file caucus before he got to be president of the steelworkers. He did what he had to do to make a name for himself. Now he's in, and he hasn't made a damn difference. Even if Able had the purest heart in the world, it wouldn't mean a damn, because it's the whole union System that's wrong. We have to organize workers' power right on the shop floor. Wildcats, job actions, whatever. No contracts. No white-shirted men in offices. It's the workers who are going to have to overthrow the place and run it."

As we drive through the gates of U.S. Steel, armed guards direct us from the little pill boxes they inhabit. We and about forty other applicants are sent to the reception center, where we watch a U.S. Steel propaganda film, and listen to a lecture about hard work and how all the country's problems are because workers are lazy. All we have to do is to get through this stuff without throwing up, and they hire practically everyone.

When you get a new job, so many things are happening at the same time that it makes you feel a little stoned. You manage to steer your way through, but for a while you're only vaguely in touch with what's passing by.

I work in Merchant Mills. A big warehouse building, only a couple of blocks wide. But it's so long that if you stand in the middle you can't see halfway through the gloom to either end. There are big doors all around it, so semi-trucks and even trains can pull in and out to take away our steel.

On the long east side of the place are the twelve "mills," sticking out from the main building like the teeth of a comb. Each one of these long skinny rolling mills is the length of a football field. Red-hot ribbons of steel come snaking down them. By the time the ribbons reach us they usually turn gray again, but they are still hot enough to cook your lunch on. Our job is to cut them into the right lengths. To test and inspect them for special uses. To straighten or flatten them in enormous noisy machines. To tie piles of them with steel wires, or bind them with metal bands.

Every morning, I get to Gary about fifteen minutes before work. The whole plant is surrounded by a metal fence, like a penitentiary. I go through the gate with the crowd, guards look at my I.D. card and make sure I match my picture, then they give me an IBM card. I write my name and company number on the top of it.

I go to the wash-house and change into my filthy clothes. After one day, my clothes are the kind of dirty that lets them stand up by themselves. I put on my regulation metatarsal shoes that have plates over the top so it's harder to break your foot. I put on a couple of sweatshirts and my army coat.

On my way over to the Merchant Mills, I gather the long hair off my shoulders, twist it around a few times, and trap it under my hard-hat where it stays all day. My hair is so long that not a bit falls back out. Finally come my safety glasses with little wire screens that fold back against my temples; they are specially constructed with adjustable rims that curl around your ears and hurt in every possible position.

The foreman's name is Chuck. He looks us over, who's here today and who's not. Then he mentally figures everyone's seniority against the jobs that need doing. He makes notes on his clipboard, and reads off the jobs. "Packard, Quintana, Lewis, Pritchet: coil trimmer!" We give him our IBM cards and he makes a note on each, since different jobs get different pay. Most of the jobs I get are rated $2.81 per hour for day shift and $2.89 at night.

As each of us hands him our IBM card, the foreman reads aloud the top "safety check" card on his desk, and then puts it on the bottom of the pile. It's like the Community Chest pile in a Monopoly game: "Watch for slippery grease spots on Floor" . . . "Wear your hard-hat at all times."

For the first two weeks, I ride to work with Matt. In the mornings he's usually in a quiet mood, and on the way home we get into fights. John says with disgust that all the guys he works with hate him; they all seem to be racists and right-wingers. I think he just talks leftist jargon at them, and that's what they hate. But when I try to rap about how I'm talking common sense to everyone and how fast I'm making friends and how much everyone seems ready to agree when you come on plain and friendly, Matt turns up the radio.

Then he jumps on me. "You think you're getting somewhere, Steve, but you're wasting your time on these hippies." I've told him about my co-worker on the coil-trimmer who reads Herman Hesse. And the mill-wright who wants to send his kid to a Free School. And Jose who reads Che Guevara and who resisted the draft. "These guys won't stick around," he says. "It's the Negroes and older workers—the guys who are going to be here for their life—that have a real sense of responsibility for this place."

I try to throw in a good word for Youth Culture. Matt comes back with: "If I ran Chicago, the first thing I'd do is wipe out Lincoln Park and turn it back into a neighborhood." (Lincoln Park is the half-hippie area where I live.) The car rolls along in silence, not even radio-noise can fill it up.

We're riding north on 94. It's March, and today a little flock of goldeneyes are swimming amid beer cans and tires on what remains of Wolf Lake. These hostile chills descend on me and Matt pretty often. We try to wait them out.

Finally I try to pick it up again: "How are *you* talking to people, Matt?" He's ready for another try too. "Speed-up seems to be the issue in my part of the mill," he says with full determined sparkle back.

"Really? I've been more bored than tired," I say.

Matt is driving. But he lets the car go blind long enough to give me a powerful and hard look. "You're going to have to work up more proletarian spirit than that, my friend. Speed-up is as big a part of the class struggle as anything you can name. Always has been, always will be."

I try an appeal to the facts—although with no real confidence. "Didn't you tell me yesterday that the guys you work with spend hours fishing for perch in the creek beside their furnace? And that they have a whole library of dirty books they sit around and read? You said that they even cook up a lazy barbecue at lunch every day. Isn't that right?"

He sighs, then gives it a last try. "Steve, do the men where you are complain about working too hard?"

"Of course they do. But I get to feel it's more like a ritual. I mean, they don't really objectively work so damn much."

"Right! They complain about it! They complain because they're oppressed! See if you can't listen a tiny bit to what some plain workers are trying to tell you, Steve. If they complain about it, you can organize them around it!"

Matt's wondering why he's cursed with a collective of such drips. I don't say anything.

So he does. "You understand that?!" Threateningly.

"No, I don't think I do." Obstinately. Defensively.

In the third week, we go on different shifts, and I have to find another ride. Through asking around and putting notes on cars in the parking lot, I find enough people so that I've got a ride for any shift, and I never ride with Matt again.

Forty years ago, workers fought to unionize the steel mills. Here in Gary there is a proud powerful history, where the army was called out many times to suppress militant workers and to prevent the establishment of a union. But people continued the fight, and the union was finally established.

Or at least that's what I read in radical history books.

No one from the union has ever talked to me. I've never been issued a "union card." (What would I do with it if I had one?) I have never seen a sign, a poster, a leaflet, or an announcement passed out or posted up, by the union. People don't discuss the union. I wonder, does it have meetings? Do they vote? Is there a union hall? And the heroism and bloodshed, the years of hard organizing work, what were they for?

I had expected the union to be on the scene. I thought they'd be racist and conservative, and we would have to struggle against them. I didn't expect that there would just be no union. I ask people if they know who our grievance man is, and almost nobody does. The union takes a few bucks out of my paycheck. I can see it listed over by the taxes and the F.I.C.A. and all the other paycheck leaks. That's my only evidence it still exists.

Is this mill just unorganized chaos, basically a scene of individual workers against the company? Now I've been here awhile, and I'm slowly learning. Gary Works is a very complex organism, thousands of people and machines making up a living, changing thing. It's not organized too clearly by the company, not organized by the union at all. But very organized, just the same. I got my first sense of it from this story, told by my friend Spider, a black craneman who I often ride to work with.

Most of the cranemen are black. Although it's a pretty good job, there's no way you can 'move up' from a crane job to a softer one, which is what most white guys aim for. The blacks know they don't have a chance at the no-work-at-all jobs, so the older, smarter men go after the crane jobs.

One day, a white craneman was assigned to a good crane that should have been given to a certain black. The foreman made some little excuse to explain it, but basically, he was doing a favor for a white friend, and at the same time showing everyone who's boss. This foreman was new or he wouldn't have been so foolish.

Black cranemen decided to sabotage production until this bullshit was straightened out. They had mild support from most white cranemen, who also thought the foreman was wrong.

Nothing can operate long without the cranes bringing and taking steel, and the blacks quickly stopped the whole mill. They kept the cranes in lowest gear and worked in super-slow-motion. Foremen soon began coming out of their offices, looking around, rubbing their eyes in disbelief. It was as if the whole building had popped LSD—or the air had turned into some thick jelly: everything was moving at one-tenth normal speed.

Down below, the steel was piling up, and men were stopping work. Foremen were yelling and cranemen were explaining all the complex problems their machines had suddenly developed. Calls were coming in from the main office in Pittsburgh, where the computer showed that our statistics had all stopped. So of course the company quickly called the union.

Union sharpies swooped down magically from nowhere. "Men. Men. Come on now. What is the problem? Let's go through the channels on this thing. Right? Submit a grievance. What you're doing is an illegal strike!" But everyone knew that grievances take months, and that the day this foreman had to be wised up was today.

After a couple of hours the company backed down. Some higher-level bosses announced that the foreman had "made a mistake." As soon as they switched around the white and black cranemen, the slowness thawed right out and the mill began to hum again at its normal rate. According to the workers' rules. Big wildcats like that are less common than small, partial ones. The most used weapon is sabotage. Various kinds of sabotage—from the wholesale wrecking of machines to trickier, more selective actions—are going on every day. I'm on many jobs where the foreman tries to hustle us too much or insists that we do a job in some dangerous or unpleasant way, and somebody breaks a machine. Nothing can ever be proved—only the workers know just what combination of speed, pressure, change of pace, angle of feed, is sufficient to make some dirty old monster start to shake and throw sparks and smoke to a crunching halt. How fast the millwright fixes it depends on what vibrations he feels from the waiting men. And of course the foreman swears, and fumes, and groans, but he can't really do anything. If he is not overly dumb, he learns, after a break-down or two, the limits beyond which he cannot go.

The men don't usually talk about this stuff; communication is carried out through undercurrents and understandings. But everyone in the mill agrees that the workers are right, which is why there's nothing the boss can do. We know the ins and outs of the machines enough to use them, undetected, against the boss, whenever necessary.

The only way a foreman can survive—the only way he can get a fair amount of work done in his zone—is to understand this communication-by-sabotage. It is the workers' police and court of law, by which we struggle to enforce our code of what's right and fair. It is part of a system laboriously built up over the decades.

Our collective's strategy is that we should each become part of the direct action leadership in the mill. Then we can find ways to sharpen and intensify this struggle.

I feel like I'm doing well, so far. I've already played good roles in a number of little actions, and have growing mutual respect and good feelings with guys in all parts of our mill. This process is a tricky one though, because the place is strongly divided up into minority groups. At line-up every morning all the workers are either black, or Latin, or hillbilly, or old ethnic European, or young white hippy-type. I'm hippy-type.

Nearly every foreman is "middle-American" white. Other older whites have skilled jobs and don't line up with our "labor gang." The workers most mistrusted by the other minorities are hillbillies and hippies—because we occasionally are transformed into bosses.

Yesterday, Hendrickson, one of the foreman's sidekicks and henchmen, drew me aside and gave me a little pep talk about a new job he wants me to learn: the job of "inspector."

Hendrickson explains that "it's a real smart job to learn, Steve, and I think you can do it. The work's not hard. You don't have much time (seniority), that's true. But people here like you; I don't think anyone will complain. And it's a good way for you to get started out of this labor gang." What he means is that young whites should want to get ahead, and this inspector's job is a first step toward having my head fitted for a foreman's blue hat.

Today Chuck, the foreman, sends my friend Chico and me to the inspection tables, together. Hendrickson takes me aside again and says, "Look Steve, here's your clipboard, and I'm going to show you how to do this job. Give it your best, son, O.K.? We really could use another inspector. Most of these guys, you know . . ." He looks around to see that no one is listening and then says, "Most of these guys, . . .fucking Puerto Rican and the colored . . . don't even know how to read and write."

The picture becomes even clearer. Hendrickson shows me a couple of simple-minded things to do, with a micrometer, a pencil,

and that clipboard. Then he says, "Sanchez here is your helper."
That's my friend Chico, who is scowling. "Your job, Packard, is to
tell him when to move steel for you. Have him spread out each
bundle of rods on this bed. Then you check them, and have Sanchez
pull them down into that trough and wire them up again. You
inspect. That's all. You don't do this other work. Understand?"

Once or twice the thought flashes through my mind, why not
become an inspector? Get a little more pay, maybe even more
freedom to organize. (In his last job, Matt organized from the
privileged position of a tool-and-die-maker, and did well.)

But this ambitious thought doesn't trouble me for long. I decide to
do the job badly, so I won't be asked to do it again, and Chico is a big
help in this. He won't work.

I say, "What a drag. I can't dig this inspecting bullshit. But I've
got to finish out the day at it. Let's work slow." Chico doesn't go for
this line. No matter what I do or say, I am neck deep in hostility.
Chico doesn't lift a finger. He says, "I don't think you make a good
inspector, hippy." The other two Spanish guys always call me hippy,
but Chico never has before.

He moves slowly, uncooperative, messes things up on purpose.
Most of the time he's in the wash house or canteen or sitting down
half asleep. He teases me, wants me to break down and order him to
work. Chico was my friend, but now he's baiting me—waiting,
almost wanting me to use that angry pissed-off commanding voice. I
think that if I say, "For Christ sakes, Chico, we got to do some work
today! Let's go!" he'll start to work, and be my enemy forever.

Twice they catch me doing the job Chico is supposed to do. "Oh!
Packard. I guess you didn't understand. You don't move the steel,
you have your helper do that. You inspect, all right? Have Sanchez
do the rest." Sure.

I don't push Chico. We get almost nothing done, and Chuck is
freaked. The next day he puts me back on inspecting with a new
helper, a black man about forty years old. For some reason this guy
thinks he's supposed to work hard. Has he just arrived from the
South? I can't talk to him very well.

We do five or six times as much steel as I did with Chico, but I save
my skin by rejecting two thirds of the steel I inspect. The reject pile
grows bigger than I've ever seen it. Chuck comes, furious. He's with
the chief inspector, who is friendly and fatherly. The chief looks over
my steel and admits that it doesn't quite come up to the specifica-

tions in the book, but sort of winks and says that we might stretch the limits just a bit and go ahead and accept most of this stuff.

I say thanks. And continue rejecting two out of three loads. I think of the various bombshells or defoliation sprayers this steel might be destined to make. I think about how much I hate being Mr. Inspector. The cranes hoist load after shiny load back to the scrap cars.

Days come and days go. I never get an upwardly mobile job again.

One of my favorite guys to work with is Billy. Billy will be a skilled worker one day, but he's in no hurry. He's generous, hates privilege, learned a lot of politics in Vietnam, always sides with the minorities against the foreman.

To watch him work is like watching a performance. He's a master. Billy runs his gray hulking band-leveler like he's playing the violin. He knows every possible subtle adjustment, combination of lubricants, point of strain, and everything else necessary to play this massive machine like no one else alive.

He knows what effects what, in every combination (and of course how to use any and all elements to cripple it any day the foreman gets on his case).

Another area of his brilliance is the contraptions he invents out of coke cans, scrap wood, cardboard, and whatever. Once he rigged up a plastic milk carton and a long nail to do 95% of the job I was assigned that day (removed when foremen lurked about, of course). He'd tell you he does these tricks to make his work easier, but he clearly does them for the sheer joy and challenge.

Billy doesn't produce much steel. He quickly admits he could get out two or three or more times as much with little sweat. But every experienced man who works this machine turns out the same small amount. It's part of our speed-up war with the company, and it would betray the other workers if you did more.

So my friend uses his energy to teach new people (me), or to build a fire for the crew on the next shift, to perform, and to clean his machine with thorough tenderness, like it was a prized sports car, or a precious baby, for a good hour at the end of every day.

I would like to understand Billy. He talks reluctantly about his bored television-watching marriage. Less reluctantly about the nutty things he spends his money on. And then there are virtual hymns of devotion to the Lake Michigan trout and to his boat. She's the only thing in his life he really speaks of fondly, that boat, and he worked a hell of a lot of overtime to get her. (Though now Billy works overtime to get a bigger one.) I have a feeling, from Billy, and from many people here, that the things they buy with their money are often more excuses to spend, than real needs or wants. I think Billy doesn't know what to do with himself. I think he spends money so he'll have to work. I begin to toy with a new slogan: "Work is the opiate of the people."

It's lucky I feel some sense of mission in this mill. Without it I'd go nuts. A lot of young guys are doped on regular chemical opiates. I might have been too.

But the middle-agers and the older guys make me even sadder. Scattered here and there in the gloom are heavy-steel hole-filled garbage-cans packed with burning coal to provide a little heat. For some reason they're called salamanders. Circles of older guys sit on kegs and benches around the salamanders for three or four hours a day. Just sit there with their lights out. It's like they're watching TV, but with no TV.

The foreman can't make you work. They've given up trying, but they won't let you do anything else. You can't play music, you can't fool around, if they catch you reading you get yelled at. Sometimes I use my time to write all these ideas down, and I always write "Dear Carol," at the top of the page so people won't ask questions. But I can't let a foreman catch me writing. The only thing they let you do here is sit, like a vegetable.

Once a foreman came by a salamander where seven or eight of us were sitting around, one of us snoozing. The foreman kicked the guy's foot, shook him and said, "What's this?! A sleep-in?! Look a little bit alive here!!" So the guy opened his eyes and sat up straight. He looked a little bit alive. The foreman was satisfied, and didn't say anything about anyone getting back to work.

One day toward the tail end of winter, I finish my job in an hour, and go walking through the mill yards, through U.S. Steel's Forbidden City, down to the shore of Lake Michigan. I walk through enormous railroad yards, wide weedy prairies struck with room-sized blocks of black rusting solid steel. It seems like the surface of a strange planet, or the burial ground of an ancient civilization. On my walk I stop to watch the work in the wheel mill (where train wheels are made) and at the plate mill. As I watch the technology and poetry and spectacle of these places, I think of how my spirit would glow with pride at this magnificent human accomplishment if it was all being done for the good.

At the cold water's edge the winds have piled up crude icebergs bigger than the steel block behind me. Crashing waves, white and grey and winter blue-black, bright sun, purple sky with intense red-orange clouds from the mill's smokestacks. The water is filthy, and the icebergs are speckled with oil and cans and boxes and crap, but if you squint your eyes, they are towering white and beautiful. I get back to Merchant Mills two and a half hours after I left. No one has missed me. I'm bored.

The next day I begin my time-and-motion study, a little bit of "social science" like I learned in college. I walk up and down the aisles noting on a piece of paper who's doing what, being careful that no one sees me and decides I'm a company spy.

In one half-hour I collect the following data:

Men apparently working:	80
Men walking around (some may have been doing a job, but most were just killing time like me):	29
Men sitting around salamanders:	64
Men standing around doing nothing:	53
Men dancing:	1

Over half are wasting their time away. I guess I knew it would be this bad, but it's creepy, and a crime. I have no crocodile tears about how the war effort isn't getting enough steel, but these numbers are about the emptiness of people's lives.

I make this survey again, picking times when it is most likely that people will be working if they ever work. The last day I do this I have plenty of time, because my job for eight hours is to sweep a little dirt and steel filings and cigarette packages out of an area the size of a living room. Here's the total:

People working:	366
People doing nothing:	600

In other words, at the peak working times, about two thirds of *everybody* would be loafing at any given moment.

Someone's been writing chalk slogans on the wall of the wash-house. "Keep the faith, baby" . . . "Work ½ out of eight hours and you will KEEP THE FAITH" . . . "Be a soul man, not a Co. man" . . . "Work ½ out of eight hours." They are all signed by "Cadillac Louis." There's a general feeling among all but the hillbilly workers that it's right to sluff off. And there is something revolutionary about the workers controlling the pace of their work this way.

But there is something deadening and enslaving about it too. I look around at the circles of soot-black hulking shapes sitting joyless, motionless, around the salamanders. They are like the molted skins of insects left by the shore of a pond. It seems like their souls have left them.

What a strange atmosphere the coming strike makes! No one talks about it, no concern or excitement. We have been producing huge stockpiles of steel so that our strike won't hurt the company, even if we stay out for months. Everyone knows, and no one cares.

Still, a strike mentality has set in. Energy gets lower and lower as we prepare to turn ourselves off. My own life here is puttering to a stop.

In the last weeks the company has been laying off men like crazy. There is so much steel now that no one knows what to do with it, and half the men hired after me are already gone. We start having good-by parties every afternoon, taking turns bringing the treats. One day I bring a watermelon, next day Charles brings little cakes and ice cream, next day Otis brings spare ribs and cokes. About a half hour before quitting time ten of us start our party. Chuck would like to stop us, but everyone is in a weird frame of mind these days and he doesn't dare get tough. Some of the oldest men come over and ask us questions about what we're doing. We explain, and they shake their heads and walk away, thinking about the days when a layoff or strike was a serious thing, and how times have changed.

I only learn about the strike vote meeting from a radical friend who works in the coke ovens. No one else in Merchant Mills seems to know a thing about it, so I call up the union, and the voice that answers says impatiently, "Yes, the strike vote is Tuesday. Every-body's been informed." I tell her that not a damn person in Merchant Mills knows about it, and she promises that the union will look into this. That night I see there's one dim leaflet tacked up in the glass case by the foreman's office. I try to talk the meeting up, but nobody cares. One older black guy sums up the feeling pretty well: "What difference? Meeting, no meeting. Strike, no strike. They going to do it just like they want anyhow." By "they" he means the union and the company.

Tuesday. The union hall of local 1014 of the United Steelworkers of America is packed by the time I arrive, and I have to sit in the front. (I'm told later that my picture is on the cover of the union newspaper. But I've never seen our union newspaper.) About 400 people are at the meeting, out of 15,000 members.

Harry Piasecki, the union president, starts by announcing in a tough and determined voice that the company is going to be real scared to hear of the big militant turnout at this strike meeting. From what I hear, this meeting is about eight times bigger than most local meetings, which means that Piasecki is probably just as scared as the company right now.

He and other union officials give long empty reports about the strike talks, and it's obvious they want to drag this thing out until we become confused and bored and hopefully we'll go home. After a half-hour some of the guys on the floor start to yell out. Piasecki can see that people want something to happen, so he takes a big sheaf of papers out of his briefcase and shouts, "Brothers! I hope we are going to register a big strike-vote here tonight, to give our union leadership the backing they deserve.

"You men know the company is stalling and won't cooperate. And I'd bet you are wanting to know just how these negotiations stand."

"Yeah. Yeah. Tell us," the shouts ring out.

He begins. "I have a copy of our bargaining position right here. It has fourteen categories of demands on it, and the company has only agreed to talk about six of them. That's the kind of bad faith we are up against."

"What is it?" "What are they offering?" the cries go up.

"Right. Right," says the president. "And I'm going to tell you exactly what these categories are." He shuffles through these papers some more, while we wait. Finally he says loudly and decisively, "Number three!" Then silence, and, after more paper shuffling and a brief consultation with another official sitting at the microphone-covered table, "Number five! Number six!" Then more silence and more shuffling and heads out in the audience are looking back and forth, and asses are shifting around in their chairs. Eventually he gets out the rest of the six numbers. Nothing more, just the numbers. This is union democracy in action. Most of the audience is looking passive, but a few start to yell out again. "Hey, what's with these numbers?!" "What are they offering?!" "What's the old age benefit?" "Come on! What's going on?"

The gavel goes rap rap rap and Piasecki says, "O.K. brothers, let's keep it orderly, every man will have a chance to speak." But the uproar continues and finally he shouts, "Do you men want to know what's in those categories?" Obviously they do. So he consults, and shuffles more papers, and then begins to read out the answers. "Wages and Hours! Retirement Plans!" He goes on like this, with the category titles. That's all. Confusion and passivity increase. Some men yell. Some leave. Most just sit.

Now the microphone on the floor is opened up, but those who ask good questions don't get answers, and many of the speakers are minor union officials. They remind us that the union charter doesn't allow us to vote on the terms of the contract; it only allows us to authorize Piasecki to call a strike. They talk drivel, but use tough, labor-movement language: "Brothers and sisters," "Standing bravely on the picket line," "We're not going to knuckle under to that goddam company until Motherfucking Hell Freezes Over, excuse me if there are ladies present."

It's getting late, and more people leave. Those who thought this meeting was actually going to mean something are frustrated and disappointed. At just the right point, Piasecki calls the vote. "All right men, how many are in favor of authorizing a strike against this company, if the negotiators feel it is necessary? Let's hear it!" There is a thunderous "Aye." How could you vote anything else? Does anybody here want to vote in favor of the company? That's what he seems to ask as he shouts, "Those opposed?" We all look around, but no hands are raised. How could they be? This is union democracy.

Still, I can't feel too superior to the union when I look back over my six months here. The only direct actions I took part in were for more bonus money or less work, and these are things the workers have already—with their job security and other past gains protected by the union.

This current set-up can pretty much handle the traditional issues.

There's a need for radicals here, but it's around whole new types of things.

Just before the strike, Billy and I have a little talk about "life." To make some point, I ask about his boat.

He says, "When the strike comes, I may finally have time to paint it up and get it into the water." It's almost August and he hasn't used it yet. Billy gives me a sheepish look.

I think the deepest needs of my friends here, the needs that require radical changes, are those same unclear things that brought me into the Movement long ago. I felt then that history was ready for the development of a whole new kind of person. Somehow things like community, art, sex roles, justice, participatory democracy, creativity—somehow things like this were almost remolded into a new vision.

Around 1970 I began to forget or abandon those politics. But that newer, free-er, wider, higher vision is what the average people need. It's the only thing that Billy and my other friends could really throw their lives into.

On July 31, the day before the strike is to begin, newspaper headlines trumpet: the union and the company have! reached! an! agreement! At the same time the company announces a layoff of practically everybody in the plant—for three, four, possibly five months. I realize that I have just witnessed the Great 1971 Steel Strike. Or the Great 1971 Steel Layoff. It's a farce, or a ritual. Matt says we should organize unemployed-councils to demand jobs or money, but what he describes sounds grim and lifeless. He's on the wrong battlefield.

As I walk around the mill saying good-by to friends everywhere —Hester, Sammy, David, Chico, Tom-bone, Cook, and many more—there is such a mixture of hope, high spirits, and sadness. I steal my hard-hat for a keep-sake when I leave.

᛭ ᛭ ᛭

SOME QUESTIONS AND ANSWERS

a self-interview by SAUL BELLOW

from THE ONTARIO REVIEW

nominated by THE ONTARIO REVIEW

Q.   How do you, a novelist from Chicago, fit yourself into American Life? Is there a literary world to which you belong?

A.   When I entered the Restaurant Voltaire in Paris with the
novelist Louis Guilloux some years ago, the waiter addressed him as
"Maître." I didn't know whether to envy him or to smile. No one had
ever treated me so reverentially. And as a student I had sat in
Chicago reading of *salons* and *cénacles*, of evenings at Magny's with
Flaubert and Turgeniev and Sainte-Beuve—reading and sighing.
What glorious times! But Guilloux himself, a Breton and a former
leftwinger, seemed uncomfortable with his title. It may be that even

in Paris literary culture is now preserved by smarmy headwaiters. I am not altogether sure of that. What is certain is that we have nothing like it in America—no Maîtres except in dining rooms, no literary world, no literary public. Many of us read, many love literature but the traditions and institutions of literary culture are lacking. I do not say that this is bad, I only state it as a fact that ours is not a society which creates such things. Any modern country that has not inherited them simply does not have them.

American writers are not neglected, they mingle occasionally with the great, they may even be asked to the White House but no one there will talk literature to them. Mr. Nixon disliked writers and refused flatly to have them in, but Mr. Ford has invited them together with actors, musicians, television newscasters and politicians. On these great evenings the East Room fills with celebrities who become ecstatic at the sight of other celebrities. Secretary Kissinger and Danny Kaye fall into each other's arms. Cary Grant is surrounded by Senators' wives who find him wonderfully preserved, as handsome in the flesh as on film, and they can hardly bear the excitement of personal contact with greatness. People speak of their diets, of travel and holidays, of vitamins and the problems of aging. Questions of language or style, the structure of novels, trends in painting are not discussed. The writer finds this a wonderful Pop occasion. Senator Fulbright seems almost to recognize his name and says, "You write essays, don't you? I think I can remember one of them." But the Senator, as everyone knows, was once a Rhodes Scholar.

It is actually pleasant on such an evening for a writer to pass half disembodied and unmolested by small talk from room to room, looking and listening. He knows that active public men can't combine government with literature, art and philosophy. Theirs is a world of high-tension wires not of primroses on the river's brim. Ten years ago Mayor Daley in a little City Hall ceremony gave me a five hundred dollar check on behalf of the Midland Authors' Society. "Mr. Mayor, have you read *Herzog*?" asked one of the reporters standing by. "I've looked into it," said Daley, yielding no ground. Art is not the Mayor's dish. But then why should it be? I much prefer his neglect to the sort of interest Stalin took in poetry, phoning Pasternak to chat with him about Mandelstam and, shortly afterwards, sending Mandelstam to die.

Q.   Are you saying that a modern industrial society dismisses art?

A.   Not at all. Art is one of those good things towards which it feels friendly. It is quite receptive. But what Ruskin said about the English public in 1871 applies perfectly to us. "No reading is possible for a people with its mind in this state. No sentence of any great writer is intelligible to them." Ruskin blames avarice. ". . . so incapable of thought has it [the public] become in its insanity of avarice. Happily, our disease is, as yet, little worse than this incapacity of thought; it is not corruption of the inner nature; we ring true still, when anything strikes home to us . . . though the idea that everything should 'pay' has infected our every purpose so deeply. . . ."

Q.   You don't see avarice as the problem, do you?

A.   No. "A people with its mind in this state," is where I lay the stress. We are in a peculiarly revolutionary state, a critical state that never ends. Yesterday I came upon a description of a medical technique for bringing patients to themselves. They are exposed for some minutes to high-frequency sounds until they are calm enough to think and to feel out their symptoms. To possess your soul in peace for a few moments you need the help of medical technology. It is easy to observe in bars, at dinner tables, everywhere, that from flop house to White House Americans are preoccupied by the same questions. Our own American life is our passion, our social and national life against a world background, an immense spectacle presented daily by the papers and the television networks—our cities, our crime, our housing, our automobiles, our sports, our weather, our technology, our politics, our problems of sex and race and diplomacy and international relations. These realities are real enough. But what of the formulae, the jargon, the principles of selection the media prefer? T.V. creates the exciting fictions, the heightened and dramatized shadow events accepted by the great public and believed by almost everyone to be real. Is reading possible for a people with its mind in this state?

Q.   Still a book of good quality can find a hundred thousand readers. But you say that there is no literary public.

A.   An influential book appears to create its own public. When *Herzog* was published I became aware that there were some fifty thousand people in the United States who wanted to read my novel. They had evidently been waiting for something like it. Other writers have certainly had the same experience. But such a public is a temporary one. There is no literary culture that permanently contains all of these readers. Remarkably steady and intelligent people emerge from the heaving wastes of the American educational system. They survive by strength, luck and cunning.

Q.   What do they do while waiting for the next important event?

A.   Exactly. What can they read month in, month out? In what journals do they keep up with what matters in contemporary literature?

Q.   What about the universities? Haven't they done anything to train judgment and develop taste?

A.   To most Professors of English a novel is an object of the highest cultural importance. Its ideas, its symbolic structure, its position in the history of Romanticism or Realism or Modernism, its higher relevance require devout study. But what has this sort of cultural study to do with novelists and readers? What they want is the living moment, they want men and women alive, and a circumambient world. The teaching of literature has been a disaster. Between the student and the book he reads lies a gloomy preparatory region, a perfect swamp. He must cross this cultural swamp before he is allowed to open his *Moby Dick* and read, "Call me Ishmael." He is made to feel ignorant before masterpieces, unworthy, he is frightened and repelled. And if the method succeeds it produces B.A.'s who can tell you why the *Pequod* leaves port on Christmas morning. What else can they tell you? No feeling for the book has been communicated, only a lot of pseudo-learned interpretation. What has been substituted for the novel itself is what can be said about the novel by the "educated." Some professors find educated discourse of this kind more interesting by far than novels. They take the attitude towards fiction that one of the Church Fathers took towards the Bible. Origen of Alexandria asked whether we were really to imagine that God walked in a Garden while Adam and Eve hid under a bush. Scripture could not be taken literally. It must yield higher meanings.

Q. Are you equating Church Fathers with Professors of Literature?

A. Not exactly. The Fathers had sublime conceptions of God and Man. If Professors of Humanities were moved by the sublimity of the poets and philosophers they teach they would be the most powerful men in the university and the most fervent. But they are at the lower end of the hierarchy, at the bottom of the pile.

Q. Then why are there so many writers at the universities?

A. A good question. Writers have no independent ground to stand on. They belong to institutions. They work for newsmagazines and publishing houses, for cultural foundations, advertising agencies, television networks. And they teach. There are only a few literary journals left and those are now academic quarterlies. The big national magazines don't want to publish fiction. Their editors want to discuss only the most significant national and international questions and concentrate on "relevant" cultural matters. By "relevant" they mean political. The "real" questions facing us are questions of business and politics—energy, war, sex, race, cities, education, technology, ecology, the fate of the automobile industry, the Middle East crisis, the dominoes of Southeast Asia, the moves of the Russian politburo. These are, of course, matters of the highest importance. More accurately, there are questions of life and death at the heart of such important public matters. But these life and death questions are not discussed. What we hear and read is crisis-chatter. And it is the business of the cultural-intelligentsia (professors, commentators, editors) to produce such chatter. Our intelligentsia, completely politicized and analytical in temper, does not take much interest in literature. The members of this elite *had* literature in their student days and are now well beyond it. At Harvard or Columbia they read, studied, absorbed the classics, especially the modernist classics. These prepared them for the important, the essential, the incomparable tasks they were destined to perform as functionaries in the media, the managers of scores of new enterprises. Sometimes I sense that they feel they have replaced writers.

The cultural business they do is tinged by literature, or rather the memory of literature. I said before that our common life had become our most passionate concern. Can an individual, the subject of a novel, compete in interest with corporate destinies, with the rise of a new class, a cultural intelligentsia?

Q.   Do you suggest that when we become so extremely politicized we lose interest in the individual?

A.   Exactly. And that a liberal society so intensely political can't remain liberal for very long. I take it for granted that an attack on the novel is also an attack on liberal principles. I view "activist" art theories in the same way. The power of a true work of art is such that it induces a temporary suspension of activities. It leads to contemplative states, to wonderful and, to my mind, sacred states of the soul.

Q.   And what you call crisis-chatter creates a contrary condition?

A.   I should like to add that the truth is not loved because it is *better* for us. We hunger and thirst for it. And the appetite for truthful books is greater than ever, sharpened by privation.

Q.   To return for a moment to the subject of a literary world . . .

A.   No tea at Gertrude Stein's, no Closerie de Lilas, no Bloomsbury evenings, no charming and wicked encounters between George Moore and W. B. Yeats. Reading of such things is very pleasant indeed. I can't say that I miss them, because I never knew anything like them. I miss certain dead friends. Writers. That Molière put on the plays of Corneille, that Louis XIV himself may have appeared, disguised, in one of Molière's farces—such facts are lovely to read in books. I'd hardly expect Mayor Daley to take part in any farce of mine. He performs in his own farces only. I have, however, visited writers' clubs in Communist countries and can't say that I'm sorry we have no such institutions here. When I was in Addis Ababa I went to the Emperor's Zoo. As Selassie was the Lion of Judah he was perhaps bound to keep a large collection of lions. These poor animals lay in the filth of dim green cages too small for pacing, mere coops. The leonine brown of their eyes had turned blank and yellow, their heads were on their paws and they were sighing. Bad as things are here they are not so bad as in the Emperor's Zoo or in writers' centers behind the Iron Curtain.

Q. Not so bad is not the same as good. What of the disadvantages of your condition?

A. There are moments of sorrow, I admit. George Sand wrote to Flaubert, in a collection of letters I looked into the other day, that she hoped he would bring his copy of her latest book on his next visit. "Put in it all the criticisms which occur to you," she said. "That will be very good for me. People ought to do that for each other as Balzac and I used to do. That doesn't make one person alter the other; quite the contrary, for in general one gets more determined in one's *moi*, one completes it, explains it better, entirely develops it, and that is why friendship is good, even in literature, where the first condition of any worth is to be one's self." How nice it would be to hear this from a writer. But no such letters arrive. Friendships and a common purpose belong to a nineteenth-century French dream world. The physicist Heisenberg in a recent article in *Encounter* speaks of the kindly and even brotherly collaboration among scientists of the generation of Einstein and Bohr. Their personal letters were quoted in seminars and discussed by the entire scientific community. Heisenberg believes that in the musical world something of the same spirit appeared in the eighteenth century. Haydn's relations with Mozart were of this generous affectionate kind. But when large creative opportunities are lacking there is no generosity visible. Heisenberg says nothing about the malice and hostility of less lucky times. Writers today seldom wish other writers well. Critics use strength gathered from the past to pummel the present. Edmund Wilson wouldn't read his contemporaries at all. He stopped with Eliot and Hemingway. The rest he dismissed. The lack of goodwill, to put it at its mildest, was much admired. The fact speaks for itself. Curious about Canadians, Indians, Haitians, Russians, studying Marxism and the Dead Sea scrolls, he was the Protestant majority's big literary figure. I have sometimes thought that he was challenged by Marxism or Modernism in the same way that I have seen the descendants of Orthodox Jews challenged by oysters. Historical progress demands that our revulsions be overcome. A man like Wilson might have done much to strengthen literary culture, but he dismissed all that, he would have nothing to do with

it. For temperamental reasons. Or Protestant majority reasons. Or
perhaps the Heisenberg principle applies—men are generous when
there are creative opportunities, and when such opportunities
dwindle they are . . . something else. But it would have made little
difference. At this moment in human evolution, so miraculous,
atrocious, glorious and hellish, the firmly established literary cultures of France and England, Italy and Germany can originate
nothing. They look to us, to the "disadvantaged" Americans, and to
the Russians. From America have come a number of great irrepressible solitaries like Poe or Melville or Whitman, alcoholics, obscure
government employees. In busy America there was no Weimar,
there were no cultivated princes. There were only these obstinate
geniuses writing—why? For whom? There is the real *acte gratuite*
for you. Unthanked, these writers augmented life marvelously.
They did not emerge from a literary culture nor did they create any
such thing. Irrepressible individuals of a similar type have lately
begun to show themselves in Russia. There Stalinism utterly destroyed a thriving literary culture and replaced it with a horrible
bureaucracy. But in spite of this and in spite of forced labor and
murder the feeling for what is true and just has not been put out. I
don't see, in short, why we should continue to dream of what we
have never had. To have it would not help us. Perhaps if we were to
purge ourselves of nostalgia and stopped longing for a literary world
we would see a fresh opportunity to extend the imagination and
resume imaginative contact with nature and society.

Q.   Other people, scholars and scientists, know a great deal about
nature and society. More than you know.

A.   True. And I suppose I sound like a fool but I nevertheless object
that their knowledge is defective—something is lacking. That something poetry. Huizinga, the Dutch historian, in his recently published book on America says that the learned Americans he met in
the Twenties could speak fluently and stimulatingly, but he adds,
"More than once I could not recognize in what he wrote the living
man who had held my interest. Frequently repeated experience
makes me hold the view that my personal reaction to American
scholarly prose must still rest upon the qualities of the prose itself. I
read it with the greatest difficulty; I have no sense of contact with it
and cannot keep my attention fixed on it. It is for me as if I had to do

with a deviant system of expression in which the concepts are not equivalent to mine, or are arranged differently." The system has become more deviant during the last fifty years. I want information and ideas, and I know that certain highly trained and intelligent people have it—economists, sociologists, lawyers, historians, natural scientists. But I read them with the greatest difficulty, exasperated, tormented, despairing. And I say to myself, "These writers are part of the educated public, your readers. You make your best efforts for them, these unpoetic or anti-poetic people. You've forgotten Ortega's philistine professional, the educated Mass-Man . . . etcetera." But none of this matters. Philistine intellectuals don't make you stop writing. Writing is your *acte gratuite*. Besides, those you address are there. If you exist, then they exist. You can be more certain of their existence than of your own.

Q.   But whether or not a literary culture exists . . .

A.   Excuse me for interrupting but it occurs to me that Tolstoi would probably have approved of this and seen new opportunities in it. He had no use for literary culture and detested professionalism in the arts.

Q.   But should writers make their peace with the academic Ivory Tower?

A.   In his essay "Bethink Yourselves" Tolstoi advises each man to begin at the point at which he finds himself. Better such Towers than the Cellar alternatives some writers choose. Besides, the university is no more an Ivory Tower than *Time* magazine with its strangely artificial approach to the world, its remote-making managerial arrangements. A writer is offered more money, bigger pensions, richer security-plans by Luce enterprises than by any university. The Ivory Tower is one of those platitudes that haunt the uneasy minds of writers. Since we have none of the advantages of a literary world we may as well free ourselves from its banalities. Spiritual independence requires that we bethink ourselves. The university is as good a place for such thinking as any other. But while we think hard about the next step we should avoid becoming academics. Teachers, yes. Some are even moved to become scholars. The great danger for writers in the university is the academic danger.

Q. Can you conveniently give a brief definition of academic?

A. I limit myself arbitrarily to a professorial type to be found in the Humanities. Owen Barfield refers in one of his books to "the everlasting professional device for substituting a plethora of *talk*" about what matters for—what actually matters. He is sick of it, he says. Many of us are sick of it.

VETERAN'S HEAD

by DIANE CHAPMAN

from XANADU

nominated by XANADU

Parents and kid brother meet him at the airport
The veteran's head nods
  bends for kisses
  the mouth smiles
On the highway home a helicopter whumps over
the head remains motionless
  facing the windshield
while stomach in body under it flinches
the kid brother chatters into a carved ear
Strange hills roll by

Though it is only October
a thanksgiving feast is prepared
Aunts/uncles/cousins crowd the house
The head allows itself to be caressed
  cupped between sets of soft palms
  waits while its hair is rumpled
Finally they let go

Nostrils grabbing for air
the veteran's head stumbles to his old room
Posters/model planes/on the wall fishing pole and .22
As mouth gapes silently
hands tear the head from shaking shoulders
hurl it into the closet
where it lodges between hockey stick and record player
A bright plaid mackinaw sways for a moment
  then hangs still

Hands fumble along the top of the dresser
feeling for the head that used to be there
Under sweating fingers a transistor radio/metal comb
        framed photograph/car keys
Wrist bumps a trophy to the floor
He turns to the desk
        covered typewriter
        pencils bristling from a chocolate syrup can

Kneeling/the body gropes beneath chenille spread
Until his mother's voice calling dinner
freezes him against the bed edge
like a child at prayer

No one notices what has happened
Air whirlpools into windpipe and a shrill sigh
Forkfuls of turkey/yam/corn relish
        drop into a drainpipe throat
Vibrations of floor and table
indicate the presence of the guests
        suggest hearty voices talking
        stock market/world series/crops

Upstairs
on the closet floor
in the dark between hockey stick and record player
the veteran's head lies
watching shattered bodies falling
and still smelling death

THE PILOT

by NAOMI LAZARD

from THE HUDSON REVIEW

nominated by Pushcart Press

You say you are a pilot on a dangerous mission.
Night after night you have to make the run
from one beleagured city to another,
flying through enemy flak, the red and orange
bursts, the air shuddering and tilting.
Those experts manning the anti-aircraft
are incredible sharp-shooters.

Just a few nights ago your plane was hit.
Only your courage, your daring and expertise,
brought the old crate in.
And all the crew was safe.

I understand about your terrible work,
how much it takes out of you,
the nightmares that scream in your sleep.
I sympathize with your burden of responsibility
for the out-dated crate you must fly,
and the crew. I've even grown to admire
that despot, the sour-faced navigator
without whom, as you've told me
with characteristic modesty,
you might never make it.

I know you are a hero.
I know these flights are genuinely frightening.
I know they take your breath away
and make you speechless. I know your silences

are a burden to you; sometimes
you are suddenly stricken by one of them.
Then you sit there, your mouth locked
in the open position, locked like your plane
zooming down with the throttle all the way
forward, in order to ride with the plunge
through the sound barrier.

Because of all this I want to make it easy
for you. This is the way it works.
It isn't necessary to say anything.
With this code I've invented,
if you love me, just tap one time
with a finger or a foot.

𝄞 𝄞 𝄞

FICTION HOT AND KOOL: DILEMMAS OF THE EXPERIMENTAL WRITER

by MORRIS DICKSTEIN

from TRIQUARTERLY

nominated by Nona Balakian

I noticed that howls and rattles had been added
to whistles and drums. Is it some kind of
revolution? . . .

Cynthia formerly believed in the "enormous
diversity of things"; now she believes in Kong.
The man whose pronunciation I had corrected
emerged from the kitchen. "Probably it is
music," he said, nodding at the windows. "the
new music, which we older men are too old to
understand."

— DONALD BARTHELME, "THE PARTY"

THE TRIBULATIONS OF FICTION in the early seventies have
been (as the phrase goes) fatal but not serious. If practitioners of
fiction no longer believe in the "enormous diversity of things,"
the blessed abundance of God's creation, they have filled the void
with an astonishing variety of their own artifacts. Today's writers
are heirs to a liberating chaos of new forms, running from the
Borgesian miniatures of Donald Barthelme to gargantuan mis-
cellanies like Nabokov's *Ada*, Alan Friedman's *Hermaphrodeity*,

and Pynchon's *Gravity's Rainbow*. But freedom can be a burden and a terror as well as an exhilarating opportunity, and in the following pages I'd like to look again at some of the experimental short fiction of our period to see how the liberated writer has dealt with his dilemma. What all these novels and stories have in common is a degree of creative freedom and seriousness about art that was alien to the generation of John O' Hara. American fiction has joined the camp of modernism with a vengeance, just at a time when the modernist impulse seemed to be exhausted.

But modernist writing does not sell, or sells only to intellectuals and to posterity; the dark side of the healthy abundance and variety of fiction is the collapse of the commercial market, which has driven novelists to little magazines with a minuscule audience and even to self-publishing, an "underground" usually inhabited only by the poets. Publishers stop buying novels or hesitate to promote those they do buy; they retreat to old middlebrow staples like history, biography, and reportage, which provide the narrative element many of the novelists have abandoned, and sometimes even deliver news about a world outside the writer's head. A recent *Newsweek* issue on "The Arts in America" gave all its emphasis to the performing arts, almost none to writing. Along with professional sports, the performing arts at least convey a solid reality, a kinetic human presence that today's writers often refuse even to simulate.

How much are writers, then, responsible for their own commercial decline? More seriously, how well has the newest experimental work delivered on the promises of the tumultuous sixties? How do the aims of the younger writers compare with those of classical modernists, who themselves endured opprobrium and neglect before achieving wide recognition? I won't really answer the last question, except to point out that an experimental attitude and a rebellion against nineteenth-century realism were important features of the modernist achievement. But they were accompanied by a heroic effort to master reality, to interpret the world in new ways, through new forms. Though a writer like Kafka may feel anything but heroic, may feel the victim of circumstances at every turn, as an artist he turns his helplessness into mastery by creating a mode of apprehension that we recognize on every page, in every sentence. His work has become a way that *we* see reality, which helps us to grapple with it too. But in the 1960s an impressive and influential body of fictional theory codified the modernist attitude in a way that almost leaves reality out of account. The essays collected in Alain Robbe-Grillet's *For a New Novel,* Richard Gilman's *The Confusion of Realms*, and William H. Gass's *Fiction and the Figures of Life* all stress the esthetic autonomy of the work of art, its nonreferential status as an object in itself—neither mirror nor lamp, neither imitation of life nor emanation of the self—a new reality bodied forth in words.

Robbe-Grillet had the example of the *nouveau roman*, which his essays aimed to validate, but there was little in American fiction in the early sixties to justify so extravagant a theory. The characteristic novels of the period, by men like Barth, Berger, Pynchon, Heller and Vonnegut, had indeed broken with the realistic conventions that predominated in the forties and fifties—not by junking them, however, but by subsuming them, as Kafka and Joyce had done, in an immense ironic structure. The worlds they created were virtual or contingent ones, which oddly mixed fact and fantasy and directed much attention to the artist's own ingenuity, but they were worlds nonetheless, full of the same "solidity of specification" that James called the hallmark of the realistic novelist.

It remained for the writers of the late sixties to press toward a mode of fiction that would make the novel a body of words *and no more*: its own devices would become its only subject. Using techniques of abstraction, fragmentation, and discontinuity— borrowed from sources as diverse as Dada painters, surrealist poets, New Wave filmmakers, Brechtian dramatists, as well as modernist writers of fiction—the stories they wrote deliberately alienate the reader, inhabiting his identification with the "characters" of the story, short-circuiting his suspension of disbelief. Barthelme's recent stories, whose protagonists have names like Perpetua, "the genius," or "the catechist," announce themselves immediately as fictive constructs, verbal machines with all their gears exposed. Yet all sorts of words and deeds are attributed to the puppet-characters, who imitate life so inexactly that they mock the very principle of imitation. Reduced to a collection of verbal and emotional mannerisms, tics of behavior severed from an elaborated human context, Barthelme's world foppishly parades its superficiality; yet with such themes as "the rise of capitalism" it also toys with an air of portentous generality, even of parable, teasing us with Kafkaseque hints of remote, inaccessible symbolic depths.

All things considered, however, the freshest and most boldly

realized experimental fiction of the late sixties, such as Barthelme's
earlier stories collected in *City Life* (1970), does not correspond to
the astringent formalism of such critics as Robbe-Grillet, Gilman,
Gass, and Susan Sontag. It is not free of that "heavy burden of
'content' and moral seriousness" that Miss Sontag deplores in contemporary literature: it has not abandoned worldy ambition for a
purer realm of style. I can explain this by citing some comments
made by Philip Rahv in 1949 on the Kafka vogue of the late forties,
which resulted in some good examples of the fake modernism,
misconceived imitations of that most elusive models.

To know how to take apart the recognizable world is not enough, is in fact
merely a way of letting oneself go and striving for originality at all costs. But
orginality of this sort is nothing but a professional mannerism of the
avant-garde. The genuine innovator is always trying to make us actually
experience his creative contradictions. He therefore employs means that
are subtler and more complex: *at the very same time that he takes the world
apart he puts it together again.* For to proceed otherwise is to dissipate
rather than alter our sense of reality, to weaken and compromise rather
than change in any significant fashion our feeling of relatedness of the
world. ("Notes on the Decline of Naturalism")

The limitations of this position are evident enough. Under the guise
of high standards of loyalty to the "true" avant-garde (read: some
previous avant-garde), it can become a conservative defense of
established forms and of acceptably humanist feelings of "relatedness to the world." Much later in the sixties, Rahv himself fell victim
to this sort of embattled traditionalism, and became an indiscrimi-
nate foe of all attempts at innovation in literature. The seeds of this
decline are already present in these earlier gibes at "letting oneself
go," originality at all costs," and the "professional.mannerism of the
avant-garde."

Yet however easily misapplied, Rahv's dictum is basically sound.
All modernist writing is in some ways experimental and revisionary,
thriving on the decadence of previous forms and norms like Swift's
tulips rising out of dung. Modernist writing is ebulliently parricidal
and cannibalistic. It revels apocalyptically in the end of culture—
the death of the novel, the death of rhyme, the exhaustion of
narrative, the end of the nineteenth century—yet feeds lustily on its
murdered forebears, as Kafka sups ironically on the techniques of
realism while undermining their grip on causality and "reality," as

Joyce turns *Ulysses* into a parodistic anthology of traditional styles.

But in all the best modernist writing this negative and parodistic element never predominates, however large it bulks. Some modernist techniques do aim at pure destruction and chaos, a form of esthetic terrorism, but where this polemical side is dominant we often find publicists rather than artists, Dada rather than symbolism, Dali rather than Picasso. Otherwise, where modernist or experimental art seems unstructured, incoherent, anarchic, even nihilistic, as is often the case, it usually means that we have not yet recognized the new norm, the new principle of coherence or mode of awareness that the artist has invented. Often enough, though, we *sense* that it is there, for our instinct is sounder than our esthetic, which is still grounded in the *idées rescues* of the past. The function of criticism is to interrogate that feeling, to turn into new categories, a new esthetic. Bad criticism spins clever theories; good criticism justifies unexpected intuitions.

In the experimental fiction of the late sixties, the largely negative strain shows itself most clearly in John Barth's stories in *Lost in the Funhouse*, in Robert Coover's *Pricksongs & Descants*, in Barthelme's novella *Snow White*, in the insubstantial and self-indulgent anti-world ("Antiterra") of Nabokov's *Ada*, and in the catatonic ambience of Rudolph Wurlitzer's *Nog* and *Flats*, to name only a few examples.* There is much to praise in all these books: corrosive ironies, flights of fantasy, nuance of language that we expect more from poetry than fiction. What they too frequently lack is poignancy, intensity, a recognizably human framework. I don't mean realism, which is only one of many conventions by which art approximates the human. Without being representational, the paintings of Kline and Pollock, with their sweeping swathes or dense multiple layers of paint, boldy suggest the energies of their composition, the turbulent circumstances of their own inception. These works are not really "about" themselves, however, because their reflexiveness takes us through and beyond technique, back to a world of gesture, feeling, and movement as well as shape and color. But some of the new fiction is really about fiction itself, paralyzed by self-consciousness, caught

*I have discussed most of these works in previous articles, including a review of *Ada* in *The New Republic* (June 28, 1969), a review-essay on Barthelme in *The New York Times Book Review* (April 26, 1970), and a review of Wurlitzer's *Quake*, also in the *Times Book Review* (October 22, 1972).

in an infinite regress of writing about writing. Thus, bereft of all full human subject, embroiled in problems of craft rather than art, it readily devolves into a parochial whine or ascends to a cerebral high, manipulating words and worlds with a meaningless impunity.

At its best, this fiction evades such criticism to achieve a genuine if narrow intensity. Nabokov's *Pale Fire* is partly saved from mere cleverness by its obsessiveness, which well accords with the problem-solving mania it depicts. Some of Barth's stories, like "Lost in the Funhouse," "Title," and "Life-Story," turn the prison house of authorial selfconsciousness into an almost adequate subject, especially when set off against an impotent nostalgia for the happy credulities of tradition:

Another story about a writer writing a story! Another regressus in infinitum! Who doesn't prefer art that at least overtly imitates something other than its own processes? That doesn't continually proclaim "Don't forget I'm an artifice!"? . . . Though his critics sympathetic and otherwise described his own work as avant-garde, in his heart of hearts he disliked literature of an experimental, self-despising, or overtly metaphysical character, like Samuel Beckett's, Marian Cutler's, Jorge Borge's. The logical fantasies of Lewis Carroll please him less than straightforward tales of adventure, subtly sentimental romances, even densely circumstantial realisms like Tolstoy's . . . .

By Jove he exclaimed to himself. It's particularly disquieting to suspect not only that one is a fictional character but that the fiction one's in—the fiction one is—is quite the sort one least prefers.

("Life-Story")

This may not be great fiction—what is?—but it has a certain wry precision and point. Its self-referential quality is earned, dramatized, by the playful dialectic of unwillingness. Like the proverbial cynic with a sentimental core, Barth in all his fiction oscillates between a mock traditionalism and a coyly hesitant vanguardism, in a way that at least approximates Rahv's formula that "the genuine innovator is always trying to make us actually experience his creative contradictions."

The weakness of such writing, as Barth himself indicates, is that it has no subject apart from the writer's problem in being a writer. This can be a rich theme, as it is for Henry James in his fable about artists and writers, but only if problems of technique and creative choice come to represent more general features of our common fate. Since the early Romantics of the late eighteenth century, the fate of the artist has repeatedly become an intensified version of the whole human situation. For this to happen convincingly, however, the writer must genuinely risk and expose himself; he cannot simply dawdle about the private, parochial problems of his craft, no matter how apocalyptically he interprets them. But the Barthian apocalypse is a game without risk, a purely intellectual game that scribbles in the margins of the history of art without adding to the basic text. Recent critical theory endows fiction with total imaginative freedom, making it no longer "subservient to the actuality from which it draws its instigations and energies." But what the Barthian writer caught in his dead-end self-consciousness most completely lacks is imagination, the deep subjectivity that enables the imagination to take wing. For all their personal reference his cerebral musings about art foster an escape from subjectivity, an escape from personality. He eschews not only characters but character, including his own; his incursions into the self are as hollow as his excursuses into the world.

This escape from personality, perhaps an understandable reaction to the fury of self-assertion that predominated in the sixties, threatens to rob the writer of everything but his "voice," the distinctive accent of his prose (distinctiveness we associate with poetry more than with fiction). At the same time it makes possible the celebrated "cool" tone of much recent experimental fiction, a cleanness of manner that partly redeems the pervasive irony and emotional distance. Experimental fiction clears away the debris of prevailing styles—such as popular realism—which are usually debased versions of styles that were radical in their own day. (Eliot's poetry challenges Swinburne and Robert Bridges, not Blake and Wordsworth; Barthelme undermines Bellow, not Balzac.) After we've read Barthelme and Borges it's hard to be told that so-and-so got into a car, slammed the door, turned his key in the ignition, pressed his foot on the gas pedal, etc., unless this sequence of gestures advances the meaning (as it does, for example, in Truffaut's neo-Hitchcock film *The Soft Skin*). In most popular (and some serious) fiction, however, such filler merely aspires to verisimilitude —to convince the reader, as Robbe-Grillet remarks, "that the adventures he is hearing about have really happened to real characters." In Balzac, setting and description are like an overture which introduces a set of musical themes; in contemporary realism they merely strain to convince us we're in a world.

Faced with the debasement of realism into lazy conventions, the writer can clear the ground by abstracting from reality, perhaps by condensing the story from thirty to three pages, essentializing it into pure narration; but unlike the painter he cannot recoil wholly from representation into pure abstraction. A painting by Jules Olitski can be "about" its acrylic surface or other layers of paint the surface suggests but half-conceals. Still the canvas remains an object of sensuous contemplation. But words are abstract to begin with; they lack sensuous address. The pulpiest novel, dead on the page, can make a good movie: the sounds and images, the moving presence of the actors, can bring the thing to life. As Mary McCarthy puts it, "language, unlike paint and sound, cannot slough off its primary function of saying something. When it tries, we simply stop listening. This is why large audiences cannot be attracted by every sort of non-objective art and 'concrete' music but so very few people will consent to turn pages from which no meaning emerges."

Admittedly Miss McCarthy is discussing an extreme example, the French "*new* new novel," which, like so many other "new" developments in French cultural life, is more a triumph of publicity and fashion than a true avant-garde. But some of the younger American writers of the seventies *have* been moving toward this kind of abstraction, insulating themselves from criticism by a coterie mentality and donning tattered modernist robes of neglect and artistic martyrdom. Abetted by the genuine foolishness of publishers, critics, and lazy readers, they have begun to create an underground fiction that even in its weaknesses resembles the so-called underground cinema of the early sixties, and that will remain underground until it overcomes its own conceptual limitations. Few will consent to turn the pages because their work neglects the sequential, durational element which is much more important in fiction than in painting or poetry, and more important in long fiction (or films) than in short.

As John Barth's *Chimera* (1972) made clear, even a novella can seem interminable when it doesn't move on its own—when the author must prod it onward, like a stubborn nag, from page to page. And arbitrary sequence is related to lack of affect, the absence of deep subjectivity, the failure to engage the reader's full being.

Philip Stevick, in his fine essay on the new fiction in *TriQuarterly* 30 (Spring 1974), acknowledges this when he quotes Kenneth Burke's point that "*Form* in literature is an arousing and fulfillment of desires. A work has form in so far as one part of it leads a reader to anticipate another part, to be gratified by the sequence." Barth, whose recent work almost disarms criticism by forever saying the worst that can be said about it, himself admits as much in one of his self-reflective digressions:

How does one write a novella? How find the channel, bewildered in these creeks and crannies? Storytelling isn't my cup of wine; isn't somebody's; my plot doesn't rise and fall in meaningful stages but winds upon itself like a whelk-shell or the snakes on Hermes's caduceus: digresses, retreats, hesitates, groans from its utter et cetera, collapses, dies.

("Bellerophoniad")

Barth deliberately directs the three novellas in *Chimera* at the crisis of self-consciousness that he perceives in experimental writing, which had been the problematic subject of *Lost in the Funhouse* and had subsequently given him his first taste of writer's block. He is caught in conflict between his affinity for traditional fiction and his acute sense of its exhaustion, a feeling that its historical moment has passed. His solution in *The Sot-Weed Factor* (1960) was to outflank the social and psychological realism of the nineteenth century by mimicking an earlier mode. His solution in *Chimera* is to leapfrog even further beyond the conventional novel, "back to the original springs of narrative"; he will return to the earliest myths and legends like those of Scheherazade and Greek mythology, whose patterns, repeated instinctively in so many later stories, he will *consciously* develop and modernize (on the premise, false in my view, that "to write realistic fictions which point always to mythic archetypes is in my opinion to take the wrong end of the mythopoeic stick. . . . Better to address the archetypes directly"). As Barth puts it earlier, "He declared with pleasure that thanks to the inspiration of Scheherazade and to the thousand comforts of his loving wife he believed he had found his way out of that slough of imagination in which he'd found himself bogged: . . . he had gone forward by going back, to the very roots and springs of story." Thus, he hopes, without smothering his self-consciousness, by mimicking an archaic mode he can write stories that are aware that they are stories but also "manage to be seriously, even passionately, *about* some things as well."

Barth's recognition of the value of a subject makes him something of a conservative of the fiction scene of the early seventies, but it does little to save his book. Greek mythology and the Arabian Nights are tough leagues to bat in, and Barth's three novellas manage few palpable hits. Caught between the simple integrity of traditional stories and the demystifying problematic and modernist self-consciousness, Barth realizes neither one nor the other. In *The Sot-Weed Factor*, whatever its limitations, Barth almost had it *both ways*, by writing a half-loving, half-mocking version of the eighteenth-century novel. There he invented stories, not yet knowing it couldn't be done. But nothing could seem further from "the original springs of narrative" than the chatty, trivializing tone of *Chimera*, punctuated only by mock-literary pomposities, never by the unselfconscious simplicity of the storyteller. Storytelling is rooted in wonder, in the marvelous, in magical charm, enchantment, even possession. Barth's versions utterly lack vividness, let alone the power to charm or possess. The stories themselves are pallid and hard to follow, swamped by digression and commentary. Barth babbles on about domestic problems, his writer's block, quotes verbatim from his sources, even delivers a critical lecture on his work to date. Some of this is funny, ingenious, and even enlightening, but it all belongs to what Walter Benjamin calls "information," the modern journalistic mode that is the fatal enemy of traditional storytelling, however many stories it claims to tell. As Benjamin puts it,

Every morning brings us news of the globe, and yet we are poor in noteworthy stories. This is because no event any longer comes to us without being shot through with explanation. . . . Actually, it is half the art of storytelling to keep a story free from explanation as one reproduces it. . . . The most extraordinary things, marvelous things, are related with the greatest accuracy, but the psychological connection of the events is not forced on the reader.

("The Storyteller")

Instead Barth tries to control the reader's response at every turn, substituting cleverness for imagination, gossipy prattle for myth, the manipulations of the will for spontaneous affect (or effect).

There's more feeling for Greek myth in the two pages of Freud's little essay on "Medusa's Head," though Freud makes no pretense at storytelling, than in Barth's laborious novelistic version of the same myth. Barth frequently tries to identify his characters' situation with his own—they too are storytellers, or are entering middle age, or are minor celebrities and feel past it, etc.—but the connections are willed and superficial. For all their comic intent, the three stories betray that fear of intersubjectivity which Paul Goodman identified as a prime cause of writer's block.

The relative failure of *Chimera* underlines the limitations of nostalgia as a solution to the dilemmas of experimental fiction. Nostalgia really does take the writer backward rather than forward. Traditional stories, however conscious they may make us of the writer's "creative contradictions," in themselves provide no instrument of creative breakthrough unless the writer experiences them in a new way. Barthelme's *Snow White* (1967), though circumscribed, is a much more successful book, for in its purity of intention it breaks more drastically with its traditional source. Where Barth's style is mock-dainty, or chatty and low, a lesson in the art of sinking in fiction, Barthelme's language is a model of planned incongruity. Like some of the New York poets, whose playfully surreal styles have similar roots, Barthelme has a background in the visual arts; he has edited art journals, done the design for *Fiction* magazine, and illustrated many of his own stories, including a children's book. All his books are attractive objects, informed by an easy elegance and urbanity, and his fictional method is similar to his visual one. Barthelme the designer is primarily a collector, who does bizarre collages of nineteenth-century engravings, the effect of which is neither wholly satiric, nor antiquarian, not camp, but poised in a vacant, eerie zone between nostalgia and irony, mad and mod. Barthelme the writer is also a connoisseur of other people's styles, not so much literary as subliterary ones—the punishment corner of language, where curious things happen—from Victorian kitsch to modern pop, from professional jargon and journalistic formula to the capacious regions of contemporary cliché. *Snow White* is a book about language, a collage of styles bleached and truncated into one pure and rigorous style of its own. Its fairy-tale subject is a hollow sham, the eye of a word-storm, the common theme of an anthology of ways of not saying anything. Its purity of purpose is cold and bracing: a good book for writers to read, like a verbal purge; or like ordinary-language philosophy, always sharpening the tools. But the book suits the theory of the new fiction a little too well; its surface is rarely ruffled, let alone subverted, by any actuality.

Snow White is an extreme case. Dominated by an austere, bookish wit and a negative appetite for verbal trash, it is a work of severe ironic distance. The perfection of Barthelme's method, now so widely and ineptly imitated, comes in half a dozen stories of *Unspeakable Practices, Unnatural Acts* (1968), and nearly everything in its successor, *City Life*, still the most brilliant collection of experimental fiction these last years have produced. In stories like "Brain Damage," "At the Tolstoy Museum," and "Robert Kennedy Saved from Drowning" the cool mode heats up electrically, and experimental writing proceeds from critique to creation. Where *Snow White* is a clearing of the ground, these stories construct a new fictional reality. They show what even *Snow White* made clear, that Barthelme is no mere collector but a writer who juxtaposes strange forms and fragments in a way that creates new form and releases new meanings. Where *Snow White* is mainly an ironic book, *City Life* is also an impassioned one. *Snow White* is more sophisticated and condescending, but experientially vacuous; *City Life* gives free play to another side of his temperament, a melancholy nostalgia for traditional art and old-fashioned feelings—unlike Barth's, a nostalgia that animates rather than inhibits him. The longing is hopeless, of course—he can't try to be Tolstoy. But he can plumb his ambivalence and make that contribute to the enigma, adding thick shadows to his subject. The Barthian writer escapes from personality; though he babbles about himself incessantly he discovers very little and achieves no deep subjectivity; his self-consciousness tells him that no art, no imagination, is still possible, and the prophecy is self-fulfilling. The Barthelmian writer is scarcely ever present; he loses himself in the oddest, most unpromising subjects: Kierkegaard, Robert Kennedy, angels, the Phantom of the Opera; but the space between passion and irony is filled with new perceptions and connections, self-discoveries, as in all the best fiction. The art is not confessional but it is hauntingly personal, full of mood and mystery, and the author is arrestingly present. Where writers like Wurlitzer, proclaiming the death of feeling, merely betray their own emotional poverty, Barthelme finds new imaginative life in the heart of the contemporary wasteland, in the land of "brain damage," where art shacks up with kitsch and tradition lies down with the New. This art of incongruity brings Barthelme's stories closer to the comic-apocalyptic writers of the early sixties—such as Pynchon, Heller, and Vonnegut, who meet reality halfway and strike a Faustian bargain—than to the verbal austerities of, say, Gass's fiction or of his own younger admirers.

Unfortunately Barthelme has so far been unable to sustain his creative élan in the early seventies, and his difficulties are symptomatic of the problems of experimental writing during this period. Fiction is one of the few areas of our cultural life where the breakthroughs of the sixties have been sustained, if not carried forward. *Newsweek* tells us that Barthelme has become the greatest influence on our developing writers, but neither the established nor the younger writers have delivered the body of innovative work that the late sixties seemed to promise. Other writers imitate Barthelme's manner rather than his inventive rigor, while he himself has frequently fallen into shallowness, decadence, and self-imitation. On both sides this has resulted not in the kinds of stunning collage and fable that made *City Life* fresh and important, but in an epidemic of the easy-to write pastiche or put-on, many of which would have been at home in a college humor magazine of the 1950s.

It's to the credit of Barthelme's latest collection of stories, *Sadness* (1972), that he's very conscious of the perils of repetition and self-parody. His main sadness is the fear that he's already said what he has to say:

When one has spoken a lot one has already used up all of the ideas one has. You must change the people you are speaking to so that you appear, to yourself, to be still alive.

("The Party")

It is difficult to keep the public interested.
  The public demands new wonders piled on new wonders.
  Often we don't know where our next marvel is coming from.
  The supply of strange ideas is not endless. . . .
The new volcano we have just placed under contract seems very promising.

("The Flight of the Pigeons from the Palace")

The realistic writer, who may take his form for granted, in principle need only find another corner of reality to portray, another "subject" for a novel. If he has the energy, he can can write a *Comédie Humaine*; this may be why writers like Updike and Joyce Carol

Oates are so prolific. But the writer who interrogates and subverts his form at every turn has no such luck. He can run out of new wonders very easily. Or stick to a manner that quickly degenerates into mannerisms.

Though it contains a few good stories, *Sadness* is a sad case in point, for it exposes the underside of all the writer's virtues. It shows how the collage method fails when the fragments remain disjunctive, unillumined. It shows how the fascination with cultural trash can devolve into a taste for trivia, lovingly collected but barely transformed. It exposes the merely campy side of Barthelme's interest in melodrama, kitsch, and old-fashioned iconography, or the snobbish side, in which the artist flaunts his cultural status while slumming and loving it. The book even betrays the limitations of Barthelme's most basic virtue, his purity of language and narrative technique, which cleans up too much—psychology, description, interaction—leaving only plastic figures with curious names, leaving elegant surfaces which, in the pages of *The New Yorker*, mesh all too well with that magazine's waning cult of style.

Barthelme is at his worst where the realistic writer is best—in describing the relations between men and women. There he retreats entirely into the satiric and ironic mode of *Snow White* but without that book's freshness and wit. (I suspect this is why he has not yet delivered his long-promised novel.) *Sadness* is much too full of the trivial and the inconsequential, the merely decorative or the merely enigmatic. I have no idea why Barthelme has regressed from the passionate fabulistic manner of his two previous books, except for the reasons he himself suggests, but the lesson for experimental fiction is clear enough. The "cool" mode has its limitations, especially in a period of disengagement and disintegration like our own. When "Robert Kennedy Saved from Drowning" (arguably Barthelme's best story) appeared in book form in the late sixties, William Gass dismissed it, no doubt in alarm over its topicality. But the story is both fervently engaged and formally daring. Barthelme needs a great subject, an immediate subject, to draw him at least halfway out of his irony and esthetic detachment. The feverish immediacy of life in the late sixties, the energy and pressure and swirl, which affected all of us, worked its way into his fiction with a fascinating indirection, just as it ruined some writers who tried to devour it too directly. Now, without that stimulus, without the pull of social ferment and spiritual possibility, Barthelme's work looks the same but feels listless and remote, sketched rather than imagined.

Given the fetid character of the age, the young writer is at a dangerous crossroads. He can pursue his quest for new forms, new spectacles, new shapes for our consciousness, but he must try to do so without abandoning experiential vividness, emotion, actuality. (I assume, perhaps wrongly, that he has a choice.) Whether or not he makes peace with realism he must somehow cope with reality—if possible in a fresh way—as the early sixties writers did, as the Latin American novelists do. If the sixties were hysterical (in more ways than one), the seventies risk becoming sterile and catatonic, and the writer, bent on refining his instruments, risks becoming part of that reaction. The times have gone from bad to worse, but the artist who is not part of the solution may become part of the problem.

BAD POEMS

by MICHAEL DENNIS BROWNE

from DACOTAH TERRITORY

nominated by Leonard Randolph

Bad poems are lying around
in huge jugs; I will not drink them!
I take a piece of beer
& nail it to the sky.
Driving, I see a nun crossing the road
& step on the gas-pedal, & get her;
these bad poems will disguise themselves
as anything!
I wake one morning
with cobwebs between my thighs;
I rush to the bathroom—
the dentures of hundreds of bad poems
piled in the bath-tub.
That night, when I switch on
my lamps, bad poem moths
storm them again & again,
as if there were a sale on light.
And just when I can begin
to forget, to concentrate, the phone goes
it is a whole troop of giggling
bad poems on the other end,
and they are calling, of course, Collect.

🔥 🔥 🔥

CLOE MORGAN

by KARL KOPP

from NEWSART/The Smith

nominated by H.L. Van Brunt

Black poets. Women poets. Gay poets. Indian poets. Academic poets. Convict poets. Chicano poets. Canadian poets. Whatever happened to Walt's dream of everyone—black/white/gay/straight/men/women—thronging the technicolored highways, arms 'round each other's waists, singing his lines *en masse?*

The average American (average anybody—including Yeats's ideal fisherman and Thomas's lovers under the raging moon) is still illiterate. And getting more so.

So this energy, this poetic radium, fizzes into the little magazines—to dissipate there in the minds of primarily white, college-educated, fellow poets at approximately the same level of fragmented consciousness.

This bothers me. Poetry is nowhere—like graduate school—unless we energize more than a handful of friends and rivals. Black/white/gay/straight be damned.

To have a locus. Walden Pond. Paterson, New Jersey. Mountain Top, Arkansas. Thebes. The universal *is* in the local. With or without Williams, we should know this by now. Then why so much *verbal* imagery merely, so much *featureless* rhythm, so much *unfixed* emotion? To invest in a place, to decipher and to speak its many voices, you have to love it. Who loves where he is in America? What purely "academic" poet, for example (and there are some), can love his interchangeable college town? Hate walls, yes. Hate boredom even more. Hate cruelty. Hate shackles and confinement. But love is the solar ray of poetry. CHOOSE a place—to go to or stay in—and Love the space, horizontal/vertical, in which your body moves.

But it's one thing to write *in* a place—to "reply to Greek and Latin with the bare hands"—and another to find an *audience* there.

The average American is still illiterate.

After having chosen to live on Yarbrough Mountain, in Arkansas, on a piece of land I in fact "own" (it has since come to own me, an "interpenetration both ways"), I can write a poem about this man:

He came of age (American-style)
in the Battle of the Bulge
which makes him roughly fifty
though he looks much younger

in and out of jail/work/wife
and house since then
more out than in

slept in his clothes
every night for five months
on Clarence's couch
the last time he left her
(Rip Van Winkle)
when he wasn't

drinking from a jug
remembering the army
and his son who'd rather
play ball and screw
than go to college

when he wasn't

watching *Bonanza &*
Gunsmoke
or fishing
or hunting coon and possum
out of season

no better shot than Cloe on
this mountain

and see him string that line
one fine March day
in Clarence's yard tight-lipped
in concentration sober
for fishing
                    happiest
when still
playing hookey

𝅥 𝅥 𝅥

STYLE THREE and STYLE FIVE

by WILLIAM WANTLING

from SEVEN ON STYLE (Second Coming Press)

nominated by Len Fulton and Leonard Randolph

STYLE 3

"Style is the selection of words which have the desired effect on the
reader and give the expression a distinctive air."
—Aristotle

Our sample stylist for today's lesson
is Chas Bukowski. you are, by now
familiar with the work of Chas Bukowski
we will, of course, study the work & ignore
the man. as graduate students in Rational Behavior
we should be, by now, adept at this. Bukowski
himself is said to prefer it. remember, last week
we learned that Poetry is Style, & Style, Intensity
therefore; imbuing Aristotle with intensity, we
arrive again at Style. thank you. today's . . .
thank you. you don't have to applaud, it won't
affect your grades. today's example, however
is not a deliberately crafted work of art
but a letter of rejection
upon submission of certain poems
to LAFF LITERARY & MAN THE HUMPING GUNS, an
intellectually esoteric little magazine of ill repute
& short duration. now, a real poet, that is, a real
stylist, cannot avoid using his blade of style under
pressure of intensity. the intensity stimuli
in this example were

1) a passionate, pissed-off
inner nature & 2) an irrational, all-consuming love
affair with the great bitch Style:

June 28, 1969

Hello Wantling:
     what the hell have you been doing to yourself,
man? this stuff very thin. since you've been going through
this college thing, babe, your writing has changed, softened.
and it was never really great, you know that. you need a
wake-up. I don't know if you can be saved. Check your
wife. I'm sure she has detected a change. I talk to you straight,
man, like a father because nobody else is going to. It's not a
crime to slip as a writer, but you went so fast. Get a ring &
valve job, joker, or do more time. Neeli says he is going to
whip your ass unless you shape up, motherfucker. If you think
I am kidding, he ain't. N. fucking with my bookcase saying, shit
shit we can sell this stuff.

     yeah?

     yeah.

     Dropped a hundred at the track today. So I am a nasty old
man. But you've written better stuff than this, sport.
     Also, tho you enclosed a stamped self-addressed, you glued
the damn thing together, so it was useless.
                              Yours,

                         Charles Bukowski

STYLE 5

   I tell it to the Freshmen
(I got it from a Master)
the first 3 rules of writing:
   CHOP Chop! *chop*

we dont wanta waste those hard-
won words, those brilliant precious gems, we
clog the nostrils of the world with snot

reminds me of the can of chicken soup I
had last night: I stare into my spoon
theres this tiny grey-green rubbery thing
I think its a booger or a pepper-corn, put
it under the reading glass, its a

    b.b. size chicken heart

now, it makes no sense to slaughter
   baby chicks
not money sense, I
know these gotta be the lil tads
that died of chickenpox, the plague, whatever, right?
somebody on that soup farm
wouldnt bury those plague-ridden little corpses
they hadda sell em, those
    b.b. size chicken hearts

waste not, the poet sd, &
               gibbered on . . .

sure, it *can* get precious, like a
speed freak crashing, like
Oscar Wilde, spending a morning
putting in a comma, an afternoon
taking one out
but there *is* a surly rat
in the rhythm of our blood
who gnaws & gnaws the night away

say it like it is & tell us where its coming from
cut clean & quick—adorn
only in the cause of intensity
(intensity comes mostly from *Chop*)

sure
theres consonantal assonance
theres vowel dance & rhyme, but
if you dont break a finger in excitement
working on the 2nd stanza
if you dont pick yr nose & ass
& smear it on a page or 2
& laugh & howl & weep with sullen anger
if you dont see God
during 1st revision
& vomit on the 2nd draft
faint from the stench of
butchered words & flesh, if
you dont howl & laugh some more
then you havent played it honest
you havent got a poem . . .

the clearest, cleanest notes in english
come from the Angles & the Saxons
those short harsh notes
forced thru the throats
of red & random horns: the
minds which sound our language-call, our

Scorpio-styled reality: Iron, Diamond
Red, the Vulture & the Wolf (the inner logic
which stands an ear on end . . . for there *is*
a surly rat
    in the rhythm of our blood
which gnaws & gnaws the night away)
& Aquarius with its phone tapped
its crotch cancer
buried under cola cans, strangled
by bureaucrats, raped
by politicians, perjured by the F.B.I.

but it *is* beautiful at times, like
a cat or a hornet or a
ground-to-air missile

whether its Emily Dickinson in the universe
of her interior rooms or Vachel Lindsay
on his ululating platform, poetry
must come from Life and the ones
who live it
    we cant make Life
come out of poems, no matter how
much we study, explicate
                or imitate
this separates
        the serious artist
from the merely serious man, &
art from the artistic
        now
I feel the universe as foolish, in a grand
& holy way, full of pain & laughter—& I
imitate it so
    I am not, however, a serious
man, I hope. rather, I've cavorted as Fool
for gods & men
    hoping that, at times, my
lunacy may touch upon the Holy (but
this is not the goal)
        & I am a serious
artist
    & the double mind is split upon
itself
    & creates its own reality—*this*
is the surly rat in the rhythm of our
blood
    who gnaws & gnaws the night away . . .

𝅘𝅥 𝅘𝅥 𝅘𝅥

EXPERIMENTAL LANGUAGE

by TONY QUAGLIANO

from GHOST DANCE

nominated by Hugh Fox

An Investigation of Eye Movement
During the Autokinetic Phenomenon
Utilizing Electrically Recorded Changes
in the Corneal-Retinal Potential
      Exploratory Behavior
      in Cockroaches
        (Blatta Orientalis)
   The Ability of Human Subjects
   to Attend to Visual Stimuli
   Not Centrally Fixated
Sign Stimuli Affecting Aggressive Behavior
in the Cichlid Fish
   (Chichlasoma Meeki)
       The Nature of Love
       Love-objects and
        Surrogates

LIKE A GOOD UNKNOWN POET

by ART CUELHO

from THE LAST FOOT OF SHADE (Holmgangers Press)

nominated by Holmgangers Press

I play my blues harmonica
to the McGuire killer horses
that go to Canada each
week to be made into dogfood.
The horses are sold by the pound
depending on how much horse flesh
dealing McGuire has with his customers—
four and five and six cents a pound,
that's the going rate of last ride death horses.

I give these shitter horses their
last bale of hay and their last song.
Their last pat on the head comes from me.
My two dollars an hour does not include
my stroking the McGuire killer horses.
This is at my own expense
because it's extremely hard to love
something beaten and finished.

You really can take pity on the horses.
They got broken legs, some are too old,
only have one eye, diseased, unwanted;
but every once in a while
like a good unknown poet
a good horse slips through

because the owner doesn't want to push
the high-priced hay into him all winter and
McGuire can't save him because
horses are a business
and remember up above all else
that McGuire gets paid by the pound
like I get my two dollars an hour
for the shit shovel and fate.

AFRIKAAN BOTTLES

fiction by G.K. WUORI

from CIMARRON REVIEW

nominated by CIMARRON REVIEW

Henry blackchick started to cross the highway but he couldn't so he stopped. Darn dumb. He looked one way and then the other. The tar band was clear, white stripe white and regular. Again he tried to move across it and again could not. Was it the press of air, the tingling in his feet? Blackchick could not move and knew not why.

During the first day (it would drag on) Blackchick was undiscouraged because of his own curiosity. The weather was good to him as well, neither hot nor cold and no sun. Blackchick hated the sun. Eventually, he spoke aloud, saying:

"I want but one quart of beer. The store is right there. Let me cross, please," Who was to hear those words he was not sure, but he thought he'd handled it right.

For twelve hours he stood there and whenever there were no machines on the road he would try to cross and could not. In the evening the storeowner closed his store and came to his edge of the highway and spoke to Blackchick.

"What's the matter with you?" he asked.

Blackchick told him. Then the man remarked how long a day it must have been for him. "I was going to drink it and watch television," he said. "I was going to relax and enjoy myself for a change. I'm out of work. Life has been difficult."

The storeowner agreed about the difficulties of life and finally said that if Blackchick would throw the money across the road he could go and get him his quart of beer.

They tried several things. First, the storeowner, whose name Henry thought was CashBrand, wrapped the bottle in a towel and tried to roll it across to Blackchick. The bottle, however, reached the centerline and rolled back. Several times he rolled it, harder and harder each time, and each time it rolled back.

Then, in a stroke of cleverness, he stopped a car. It was a friend of his, he said. Through the window he passed the bottle and Blackchick reached out to the driver's window to receive the beer. The man, however, found that his window was jammed and when he tried to open his door that was stuck too. So he gave the beer back to CashBrand and drove off to his regular service station to have the door and window repaired.

By this time CashBrand was, frankly, angered, and he took from his pocket a small knife with a bottle opener on it. With the bottle open, he stuck his thumb to the top and shook the bottle as hard as he could until it was all foamy and pressured inside. He aimed for Blackchick and released his thumb. The beer arced all golden and beautiful, like a pee in the sunset, but a wind came up just then and met the foamy arc and drove it back to CashBrand. Not a drop had touched Henry Blackchick.

"Did you think I would drink it in the air?" asked Blackchick.

The night was not as pleasant for Blackchick as he had hoped it would be. He returned to his apartment, which was in a large complex adjacent to the highway, told his wife, Regina, about his day, then collapsed into his chair without turning on his television, without smoking or reading his newspaper or even drinking the one can of beer remaining in the refrigerator. One can he did not want.

In the morning he was standing on the highway even before CashBrand arrived. He watched the early morning diesel trucks pumping by, noted how they seemed to run in packs like big tin dogs and thought their stench pleasant. Henry had always liked the smell of fuels. The roaring of the trucks thoroughly woke him and by eight o'clock when CashBrand drove in he was in good spirits, regardless of the rain which had begun falling and the general rawness of the day.

Somberly, CashBrand walked to the edge of the highway and looked at Blackchick. "I don't think ingenuity is the answer," said Blackchick.

"Devices?"

"Yeah, that's not it."

"It's all we got. We got to try."

"I suppose."

"This ever happened before?"

"Once."

Until that moment he had not even connected the two events. But it was a time Regina had sent him to the store for some cigarettes. He had gone downtown because it was always quiet and pleasant there now, and was on the corner across from the tobacco shop— when everything had suddenly seemed quite unredeemably funny, humorous, a very wholesome kind of humorous. Buildings standing before a man, such dainty concrete paths at his feet. Yes, dainty! Clay blocks festooned with ribbons, clay sound he did not need to hear. The traffic light had changed again and again and from time to time—he stood for over an hour—someone he knew would come up to him, say hello, and he would answer, not confused at all, quite coherent, they would talk for a moment and whoever it was would go on. But he could not cross the street, and he thought it was really greatly terribly funny. A man trapped by his own forces and like a surgeon reaching into a gut he could point inward and identify all of his problems but that didn't seem to make any difference. He stood and he stood until finally he simply turned and walked back to his car. When he got home he found that Regina had gone across to the CashBrand's herself and had gotten her own cigarettes.

He could point to a snapped linkage between will and deed; now and then a man didn't have the heart to do what he set his mind to do because that was all too neat. Again, the pointing did no good, but it killed the worry, like saying to yourself I've got a problem and it's damn serious but I always prevail over my own weaknesses. I always do. Yet, who was prevailing over whom here? CashBrand's face had received the spray of beer. It had been that other nameless man who'd paid for his spirit by a broken car. More and more, Blackchick began to feel like a mere bystander in a situation where people were trying their hardest to help him and ended by getting so bound into their own frustrations that his problem became theirs. They entered with sympathy and left with anger, no longer caring about him and about the quart of beer he wanted because times were difficult and he wanted only to sit by his television and be nothing at all for a short time, just a man who was enjoying something privately and not hurting anyone.

At noon that day Regina joined him and surveyed the litter of the morning's attempts. There were more towels. There was a complicated stick-and-wire apparatus that had not even begun to work. There was an automobile tire. That had almost done it. CashBrand had taped the bottle inside and had rolled it in Blackchick's direction. On the first try it had collapsed in a circling roll on the centerline. A trucker stopped then and brought the tire back to CashBrand, even though both of them were trying frantically to tell him to give it to Blackchick. He had just not understood and seemed rather angry. On the second try the tire made it to Blackchick but at the centerline, where it all seemed to be happening the tape loosened and the bottle fell out, somewhat remarkably not breaking.

"You know, I feel awful about this," he said. But Regina said nothing.

She was his wife so she sympathized, stood beside him, a woman taller than he with angle-iron bones and gray eyes, a women of strong intelligence and no ambition, who made it a point to know what Blackchick wanted and yet who'd always stood just far enough out of his way to be unable to help at, say, crucial moments. She was no heroine, at least not until now.

By the third day some of the regular truckers had begun to notice Henry Blackchick, enjoyed the sight of Regina Blackchick too, dressed in shorts and halter and sandals as the rain passed and the weather warmed. They stood—sentinels, thought Henry—they seemed not to move at all while all about them the car lots, hamburger shacks, and pizza parlors spun with activity.

By the end of the third day Blackchick was nearly paralyzed, his long forehead a badlands of wrinkled concentration. Schoolbuses passed by regularly and the students waved at them, and some threw things, wads of paper with the red marks of error, applecores scarred by the dents of loose baby teeth. Neither Blackchick nor Regina smiled, neither of them returned the waves and shouts.

On the morning of the fourth day Blackchick lost his odd resolve and asked Regina to try. There was no reply, no hesitation. She was, it seemed, quite ready to help him this time. Once inside the store she nodded in agreement as CashBrand said: "That's some man you've got there. A will like that moves mountains. Fifty cents with the tax please."

"My husband paid you four days ago," she said. CashBrand seemed honestly sincere as he apologized, and even walked her back to the edge of the highway, muttering his sympathies and his understandings over her husband's dilemma.

"He's not alone, Mrs. Blackchick," he said. "But a lot are keeping it to themselves and keeping it in private places. I admire your husband for bringing it out."

As they returned to the highway a long pack of the diesels crossed in front of them, their roar threatening to erase not only words but even vision. Regina's eyes filled and the parking lot suddenly seemed cratered and dangerous. The man beside her a vain creature mumbling things he did not know, assuming knowledge about her husband he had no right to assume.

This pack of trucks seemed truly endless and Regina wondered if there were not an accident somewhere down the road. They slowed to a crawl and CashBrand went on and on. The bottle cradled in her arm was leaking in coolness through the paper sack. It would be warm by the time she got it to him.

She stepped onto the highway, leaving CashBrand behind. Edging toward the centerline, she looked up to the cabs of the trucks, urging, almost pleading for one moment, a second break in the bumper-to-bumper chain while she dashed through with the beer still cool and refreshing for her husband. It was the least she could do for him these days, she thought.

"Henry!" she yelled, stooping over and trying to see his legs through the trucks. She couldn't spot him. Looking up again, she shouted to one of the truckers but his window was closed for his air-conditioning and he could not hear.

CashBrand screamed as she grabbed the tail of one of the trucks, held his breath as he watched her dancing across the bumper of the next truck, nearly ground his fingers into his palms when she fell beneath the wheels of the machine.

Bending over, he could see her lying on the shoulder of the road, legs twisted all wrong yet both hands grasped around the upright bottle. He stayed bending over as he waited for Henry Blackchick to come running frantically to his injured wife, a woman maybe dead who'd maybe died trying to do a good thing for her husband. He remained stooped for a long time looking for Henry, and when the line finally passed and he could cross over and take the silly-looking bag of beer from the woman's hands he was not surprised that Henry Blackchick was nowhere to be seen.

THE ELEPHANT

by CARLOS DRUMMOND DE ANDRADE

(translated by Mark Strand)

from PLOUGHSHARES

nominated by Daniel Halpern

I make an elephant
from the little
I have. Wood
from old furniture
holds him up,
and I fill him
with cotton, silk,
and sweetness.
Glue keeps his heavy
ears in place.
His rolled-up trunk
is the happiest part
of his architecture.
But there are also
his tusks made
of that rare material
I cannot fake.
What a white fortune
to be rolling around
in the dust of the circus
without being stolen or lost!
And finally there are
the eyes where the most
fluid and permanent
part of the elephant
stays, free of all fraud.

Here's my poor elephant
ready to leave
to find friends
in a jaded world
that no longer believes
in animals and doesn't
trust things.
Here he is: an imposing
and fragile hulk,
who shakes his head
and moves slowly,
his hide stitched
with cloth flowers
and clouds, allusions
to a more poetic world
where love reassembles
the natural forms.

My elephant goes
down a crowded street,
but nobody looks
not even to laugh
at his tail that threatens
to leave him.
He is all grace, except
his legs don't help
and his swollen belly
is about to collapse
at the slightest touch.
He expresses
with elegance
his minimal life
and no one in town
is willing to take
to himself
from that tender body
the fugitive image,
the clumsy walk,
hungry and touching,

but hungry for pitiful
people and situations,
for moonlit encounters
in the deepest ocean,
under the roots of trees
or in the bosom of shells,
for lights that do not blind
yet shine through
the thickest trunks.
That walk which goes
without crushing plants
on the battlefield,
searching for places,
secrets, stories
untold in any book,
whose style only the wind,
the leaves, the ant
recognize, but men
ignore since they dare
show themselves only
under a veiled peace
and to closed eyes.

And now late at night
my elephant returns,
but returns tired out,
his shaky legs
break down in the dust.
He didn't find
what he wanted,
what we wanted,
I and my elephant,
in whom I love
to disguise myself.
Tired of searching,
his huge machinery
collapses like paper.
The paste gives way
and all his contents,

forgiveness, sweetness,
feathers, cotton,
burst out on the rug,
like a myth torn apart.
Tomorrow I begin again.

BROKEN PORTRAITURE

fiction by BRUCE BOSTON

from GALLIMAUFRY

nominated by Len Fulton

RED PETALS ON A VARIEGATED GROUND

Rolling, turning, spitting out words, going up and down the coast, getting drunk, vomiting in bus stations, dying train stations, thumb aching in cold highway wind, staying with friends, believing, imbibing the sacrament, sitting in the circles in the cities passing the burning stick, warm skies blending to grey drizzle matting his unkempt hair against frayed denim collar, cracked leather collar, dirty and knotted fur collar, staying with friends, finding another woman, sitting in the circles in the country with the city-fled, imbibing the sacrament gone sour, staying up all night, jangling reds three for a dollar, going inland, up and down the central valley, talking, talking, spitting out words, leaving nothing unsaid, double-said, triple-said, losing the sense of things, standing on the beach at Sur and letting his mind unzippered turn the white wave froth to Chinese dragons on a 14th century scroll, dodging the draft and beating it, going down in the files of national security as a c.o. addict with a trick knee and too much sugar in his urine, dropping out of school for good, standing alone in a street outside a bar or an all-night coffee shop or the 16th avenue laundromat where he'd caught a few hours of sleep beneath the droning dryers, B-52s in his dreams, marching for the napalmed dead, marching for something else and something again and for the faces on the street, looking for Billie or Marilyn or Rider, listening to the radio, cursing the powers that be, making the connections, watching the records stack and fall, lighting the incense a red pin-star dance in the blackness of the windowless basement bedroom, reading the books of illumination, forgetting the words, talking, saying it again, losing the friends gone straight, burnt out, spitting the words like a plasmic stream, vomiting the music, imbibing the sacrament bastardized with killing chemicals, the words laid down to the beast, bum-tripping once more, feeding his ego. losing the friends gone sour and scared, finding others less certain, more confused, watching the records fall, breaking the penultimate capsule with his teeth and discovering the soul of bitterness within . . .

MONDRIAN MONOCHROME

Once he became like so many others, aping the accepted externals of existence, life reduced itself to a simpler matter. His oscillations, which had once soared and plummeted beyond the limits of any standardized graph, now performed a gentle sine weaving about the x-axis. Now he chose to see all things as solid and well-defined. When their outlines began to waver and threaten other forms he feigned ignorance of their vagrancy. CONTROL was a key word; CALCULATION was another. It was important to think in numerical terms since it gave one a proper sense for the grouping of priorities. As for his idealism, once he ranked it as pubescent nonsense he could dismiss its relevance with respect to decision-making processes. As for his rage (at the hypocrisy), at first he kept it in a green bottle, nearly opaque due to the darkness of the glass, stoppered with an oversized cork. His further differences he set apart to occupy private barred chambers within his mind. Other respectable men had their secrets, the afternoons in uptown apartments the late evening business engagements, even if they were of a less metaphysical bend. And weren't such indiscretions as those more likely to be uncovered than those locked totally within the self.

Bizarre intoxicants he abandoned for the everyday variety: alcohol, tobacco, coffee, commercial tranquillizers and vitalizers. Socially these were less harmful and with a proper dosage could be effective in their own ways. He adopted a SCHEDULE to finalize the regularity of his days and as the years began to accumulate it encouraged the sum of his visible life. Naturally there were additions—a wife, a house, advancement in his chosen field of endeavor, a budding family—all pointing in one direction, toward a red letter calibration of normality at the peak of the bell curve.

As for his wife, she was sleek and polished. She was well-born to her role in life without the adjustments he had found necessary. Her breasts were full, her legs clean as marble. Her eyes shimmered like nickels coated with mercury. When her mouth closed upon him it moved with the accuracy of a machine.

As for his office, the walls were grey-green. He was never sure of what material they were composed since he did not focus on them directly. Certain things were better left without attention, like the illusions which distracted him at the corners of his vision but which he refused to turn his head to confront. His rage (at the corpulent amid the hungry) was not like that; it required constant attention. It proved to have tumerous inclinations. Benign enough he was sure, yet growing nonetheless. He transferred it to a larger flask, one of slate grey pottery fired to a high gloss at 4000° fahrenheit so that the contents remained invisible. A stopper of the same material was heat-sealed in place and he mounted the oversized vessel atop the mantle in his livingroom as a weighty reminder of the errors of his past.

His desk changed from metal to oak as his prominence grew. Not all at once. First a handle here or there made the transformation, next an entire drawer or a segment of the side paneling. Finally one morning he entered his office to find the completed product, its richly-grained surfaces shining softly and perfectly as if in celebration of his own perfection. From that day on, his lesser needs were supplied by others. His desk was always fully stocked without him lifting a finger. Pencils, pens, erasers, paper clips, rubber bands, scotch tape, masking tape, scissors large and small, datebooks, rule books, memos, specifications, and six grades of paper each with its assigned use. This desk provided a parallel to his life, right down to the locked-off compartment on the lower left in which he stored confidential papers. As for the locked-off compartments in his mind, these he visited less often—only in the moments before sleep when he began to give up CONTROL, or in his dreams. But dreams were of no matter and could be dismissed upon awakening.

Still, there remained his rage (at the separateness). He knew that any piece of pottery, even heavily cast and perfectly fired, could be shattered in a moment of carelessness. Thus at last he came upon the box. It was a wooden box with a velvet interior and had once held a matched set of long-nosed dueling pistols. It was an appropriate box in which to store and imprison one's rage (at the patronage). A fall could not break it, and the metal sheeting between the lining and the wood made it impervious to fire. There was a sturdy clasp of solid silver with a secret fastening so that no chance guest or curious servant might pry within. Its sole disadvantage lay in the fact that unlike a corked bottle or stoppered flask, he could open it at a moment's notice. Surely, this was temptation.

SNOW LIKE STATIC, LIKE BEAST-ROAR

He sees the faces which are no longer faces which are blocks of meat, dark and radiant buttons for eyes, empty hooks for teeth. Is it a word which sets him off? An unrecordable chemical accident within the brain, the twitching of a face muscle beneath a razored jowl? No matter. Although he has compromised again and again and it is but a single moment among many, this once he fails.

In the hall the hose lies curled, a bland and dusty snake within its cage. Beside it rests the axe, potent, shining dully. His hand has forgotten the ways of glass and passing through it bleeds. The axe within his bloodied grip dominates the entire room. With this one action he has brought them instantly alive, all of them, and they scatter like bugs before him as he goes to work. One, two, one, two.

So easy, he thinks. Lift and swing. Lift high and deliver the blow and the desk resonates, splits, and begins to crumple. The life of its polished grain is only deception, a surface life. Within, the wood is too dead for sap to flow. Rotted and fibrous it topples away in crackling chunks. Yet his eyes of sweat and rage can perceive another kind of flowing: clips, staples, pennons of unreeling tape, scissors double-jackknifing through the air, six grades of paper, manila folders stamped CONFIDENTIAL and shredded roughly in two.

So easy, he thinks, lift and swing and the pressure wells up and finds release again and again. This was the kind of work any soul could comprehend, destruction clean and simple.

He vaults the midden of the desk and delivers a deft blow to the window. It splinters outward to sprinkle the street far below, soundlessly. He gashes the walls with his own brand of abstract expression, sends a filing cabinet on a clattering journey from one scarred corner to another. He laughs completely and steps into the hall.

Now their eyes are buttons broken, wax grapes crushed underfoot, cheap glazed candies with their tasteless centers exploded. They have retreated and grouped at each end of the corridor, two mindless tides reflecting one another. He controls these tides: when he advances, they retreat. Whirling the axe above his head, sensing its whistle in the programmed air, laughing again, he charges and they disperse to individual droplets running for open elevators and stairwells. He continues his abstract on the corridor walls, in the deserted offices. The artist alone with himself: the axe his brush, all of the immediate world his canvas. This could rival Kokoschka, dwarf Pollack. He is laughing more completely than he has in years. And that is how they find him, laughing still, lift and swing, lift and swing, as they surround him from behind like a cautious hunting pack and drive the needle within.

THE COLORS ARE IN HIS HEAD

The plays within his mind, the brainreel running unspliced and without commercial breaks, becomes far more fascinating than anything on the outside. At times the externals of his existence provide the ground work for these internal fantasies; yet often they seem born unto themselves, or drawn from another reality he has experienced in some other life or plane of being. His waking dreams take on the quality and intensity of sleeping dreams. His unreasoning unconscious holds the reins and the whip and together they travel mightily, with no chosen direction on his part whatsoever.

Example: a dark tree and fern landscape which he has never visited before, a tiger docile as a lamb, a sun which pokes about in the hairy branches this way and that as if it has lost all sense of time and does not know setting from rising from burning noon meridian. Right side up and upside down reverse, become as aberrant and interchangeable as the rise-up-fall-down constructions of toy blocks. Here or there a tree chooses to grow into the ground and send its roots uselessly soil-searching toward the sky. By night, moonless, the constellation of Orion burns brightly in the lake and casts its reflection like an afterthought, tenuous, rippling overhead in the smoky waters of the firmament.

AUTUMN EVENING

by JOHN H. BEAUVAIS

from A FLIGHT OF ARROWS (Pitcairn Press)

nominated by Pitcairn Press

Young women
who have given eight hours
of hope to a bright office
come up out of the subway,
figureheads
on that invisible ship
The American Dream.

Going home,
carrying groceries and cut flowers,
the cool kiss of rain is like a wish.

> Women from offices
> come out of the subway
> into the bounty of streetlights
> going back to their rooms
> breaking in and out of shadows quietly.

> Press your heart
> in these wet autumn leaves
> and put it away in a book.

🔥 🔥 🔥

ENCOUNTERS WITH EZRA POUND

by CHARLES OLSON

from ANTAEUS

nominated by Leonard Randolph

CANTO 3, JANUARY 24, 1946, 3:10-3:30

T ODAY'S MEETING WAS completely different in tone. It is strange, but the only word is gay. Right from the start it was wild and strong. I brought myself forward more, and Pound did too.

This time we were in the second of the two visiting cubicles, and the stair didn't spill away behind me, he was backed up by the heavy ward wall, and it seemed to create a more explosive character to our meeting. The guard was different too, less interesting than the

This manuscript was found among Charles Olson's papers, and has not been revised in any way, in accordance with the Charles Olson estate.

353

regular one, so we sort of forgot him. Except when Pound, as always so instantly gracious, was quick to suggest he have a cigarette as I was opening a package to give me one to Pound. The guard declined, and with that Pound says, CHAW CUT PLUG. And repeated it, CHAW CUT PLUG. Explaining to the guard he meant that's the only thing he guessed the guard did. The sudden explosion of Pound's voice in this phrase was quite total to me. It was the poet making sounds, trying them out to see if they warmed his ear. But it was the fascist too, as snob, classing the guard. And it was Pound's old spit at America. Add an ounce of courtesy in it, and you have something like what I mean.

I had provoked this tobacco business when I gave Pound the dates I had brought. Connie[1] and I had wondered if we couldn't bring him some of bertram's stuff.[2] So I asked him if he smoked. He said no, it made him nervous the next day. Then quite soon after, when he was rubbing his forehead with the heel of his hand, troubled by his lack of ability to concentrate, he had asked me for a cigarette, which he smoked like a woman who does it to be free.

But this is where the business led:

From cut plug, Pound suddenly said: "I suppose if I had used————(a brand of plug, I gathered, which I didn't catch) I'd be a Senator today!" It was too much for me! I said, "But you remember, Yeats warned you about that. Do not be a Senator, he said in the Packet. . . ."[3]Pound didn't say anything, looked at me sharp, and I went on; "That remark always seems funny to me, the difference between an Irish senator and an American is like a . . . planet . . . and a pumpkin." And then Pound, quite seriously and up out of his depths said, "I guess I never understand that." As though it had been a mistake of his. Of course what he was feeling was revealed in what he then launched into, a swift autobiography.

Before I record it, I should say that it was prepared by my chance meeting with Miss Maple, one of the two old ladies who have been also visiting him. While I was waiting downstairs to go up to visit, she came down, and asked the guard who it was that was waiting to see Mr. Pound. He pointed me out, she asked me my name, said are you a journalist, I said no, a poet, o, she said, that's different, I said, He looks good physically, don't you think, she demurred, and was thinking of him when she saw him in 1939, and all the years back. I asked her how long she had known him, she said all her life, that is since 1906. I said, most of his life then too. I said, did you meet him

in Idaho. And then she almost querulously corrected me, by explaining that it was an accident he had been born there, that it was
because Pres. McKinley had sent his father out to survey the territory, and that Pound had actually been brought up in Philadelphia.
Then, as people will, when they want to establish the propriety of
someone, she started to tell me he had gone to Hamilton, Columbia.
. . .[4] I indicated I knew of that, at least. She sort of muttered, "Even
then he was unusual." There was distress in her, over his plight. But
an air about her at the same time, which her visits prove. She asked
me a strange question, Was I English? I answered no, American,
and perhaps because I had felt the sting the last time of Pound's
praise of Pegler, I went on, my father was Swedish and my mother
Irish, which makes me very American. She looks up at me, and says,
"Then you must have a sense of humor!"

The point is, I had recounted some of this, especially about my
ancestry, to Pound when I had come up. He had apparently taken
me for Norwegian. Said, apropos of her remark you are English,
well, your face could be, and I said yes, I carry no marks of my blood,
except possibly my height and there I outstripped my father. (It felt
good to get the ancestry across to Pound for reasons aforesaid.)

So that there was preparation for Pound to go on from the Senator
business thus: I was raised in an atmosphere of the civic Congressman. Of course I was only a child but . . . (Instantly the feeling
of *Confucius* and his *Jeff and/ or Muss*.)[5] My father met my mother
here (Washington) when he was congressman. And after he was sent
out to Idaho, he got appointed as assayer at the Mint. My mother
tried to urge him to get out (and follow a career of public service, I
gathered) but he refused. He was probably wise. He didn't say any
more than I remember, yet I have the feeling of a large passage here.
It is probably the intensity of Pound's feeling for civic responsibility,
made painful now by where it has brought him.

His plea his broadcasts be examined is not without point. Wrong
as he is, to my mind, in his conclusions on authority, and obscured,
as fascists can be, by a mania to save the Constitution, no one can
deny the seriousness with which he has examined civic responsibility. The personal sources of his obsession were revealed to me
yesterday. It is a little like Biddle,[6] when I talked to him in his office,
pointing out the engraving of Washington's cabinet, and proudly
indicating his ancestor as one of the four. Though it must be said for
Pound that his sense is not social, but societal, more John Adams,

and the Adams' family sense. What's shallow about it is the deadness of it, the 18th century *lag* in it, the moan for the lost republican purity, the wish to return America to its condition of a small nation of farmers and city-state patricians, all Boston brahmin, and Philadelphia brick. Nothing wrong in that either, except what happens to political action now if it is so motivated. It turns out to be reactionary and fascist. For what are the positions it leads to? (1) an antagonism to immigration; (2) a hate for "foreign" elements; (3) a feeling of a Jewish conspiracy; (4) the old ways of "free enterprise"; (5) a Civil Liberties Union concept of the bill of rights; etc. In other words, a pitiful, sick and dangerous defense of all that *was*, which forever and anywhere and in all things, fears anything forward. Pound can talk all he likes about the *cultural lag* in America (he was at it again yesterday as of the Vanguard Press announcements, the 20 years lag) but he's got a 200 year *political lag* in himself. It comes down to this: a rejection of the single most important fact of the last 100 years, the most important human fact between Newton and the Atomic Bomb—the sudden multiple increase of the earth's population, the coming into existence of the MASSES. Pound and his kind want to ignore them. They try to lock them out. But they swarm at the windows in such numbers they black out the light and the air. And in their little place Pound and his kind suffocate, their fear turns to hate. And their hate breeds death. They want to kill. And, organized by Hitler and Mussolini, they do kill—millions. But the breeding goes on. And with it such social and political change as they shall not understand.

It is *economics* that finally confronts them, this science of the *masses*. And it is economic necessities which underlie the revolution in society and politics.

In Pound I am confronted by the tragic Double of our day. He is the demonstration of our duality. In Language and form he is as forward, as much the revolutionist as Lenin. But in social, economic and political action he is as retrogressive as the Czar.

And then Pound jumped ahead to 1914 and Poland, and something about they were wise enough to get out. Or he was, I couldn't quite get it clear. (This date seemed to be important, for Pound there took a swing at the doctor Kavka, who, he said, thinks that all my trouble starts there, 1914, Poland.)[7]

I believe it was here too that Pound said, "I told Potocki,[8] is that

how you pronouce it?" I said, Potostcki, and he went on, "I told him
not to trust England." (Familiar?)

Pound's complaint about the doctor served somehow to create the
gaiety of the meeting, despite the anti-semitism which mixed itself
into it. For poor Kavka does seem to be scared to death of this Pound
business, and to be handling it in an absurd way because of his fear
and uncertainty. God knows it is causing Pound a good deal of what
I'm sure is unnecessary pain. He says Kavka keeps pounding questions at him. . . . and punched his fist against the wall of his other
hand to illustrate the effect. He says he wakes up the following
morning exhausted from trying to think back and work out the
answers to his questions.

I tried to get him to take Kavka less seriously, telling Pound K is
frightened to death, not of him so much as of the fact it is the Ezra
Pound case. And that he's no more than a graduate student, trying to
act professional.

At this Pound says, I never knew a doctor less scientific. If they
want to examine me, why don't they give me some scientist, I
wouldn't mind. He merely acts like a goddamn bureaucrat. But his
intolerable questioning, Good god, what the hell, what the hell
difference does it make what I was reading in 1902! (At this point
Pound just continued to swear, and wondering if there was any
"lady" in the next cubicle, saying he wouldn't want to shock them,
he jumps up and looks around the corner, and finding none, continues to let it rip.

"With ANTISEMITE spread all over the front page of PM, you
can't expect much else," he said, alluding to K., who was born
Jonah Kafka, and is now Jerome Kavka,[9] as he told me when I
gave him Pound's *Kulch* and *Cantos*—. (At that time K said, it
hadn't made any impression on EP when he had learned his name
was Kafka.)

Pound then followed up, "The other doctor I didn't mind." He
meant Tiny, who had been in charge that one Sunday CC had
visited. Tiny Ziman.[10] I point out to Pound that Tiny used to be a
master of ceremonies in a night club, and had some experience of
people. But that K was just a kid. Told him I had tried to get Tiny to
bring K and me together informally.[11] And would try again. But that
K has so far backed away from me. Probably K is also scared of that
s.o.b. Griffin,[12] who is his boss.

Pound said, "They (meaning Jews) were nice to me at the DDC[13] (jail?).

"I guess the definition of a lunatic is a man surrounded by them."

He was quiet for a minute, working his forehead, when he started out, talking down and away toward the window to his right and my left: "There was a Jew, in London, Obermayer, a doctor of comparative. . . . of the endocrines, and I used to ask him what is the effect of circumcision. That's the question that gets them sore," and he begins to be impish as hell, "that sends them right up the pole. Try it, don't take my word, try it." And then, with a pitiful seriousness, turning directly toward me and says: "It must do something, after all these years and years, where the most sensitive nerves in the body are, rubbing them off, over and over again." (It was fantastic, again the fascist bastard, the same god damned kind of medical nonsense Hitler and the gang used with the same seriousness, the same sick conviction.) It was so cockeyed for the moment it was funny actually, absurd, and I was carried along by this swearing, swift, slashing creature.

I record it, but here as elsewhere, it is impossible to give a true impression. For at any given point, always, there is the presence of the seriousness of the man. Even in his sickest and most evil moments. He is always a man at work, examining, examining. Here, for example, on the one hand he is attacking K as a Jew, when the truth is K is making the mistakes of any young man, and Pound is god dammed well lucky it is K and not the monster Griffin who is questioning him, is in charge. I could not help feeling during this whole line of Pound's, how it was precisely the Jews around him and in the DDC[14] who gave him some warmth and help, how it was through Tiny and K that I had got drawers issued to him, how it was K who at least had the curiosity to read his verse, and that K, in Chicago, when the bookstores said they wouldn't carry the books of a fascist, objected and damn well told them that was the same as burning books, and plain out and out fascist. On top of that that it was Rahv,[15] another Jew, who had accepted my Yeats thing on EP, when all the blessed Christian editors took it as offering Pound an out, an intellectual excuse.

Hate blinds. It makes this man of exquisite sense a false instrument. It makes a lie of perception. It empties Pound as completely as Oscar's pitiful ego prevents him from any illumination of the human beings around him.[16] Where all that Oscar takes in has to come by way of the brain, as though he were some cathode tube without eyes, ears, skin to record, flesh to touch. Pound is become the same thing in reverse, with eyes, ears, touch gone, and only gangrenous bowels left, rotted from fear, and giving off nothing but the stink of hate.

Yet you see this isn't all, despite everything. For Pound will spend his night honestly seeking answers to K's questions, genuinely trying to give this Jew what he wants. He will mention his debt to the Jew in Rome who suggested to him to translate Confucius. He remains, on the creative side of him, whole, and as charming and open and warm a human being as I know. Despite all the corruption of his body politic.

It is this contradiction which keeps me from turning my back on him. I imagine that is why when suddenly he throws his bowels in my face I am forever surprised and react too late for anger and disgust to strike back. I am carried on by the gravity and intensity of the man, now as ever examining, examining, as puzzled as ever to the questions, as naive as your skin and mine to a new rain, an open man, the poet, who does not hide his pain, joy, doubt, pride,—or hate. Sick he had made himself, finally a menace, yet point by point, cornered as he is, I shall still hold out the hand.

He gave me a chance to catch up with myself at one point yesterday, when he again mentioned Austine Cassini. It came early in the conversation, when he said: "It is time someone examined my broadcasts." He had in mind a defense, in the press. I was again off guard, in this instance, because I go to Pound as a writer and go on the assumption we can talk without his trial coming in. Which is of course utterly silly. And ignores the fact that Pound has nothing else on his mind. Anything else is accidental, and leads back in any case to the sore place inside him. So all I said, was, weakly, "But I don't think they are available."[17] He said yes, and mentioned the name of some woman who had examined them. It was then he asked if anyone knew Austine Cassini, and quickly said, But I mentioned her to you last time.

This time I couldn't let it go. I said, Such people are not your friends, Mr. Pound. They do you no good outside. For their interest in your case is false, and they misuse you. They have not examined things as you have, lack the intellectual grounds you establish. (God

knows I felt as I said this that to him, alone and isolated in prison
with one thought only, how to get out of this mess, an Austine
Cassini or a John O'Donnell are the only ones who appear as friends.
And I also thought, yes, and in the straight fascist sense, they are
your friends, and the only ones. And I dare say my sense of a total
Pound, or Bill Williams, doesn't mean now a goddamnedthing to
Pound, really. But there it is, I am the friend of the man. (When I
signed the register, the new guard couldn't read my name or the
word "friend" written in the space for relation, and interrupted to
say, are you his brother, was it?)

I went on: "Actually, your sense of the civic responsibility is the
strongest base on which your case rests," contrasting it by the tone of
my voice to the Cassinis and Peglers.

I paid him one compliment, when he complained he couldn't
concentrate, and make a coherent conversation. (It was about this
time he asked for a cigarette.) Actually, in these conversations, he
has seemed to me to be quite coherent and consecutive, and I said
so, in hopes he would take the judgment of someone outside himself, someone admittedly "fresh" to him as myself, but a reasonable
judge. He made nothing of it, as he doesn't of any remark to him,
actually. You can see him take such things into himself, and know he
hears, but that's all. The only instance I can recall now where I did
get an immediate response was on the difference between an Irish
and an American Senator.

When he was sounding off about the doctor, he pleaded convincingly that what he most needed was to be led away from the subject
of himself, to be given rest from this question of why he was what he
has become, just the opposite of what Kavka was doing. It was then
he said, "Ford, I happened on a novel of his, and it did me more
good than anything has, to restore me, except Katherine." It turned
out he meant Fordm-Ford's SO. . . . ,[18] for as I was leaving he said,
read it, the second volume isn't as good as the first, but I had
forgotten what a fine novelist he was.

I asked him: "Katherine?" He said: "O, Katherine Proctor, didn't
I tell you about her visit to me at the Jail. Yes, I've known her for 40
years. Of course then she was full of Wellesley and that stuff. But she
had married the man who did the stained glass windows in the
Cathedral here, and had done nothing all these 40 years but read the
Bible. Of course it's Bibles only that I have had. First, it was a Jewish

Testament, the manual they use in the Army. Then a priest brought me a new Catholic version, a little bigger, but the translation not as good as the old Version. And then the regular one bigger than that. I had a pile so big it crowded what little room there was on the table beside my cot. So in comes Katherine, with a couple of her fat children, to reform the old reprobate, to save the sinner's soul, despite the fact he might not want to be saved. (Laughing, laughing, full of red-beard, redhead, red tongue laughing) Swearing, slashing, but at the same time telling how good it was to see her and why it was she and Ford only that have done anything to give him rest and restore him to some equanimity in the midst of these, his troubles.

I can't for the life of me remember what it was that provoked the 20 year lag again business, but he said, indicating with his hands the closing of a gap, "I have tried to bring them up . . .," meaning even with themselves. Then he, why, I don't know unless he has just seen their catalogue, but he says: "Look at Vanguard's list, just look at it, don't say anything, just look, and then Vanguard's list 20 years ago."

As of dates I brought, "I eat anything."

As I was leaving half to me and half to the guard, swearing away, he was half complaining, half laughing at the way the whole ward and its troubles seems to have to go through his room, by his door, illustrating "poor guy in the next cell" by suddenly going down on his heels, and squatting all bent over, his hands over his head, as agile and quick as you please, a Kollwitz pose of misery. And coming up, saying "And Wahoo," meaning I suppose the Indian who talked about bumping off 10,000 people.

I had assumed he was in an open ward, but he spoke of the heat apropos of my telling him I couldn't get him long drawers, there were no wool ones, saying he didn't want wool, too hot, they keep the. . . . (same hall) too hot. I asked about the courtyard for walking and he said, horrible. Then he told me he had a room to himself and all the ventilation he needed. "Only if they wouldn't have to lock the door at night. Of course I'm getting better. I only have to go to the toilet two times now."

I told him I had seen CC and reported on the Gaudier Brzescas. He said, yes, and launched again into what he would do with them: "I'd put some 24 of them up in a large room like a frieze." I said, "How many of them are there anyhow?" And he, indicating piles, said, "All his charcoal drawings. She ought to be able to sell them to some gallery. . . ."

I said, "You make Gaudier seem so young"—and I went on with what I have thought so often, "as you seem to me yourself, so young." And he crushes his head and face in his hands, and says nothing.

NOTES

1. Constance Wilcock Bunker, Olson's first wife.
2. Bertram's is a tobacco shop in Washington.
3. "Do not be elected to the Senate of your country. I think myself, after six years, well out of that of mine. Neither you nor I, nor any other of our excitable profession, can match these old lawyers, old bankers, old business men, who, because all habit and memory, have begun to govern the world." William Butler Yeats, *A Packet for Ezra Pound* (Dublin, 1929), p. 33.
4. Pound attended Hamilton College and the University of Pennsylvania.
5. *Jefferson and /or Mussolini: L'Idea Statale; Fascism as I Have Seen It* (London, 1935; New York [1936]).
6. Francis Biddle, U.S. Attorney General, 1941–1945, who handed down Pound's indictment in 1943.
7. Dr. Jerome Kavka, a psychiatrist on the staff of St. Elizabeths Hospital, does not recall any particular reference to Poland by Pound except in reference to Kavka's Polish origins on those occasions when Pound felt a need to strike back at his questioner. Kavka does believe that Pound's bitterness over the outbreak of World War I in 1914 and the resulting deaths of Gaudier and Hulme had much to do with his later problems. (Conversation between Dr. Kavka and Catherine Seelye, Dec. 28, 1973.)
8. Count Jerzy Potocki (1889–1961), Polish ambassador to the United States, 1936–1940. Pound lunched with Potocki while in Washington in 1939.
9. Max Brod, in *Franz Kafka: Eine Biographie*, points out that Kavka is the correct spelling of his name.
10. Dr. Edmund Ziman "was called Tiny because he was a very portly man resembling to some extent one of his close personal friends, Zero Mostel. He had a great sense of humor and was most articulate." Letter to Catherine Seelye from Dr. Jerome Kavka, August 21, 1973.
11. Olson invited Kavka to dinner on January 4, 1946 (the day of Olson's first visit to Pound). Kavka declined "for fear of compromising the case." *Ibid.*
12. Dr. Edgar D. Griffin, Clinical Director of Clinical Branch II, St. Elizabeths Hospital.
13. DTC. Disciplinary Training Center, Mediterranean Theater of Operations USA, near Pisa.
14. *Ibid.*
15. Philip Rahv, editor of *The Partisan Review*, accepted Olson's "This Is Yeats Speaking."
16. Probably Olson's friend Oscar Lange (1904–1965), a Pole by birth, one-time professor of economics, University of Chicago, who renounced his naturalized U. S. citizenship in 1945 to become Poland's ambassador to the United Nations. Olson met Lange through Adam Kulikowski, a consultant to the OWI.
17. Olson wrote Donald Allen of Grove Press in April 1958: "Publishing coup of present (now that Pound's out of hospital and indictment dismissed) is the *full* transcript of his *broadcasts*—without alleviation or explanations. Document #1 of American *literary* Republic. Cannot urge on you, and thru you on Barney [Rosset], anything equal to it text-wise for our times."
18. *Some Do Not*, published in 1925, followed by *No More Parades* in 1926, the first two volumes of the "Tietjens Tetralogy."

CANTO 5, FEBRUARY 7, 1946, 3:15-3:30

T ODAY POUND WAS in bad condition, his eyes worried and muddy, his flesh puffy and old. It appears again to have been too much "hammering" at him. He started out by saying: "4 medicos at me this morning."[1] I tried to suggest it might end once the sanity hearing was over. He said they had had him dressed and waiting to go all last Tuesday, even after the hearing had been cancelled, but no one apparently had thought to let him or Howard Hall know. As he said: "I don't [know] what goes on. Who to believe. Cornell writes that the hearing will be next week.[2] But what is going on." He kept rubbing his head upwards with his hands. Wrought up, until it would squeeze your heart of blood. For this is all unnecessary, all the result of the negligence, thoughtlessness, carelessness, let things drift. Laughlin has not come, has not sent him the proofs of the *Confucius:* "which is the base of my defense." And of course from his point of view—and mine—he is right. His defense is the intellectual grounds of his examination into what is wrong with contemporary whig society. His conclusions may be wrong. But the process is a thing to protect. Which when mentioned is laughed at, as K did, for no court will try him on such grounds.

He announced that the best defense of him had appeared in Farc's paper (?), a Gesell organ in San Antonio, Texas, though it was harmed by a confusion of Tremaine & Truman (?).[3]

Connie was with me, and we brought a bottle of wine, but he was not allowed to have it. I sought to get his mind off and back to writing. Mentioned I had stolen a poem from him. At which he made a gesture like a salute with the right hand, as much as to say, take it away. I said it was King Tching T'ang's inscription, apologizing for my Chinese.[4] He expressed his belief again that the inscription was important, saying Confucius is not understood, that that's what he stood for. I said I had tried to give in English some of the effect of the ideograph by using the words bare: AXE TREE SUN, but admitting how difficult it is, though challenging him a little by saying he has as much trouble by using the Chinese character. I went on to make clear it was the only time I had rifled him, directly, anyhow.

He got on the subject of the Cantos. I asked him which were the 10 he had done at Pisa. 73-83, the two in Italian, 71, 72 cannot be published in America at the present time.[5] One is Guido's ghost, and (Ambrogo[6] or something I did not recognize). They are buttressed in the Inferno. Pound kept emphasizing the way they back up against Dante, come from him, even to terza rima. And gave me the sense that only Pound of all Dante's followers has picked up where Dante left off. Not that Pound said any such thing. Perhaps it was just that his emphasis on the way he has in these cantos gone back to stem from the Inferno suddenly gave me the sense of an unused method. No, Pound put it in this way. He is himself excited at having rediscovered and used a Dante method. He especially mentioned the use of a ghost to speak, repeating Guido.

Then he made clear why they cannot be published now. Smothering the facts from the sailor who was the attendant today, he told Connie and me that one of the cantos contains the tale of a girl of Rimini who has been raped and who leads a company of Canadians who had asked to be directed to————across a mine field instead. She also was blown up, both legs off. But it enabled two German prisoners to escape. The payoff came when Pound says, "She was one of the resistance."

It amazed both of us. Here we were listening not only to a fascist, but the ENEMY! The resistance was patently the German-Italian gang behind Allied lines. Pound was talking like no American but an out and out enemy. The strange thing was there was no awareness of his part that we might take this as what for the very first time I have seen: TREASON. There it was staring us in the face and speaking straight out bold. And yet let me record: merely there it was. A fact. I felt no surprise. Nor, I confess, did it shock and repel me as did his reference to Pegler or his antisemitism. I am bewildered. He makes no heroine of her. (One could not judge until one read the canto.) He told it as a tale of war. But he also told it as a deed of one of his side. These were soldiers who were fighting against the Axis who died because of her betrayal.

I asked him if he still intended his original schema, of 100 Cantos, and he said yes. In other words 17 Cantos remain undone as of now. He gave the sense of the Dante between as a returning theme. I wanted to go on and ask if Yeat's description of the form is accurate.[7] We didn't get to that.

At one point I told him that CC was going to Italy to get out an issue of PORTFOLIO.[8] (She had brought him over a copy.) He mentioned Gaudier again, and other Italian painters. It suddenly occurred to me he might have known Cagli. He said: "I think he tried to do a portrait of me, but it didn't come off. He was a Jew, wasn't he?" I said yes, his mother was, his father a Milanese. P said: "He came to me from Rome. I think he was interested in me because he thought I was a Jew, my first name . . ." (!) I protested it couldn't be Cagli, for he didn't work that way. But P insisted he thought it was the same person, and that he was a man who made racial judgments! (or a phrase similar to that!) (How about that!) I said, "A Chirico man . . ."[9] but it didn't register on P. I went on to say Ciano had confiscated his work and driven him out,[10] and that here he had gone into the Army.

Ford again came up—"Fordey," as P calls him. As of his influence on the American novels. *Whistle-Stop*,[11] for example, which P thinks good "unless I have lost my critical sense" he observed, in one of the several examples of his collapsed present state. In fact the whole effect today was of a demoralized man. He had nothing but tatters of dignity left. It was all, over my brother's nakedness, with me. Even his parting remark: "Thank you for coming. You have saved my life more than once. Come again when you have the energy." (!) It was very unpleasant. I couldn't say anything but: "I can hold out a hand."

At another point, he came up from his hands on his head, to sway out with, "I'm sorry to be so lachrymose."

On Ford he is bothered by some sense of guilt, apparently at either not having attacked him, though he insisted—" no backbiting." Something in the Ford matter is bothering him. He again said *So Let It Be* is fine, the second volume, ———,[12] not so good. But he kept reiterating: He knew how to write.

I told him the story of how I was impelled to write to Ford the night before he was leaving for Europe. How much it had meant to us younger men to have him in N.Y. Pointing out that only he and Bill Williams were there for us among Pound's generation. I did not realize at the time I said it that it was a sort of comment on Pound being in Rapallo, exile.

He mentioned Frobenius as another he had missed. I asked if F was alive. He said: "No, he had come to (France?) for his 65th birthday." (Apparently P had wanted to be there, and couldn't.) And died. There was some mention also of Yeats' death.

(I had been recording some passages from the Cantos the night before, and feel now the Canto on love is an intellectual performance, but the Artemis hymn against Pity is true,[13] straight out of

Pound. He is a hunter. He is inside a man who enjoys to close & kill
the game. His attraction to Confucius must be the old thing, what
we all do, confuse our opposite with ourselves.)

NOTES

1. The four psychiatrists who were appointed by the Court to judge Pound's competency to
stand trial: Joseph L. Gilbert, Marion R. King, Wendell Muncie, and Winfred Overholzer.
2. The hearing was held February 13, 1946.
3. Dr. Hugo R. Fack (whom Pound called a " country physician" in *Guide to Kulchure*)
published from 1931 to 1950 a paper under the titles of (1) *Freedom and Plenty*, (2) *The Way
Out*, and (3) *Free-Economy: The Way Out of Democracy*. Fack devoted his publishing
activities to the espousal of Silvio Gesell and his theories, publishing Gesell's *The Natural
Economic Order* and a series of pamphlets entitled "Neo-Economic Series of Freedom and
Plenty." *Freedom and Plenty* 16, No. 2 (February 1946) contained an article called "Ezra
Pound—Poet and Money Reformer: Traitor or Patriot? " in which Pound was quoted as
saying. "If only Vinson knew Truman didn't think me an idiot." "Truman" should have read
"Tremaine," probably Morris S. Tremaine, the highly respected controller of the state of New
York for many years.
4. See Pound's Canto XIII for the source of Olson's poem below.

A Translation

King Tching T'ang's inscription:
AXE TREE SUN

> The AXE to put away old habit
> new as the young grass shoot
> wrote Kung interpreting TREE
> look to a constant renovation LOOK to
> as each new day
> look: the sun!

on the bathtub:
AXE TREE SUN

5. Cantos LXXI and LXXII have not yet been published.
6. Probably Ambrogio Praedis. See Pound's Canto XLV.
7. Yeat's description of the cantos is found in his *A Packet for Ezra Pound* (Dublin, 1929),
pp. 2–4.
8. *Portfolio: An Intercontinental Quarterly* (published in Washington, D.C.., and Paris by
the Sun Press, 1945–1948). Olson's poem "Upon a Moebius Strip" appeared in the Spring
1947 issue.
9. Giorgio di Chirico, Italian surrealist painter.
10. Cagli's murals decorating the lobby of the Italian Pavilion of the Paris Exposition of 1937
were partly destroyed when the exhibition was ordered closed by Ciano. Cagli left Italy in
1938 for Paris, and then the United States, where he lived until 1948.
11. *Whistle Shop*, a novel of an American degenerate family, by Maritta Martin Wolff, first
published in 1941.
12. *Some Do Not* and *No More Parades*.
13. The canto on love is Canto XXXVI; the canto on Artemis is Canto XXX.

CANTO 6, FEBRUARY 14, 2:30–2:45

It was the day after the hearing which declared Pound mentally unfit for trial on charges of treason. He came in with his bounce back, carrying the Pisa Cantos in his hand which Laughlin had delivered to him this morning. He had already corrected the typed copies of Cantos 74 and 75 (1 page job with music) and wanted me to either send them on or put them in JL's hands if he were still in town. Which he was. And which I did later in the afternoon.

The sense, the whole sense of this meeting was Pound in power, anew. Flushed with his return to work. Full of plans to get on with things, now that his fate was settled for awhile.

He had one complaint, a fistula which I gathered had been operated on three times, but continued bad because of sitting "two or three hours on the concrete" (?).[2] And "I want to get out into the yard," indicating the space inside the wall of Howard Hall. Apparently walking in the courtyard is unsatisfactory to him. At this point I believe it was he repeated his definition of a lunatic: "an animal somewhat surrounded by Jews."

He was full of the need to "close the gap" in America. This time I spoke up: "Work to do it, but don't expect it to be closed for a hundred years more. It goes deep." In here he threw out the remark: "Mussolini tried to push Italy too fast."

He gave up talking suddenly and said, "You talk. What exactly do you do." I begged off, saying I was tired, too much doing this week, that I was down like the earth waiting for the rain. But he persisted, kindly. I said writing. He asked how Connie and I lived. I said she worked, had to, with my income of '45 $60. He laughed and said, "I got mine up to £200 once, then it fell off to £40 something, that was in the last war." In answer to further questions, I said my book, CALL ME ISHMAEL, was not getting anywhere with the publishers.[3] Told him of the new deal on it. He suggested I send it to Eliot with a covering letter to Ron Duncan.[4] I thanked him. He said he didn't think Duncan could write poems, but that Eliot had liked his last play.[5]

Then we returned to America and I let go with my SPACE idea, indicating it was why I wanted to get this book out. I quoted the first sentence,[6] and went on to add I thought it was only the Indians, and not Pueblo or Navaho, but Aztec and Mexican Valley Indians that had done anything with the cruelty consequent to Space. At that

Pound exclaimed: FROBENIUS! I said, I did not know his work, only as I had it from him, Pound. I did not know of any translation. He agreed and went on about some guy named Fox who had been translating but the war had come along and, I gathered, Fox had died.[7] Later on Pound spoke of the 30 volumes and spattered off the German title which I missed.[8]

We spoke also for the market for verse and I complained there was no magazine which was a frame for work, that they all had political positions, and that such positions made it impossible to get your things published properly. I went further to say politics belonged below, not on the surfaces of policy. I said *Harper's Bazaar* was my best market. He said, what about *Esquire*. I replied I had just sent them something including a nasty thing I had done last year in Key West.

He too seemed to think JL was tied up with VIEW, and said he had called it "shit" to JL that morning. Went on to say JL had no flair as a publisher.

As of the psychiatrists, he said he always forgot the important thing to say to them until the next day when it was too late.

As of publishers told me the story of Kewpie Reynal[9] coming to him in Italy and offering $5000 for his autobiography, something like Gertrude Stein's etc. And how when he heard what would go into it, cooling off more and more. Calling him Kewpie didn't help. But, says Pound, that's what Morley had called him,[10] and I thought that was his name. But I've done that all my life, said the wrong things, and bring the whole fucking crockery down around me.

But I pointed to the Canto copy I was to take away and said so this is the other side of your sharp tongue.

He kept talking about me as a container for him, making this drawing on the envelope of the Cantos to indicate what he meant.

As of the two old ladies, the Maple sisters, he says "it's like trying to ride a cat!"

It was too bad we had to be cut off by the guard, for we were steaming along. I asked for more time but the s.o.b. went official on us. I told Pound when I would be back in answer to his eager question, for he wants me to pick up the rest of the corrected copy on the Cantos in order to send it to JL.

*　　　*　　　*

Saw JL, and he was all excited about the examination the day before, stating the discussion got to the point where they were asking: What the hell is reality anyhow.

As I was leaving him I asked how much the unfit plea had been planned. And JL allowed he had from the beginning thought the thing was to get P out of trial, the easiest way. He appeared to have been surprised they found him "insane." I demurred. But he came back with this remark: "But this morning he came up with a remark like this, over the Jewish question: 'It's too bad, and just when I had plans to rebuild the Temple in Jerusalem for them.'" I said, sure, he's crazy like a fascist, but shall we put this on rational or moral grounds.

NOTES

1. The version here differs from the published text, as Pound made changes on the proofs.

2. The "Gorilla cage" had a cement floor upon which Pound sat and slept. A cot was added later (along with a pup tent which Pound could erect to keep out the elements).

3. *Call Me Ishmael* was published by Reynal & Hitchcock the following year.

4. Olson sent the manuscript to Eliot, who rejected it as being too sophisticated a treatment of Melville for an English audience.

5. *This Way to the Tomb*. See Ronald Duncan's Introduction to his *Collected Plays* (New York, 1970) for a discussion of the forces which led Duncan to write the play and to Eliot's part in the writing of it.

6. "I take SPACE to be the central fact to man born in America, from Folsom cave to now."

7. Douglas Fox, Frobenius's American assistant and collaborator on *African Genesis* and *Prehistoric Rock Pictures in Europe and Africa*. Fox was alive at this time and in fact he and Olson shortly thereafter exchanged a few letters, Olson suggesting that Fox's NEW ENGLISH WEEKLY articles be collected and republished and that Fox continue his translations of the Atlantis series.

8. There is no thirty-volume work of Frobenius of which I am aware. Pound may have been referring to Frobenius's total published output or perhaps to the publications of the Forschungsinstitute für Kulturmorphologie. Pound considered *Paideuma* (vol. 4 of *Erlebte Erdteile*) to be Frobenius's most important work and had planned to translate it in 1929 but could find no publisher for it. See New Stock, *The Life of Ezra Pound* (New York, N.Y.), p. 285.

9. Eugene Reynal of Reynal & Hitchcock.

10. F. V. Morley, a director of Faber & Faber.

CANTO 9, JUNE 18, 1946: WITH EP FROM 1:20–1:45

I RETURNED TO SEE Pound yesterday. He has such charm. It is his
charm which has betrayed him, for he assumes it can manage
people. In itself, it is lovely, young, his maintaining of youth a rare
thing. I do not know anyone who could be in a prison and stay as he:
it was young of him, as Constance observes, to remark to Griffin, the
doctor, as we spoke to him when he went through the visiting room
yesterday " . . . before I got myself into the mess." As far as I can
judge Pound acts within the wall much as he acted outside, the
difference only of degree. Yet the Griffin incident also suggested the
misuse of his charm which I feel has led Pound into snobbery, and
the company of shits and fascists. It is clear he has Griffin pegged for
the white trash he is. Yet he can traffic with him. And so that I shall
not be misunderstood—Griffin is the boss of the prison—I shall also
mention Pound on Ted Spencer, to whom he is not prisoner, and
only beholden as he allows himself to be as writer to professor-critic.
He told me Spencer had been to see him, and seemed impressed
that Spencer could "take it," catch on when Pound told him "Eliot is
fatal to you, Ted." I pointed out it was all intellectual with S, it would
never lead to an intuition, point by point it could never form a curve
when plotted which would lead S anywhere. So what the hell good
was it? The truth is, S is flattered to be in the company of Eliot or
Pound, without regard to life or feeling. It is a triumph for him, even
to have Eliot fatal to him. That he should "take it" is all so kittenish.
I told Pound what S had done to little Ellery Sedgwick, with his
mean will, said El was the sweetest thing ever to come out of the
old N.E. tradition. And Spencer bedevilled him. Along with
Catholicism.

There is an assumption on Pound's part that he can traffic with
snobs and bastards, and get away with it. I don't believe he or any
man can, and I figure on this path he went to fascism. Or is it simply
that he prefers such people, Princesses, and the rest of the fawners.
For he has a hunger for power and name, and maybe he likes such
creatures because somewhere in him unrecognized is a sense he
never could make it. Maybe Yeats' warning: Do not be a Senator was
more than an image, was a personal observation, and was meant to
indicate to Pound: Reform it altogether.

The trouble with it is, he cuts the ground out of any relation. You

come to distrust the nice things he says, look upon all his conduct as
a wheedling or a blackmail. He becomes in fact not a Senator but a
politician of friendship, and it's no good.

I enjoyed myself of course. For he is swift, and his wit is sure. He
mentioned that Eliot was in this country. I said I understood one of
his purposes was Pound. I said everyone in N.Y. and Cambridge was
atwitter at his Second Coming, the Messiah, and that one of them, a
publisher, as I remembered, had said his purpose was Pound.
Pound smiled, turned himself out of the ease of the rocker he was
sitting in, twisted towards the window and away to [from] me, and
remarked: "I have known Eliot for thirty years, and you are never
sure. You know when he says 'No,' he won't do the thing, but when
he says, 'Yes,' you are never sure he will." It was a shrug, a tolerance, one of Pound's bites.

In Pound's case, however, I feel he has not cleared his course of
the dangers. I think of the presence in his work of the worship for
past accomplishments and a kind of blindness to the underground
vigor of a present. Yesterday we batted around the radio, the
movies, the magazines, and national advertising, the 4 Plagues of
our time. I had in the morning, after Ziegfeld Follies, been wondering how deep the effects go, had recalled that, in time terms, the
existence of these 4 was short, about the span of my own life, 35
years. I had been turning over in my mind how much actual rejection there was on the people's part, how much hope there was all 4
might in another measurable period be swept away.

Pound had made an observation about the expatriate, around the
time we spoke of Eliot. Mentioned a story of James in which.
No. . . . I remember. . . .

It was a pick-up on his part to my observation about Spencer. He
went on to wonder if Henry Adams had the same intellectual complaint. We both admitted, of course, the difference in dimension.
No . . . the Henrys have tricked my memory. . . .

Anyway, Pound spoke of a story of James', in which James imagines what he would have been like if he had not left his own
country. *The Jolly Corner*.[2] It was clear that Pound had been brood-
ing (as much as he ever broods) about himself in this respect. I could
not resist, because of some irritation I have with him over his politi
s, to say: "In your case what you would have run into around the
corner was radar." He had in one of our earlier conversations

admitted his surprise at it, and American production. It was his
failure to calculate it that had led him to broadcast after Pearl
Harbor, and put him here in St. Elizabeths.

It was a pleasure to listen to him on our Plagues, for he was talking
out his direct impressions and actions, not going over into generali-
zations, so many of which or all of them become fascist and cliche. To
suggest the difference from his usual dish, listen to this: "That
Consummate Shit, in New York, on the radio, that provincial Winchell, how can people listen to him, no matter what he says, when
they hear the Jew, no yaw-yaw, ja-ja, even the parenthesis exclud-
ing a measurement based on Winchell's doctrines![3]

It appears the fact the man in the next cell reads *Collier's* (the way
it loosens, softens up the mind) etc all the time had stirred up this
business, as well as Pound's hearing a Winchell broadcast on the
radio. He said: "I first sensed it in 1910, when I made a crossing, and
in the lounge saw men sitting around reading some 40 different
magazines."[14] He went on to recall that he had been after it when he
had first attacked Henry Van Dyke and *Harper's*.[5] (I gathered that
was earlier than 1910.) Again I wanted to make him see the difference for us younger men, and why we don't arrive at the same
conclusions as he does. I said: "But I, the men of my age, we didn't
have the comparison you had to start with. We have had to work our
way through, discarding each as we went, immunizing ourselves,
the radio, the movies, magazines, advertising, until we come
out to an island such as you started from." Pound: "Yes, Paris, the
island, I called it, THE ISLE DE PARIS,[6] in an article I wrote
then. Yes, Van Dyke was a daisy compared to the rubbish cans you
men have."

It was fun to talk to him yesterday. He seemed in good health, and
explained: "I've been all right since I got out of that courtyard." And
he was. The coversation ran on, pushed against the guard who
wanted us to quit. At the end I tried to get in this: "I've talked to alot
of the returning soldiers, and they seem to have come to rejections
too, but the only alternative they grasp is the cynical."

(When we were discussing movies, he mentioned a film he saw in
Italy on submarines, made by the actual officers and crews, which he
said was fine, none of that poetic stuff, only one figure against the
sky, and something about a review he [had] done about the thing,
remarking that it was no wonder the director, ?Favellini?, hadn't

any interest in movies, which the censor had scratched out so as to take the paper away. When I said it had not been shown here, he said O of course not, it must have been very liberated, destroyed altogether!)[7]

NOTES

1. *Wake* did not devote an issue to Pound. This may account for Pound's coolness to Spencer on his visit to Pound early in 1949. See Noel Stock, *The Life of Ezra Pound* (New York, 1970), p. 427.

2. "The Jolly Corner" appeared in the first number of Ford's *English Review* (December 1908).

3. Walter Winchell (1892–1972) was a gossip columnist and radio commentator who had a rather nasal voice and a strident delivery. He was an early hater of the Nazis (whom he called "Ratzis") and a strong supporter of Roosevelt.

4. "'the awafulness that engulfs one when one comes, for the first time unexpectedly on a pile of all the *Murkhn* magazines laid, shinglewise, on a brass-studded, screwed-into-place, baize-covered steamer table. The first glitter of the national weapons for driving off quiet and all closer signs of intelligence.'" Stock, *Life*, p. 87.

5. In "Patria Mia," first published in London in *The New Age*, November 14, 1912.

6. "The Island of Paris: A Letter," *The Dial* 69 (October, November, December 1920).

7. The film was a newsreel of Hitler's visit with Mussolini in 1938. In honor of the occasion, the fleet of Italian submarines, positioned 100 feet apart, dived and surfaced simultaneously. Neither the director of the film nor Pound's review has been identified.

CITY JOYS

by JACK ANDERSON

from CITY JOYS (Release Press)

nominated by Release Press

In cities at night
you can sit in the luxury
of a darkened room
where objects become feelings
in the shadows around you
and there is no more piano,
no more plants, no more desk,
and the only light
is the light of the dial
on the FM radio:

you can sit at a table
and look outside
and watch the night like a movie,
the traffic light
changing, a late bus
passing through the intersection,
and how someone's window goes blank
to be perfectly night.

Now he comes home, his key is in the lock.
He has closed the door behind him.
He walks about some other room,
then goes to the kitchen.
He wants something to eat.
He carries in a tray
to the table where I'm sitting,
still in the dark.

On the tray are cups
steaming with coffee,
slices of coffee cake,
and a book.
He gives me the book:
it is dark.
I set it beside my cup.
I touch his sweater.
We kiss.
We talk and we watch
the traffic light change.

We are eating the luxury
of cake at night
and talking, smiling,
staring into the dark
at Telegraph Hill
leaning down toward the lakefront
where cars on the Outer Drive
sweep by like thoughts,
and across the river, always present
in its own light
shining through the dark, rises
the Empire State Building,
God.

LOST COLONY

by MARVIN WEAVER

from ST. ANDREWS REVIEW

nominated by Reynolds Price

They passed the pop bottle between them
at arm's length as if it were a calumet
black hair smoked their faces as they breathed
and twisted over upon their sides
and twitched their legs like insects

three of them there under the bridge
Simon Locklear, Willie Sampson, Rudolph Oxendine
Tuscarora, Lumbee, Croatan
whose old chiefs ate the first white spirits
beached behind the cape on Roanoke

rendered the medicine in their blood
who drank the strong mixture
half paint thinner half Mountain Dew
they called smoke-on-the-water
for reasons that ceased to matter.

THE DAY OF THE NIGHT

(SANTIAGO DE CHILE XII.73)

by JAMES SCULLY

from SANTIAGO POEMS (Curbstone Press)

nominated by Curbstone Press

The day of the night
they arrested Fernando:
I'm lounging on a bench,
among retired old men
and purple flowers
in the Plaza de Armas.

A one-legged man
rolls his sleeves up
and hums: over
an iron water bubbler
bubbling over
his hands and forearms.
Having dropped his crutch
he's washing away.
The wornout
blue of his shirt
is gray as the overworked sky.
He could be a cloud
      blue
bird with spindly legs,
standing, one leg
more or less straight,
the other tucked up
under its belly:
tossing a splat of drops
off, onto the packed dirt

under a huge leafy palm
that droops and crests
—but motionless—
in carbon monoxide
it can live with,
the way an oasis
lives with desert.

He will stand
72 hours, without
a thing to eat,
a black
hood over his head.

If we had wings, roots, petals
we would not be men.

WHITMAN'S SONG OF MYSELF: HOMOSEXUAL DREAM AND VISION

by ROBERT K. MARTIN

from PARTISAN REVIEW

nominated by William Phillips

IT HAS BECOME COMMON among critics of Walt Whitman to argue that the protracted debate over the nature of the poet's sexuality, whether he may have been homosexual, heterosexual, or bisexual, is essentially beside the point. This argument has not been based on any reading of the poetry, but rather on the general modern and "liberal" tendency towards acceptance and tolerance. Acceptance and tolerance of homosexuality have not only been disastrous for the development of a homosexual consciousness; they have also led to a critical irresponsibility which seeks to equate all experience and to deny that homosexuals are "really" different from heterosexuals (to test the absurdity, substitute women and men, or blacks and whites).

Homosexuality shares a number of the general functions of all sexuality, but it bears a particular burden, given the social view of homosexuality and the virtual universality of repression of homosexual desires, at least in their most overt or public manifestations. The homosexual artist has a double need to express his sexual drives through his art because he is (or was) far less able than his heterosexual brother to give expression to these drives in his own life. In a society which attaches serious penalties to the open practice of homosexuality, the homosexual will often turn to art as a way of confronting those desires that he cannot acknowledge through action. Through the symbolism of his art he can communicate the facts of his homosexuality to his readers, knowing that those of them who are similarly homosexual will read the signs properly. Thus it was certainly with Whitman. He wrote a large part of his poetry directly out of his own sexual conflicts and fantasies, and he used his poetry to convey the news of his homosexuality to his readers. He knew that they were to be his "cameradoes," his only faithful lovers and only true readers, for all others would (Whitman predicted accurately) fail to see the "message" that would be unmistakable to some:

This hour I tell things in confidence,
I might not tell everybody, but I will tell you.
          (Song of Myself, sec. 19)

WHITMAN'S (MIS)READERS

Whatever homosexual readers may have thought (and John Addington Symonds was but the first to have recognized Whitman's homosexual meanings; he has been echoed by gay writers from André Gide to Allen Ginsberg to any of a large number of young American poets all of whom take Whitman as a point of reference, exceeded by no other American gay poet with the possible exception of Hart Crane), Whitman's readers in general have made a sorry record of misreading Whitman's poems. If one is charitable, one can suggest that these readers were simply unable to see the homosexual meanings, which were so divorced from their own experiences. But I am not inclined to be charitable. The record of absolute lies and half-truths and distortions is so shameful as to amount to a deliberate attempt to alter reality to suit a particular view of normality. If Whitman is to be a great poet, then he must be straight. If the poetry shows something else, Whitman must be made to alter his own poetry, censor himself. Despite considerable concessions made by Whitman during the course of his career, and the removal of a number of passages, the rabid heterosexualists were not satisfied. Whitman's life must be betrayed, rewritten, and his poems reread in a "safe" manner. Whitman must be saved from himself.

The process of this creation of a new, false Whitman is so well known that I will not spend too much time recounting its details. But it is important to note the extent to which otherwise respectable and reliable critics went in their efforts to "clean" Whitman up. The first stage, the most overt, was directed toward biography, toward proving that Whitman was actively heterosexual in his personal life. In part this stage was provoked by Symonds' famous letter to Whitman and Whitman's equally famous (and comic) reply, in which he boasted of having fathered six illegitimate children. Whitman had played the role of good citizen, especially in his old age, despite the barely concealed friendships with younger men (which are discussed in some detail by Edwin Haviland Miller), and his older friends continued the fiction of his life. But the first critics were not content with such an absence of open homosexuality: they needed proof of heterosexuality. So the New Orleans story was invented, out of nothing but a desire to prove that Whitman was normal. And even otherwise sensitive readers of Whitman, such as Emory Holloway, William Carlos Williams, and Babette Deutsch, continued to believe in the story long after its total fictitiousness had been demonstrated. Doubtless many still do.

The case of Holloway was particularly disappointing since it was he who was responsible, in 1920, for revealing that the poem which seemed to give rise to the New Orleans story, "Once I Pass'd Through a Populous City," had been changed prior to publication by Whitman to alter "I remember only the man who wandered with me there for love of me," to "I remember only a woman I casually met there who detain'd me for love of me." One would have thought that such evidence would have been conclusive. But no, the New Orleans story blooms again whenever someone wants to refuse to believe that Whitman loved other men. Even those critics who must of course admit the textual evidence refuse to accord any significance to it: James E. Miller, Jr., in his important book on *Leaves of Grass*, published in 1957, commented, "Although Holloway's discovery may be biographically revealing, the poem has the 'meaning,' surely of its final version." How convenient when a new-critical principle can be used to buttress what is essentially nothing more than a refusal to admit an unpleasant truth! One wonders what argument would have been used if the homosexual meaning were in fact the published version—as is the case of virtually all the Calamus poems as well as of large numbers of poems scattered throughout the *Leaves of Grass*.

Many critics have at least been honest about this prejudice. Whitman criticism is full of the vocabulary of social opprobrium and the clichés of undigested psychoanalysis. Even homosexuals themselves have used words of scorn—Symonds says "symptoms of emotional abnormality" and Newton Arvin spoke of a "core of abnormality." Others have been more vicious. Mark Van Doren in 1942 was able to write, "Manly love is neither more nor less than an abnormal and deficient love."

Since that time the heterosexual attacks on Whitman have become more subtle, and perhaps ultimately more damaging. They have used sophisticated techniques of literary analysis to demonstrate that sexuality is not an important aspect of Whitman's poetry. The most insistent of these arguments is that advanced by James Miller, in his reading of "Song of Myself," for instance, as an "inverted mystical experience" (he didn't mean the pun on invert there). By seeing patterns of mystic symbolism (which is identical to erotic imagery, except that it does not mean what it purports to mean, but only uses sex to talk about God) at crucial points in the poem, Miller diverts the reader's attention from the poetry's frankly and directly sexual nature. Miller's argument at least had the virtue of making us look again at the "mystical" Whitman and making us return to the visionary poet; in the hands of his less talented followers, the arguments singularly lack charm, as in this recent example from Thomas E. Crawley's *The Structure of Leaves of Grass* (1970): "To associate it (These I Singing in Spring) with any crude, sensuous interpretation of the calamus-symbol is to miss the mystical beauty" or again "the gross interpretation . . . that the root is a symbol of the male sexual organ."

A recent, "liberated" version of Whitman's poetry illustrates the failure of the "liberal" reading. Walter Lowenfels' edition of *The*

Tenderest Lover: The Erotic Poetry of Walt Whitman purports to be honest. Lowenfels maintains with pride, "Our text . . . is unexpurgated; erotic lines and passages that Whitman changed or deleted have been restored." But although the text is restored, the editor feels obliged to insist on the interchangeability of the sexes. He writes of the famous "Once I Pass'd Through a Populous City" text, "What is intrinsic to the poem is not the sex of the loved one but the love itself."

Such intellectual softheadedness is characteristic of this reprehensible edition which is only possible because of the critic's need to romanticize (i.e. render abstract) a sexuality which he finds distasteful. One can hardly expect much of anyone who can write such garbage as "Whitman was a prophet of today's sexual revolution . . . In his love poems, youth speaks to youth of all ages, across all centuries and languages." But he goes on to ignore crucial and obvious evidence, and refers to "the unnamed him or her whom Whitman identified only by the number '16' or '164.'" The rankest amateur in cryptography knows that Whitman meant P or PD, Peter Doyle.

The history of Whitman criticism in this connection is shameful. I can think of no parallel example of the willful distortion of meaning and the willful misreading of a poet in order to suit critics' own social or moral prejudices. And it must be added that the very few critics who spoke against this tradition of distortion were generally Europeans, who perhaps did not totally share American Society's total and relentless hostility to the homosexual. It is thanks to the work of Jean Catel, Roger Asselineau, and Frederik Schyberg that Whitman finally can be seen as a poet of sexual love between men. In the last few years there has been the important work done by Edwin Haviland Miller, which has unfortunately not received the attention it deserves (despite his overly normative Freudian bias). One begins to suspect that the history of Whitman misreading is not over.

Whitman's own life was marked by the same pressures toward sexual conformity that now lead to critical distortions. He seems to have felt the need to act out a role, to hide behind the mask of the tough. And he had to learn the strategies of concealment, strategies that, until recently at least, all of us had to learn in order to succeed as homosexuals in a heterosexual world. The changing of texts, the excision of passages, these are but the most obvious of what must have been enormously painful series of acts performed almost daily in order to conform to someone else's version of normality. And how painful they must have been to the man who was able to give another man a wedding band, who from his youth on wrote with passion only of friendship between men, who cried out in suffering "O unspeakable passionate love" (Song of Myself, sec. 21) for the love, "the secret of my nights and days," which lay hidden "in paths untrodden."

One important consequence of his homosexuality is that Whitman, unlike so many male poets, does not see women as sexual objects even in his ostensibly heterosexual poems. Freed of the need to enslave the opposite sex, the homosexual is free to see women as human beings, and thus we find in Whitman a strong sense of compassion for suffering figures of women—the mother, the prostitute, the spinster. It is not only that he does not see woman as sex object, but that he can thereby see himself as self-enjoying. Whitman's poetry is frequently auto-erotic in the sense that he takes his own body as a source of sexual pleasure much as Freud's famous polymorphously perverse child does, and derives pleasure from his own orgasm, rather than from any sense of conquest or aggression.

Whitman makes no distinction between subject and object (a distinction necessary to the position of woman as "other" and as property). All experience becomes a part of himself—"Absorbing all to myself and for this song" (sec. 13)—as the total egotism of the child is restored. The "Song of Myself" is the song of the world, as seer and seen, male and female become one. If Whitman's vision is regressive, it looks back to an earlier ideal of play. We need to see the sensitivity, the *finesse* of Whitman, a sensitivity which has too long been obscured by the image of him as

> *Walt Whitman, A Kosmos, of Manhattan the son,*
> *Turbulent, fleshy, sensual, eating, drinking and breeding*
>   (Song of Myself, sec. 24)

This was what Whitman wanted to seem to be; but the poetry reveals the happy truth that he was indeed a much deeper, more sensitive person than he dared admit.

WHITMAN'S DREAM—VISION POETRY

The great debate over homosexuality in Whitman's poetry has generally centered on the poems in the Calamus section or those poems which, although not actually placed in that section, seemed to belong there, by similarity of theme or imagery. But this emphasis is somewhat unfortunate for two reasons. First it tends to isolate the "homosexual" poems of Whitman into one neat category which can be labelled and then safely forgotten and put away. Second it tends to assume that Whitman's sexuality is only relevant to his most explicit and frequently didactic poems. On the (hopeful) assumption that most readers are capable of reading Calamus themselves, I have therefore preferred to center my discussion here on another mode of Whitman's poetry, which is perhaps slightly more elusive and yet which seems to me essential to an understanding of the whole body of his work. I refer to what I have called Whitman's dream-vision poems, those poems which are written in a state of the mind somewhere beneath full consciousness and which invoke the experience of the mind in that state.

"The Sleepers" has received a fair amount of attention in recent years, probably due to the general interest in stream of consciousness techniques and also to a new willingness to look more carefully at explicit sexual imagery. I do not wish to give a full reading of the poem here—one may be referred to the helpful comments of Leslie Fiedler and Edwin Haviland Miller in particular, as well as to the reading of James E. Miller—but I do want to look at it sufficiently to suggest that it is similar to "Song of Myself" in its sense of wavering consciousness, in its use of cosmic observation, in its shifts through time and space, and in its sexual imagery.

"The Sleepers" is explicitly about a vision, as the first line informs us, and its action is the movement of the poet within his vision,

> *I wander all night in my vision,*
> *Stepping with light feet, swiftly and noiselessly stepping*
>   *and stopping,*
> *Bending with open eyes over the shut eyes of sleepers,*
> *Wandering and confused, lost to myself, ill-assorted,*
>   *contradictory,*
> *Pausing, gazing, bending, and stopping.*

The first section of the poem is agitated, marked by continual movement. The poet uses the game metaphor to depict the atmosphere of levity which prevails as the covers are lifted and the genitals are revealed.

> *wild-flapping pennants of joy!*

It concludes with a remarkable depiction of orgasm, in which it becomes clear that the naked speaker who has been exposed is using his body as a metaphor for his penis and that the entire exposure motif of the poem operates on these two levels (the exposure of the poet for what he is—the fear of being revealed as a homosexual— and the exposure of the penis which may bring forth castration anxiety in a hostile world). The text is worth quoting in full, especially since Whitman later removed these lines from the 1855 edition and they are therefore not present in most of the edition regularly used.

> *O hotcheeked and blushing! O foolish hectic!*
> *O for pity's sake, no one must see me now! . . . my*
>   *clothes were stolen while I was abed,*
> *Now I am thrust forth, where shall I run?*
>
> *Pier that I saw dimly last night when I looked from the*
>   *windows*
> *Pier out from the main, let me catch myself with you and*
>   *stay. . . . I will not chafe you;*
> *I feel ashamed to go naked about the world,*
> *And am curious to know where my feet stand. . . . and*
>   *what is this flooding me, childhood or manhood.*
>   *. . . . and the hunger that crosses the bridge between.*
>
> *The cloth laps a first sweet eating and drinking,*
> *Laps life-swelling yolks. . . . laps ear of rose-corn, milky*
>   *and just ripened:*
> *The white teeth stay, and the boss-tooth advances in darkness,*
> *And liquor is spilled on lips and bosoms by touching*
>   *glasses, and the best liquor afterward.*

Miller manages to see vaginal imagery here, but I do not see it. It seems clear to me that what is being depicted is the act known politely as fellatio—the penis protrudes from the foreskin, the balls are sucked, the penis is sucked, and finally there is ejaculation in the mouth. The sexual experience is the starting place for the poem, and the poet begins his vision with the second section, after the orgasm when "my sinews are flaccid/Perfume and youth course through me, and I am their wake." The physical experience leads toward the spiritual experience which is the dream, and which is also in its turn physical and sexual.

The third section brings a fantasy of the destruction of the "beautiful gigantic swimmer," a warning in dream terms of the dangers in the unconscious world of the sea with its "swift-running eddies." The swimmer seems to be a sexual object, but is also an ideal presentation of the self. The dream of the third section is a dream of the destruction of the self—the clue lies in Whitman's surprising line "will you kill him in the prime of his middle age?" (Whitman was 35 at the time) and in the transition to the next section through its first line, "I turn but do not extricate myself." The poet-dreamer wants to escape from his dream, but the nightmare is not yet over. In another key passage that was omitted from later editions Whitman introduces his conflict with the Satanic through the figure of Lucifer (whom Whitman seems perhaps to have taken in his literal sense as light-bearer, for it is the coming of dawn that will destroy the dream and take away the lover, real or imaginary).

The theme of slavery is linked to the sexual by the sequence of the poem, where the poet moves from the mother's vision of the "red squaw":

My mother looked in delight and amazement at the stranger,
She looked at the beauty of her tallborne face and full and
*   pliant limbs,*
The more she looked upon her she loved her

to his own identification with the black slaves. Both evoke guilt because of their (implicit) double violation of taboo: homosexuality and miscegenation are the twin crimes so feared in American thought. (And we recall that Whitman's famous letter implied that he had broken the lesser of the two, lest he be found guilty of the greater!)

Starting with section 7 there is a drastic change brought about by the poet's acceptance of the world, an acceptance which is possible through his perception of unity in space and time. The agitation of sexuality, the immediate sensation of guilt following it, and the fantasy of death and loss which accompany its completion give way to a sense of sexual calm and peace. The poet learns to accept the daytime world of disunity ("the rich running day") because it is part of the cycle which always leads back to the night and love and the

Great Mother. His love of experience and diversity does not lead him to forget the world of unity and calm, but rather to accept both:

> I love the rich running day, but I do not desert her
>   in whom I lay so long:
> . . .
> I will stop only a time with the night, and rise bedtimes.
> I will duly pass the day O my mother and duly return to you.

Much as I am indebted to the thoughtful book of Edwin Haviland Miller (*Walt Whitman's Poetry: A Psychological Journey*), I must take issue with his particular emphasis on such a passage as evidence of Whitman's regressive patterns and what he implies to be an unresolved oedipal situation. I do not feel any *personal* maternal qualities in his poem. The mother addressed here seems to me to be a universal mother, goddess of the night, of the dream, of the vision, of all that is excluded from the daylight world of jobs, reason, and fathers. Reading the poem in terms of personal psychology seems to me to miss the essential significance of Whitman's vision, which achieves a return to a state of primal consciousness, which is pre-patriarchal, and cyclical rather than linear. His essentially matriarchal vision leads him to send the poet back to the Night-Mother (forces of darkness, mystery, and the unknown) to be reborn from her. The Mother is the death-sleep which follows upon the male striving of sexuality, but it is also the repose that heals and out of which the fallen penis may rise again:

> Not you will yield forth the dawn again more surely than
>   you will yield forth me again,
> Not the womb yields the babe in its time more surely than
>   I shall be yielded from you in my time.

The sexual experience is revealed by this poem to be the gateway to the visionary—literally because enjaculation leads to sleep and thus to dream, but metaphorically because it is the realization of the possibility of transcending the self through sexual ecstasy which leads to an acceptance of the world. As we fall off to sleep following orgasm, we are able to see a kind of inner sense in the world, a world freed from the pressures of the day and in which we have regained a kind of repose that Freud thought found its only model in intrauterine existence. Through that vision Whitman could come to his understanding of the world and greet all men and women as sleepers, each dreaming his own dream, but each dream like the others.

"SONG OF MYSELF"

Whitman's most important poem, in terms of length, and in terms of the themes broached there, is clearly his "Song of Myself." Critics have attempted to find an adequate way of understanding the poem's strength and sense of inner unity despite an appearance of disorder, but no one has fully explained the poem's patterns by looking at it in the light of "The Sleepers" as a dream-vision based on sexual experience. I would like to attempt such a reading now with the clear understanding that I am not denying any epic or mystic or democratic elements—they are clearly all there but they do not explain how the poem works, nor do they deal with any of the sexual structure.

The poem appears, at first glance, to be very unlike "The Sleepers" in that it seems to be the product of a wholly conscious mind which is engaged in a number of identifiable traditional poetic functions—e.g. singing, being an epic poet; debating, being a metaphysical poet. But a careful look at the poem will reveal that the poem is a monologue posing as a dialogue, or perhaps a dialogue which turns out to be a monologue. A dialogue for one speaker might be a nice way of putting it. The second role is clearly nonspeaking.

The mode of the poem seems to be a body/soul dialogue, such as those popular in the Renaissance, and known in American poetry through the example of Anne Bradstreet. But the body does most of the talking, the soul does not seem to respond, and the reader is addressed so often and so insistently as "you" that he indeed becomes a part of the poem. The poem is cast as a love poem; it involves a seduction, a growing desire which leads to final fulfillment and then to the vision which follows on sexual experience and which, as in "The Sleepers", permits the poet to perceive the unity of all things. The poem also ends with a sense of contentment brought on by acceptance but not until the poet has marked the end of the night by bidding farewell to his lover.

The structure of the poem is loose, but nonetheless clear if one follows the basic themes which are developed. I can only outline a

few of them here and suggest their similarity to the patterns we have
already seen in "The Sleepers." The first section is a very brief
introduction, particularly in the 1855 edition, where it consists of
only five lines which provide a setting and the argument. In the
second section, the process of natural intoxication has begun. The
poet concludes this section by asking the you-reader to "stop this
day and night with me." It is clear that, in fantasy at least, the
request is granted, and the rest of the poem is an account of that day
and night. At this very early stage of the poem it is clear that the poet
has a sense of acceptance—"I am satisfied" he writes—and that
acceptance is based on the metaphor of God as the lover who sleeps
with him by night, leaving him "baskets covered with white towels
bulging the house with their plenty." In the scarcely concealed
sexual symbolism of this section, the genitals are hidden by white
towels, not unlike the "cunning covers" of "The Sleepers." It is the
coming of God at night which gives the poet a "bulging basket" and
permits him to accept the day in the knowledge of a forthcoming
night and permits him to ask whether in fact he should

> *postpone by acceptation and realization and scream at my eyes,*
> *That they turn from gazing after and down the road,*
>   *And forthwith cipher and show me to a cent,*
> *Exactly the value of one and exactly the value of two,*
>   *and which is ahead?*

In the world of nighttime vision there is no counting, one and two
are the same, real and imaginary lovers are equal.

The poet continues his address to you, through the recollection of
a previous sexual experience which is the source of his first knowledge of peace:

> *I mind how once we lay such a transparent summer morning,*
> *How you settled your head athwart my hips and gently turn'd*
>   *upon me,*
> *And parted the shirt from my bosom-bone, and plunged*
>   *your tongue to my bare-stript heart,*
> *And reach'd till you felt my beard, and reach'd till you held my*
>   *feet.*

From this reminder of previous love and the insights it gave, the poet turns to the beginning of a new sexual experience, which begins with undressing of the you; "undrape!" Once undraped the loved one is subject of one of the most interesting passages of this poem, section 8, which depicts the progress of life through sexual metaphor.

> *The little one sleeps in its cradle,*
> *I lift the gauze and look a long time, and silently brush away flies*
> *   with my hand.*

> *The youngster and the red-faced girl turn aside up the bushy hill,*
> *I peeringly view them from the top.*

> *The suicide sprawls on the bloody floor of the bedroom,*
> *I witness the corpse with its dabbled hair, I note where the pistol*
> *   has fallen.*

From childhood to adolescence to death; from birth to reproduction to death; from the "little one . . . in its cradle" to the "bushy hill" to "the bloody floor . . . the pistol has fallen." The sight of nakedness leads in visual terms to a realization of death and suggests the ambivalent attitude toward the male genitals. But it is crucial to see that if one "cannot be shaken away" then one must accept all. He must accept the penis beneath the foreskin, the erect penis, and the penis after coitus. The acceptance of these three stages can lead to an acceptance of the same three stages of life and thereby to an acceptance of life as a whole in all its multiplicity, and so the second half of this leads to the first catalogue, and we begin to understand the meaning in Whitman's work of the catalogue—the expression of ultimate unity of things seen not on their surface but seen *sub specie aeternitatae*, a point of view that for Whitman was best arrived at through a sexual experience.

The following sections of the poem go out, literally, into the world and lead, for instance, to the celebrated section 11, where the abstract vision of section 8 is transformed into a very specific vision of masturbation.

Twenty-eight young men bathe by the shore,
Twenty-eight young men and all so friendly;
Twenty-eight years of womanly life and all so lonesome.

She owns the fine house by the rise of the bank
She hides handsome and richly drest aft the blinds of the window.

Which of the young men does she like the best?
Ah the homeliest of them is beautiful to her.

Where are you off to, lady? for I see you,
You splash in the water there, yet stay stock still in your room

Dancing and laughing along the beach came the twenty-ninth
  bather,
The rest did not see her, but she saw them and loved them.

The beards of the young men glisten'd with wet, it ran from
  their long hair,
Little streams pass'd all over their bodies.

An unseen hand also pass'd over their bodies,
It descended trembling from their temples and ribs.

The young men flat on their backs, their white bellies bulge
  to the sun, they do not ask who seizes fast to them,
They do not know who puffs and declines with pendant and
  bending arch,
They do not think whom they souse with spray.

This poem, or part of the poem, is exquisite in its evocation of the mood of sexual arousal. As many readers have pointed out, Whitman achieves the feat here of being both subject and object, of being the woman voyeur, and also of being the men who are masturbated. Not only is this one of the loveliest sexual poems I know, it is also a clear defense of the anonymity of sexual encounter. In the dream-vision of Whitman there are no persons, but rather a general feeling of the delight of sexual experience regardless of the partner. They are totally tactile, since they take place in the dream-world of closed eyes. The experience could well be repeated in almost any steam bath of a modern large city. But the important point to see is that not asking, not knowing and not thinking are integral parts of Whitman's *democratic* vision, and anonymous sexuality is an important way-station on the path to the destruction of distinctions of age, class, beauty, *and* sex. Whitman loves all being, and will love, and be loved by, all being. It is perhaps at this juncture that the implications of Whitman's perspective become most revolutionary.

The sense of universality of experience leads to the long catalogues of the following sections, which introduce the transitional sections 21 and 22, concerned with the yearning for love. In section 21, Whitman returns to his Body-Soul division to express his desire to return to the bodily. He concludes the section with the line I have quoted earlier:

unspeakable passionate love

and then 2 lines omitted in later editions but which make the sexual male marriage metaphor clear:

Thruster holding me tight and that I hold tight
We hurt each other as the bridegroom and the bride hurt each
   other.

The sense of growing desire and longing culminates in section 24, where playing gives way to direct phallic arousal, and introduction of the calamus theme. The sperm is risen up:

You my rich blood! Your milky stream pale strippings of my life.

As the poet imagines himself making love, his assertions become bolder. He refuses the stigma that society may attach: "What we do is right and what we affirm is right." The imagery becomes more violent as he asserts his right to homosexual love:

Unscrew the locks from the doors!
Unscrew the doors themselves from their jambs!

All that is hidden must be exposed; there must be no secrets, in this metaphor strikingly similar to the more modern "Out of the closets into the streets!" As his ire increases, the blood and sperm rise, he introduces his calamus symbol ("Root if washed sweet-flag, timorous pond-snipe, nest of guarded duplicate eggs") as a metaphor for his own genitals, and he is able to sing all of the body, with penis and sperm ("Your milky stream pale strippings of my life"). The extraordinary crescendo of section 24 is based in sexual ecstasy and reaches its culmination in a sexual climax: "Seas of bright juice suffuse heaven."

And yet suddenly the passage comes to an end with the apparent arrival of the dawn, which would destroy the night. The reference is at the same time ambiguous, since the physical dawn would end the nighttime vision, but the day-break of sexual ecstasy would show the poet the possibility of ultimate victory over the day through his sexual powers.

> *Dazzling and tremendous how quick the sunrise would kill me,*
> *If I could not now and always send sunrise out of me.*

> *We also ascend dazzling and tremendous as the sun*
> *We found our own my soul in the calm and cool*
>   *of the daybreak.*

Man can make his own sunrise and thereby master the natural world and escape the necessity of the cyclical pattern—recalling the first sexual experience, section 5, which also took place in the morning. Making love in the morning seems to break the tyranny of the day.

The next few sections record the poet and his playful reluctance to give in, to let himself be brought to orgasm, a coyness which is ended by rebirth of section 28.

> *Is this then a touch? quivering me to a new identity,*
> *Flames and ether making a rush for my veins,*
> *Treacherous tip of me reaching and crowding to help them,*
> *My flesh and blood playing out lightning to strike what is hardly*
>   *different from myself,*
> *On all sides prurient provokers stiffening my limbs,*
> *Straining the udder of my heart for its withheld drip,*
> *Behaving licentious toward me, taking no denial,*
> *Depriving me of my best as for a purpose,*
> *Unbuttoning my clothes, holding me by the bare waist,*
> *Deluding my confusion with the calm of the sunlight and*
>   *pasture-fields,*

Immodestly sliding the fellow-senses away,
They bribed to swap off with touch and go and graze at the edges
of me,
No consideration, no regard for my draining strength or my anger,
Fetching the rest of the herd around to enjoy them a while,
Then all uniting to stand on a headland and worry me.
The sentries desert every other part of me,
They have left me helpless to a red marauder,
They all come to the headland to witness and assist against me.
I am given up by traitors,
I talk wildly, I have lost my wits, I and nobody else am the greatest
traitor,
I went myself first to the headland, my own hands carried me
there.
You villian touch! what are you doing? my breath is tight in its
throat,
Unclench your floodgates, you are too much for me.

This most extraordinary passage is almost certainly a depiction of anal intercourse, in which Whitman has turned the entire physical experience into mythic proportions and sees himself reborn as he takes into himself the seed of the unnamed lover. The cycle is complete, the sexual anticipation is ended through fulfillment, tension gives way to satisfaction, and the pattern we have now come to recognize is again present: the orgasm is followed by passages of philosophical summary and visionary perception of unity.

Something very similar happens a few sections further on, in section 32, when he turns to the stallion, symbol of the male lover. But the poet who in section 28 was the so-called passive partner in anal intercourse has now become the active partner as Whitman makes vivid the banal sexual metaphor of "riding" someone.

A gigantic beauty of a stallion, fresh and responsive to my ca-
resses,
Head high in the forehead, wide between the ears,
Limbs glossy and supple, tail dusting the ground,
Eyes full of sparkling wickedness, ears finely cut, flexibly moving.
His nostrils dilate as my heels embrace him.
His well-built limbs tremble with pleasure as we race around and
return

Thus again the sexual leads to the visionary, in this case to the famous section 33, where the poet is "afoot in my vision," recalling the first lines of "The Sleepers."

This vision, like those in "The Sleepers," includes the negative, for the poet is not able to separate sexuality from guilt. Death images are pervasive and culminate in his vision of himself as a crucified victim, in section 38. His racial memory includes all experience, and all suffering. He becomes a sacrificial victim, taking upon himself the sins of the world, and thereby assuring the safety and the sleep of his beloved. Reborn like the resurrected Christ, he can begin his journey across the continent—"Ohio and Massachusetts and Virginia and Wisconsin and New York and New Orleans and Texas and Montreal and San Francisco and Charleston and Savannah and Mexico"—and beyond. He recognizes that his poetic mission will be carried on by his élèves, the poet's disciples, who can learn the meaning of his words only if they have followed out the sexual patterns of the poem and have in fact become the poet's lovers. He is now awake but lets the other sleep:

> Sleep—I and they keep guard all night,
> Not doubt, not decease shall dare to lay finger upon you.

He carries his message of salvation, his Christ-like role to the world and feels certain of the correctness of his mission. Thus assured, he awakens the lover in section 44. "It is time to explain myself—let us stand up." He realizes that he has escaped the trap of reality through the acceptances, including that hardest of all to accept, Death. But once he has accepted it, and acceptance was already implied in section 8, he is already out of time and out of space (to quote Poe, who sometimes seems surprisingly like Whitman). Having achieved that state of ascension, he can now say good-by to the lover, recognizing his transitoriness. The recognition of death means that no earthly love is final; that all lovers will part; and so he parts from his lover, prepared to give himself to the world rather than to any one individual. He cannot take this lover with him, but must ask him to make his own journey.

> Not I, not anyone else can travel that road for you,
> You must travel it for yourself

. . .

I kiss you a good-by kiss . . .
Long have you timidly waded holding a plank by the shore,
Now I will you to be a bold swimmer
To jump off in the midst of the sea . . .

Having made love, learned about the world, and then bid the world adieu, he is calm again, he has found happiness. Characteristically Whitman's image is physical and sensual:

Wrench'd and sweaty—calm and cool then my body becomes,
I sleep—I sleep long.

It is only after the experience of sexual gratification, achieved through the dream, that the visionary experience becomes possible. It is the euphoria of the satisfied lover that gives rise to Whitman's poetry of vision—the poems of realization of unity. Its needs fulfilled, the body expands to encompass the world, through its physical embodiment of the lover, who in his role as "other" is the world. One can accept the death of the world only after transcending unitary death, escaping beyond the fear of the "little death" into a realization that all death brings resurrection, that the penis shall indeed rise again.

* * *

Homosexuals are a constant affront to the society, because they demand to be defined in terms of their sexuality. The homosexual has no existence as a group unless it is through sexual preferences and experiences. He cannot be wished away with the thought that such matters are of no importance, or with the piety that all human experience is basically similar. Whitman's poetry, particularly "Song of Myself," shows how the poet translates his love for the world, his cosmic promiscuity, into a myth of the wandering lover seeking his partners in all places and at all times. The visionary is rooted in the sexual, and Whitman will not let his root be torn out. He remains what he is for those who will read him, despite all that has been done to him. He can be secure in the knowledge he spoke of in "Scented herbage of my breast" and which we have seen to be fundamental to his other poems as well:

Every year shall you bloom again, out from where you retired you
*   shall emerge again;*
O I do not know whether many passing by will disvover you or
*   inhale your faint odor, but I believe a few will;*

. . .

Do not fold yourself so in your pink-ringed roots timid leaves!
Do not remain down there so ashamed, herbage of my breast!
Come I am determin'd to unbare this broad chest of mine, I have
*   long enough stifled and choked;*
Emblematic and capricious blades I leave you, now you serve me
*   not*
I will say what I have to say by itself,
I will sound myself and comrades only, I will never again utter a
*   call only their call,*

Out of the cycle of the penis is born the cycle of the soul; out of his erections, ejaculations (the pun is crucial), and re-erections comes Whitman's faith in a cycle of the world which will comprehend and conquer death. The real sleep is the sleep of the contented lover who will not die.

SONG OF THE SOAPSTONE CARVER

by SHEILA NICKERSON

from TO THE WATERS AND THE WILD (Thorp Springs Press)

nominated by Thorp Springs Press

In my hand, the stone:
Already it knows its shape
And lives—an animal, a bird—
Already with its wings or feet
Set on certain flight.

Follow, fingers, the slow terrain
Of dreams within a rock.
Cut away the dark forgetting,
A geology of loss.

Come, ptarmigan or Fox released,
And know the loving knife.

RETARDED CHILDREN IN THE SNOW

by MICHAEL MCMAHON

from ASPEN LEAVES

nominated by Aspen Leaves

from my hill I shivered and thought them crows
huge   and downed
in the field for some new age of ice

they seemed to stare straight into the sun
and spun and fell   and fell

then I knew

many nights I have tried to drink enough
to lose my name   like a wallet
and enter their land
where no animals prowl   where no trees grow

where   in place of a past   a white field
without the track of a single memory
crusts with cold

where these children live
with only the pulse of their distant hearts
to keep them open-mouthed   in constant awe

FALLING TOWARD THANKSGIVING

by DAVID WEISSMANN

from FALLING TOWARD THANKSGIVING (Raincrow Press)

nominated by Raincrow Press

1
The petite, gasoline
whine of an engine
cuts my breakfast short,
forty elm feet

bouncing the cereal bowl
a quarter inch. Caught
with a mouthful
of oatmeal, I watch

the chainsaws flash
like safety razors
or Brazilian fish
taking a minute

to strip a horse. "Honey,
I can hear the coffee
boiling," my wife calls,
lurching from sleep

into the kitchen. She
turns down the range and
settles with a slightly
ruined look at me.

2
Tonight even the snowflakes
are blowing south. Under
the streetlamps they are brilliant
freights starting their long
haul toward the Gulf.

I block the wind,
slanting with abandon
into the snow, almost
like a man bent
on bringing the commerce

of our northern states
to a standstill. It is so
quiet I can hear myself
shouting at the storm
to stop falling; but faster

and purer than sawdust,
a cold prosthesis
starts to fashion over
the stump the white
first inches of a tree.

✺ ✺ ✺

BEAUTIFUL PEOPLE

by JOHN BENNETT

from GHOST DANCE

nominated by Len Fulton

Beautiful People
are self-defined,
eat the right food
& smoke the right grass
to wash their hands
of any killer instinct.

Beautiful People
sleep on water beds
& fill their heads
with Zen made easy.

It's all too good to be true,
the number painting way
to God.

Beautiful People ride the crest
of their Heritage,
backs turned to the razor reef,
looking eastward
to a salvation
that is not theirs,

🔥 🔥 🔥

THE HALLUCINATION

fiction by JOYCE CAROL OATES

from CHICAGO REVIEW

nominated anonymously

HER HUSBAND'S VOICE LIFTED THROUGH the floorboards of the old house.

She was awake, suddenly. She couldn't remember having fallen asleep—what time was it?—she sat up, shivering, and heard now the voice from downstairs, familiar, but too loud, as if Alan were on the telephone. But it was too late for him to be talking to anyone: it was nearly two o'clock in the morning.

. . . she could hear her husband's voice but could not distinguish any words.

She got out of bed, slowly.

On the landing she heard the anger in his voice. And the pleading.

" . . . why don't you go home? . . . go somewhere else?"

The lights were out downstairs. Alan stood at the front door, in the darkened hallway, talking to someone out on the porch. Joanne was fully awake now: she stared at her husband's shadowy figure, wondering if the frightened anger in his voice, in his tense body, would be enough to protect them. She could not see who was there—only a blurred form, on the porch, pushed in close in the space between the door and the screen door, which he had opened. They never bothered to latch the screen door.

". . .why don't you go home? I'm not going to let you in. What do you want? Look, I can't help you," Alan was saying. He spoke quickly, yet gave to the final words of each sentence a peculiar dragging weight, almost a plea, the way one might speak to a child. "I said I can't help you . . . What do you want?"

Outside, a man's voice—high and thin—the words unintelligible. Then a burst of laughter.

Joanne was at the foot of the stairs now, and she could see the intruder more clearly—a head of long blond hair, a face in continual movement, youthful and creased, sunburned, the mouth contorted in a wide grin. He kept jerking his head from side to side, furiously. He was arguing with Alan through the door but his words were only plunges and leaps of noise. In Joanne's panic she seemed to see him as someone come back to reclaim the farm, the old farm-house she and Alan had just moved into—six miles outside Beulah, Vermont, and a quarter-mile from the interstate highway to the south—but that was because the boy was wearing denim jeans and a vest or jacket of denim, and because of the bleached, haylike look of his wild hair.

"Alan, who is it? What does he want?" Joanne said.

He turned to her, startled. His blond, greyish-blond hair looked disheveled: she had never seen him so distraught—tense, alarmed, yet irritable too, and a little embarrassed—as if she had come upon him when he had believed himself alone, totally alone. The face on the other side of the door bobbed like a mirror's reflection, broken loose. Joanne had taken down the old, dust-yellowed white curtains of a gauzy beige material, transparent from inside, from the darkened hallway. The boy on the porch was exposed by the overhead light. He brought his face up close to the window, pressing it against the pane, while Alan, turned to her, signalled for her to stay away. "Joanne, don't let him see you! Stay back!"

"But what is it—?"

"I don't know, I don't have any idea," Alan said. He spoke in a low, distracted mutter. The boy was rapping on the door in a series of quick, shallow knocks, so rapid they sounded like a single wave, a sequence of vibrations. ". . . I was just coming up to bed, I was just putting my things away, when he knocked on the door," Alan said. In his tone, now, was a sound of innocent perplexity, a slightly accusatory note, as if he were explaining this for the second or third time, to someone who did not quite believe him. "He's in his twenties, just a kid . . . I don't know what the hell he wants or where he came from . . . unless he wandered over here from the expressway, and . . ."

"What does he want?" Joanne whispered. "Does he want to use the telephone, or . . .? Does he want help?"

"Joanne, stand back out of the light, will you? I don't want him to see you, please, for Christ's sake. I'm hoping he'll just go away—but maybe I should call the police—"

Joanne did not quite hear him, she was so distracted by the boy on the porch. He was now holding onto the doorknob with both hands, turning it from side to side, and rubbing the forehead and the crown of his head against the window. Laughing, giggling, crooning and interrupting himself with a sudden jerk of his head, a strangled shout—his shoulders were raised high and narrow, his body seemed constricted, somehow deformed—he was a stranger, he had a stranger's face, yet Joanne experienced once again the fleeting mad thought that he had come back home, back to this restored nineteenth-century farmhouse, that he had not wandered back the driveway by accident. "The police," Joanne repeated. "The police, I wonder if—I think—Did you call them yet?"

"Honey, no I've been afraid to leave the door," Alan said.

"Is he drunk? Is he crazy?"

"I think he's high on drugs," Alan said. "He must be hallucinating. Just don't let him see you—he's out of his mind, obviously, and if he wanted to he could smash the window and get in here. He doesn't seem to know what he's doing—he doesn't seem to hear me—he's arguing with someone, but it isn't me, this is the strangest thing that's ever—that's ever—"

"How long has he been out there?" Joanne asked.

"Maybe ten minutes."

The figure out there lurched away from the window, backward.

But the thatch of blond hair reappeared, almost immediately, and there was a heavier pounding on the door and the doorframe, and a sudden banging on the screen door against the side of the house, as if he were kicking it, impatiently, having just discovered it.

"Didn't you call the police?" Joanne said faintly.

"Go away! Get out of here!" Alan shouted.

The boy jumped backward.

"We're going to call the police if you don't get out of here—Go on, get out! Go home!" Alan said. His voice climbed, angrily. Joanne felt a moment of intense relief, hope, an absurd pinprick of relief, thinking that her husband's anger had driven the boy away. But he had only stumbled backward, bumping into something on the veranda—one of the old wicker rockingchairs that had come with the farm, that Alan had recently repainted a bright hunter green— and this made him more furious, so that he ran to one of the windows and began scratching at it, drawing his fingernails wildly against the glass, up and down and around in crazy desperate circles. Alan and Joanne went into the room Alan used as a kind of study, a big, cluttered, handsome room with built-in bookshelves, so that they could see what he was doing. Despite the frenzy of his head and shoulders and torso, the dancer-like contortions of his body, he seemed oddly helpless—he only clawed at the window-pane, as if he did not dare to smash it. Yet he was very angry—crazily angry— shouting something that sounded like *You, y'no, yah*—But really it was nothing at all, strangled screams in a foreign language.

"Go upstairs and call the police, Joanne," Alan said. "I'll watch him to make sure he doesn't break in."

"But—But I—"

"Look at him, look at his eyes—His eyes are rolling back up into his head," Alan whispered. "Jesus, look! Have you ever seen anything like it? He's out of his mind. He's completely out of his mind."

"But why did he come here? Do you think he knows us? Is he one of your students?"

"No, I'm sure he isn't. No. He's too old. No."

"He isn't very old—he could be eighteen or nineteen—"

"No, he's older than that."

"It looks like he's crying—"

"Why don't you go upstairs and call the police?"

"What is that, on his face? Is he crying? Is he sweating, like that?"

"He's sweating."

"His mouth is all wet—"

Joanne was clutching at the collar of the robe she'd put on, an old blue flannel bathrobe from her girlhood, years ago. She was confused but part of her mind functioned with an odd over-bright clarity: the porch light was bright, very bright, and around it moths and gnats fluttered, in the early-summer mildness of a June night, and she felt isolated and observed and eerily, inexplicably girlish, standing barefoot in her husband's study, a few feet away from a maddened boy. Something like this must have happened many years ago—otherwise, why did she seem to remember it?—and why a gradual slowing of her heartbeat, a gradual conviction that she was in no danger, really that the frenzied boy would not harm them? Her fingers relaxed. She flexed them, they were numb, the nails had dug into the flesh of her palm, tiny pricks of pain too remote to be real. Alan was instructing her to go upstairs, to call the Beulah police or the highway patrol or, if she was too nervous, to dial the operator and tell her what was wrong. And emergency. Send police out. Send help. Maybe an ambulance . . . yes, an ambulance . . . a boy out of his mind, probably on drugs. Not a drunk. "Tell them it's a boy on drugs, hallucinating," Alan whispered. "And that it's quite serious. He could really go crazy at any moment and break in here and—"

The boy had stopped clawing at the window. He backed away, slowly, until he collided with the porch railing. He turned, surprised, and yet slowly, with the mechanical, faintly ludicrous alarm of a cartoon figure. *What? What? Oh.* He touched the railing. With his left hand he stroked the uneven surface of the railing, as if he were trying to see it better. His head drooped. Joanne could see his profile—a boy's face, the jaw dropping slackly, threads of saliva on his chin.

"Isn't it terrible . . . ?" Joanne said. "Oh, it's terrible . . . terrible."

"He was trying to talk to me through the door, but he couldn't understand anything I said," Alan said. He spoke now in a more normal voice. He and Joanne stood side by side, not touching. The boy was only a few yards away, but he seemed less dangerous. He was stroking and caressing the porch railing, his head bent attentively toward it. The laughter had stopped. Evidently the railing had

taken on some important meaning to him . . . very slowly, painstak-
ingly, he drew his fingertips along it, with a delicate precision that
seemed to open, in Joanne, a swift pragmatic pity. Alan was describing how he had been clearing his desk, had just switched off his desk
lamp, when the rapping began, there had been no possibility of its
being someone in his right mind, but from the start exaggerated and
hysterical—so Alan had acted quickly, turning off the hall light so
that the boy could not see him, though he had left the porch light on,
in order to see what the boy was doing. A friend of theirs had visited,
earlier that evening, and they had forgotten to turn the porch light
off; that must have been what had attracted the boy, Alan thought,
he must have seen the light from the highway, and . . . But Joanne
felt pity for him, she interrupted her husband and said: "Alan,
please. I don't think it's so serious. I think he just wants to use the
telephone . . . look at him, he doesn't seem dangerous, does he? I
think . . . I think that. . . ."

"Still, we'd better call the police."

"He must be from around here. He must have wandered over
here by accident . . . maybe he was with some friends, boys his age,
and they left him out, as a joke? . . . or maybe he lives nearby? . . . If
we call the police they'll arrest him, won't they? Won't they take him
to jail?"

"Joanne, I think we should call the police."

"Maybe he'll just decide to leave. . . ."

"He's out of his mind," Alan said irritably, "he could do anything.
Right now he seems harmless, yet, but. . . . Can you hear what he's
saying? What is he saying?"

"Should we open the window a little?"

"But don't let him—No, wait. Wait," Alan said, pushing her back.
"No, don't open it, go on upstairs and call the police, will you? I
think it's serious enough for the police. I'm not afraid of him, I don't
think there's any danger—he's so skinny—I don't think there's any
real danger to us, but maybe we should call the police just the
same—It might be that—He could go wild and—"

"He's saying something, isn't he?"

"I can't make any sense out of it."

"Maybe we should try to help him," Joanne said uncertainly.
"I mean—I mean—What can you do for someone in his condition,
hallucinating? . . .or whatever it is? Is it like being drunk, or is it

different? I've read so much about drugs but I don't know what to do. Do you think we should call the police, Alan? Why don't we try to help him? . . . Maybe," she said, taking Alan's arm, squeezing it, "maybe he just wants us to help him, maybe call his parents for him . . . or maybe he thinks this is his house, he's just trying to get back home, and. . . ."

The boy was rocking back and forth now, his body twisted, buttocks pressed against the railing. How pale his hair was, platinum-blond hair, amazing!—like a wig that was almost glamorous. The denim jacket and jeans were filthy, streaked with mud and grease or black paint, and he wore a shirt without buttons, opened upon his sunburnt, bare chest, that looked as if it were made of some thick, canvas-like material, crude scarlet and bright green, like an Indian blanket. Out there, he was somehow over-exposed, magnified. Joanne saw clearly the foot-long tear in the left pant-leg of his jeans and even the wet bloody wound inside, a child's accident; and she saw the tension in his feet, the strain of tendons and muscles as he rocked slowly back and forth, as if with great, mysterious effort, pushing himself against an element that opposed him. He had lost his shoes some-where: he wore thick white socks, like gym or hiking socks, with tiny diamonds of black and red in them, the socks torn and filthy, one of them—the one on his left foot—ridden down to his heel. Now that he was only crooning to himself, straining his body in and out of a posture that must have hurt his spine, he seemed only pitiful; Joanne wanted to open the window a few inches and talk to him, console him. Like her husband she would tell him to go home, but gently, gently. *Go home where you belong, don't stay here, don't force us to call the police and turn you in* . . . She even made a motion toward the window, but hesitated. She was afraid. And Alan seized her by the wrist and asked her what she thought she was doing . . . she had better stay back out of the light, in case he looked this way.

"Are you sure he isn't one of your students?" Joanne whispered.

"I'm fairly sure," Alan said.

"But what if . . . what if he's one of your students?"

"Joanne, I'm sure he isn't. I'm sure he isn't. I've never seen him before. He must be from Beulah, or one of the farms around here . . . no, honey, he isn't from the college. He just doesn't look as if he would be."

Alan was Dean of Humanities at a small college in Beulah, an excellent liberal arts college that had originally been affiliated with the Anglican church, but was now a secular institution; a young dean—Alan was only thirty-nine—he tried to become acquainted with all six hundred of the boys and girls he dealt with, and he even taught an honors course, a seminar in American Civilization, though the three-hour course was not part of his regular workload as an administrator. He and Joanne had moved to Vermont two years before, and had moved out to this farmhouse only a few months ago; it looked larger than it really was, like so many of the older houses in Vermont, but it was spacious downstairs, with a big living room, a closed-in porch Alan used as a study, and a high-ceilinged, drafty kitchen. Made partly of wood and partly of stone, it gave the appearance of being a small fortress, rather sombre and crypt-like in overcast light, half-buried beneath elms and the spreading, sprawling branches of an enormous willow tree . . . hardly visible from the road, back a long cinder-strewn lane that was itself lined with elms and smaller trees. When they turned in from the narrow country road, coming back from an evening in town, Joanne experienced a faint shock of surprise, sometimes even of dread—as if they had turned up an unpaved road by mistake, leaving the public road behind. The house could hardly be seen from the road. And then it emerged slowly, reluctantly: handsome enough if you knew what to look for, but overpriced, drafty, with a cellar that leaked and a furnace that must soon be replaced and an attic in which wasps and bees had lived for decades. Friends from school had dropped in a few times, but only after having been invited to drop in, to "stop by" if they happened to be in the neighborhood . . . and only once had a student come out, to see Alan about financial difficulties concerning the college newspaper; other than that, no one had ever visited them except as party or dinner guests, and no one had ever wandered up the driveway from the road, like this boy, to take them by surprise.

"He could be from Burlington," Joanne said. "He could be far from home. Oh God . . . look at him, look at his eyes . . . Maybe we should let him in. . . ."

"You want to let him?" Alan said sharply. "You want to let him in," he repeated.

". . . maybe give him something to drink, cold water, let him run some water over his head . . . a cold cloth . . . I could soak a towel in cold water and. . . ."

"You want to let a madman in our house," Alan said.

". . . his face is all wet, that's saliva hanging down his chin, onto his chest," Joanne said. "He must be seeing things. Right there, in front of us, standing right out there . . . he's seeing things, isn't he? He's hallucinating, isn't he? I wonder what he's seeing."

"Would you like to ask him?" Alan said. "You can ask him. Invite him in, have a conversation with him . . . Get the taperecorder. You could record it. Go ahead."

"But I. . . . I. . . ."

She fell silent, hurt.

"I only want to help him," she said.

Alan pulled her back from the window. He walked her into the hall. "I'm going to call the police. The sheriff's office."

"But. . ."

"Do you want to come upstairs with me, or what? I'm going to call them," he said angrily. "I don't trust you down here. I'm afraid you'll open the door to him."

"I won't open the door to him, but. . . ."

" . . . and if he sees you, what if he goes crazy? How can you tell what he's really seeing, when he looks at us or at anything?" Alan spoke in an urgent, reasonable voice. He was a man of moderate height, Joanne's own height, though with his shoes on—she was barefoot—he seemed much taller. He still wore the dark green shirt he had worn to school that day, and the dark flannel trousers, though he had taken his tie off; in the dim, blurred light that came through the gauze curtains his face was shadowy, almost secretive, diminished. The boy, so exposed, drew Joanne's attention back that way, though her husband was arguing with her and gripping her shoulder, hard. She knew she must listen to him. She must pay attention. He rarely spoke like this, rarely with that note of drama, of warning—most of the time he was low-keyed, like Joanne himself, smoothed by early, consistent success (his in his profession, Joanne's in terms of beauty, social achievement, her very womanhood itself) and a sense of rightness, of being and inhabiting what was right. They had both been praised for their ability to be competent, but predictably competent; now, Alan's words seemed to Joanne exactly the words that must be said, that had already been said, in the past, but she balked at hearing them, a small neutral smile interrupting him: " . . . Well, what do you want me to do, then?" he said.

"I don't know. Nothing."

"I still think he's dangerous. What can we do, go to bed? . . . with him out there on the porch singing to himself?"

"He hasn't tried to break in the house."

"What do you want me to do?" Alan asked.

"Nothing."

He paused, staring at her. She saw a complex fusion of dislike, impatience, bewilderment in his face—the eyes narrowed, focussed directly upon her. In the last year or so he had begun to look his age; before that, he'd always seemed like one of his own students, a graduate student, perhaps, though more courteous and alert than the average student. "Nothing?" he said. "Go to bed and leave him out there, and try to sleep? . . . knowing he might break in at any minute?"

"I don't know," Joanne said slowly.

The after-effect of the panic spread through her now: a sensation of chill, the clarity sharp-edged, without emotion. She peered through the door window and there he was, still, yes, still out there, leaning back against the railing, his legs outspread, his head now lowered. His arms hung down limply. Moths fluttered about him but he did not seem to notice. Joanne remembered an incident she had not told Alan about: in Cambridge, down there for a visit not long ago, she had seen a nice-looking boy talking to a parking meter, then yelling at it, trying to strangle it . . . and, only a few hours later, somewhere up the turnpike where she had stopped for gas, she'd seen another boy gesticulating, pleading with, trying to get into a conversation with an ice-cube machine outside a Texaco station. The two incidents returned to her now, gracefully fused. She had half-wished the boys had been in the same dimension with her, not so that they might be sane again—what value had that, when everyone was sane!—but so that they might interpret her. How did she look, to them? What contours had her face, what elegant ghastly proportions her slender body? And her eyes—transformed weirdly by a power she would never dare take on, herself—what beauty might they have, not known to her, and certainly not to her husband? This handsome, alarmed, impatient man who argued with her, this sensitive man whom responsibility had touched so subtly—only a few silvery, curly hairs, only a few slight indentations between his eyebrows—he too was transformed, something quite exotic and unknowable, but there was no way of seeing him, no way in.

"I don't know," she repeated, staring.

Alan pushed her away, in disgust, and started up the stairs.

"I'll call the sheriff's office," he said. "I've had enough of this for one night, Goddamn it—"

Joanne saw the boy lurch forward. He took a few steps toward the door, as if to call Alan back, then he reeled around and faced the opposite way, mumbling to himself. He was still rocking, not quite forward and back; not from right to left, either; but in a clumsy, uncertain, but stubborn rhythm, like a child imitating someone he is watching closely, trying to get the movements correct. Then he bounded off the veranda, down the steps, and ran away—across the weedy front yard, toward the driveway. Joanne could see his blond hair several seconds after the rest of him seemed to disintegrate.

"Alan," she called. "Alan. . . . Alan, wait. Alan? He's gone."

At first Alan did not reply; she was afraid he had called the sheriff.

"Alan . . .? Alan, he's gone," she said triumphantly. "He's gone."

"Is he gone?" Alan asked.

He stood at the top of the stairs, crouching in order to look down. He sounded a little embarrassed. "Is he gone?"

"He ran out toward the road."

"What did he . . .? What did he do, just run away suddenly?" Alan asked, doubtfully. "Out toward the road?"

"Yes, he's gone."

Alan came back downstairs, cautiously. He opened the front door, leaned out, looked from side to side. Joanne pushed past him. Barefoot, she stood on the veranda, looking out into the darkness. She waved a moth away from her face. Alan muttered something about the surprise of it, the shock of someone banging on the door like that . . . at one-thirty in the morning . . . and he'd been so tired, so exhausted, from committee meetings that day . . . what could you expect of him, what had she expected? She did not make sense of this, but was watching to see if the boy might appear: first the glimmer of the hair, she would catch sight of that first. Running back the driveway, from the road. Running in his stockinged feet. Crying, gesturing, exploding into laughter . . . so mysterious, the bearer of so mysterious a message, and now so hopelessly lost!

"What did you care if he was dangerous or not," Alan said sullenly. "You had nothing to lose."

" . . . It's all right," Joanne said. She had begun to shiver. Still, she felt no emotion, only that clarity, as if someone had struck her and she had not fallen, but remained upright, watchful. "He's gone. There isn't even anything to show he was here."

Alan straightened the wicker chair, as if to correct her. But he said nothing.

"Had you dialed the sheriff?" she asked.

"What difference does it make?"

"When we were in London that time, and walking through the subway, at Hyde Park Corner, you were afraid of that old woman," Joanne said softly. "Remember? That old alcoholic woman with the market bags, and the scarves tied around her neck. . . ."

"I don't remember any woman," Alan said.

"She asked us for something, we couldn't understand what she was saying."

"She wanted money."

"Did she? I don't know, I don't know what she wanted," Joanne said. "You were afraid of her. . . ."

Alan went back inside, and after a few minutes she followed him. She latched the screen door and locked the inside door.

She switched off the porch light. Now she could see across the grassy front lawn, to the ridge of trees that lined the driveway. First she would catch sight of the blond hair, a glowing patch of light . . . then the body would take shape out of the confused shadows. . . .

"How do you know what any of them want from us?" she called out shrilly.

But Alan had gone upstairs. He had turned on the creaky hot-water faucet in the bathroom.

She went to bed and slept, and did not dream about the boy. The next day, she did not think about him: only the image of him, the ghostly shape he might take. But she did not think of him, really, until just before dinner when Alan came into the kitchen and thrust something at her—the Burlington newspaper, which he had folded back. His hands were shaking.

"What? What is it?" Joanne asked sharply.

She took the paper from him and read a small news item on page 9, headlined HITCH-HIKER IN CRITICAL CONDITION: an unidentified young man, about twenty-one years old, weighing about 140 pounds, had been hit by a truck heading south on the turnpike near Beulah, early that morning—he had evidently wandered onto the turnpike in the hopes of getting a ride, though the truck driver said the boy seemed to be in a daze. *Not yet identified. Believed to have been under the influence of drugs.* Joanne read the article twice, began it a third time, then broke off and stared at the dancing newsprint. Had it been real, her dream of a boy, her forlorn pitying rush of love . . . ?

Alan took the paper away; she forced herself to stare at his flushed face. He was not going to say anything. He was not going to accuse her. But she whispered just the same: "Why—why did you show this to me? Why did you show this to me? What has this got to do with me?"

He unfolded the paper, turned it back to page one, and dropped it on the cane-back chair by the rear door, where they kept the papers until Alan got rid of them each week. He did not accuse her of anything. He did not say anything at all.

MUSICAL SHUTTLE

by HARVEY SHAPIRO

from LAUDS (Sun press) and UNDINE

nominated by UNDINE

Night, expositor of love.
Seeing the sky for the first time
That year, I watched the summer constellations
Hang in air: Scorpio with
Half of heaven in his tail.
Breath, tissue of air, cat's cradle.
I walked the shore
Where cold rocks mourned in water
Like the planets lost in air.
Ocean was a low sound.
The gate-keeper suddenly gone,
Whatever the heart cried
Voice tied to dark sound.
The shuttle went way back then,
Hooking me up to the first song
That ever chimed in my head.
Under a sky gone slick with stars,
The aria tumbling forth:
Bird and star.
However those cadences
Rocked me in the learning years,
However that soft death sang—
Of star become a bird's pulse,
Of the spanned distances
Where the bird's breath eddied forth—
I recovered the lost ground.
The bird's throat
Bare as the sand on which I walked.
Love in his season
Had moved me with that song.

STATIONERY, CARDS, NOTIONS, BOOKS

by HAROLD WITT

from POETRY NOW

nominated by H. L. Van Brunt

They sank what they'd saved up
and a small inheritance—
nailed shelves for a month,
at the opening, served coffee
among the attractive displays

His wife in her handwoven skirt
and he convivial
with his pipe and English tweeds
tried to create an aura
of culture and good taste—
but except for a student or two
no one wanted Auden,
Toynbee or either James—
and the dusting they had to do!

Then after a half price sale
they did get rid of some books
and just in time not to fail
moved the rest to the back—

the greeting cards sold well
and so did the comic ceramics—
the cat with a cactus tail,
the miniature toilet ashtrays.

𝄞 𝄞 𝄞

INTRO

the opening to his new novel-in-progress

by HAROLD BRODKEY

from AMERICAN POETRY REVIEW

nominated by Gordon Lish

I CAN'T BELIEVE I'M GOING to be the hero of this book. Maybe that's because I'm from the middlewest. I think I better say now I know what I'm doing at least as far as it goes in that I haven't listened to any advice: the mistakes are mine.

Before I began to make my living as a writer, I used to think I just woke up. But it turned out that was wrong and that a great deal goes on when I wake up; there's a whole narrative to my waking up that I didn't know about until I began wondering once what my qualifications were for being a writer.

I was worried that I didn't notice more things, or if maybe I did notice more things than other people did, and didn't give myself credit for noticing stuff that wasn't in books or movies or that someone else had not spoken of in my hearing, because I was afraid to have my own consciousness—as a middlewestern American, a lecher, as my parents' child, and all that.

I started thinking about waking up because trying to decide if I was equipped to be a high-status writer was like deciding whether to wake up or not—I'll explain this—whether to wake out of being maybe falsely middle-class—and silent. I was, I thought, attached to a question of consciousness now.

It was the idea of waking up, or a summary of it, or a general law I was after, not a form or way of apprehending it so that it could be put into speech: I suddenly became very curious about the actuality—of breath and sheets, dreams, night-sweats.

No one had asked me about it; I never had wondered about it before; it was new to me as a subject of exploration.

I discovered first I couldn't be sure—consciously assured—of what I noticed until I decided to write down what I saw and to show what I wrote down to someone. It seems I don't know what I know unless I am out to answer a question with a witness there, to judge me. In answering I become, maybe fraudulently, maybe genuinely knowledgeable, about what is asked—I rally to the question.

If I don't write it down and show it, there is no discipline to my knowing things—it is all quite mystic, golden, and revelatory—and unfinal.

Part of my consciousness, my remembering-and-codifying attentiveness seemed very agreeable and anxious to co-operate: it was right there, in my dreams the next night, or morning, as I began to wake up: it said, just as if it were a separate identity among all the others congregated at that moment in my mostly sleeping self, it said Here we go—now notice this.

And it did this nearly every other night for four or five months, skipping a few now and then.

It would seem waking up for me begins when I grow to loathe the emotional bullying of dreams. All that feeling things arouses antagonism. I resist. Some dream episode, probably the eighty-ninth of the busy night, releases the blazing spread of real terror through my more or less sleeper's, or sucker's, consciousness, one of those unfair and total *oh no, oh no* terrors of a dream; and I just don't want it.

Part of it is I begin to resent the terrible conventions of narrative, of enducing emotion that my dreams use—falling in love with a woman dressed in white on a transatlantic flight or falling from a cliff. It is crass and demeaning to feel so much emotion because of a casually and fiercely irresistible situation that shows no inventiveness or reliability—(as when a counter-espionage agent and his helpers are drowning me in an old-fashioned wooden barrel: I have been caught out and am being forced into a stale or stagnant water, into unconsciousness).

I am dreaming it is the end of the world. I am in a supermarket—with a whole bunch of people—and the deluge begins. These are the last moments. The roof of the supermarket blows off, but God—the father—hovers overhead and keeps a lot of the wind, the typhoons and rain and lightning off; still, some gets in. Terror and revelation. Patience and a blankness about the bad luck.

There is a child there, a small girl: I take it on myself to comfort her—so there's all *that* sentiment, and concern for her.

Then some one insists we put on a drama, a play: I am given a good part and feel considerable stage fright *on top of all the rest*. Oh so many emotions. Then it seems the end really is close at hand; the emotions grow so intense that I say The hell with this. What it is, is I want my own emotions. I want to wake up.

Very well. But I don't know that—I don't know that I'm dreaming and so I can't know that I want to wake up. Sometimes I feel wistfully, ah, if only I was dreaming. And sometimes then, I think, maybe I am.

Sometimes it is more intellectual: sort of, have I been fooled into accepting *a dream* as real? If I have been deluded that this is reality, I can get out of this practically by snapping my fingers.

But what if my suspicions were wrong? What if my hopes are ill-founded? Suppose this event is coexistent with the universe and is in reality as I am, the reality in which I have to die someday? If I challenge it, this reality, it is so constructed, it is, in such a mean way, that I will bring on my death—or the rending of my consciousness into insanity—much sooner and with more chagrin than if I was sensible and endured my time and tried to live through this event as best I could, accepting it as all that there logically can be.

There is such shame in being wrong—at least for me—especially when I dream: I mean being wrong about what reality is, whether there is good sense and victory in revolution, salvation, anarchy, whether there *is* another life behind a membrane, another life and a different consciousness, or if I will discover I was wrong in believing any such ridiculous thing, that, since I can govern my dreams, there comes a sudden improvement in the dream's plausibility, removing all question of their being another reality: it seems I was wrong to think I was dreaming: this *is* the end of the world. Ah, thank God, I don't have to choose.

But rebellion—or incipient wakefulness as wit—sharpens my eyes and mind; as does resentment which returns as a paranoia: is that check-out clerk's hand transparent as glass? There's no such thing as a glass hand, in real reality—I know that—. One would not see a glass hand at any supermarket I go to in my waking life.

All at once, all around me, I see the quickening of signs through camouflage of delusion and cruelty and ego that my dreams used to fool me with throughout the night: everywhere are traces of the unreality of this world: a wall has no thickness and changes its shape; if God the father is there he can keep out *all* the rain—therefore, he is not there! The entire shape of a waking consciousness, of an assurance of consciousness, takes its shape and is established in me.

A fragility of logic, an illogicality of substance, a tenuity begins to make itself known in the cold, tough, earnest face of the man who is making us put on the play. Or I float swiftly through and above the overcoated Czechoslovakian (Bohemian) crowd that cares nothing about me, that does not care what becomes of me, that does not care if I write well or not.

No other reality is yet present—or even hinted at—I am still asleep, after all—but I know this one is false. There is a joy and self-satisfaction in seeing failed plausibility everywhere—all the connections of *this* world are in shreds: anarchy comes to the kingdom at the end of the night.

During the months when I was visiting my dreams, I would, a surprising number of times, now turn into Abraham Lincoln.

The main connection I think was this: my father (by adoption) when he discovered I was afraid of sleep, told me about Wynken, Blynken, and Nod, setting out to sea, to see; and he told me they came back—or perhaps I made the deduction myself. I was coming back like a Blynken, Abe Lincoln.

I am a creature who can wake.

It is wonderful to have guessed right and not to have to die just now.

Sometimes, a great many figures, perhaps all the figures from all the episodes of the night's sleep, gather then, a mob to cheer me, or just to stare at me. The ambition in waking up is very great.

For me there is the sense of advancing away from a place where explanations arouse complete emotion and therefore could not be disbelieved.

I am proceeding, on the grounds of disbelief, toward yet more disbelief.

I am rising; I am elevated to a height where there is an overriding *dreaming and now I am waking up. . . . I am coming to my senses.* This explanation for everything in my consciousness at that moment: I *was* outranks all other meanings; and in spite of the disbelief thing, it seems very religious: I suppose one does not sleep for God, one keeps a vigil, usually.

I seem to enter a light of weightless semi-consciousness, waking consciousness almost, of intelligence without locus or any sense of ignorance limiting it or creating areas or holes of shadow in it; I am innocent of exhaustion.

The light of the wind of God, it was announced one morning in a non-rhetorical voice.

The proportion of being-awake to being-asleep changes like a mixture of salt and fresh water in the lock of a canal.

At some point there is a lurch; the silken time of dreams completely gives way; and I am hooked onto the marching pulse or clicking and grinding train of that waking time that goes only in one direction and that without remission.

I am one of those people who is almost always glad to wake.

YOUNG CASANOVA: IN HIS BED—AND ELSEWHERE

When I was a child of a certain age—two, three—I woke in a house made of wood.

The feeling of being awake, my consciousness of it was a gray chamber in which something who was me now resided—as a waker, as a rememberer of things I could not name, things having to do with sleep or with sunlight and rooms and faces from the time before my adoption: I was adopted I was two years old; and since I could not name them, they were not memories but movements of consciousness, swings—as in a real swing, or as in being lifted, or as in sliding and crawling: I sat in a gray chamber and looked out into another gray chamber in which earliness and solitude were compressed, or caught, a menagerie of vague illuminations and joinings (walls to ceiling, chairs to floor) that I did not understand. I was somberly pleased to be in that room—separated from grief, from noises: again, I had no name for grief: it was somewhat an indignity, a pridelessness. My room, my shell, my outer identity—as if I found me on a beach—as if ownership and solitude made an odd mirror that reflected a knowledge that then in turn seemed physical: I *was* in a gray room, inside me, inside the outer room. I did not at that age speak aloud: I did not name things to myself very often. I did not name it room: it was an area of fact—it was where-*I*-was. It was never silent but ticked or creaked, sobbed, or dripped polka-dottedly. That room—I was its lover, its twin: my genus was determined by my shell.

It is hard for me to identify the somberness that I had—that of an Arab sheikh, was it, ruthless, with a nomad's dignity, and griefless-ness, anger and pride being substituted for grief?—somber, enshel-led, small in the bed, constrained by taut sheets and blankets and by chairs set backs to the bed: I was a somber, stilled, snobbish, nomadically or Britishly arrogant, waked up lover of the act of conscious looking, the arcs, the sparking of conscious sight, or the slower blotting up, or the silent sweeps, or the sending out on expeditions, or the brushing flights, or palpings, the hesitations, broodings over, the pressings against by a Martian, a Proust, an insect, an insect's legs and belly on the things looked at, which press back, cool and itchy, foreign, and insect-like themselves to one's senses and mind.

The chair, for instance—the chair was lit and shadowed—it was a thing Anne Marie, my nurse, dusted; the woman who was my mother by adoption (I did not know that) sat in it sometimes; its rungs had sleeves of shadow: there were shadows on its seat, smears, like tongue marks.

Night air was like a cold, half-sleeping snake; at dawn the air began to dance.

This happened in a town slowly turning into a suburb of a nearby city. The house I was in—which I know now was Edwardian and good-sized—was set on a high bluff above a large river, an American river with an Indian name.

We were about forty miles from that nearby city: its downtown towers rose out of a cornfield—that's what it looked like when my father's car drove toward it.

My family was rich, or nearly so, or pretended to be, or thought they were.

I had a patient suspiciousness, a patient incautiousness about consciousness so that wakefulness, when no one else was around, meant I was in an often increasingly large chamber of isolation—a tent turning into an enormous reception room at an airport in which there was no one at that time of day except me.

I don't think I conceived of myself as necessarily human—or as having gender—or a name, if no one was awake near me.

Until someone came into my room, I could as well have been a monkey-girl—*"Look at him—look where he's climbed to—the monkey. . . ."* (He could be a girl, so far as I knew.)

I climbed on the bureau, to its top, and out the window —and so on.

I was adopted when I was two and did not speak until I was four.

Behind our house was a little park which I did not understand to be a park but thought was part of the outdoor room of our back yard, our *property*. Proper, yes. The park ran to a wall at the edge of the bluff, a wall too high for me to see over, and which I was forbidden to climb (I still climbed it whenever I was unobserved); my father would stand me on it; he'd hold me; I'd lean against him and taste the salt of the danger, of the view, of being flicked at by narrow, abrasive bands of wind, sun-crisped, wind-cooled, veined.

The wind would push at my eyelids, my nose, my lips. I heard a buzzing in my ears which signalled how high, how alone we were: this view of (parts of) four counties was audible. I looked into the luminous hollow in *front of me, a grand hole, an immense bellying deep sheet or vast sock.* There were numinous fragments in it— birds in sunlight, bits of smoke, mist.

It had a floor on which were creeks (and the big river), rail lines, roads, highways, houses, siloes, bridges, trees, fields, everything beaded with quiet or suddenly enlarging and shrinking glitter, and bearded and stippled with shadows, of varying geometries and colors: it was almost a whole world made into a toy, a view, a panorama as a personal privilege.

My mother's family, as she would point out with an air of temperamental exasperation, as if boasting wearied her, was "influential in this town."

She used the local police force as if its members were employees of hers: a policeman, tall, silent, and obviously redolent with the violence, the force packed within his slightly casual, temporary, skimpy ordinariness and uniform, came to our house every afternoon to go with me and my nurse to the park right behind our house—this happened every day for a while. Nearby was a working class neighborhood, and my nurse, Anne Marie, was fat and pious (Lutheran) and could not bear to be teased or mocked. Also, there was some kind of threat from my real family that they would repossess me by kidnaping me.

By force.

There was a bandstand in the park, a Moorish-Victorian pergola. I climbed on its steps; another child followed me and stood nearby, in the slant of sunlight and shadow on the steps (that the roof of the pergola made). I looked at the child who stared at me: we decided, gravely, to attempt to play, to keep company, to begin the difficult project of loving someone our own size.

The policeman stood on a nearby path. I have forgotten my playmate; and I stare at the policeman (perhaps my playmate does too). If I want to mount the steps to the bandstand, I have to crawl, sort of, I have to use my hands and feet: the steps are too high for me to walk up. Sunlight obscures his nose, his chin: down his front run two rows of buttons: night-blue cloth and orange suns. His eyes are blank, largely uninterested, filled with idleness: how is it I know they mask a threat?

What does a protector protect you with.

He is a disturbance in the clear and sunlit air.

My father, if he comes home early, will come into the park, to fetch me, to see me: he will lift me; and I will sit on his arms, propped against part of his chest; and then I can see into the policeman's face which is dreadful with various obscure potentials that concern me: the holes in his face, nostrils, eye pupils, beard stubble, are very final: the careful unaliveness of the eyes announces that rage and adventure are not here—who is this man? I knew the sunlight could collapse for me into that patient and childlike horror of not knowing what was happening but knowing one was hurt.

Perhaps I had been beaten, or had seen a beating administered in the two years before I was adopted.

Sometimes my father tells me I can see the policeman's gun.

The policeman is deferential—obscurely arrogant—bored—boyish in some ways.

My father is deferential, slightly condescending—he is familiar with guns—and yet he isn't: there is some quality of *comfort*-with-a-gun-at-your-side or in-your-hand that is unutterably foreign to him. He is half-laughing at the policeman in an inevitable, maybe compulsive competition, or measuring-himself-against-him thing; but also he is full of magic, awe, discretion, boastfulness, and a hidden, lower heat.

The policeman unbuttons his sunglazed holster and pulls out a very large bluish oily reflectant heavy, heavily strange looking *thing*—object—changeable, threatened, charged with forces and possibilities: presently docile: a mysterious machine: a machine of mystery. Dismaying. Thrilling.

I touch it. I cannot bear to touch it—or not to touch it.

Strength enters me. Flees from me.

I put my arms around my father's neck and look in the other direction, over my father's shoulder, at the sun-filled expanse of air (sunlight beats upward from the river, from the cliff face, from the grass: the air is mingling of crooked spears of light, pointing down and up, and at oblique angles of all kinds).

"Are you an American boy?" my father asks me: "do you want to be a policeman when you grow up? Here's a young fella who wanted to be a policeman and I guess he was pretty stubborn because he is one."

Sometimes I stand mute, fatherless, hanging onto the railing of the Moorish pergola, observing The Nature of Reality. I think that is what I'm observing—those paths, my nursemaid on that bench, the policeman standing there.

I look at the policeman in *the children's light*—grownups are busy, older children are in school—this light belongs to us. I feel the fingering breezes at my childish face as if they meant to enter it.

I have never been hurled backward into time by a cup of tea. Lost time was always present—through a maze, through an effort of mental skills: to be a practiced rememberer is to be a wastefully overtrained acrobat in a circus of the no longer actual, of the *what is this?*

Sometimes in the mornings, when I first wake up, I don't know if I am dead or not, an animal or not, an infant, an emperor, a woman—and this happens if I wake up in the same bed as usual and at the same time. I come out of the sensual void of nurture and imprisonment which is sleep, and my consciousness jerks around like a sea thing stranded on a rock. On the circumstances of my life now which I don't yet remember—my gender—my money. Perhaps it is the *I* that in my dreaming during the night often said of some figure, That is me, and then moved inside it—maybe that *I* is what thrashes, caught in wakefulness, or it waits while my senses stumble, and other forms of consciousness do, in this time, this world. In my case, when I awake, sometimes, my mind, my consciousness, unsettled toward history and the absolute, struggles to locate and to begin, even now, each morning, at the beginning, nearly when I was born, when it was first established I was to be alive and awake in this way.

It is very brief—briefer than a twitch—and I do not have to notice it unless I want; but I have had, on awaking, what seems to be a very near, a very recent memory of hands as large as I am on me, a rough lace or hod of hands. I seem to remember recently being held by those large hands. I remember the adjoining squeaks, silent and inward, outward and aloud, of my skin.

When I am happy in my present life, and not working hard, not dwelling much in my mind, this stuff of waking up is so brief it is like a joke, a quick zipping past or flutter—life wit, morning wit. When I am unhappy, waking takes longer and is stranger and seems anxious to impart a gloomy instruction about me and my life to me with a school-like wintry weariness. I am not usually willing to receive it: I endure it. When I am happy, I have no time for instruction, I have learned enough about me, I know enough about me.

If I want to re-experience those grudging, instruction-filled moments of those sad mornings, I have to be unhappy again: I have to make it clear I am defeated and empty; and my life is hollow.

Then the morning drama aches with parables. I seem to slide along a graph of who I am and have been: it is not certain where on the graph the slide will stop: a point becomes a doorway, a room filled with waiting figures: I start to enter my life—but it turns out to be an earlier part of my life: I am too tall now for this: some of these people are dead: ah, god, the smell of tragic ardor when one pauses at the threshhold of a memory! It is as if the emotions of whole years are compacted into one still moment and impart a violence which we disguise as lyrical nostalgia.

For instance, I am running, more or less in a circle, my god, my god, in partly shadow—compacting, partly rainbowed prisms of childish sweat. The grass is not far from my eyes—is indeed much easier to see, is much nearer than would be the face of an adult standing near me even if I were standing still: grass is the level, the substance of my vision.

The air is partly daylight air, partly evening air, abrasive, resistant, hot with the day's heat and dust (thick and brick-like) but in some patches the air is smooth, moist, odorous, like some awful, fretful, enclosing flower.

The butterfly pumping of my heart signals the weak violence of my utmost physical efforts: I am made of innocence—this running is a game of effectual wickedness.

The physical flutter, the flitter, of blood, eyelids (sweat-weighted), fluttering white shoes, at the jerking edge of vision, fluttering points, ripples of white sleeves, of aimlessly bouncing white hands—bouncing on air (on the limits of the bones of my arms but I cannot comprehend that)—the skewed, scurried rhythm of my—amateurishness. . . . The world is getting to be hard to see. Darkness makes my running dangerous (hurting me is all I can hurt), sight and physical beauty are becoming mythical, a glimmer of memory like a dim glow over the veil of dark that hides faces. One runs as a particularly good-looking child does, hand-in-hand with, in connivance with the physical—it is because of my face—"You were irresistible," my mother said—that I am part of this family, run in this park, wake in that room.

My father is nearby. A huge voice, a rattling boxcar of a voice, in the twilight, rattles down toward me—as I run—it says: "Go ahead, Wiley, run—let's see you run—you run like a demon. . . ."

(My mother by adoption said that after my real mother died, "No one took good care of you—you became ill, you stopped walking —most people thought your brain had been damaged, but you were the most beautiful child I ever saw, so we took a chance on you."

(She said, "We couldn't get a child through a regular adoption agency—I'm not sure why—we didn't make a good psychological impression. . . .")

"Run. . . . Go ahead, run. . . . You little demon. . . ."

Here and there, in the dark, which gathers, like ancient Roman senators dressed in black—they move and rustle, stand closer and closer together in the senate house, fill it with a dully muttering menace, a crowd—the dark crowds in among the pillars of the bandstand, among the houses that rim the park, and in the large, middlewestern sky. A few lines and patches of peach, of pink and gold, remain, on a bush here, on the roof of the bandstand, in my father's gold-rimmed glasses, among the blackening strips of cloud near the horizon (that is to say, the wall that edges the view: it is the horizon here). My father's hat is shadowy: he wears a hat: he stands spread-legged, a splendid mass of consciousness and powers. Sometimes—when I am standing still—and see him, a broken wall of water, of affection, rushes toward him. I run. I run. On a human carpeting of breath: there is a laboring engine in front of me—I pant, a child running in the damp mouth of early darkness. Life, one's life, is in part like a sealed or closed carton—one stuffs papers in it; other people stuff papers in it—who will it turn out to be I was? What will it turn to be my life was like?

The rapt hypnosis of the novice runner is interrupted: "Wiley," my father calls: he calls my name: "Wiley. . . ." He says, "Wiley, it's time to stop."

One is wicked and a whore, like a movie star.

It occurs to me not to hear my name: anonymous, I continue to run: no one is calling *me*: I am wicked: I laugh.

Free will. Ecstasy.

My father is chasing me.

My god, I feel it up and down my spine, the thumping on the turf, the approach of his hands, his giant hands, the huge ramming increment of his breath as his breathing shifts from the near-silence of standing still to this fierce rush of competence and of widening effort. I feel it up and down my spine and in my mouth and in my belly—Daddy is so swift: whoever heard of such swiftness? Such as in stories. . . .

I can't escape him, can't fend him off, his arms, his half-laughter, his rapidity, and his will and his interest in me.

I am being lifted into the air—and even as I pant and stare blurrily, limply, mindlessly, a map appears, of the dark ground where I ran: as I hang limply and rise anyway on the fattened bar of my father's arm, I see that there's the grass, there's the path, there's a bed of flowers.

I straighten up, and there are the lighted windows of our house, some distance away; and from them hang yellow rugs which slant and are roughened by clapboard walls and by stalks and leaves of plants and bushes at the base of the wall: some of the rugs spread a yellow parallellogram over the rough-fibered, hillocky grass. My father's face, warm, full of noises—breath, ticking eyelashes, the rustle of stubble against the cloth of the shirt I wear, against the cloth of my shoulder—is near: it looms: his hidden face: is that you, old money-maker? My butt is folded on the trapeze of his arm. My father is as big as an automobile.

In the oddly shrewd-hearted torpor of being carried home in the dark, a tourist, in my father's arms, I feel myself attached by my heated-by-running damp sweatiness to him: where we are attached, there are binding oval stains of warmth.

In most social talk, most politeness, most literature, most religion, it is as if violence didn't exist—except as sin, something far away. This is flattering to woman and conducive to grace—because the heaviness of fear, the shadowy henchmen selves that fear attaches to us, that fear sees in others, is banished.

Where am I in the web of jealousy that trembles at every human movement?

What detectives we have to be.

ON GETTING READY TO BE BATHED

I do not do much toward my own disrobing. I am undressed by hands, by skills I don't comprehend—and anyway, most of the movements of those hands I can't see no matter how far into my neck I lower my chin: if I twist around so I can see, Momma or Anne Marie says, "Hold still."

In my passivity, I am like a ground beneath a large, moonish, female face, which bathes me in pleasure—small, slippery, sliding, nameless pleasures.

The face is a vast surface which I touch, lean toward, or tease, or stare at with increasingly jovial—and stilled—contentment—or I resist and stare at it with imprecise questioning which turns into acquiescence: what is *it* doing? (That face, that consciousness) is looking at a button caught in the eyelike slit of a buttonhole.

If I am standing on the floor, then Momma is stooping—her knee protrudes: her arms move complicatedly: the top of her dress or robe holds big, sleeping, stirring animals (lambs, scotties, masses of pigeons): her arms and knee—or knees—makes a filigree or loose, golden-silvery fence—(as they brush me and apply a melted foil, a gliding, or a brief moonish flare)—behind which the egg-like rollings and circuits (circuses, circles) of her drowsy belly, mounded, and yet pond-like (to be divided at, pushed into) waits and the curious sleeping animals of her breast. Time whispers. I am not to make difficulties.

You-can-wrestle-with-your-father-if-you-have-to-wrestle. . . .

Momma's attention, her *neatened*, delicate—pecking-like, birds-eye-like—attentiveness and efforts—efforts like little scissors going snip, snip—is given over to my buttons, fastenings, knitted cuffs: she pulls—then a thin, fabric-y, shimmer-noose and crawling-caterpillar or fluttering-bird's-struggle-and-flight holds, pulls, stirs my skin with messages, traces of animal life, of something held and then gone, they tug against my nose, firmly haul at my eyes, draggle and wrench my forehead, my hair.

In a peculiar mixture of being there, of being ignored, of being still and excited, of vague boredom, of pleasures, the moments pass; and at last, I am naked.

ENTERING THE WATER

Hands cup my ribs; a woman's head is near my own, facing in the same way so that her breath scores my cheek—and drums in my ears.

A woman's head and hands guide my descent through the faint steaminess of the air above the tub: I must not overbalance her by lifting my legs to delay entry in the water or to prepare for a mighty kick, to shatter the water's self-possession so that I enter it in the midst of the disturbance I have willed and made; I must not be limp as I am with Daddy: there might then be a crash into the side of the tub, and a too quick, and unplanned plunge into the motionless or shivering water.

The water rises, closes lips around my toes—I jerk—"Be careful or you'll make me drop you." Pleasure is difficult—is this pleasure? One's shoulders fold up alongside one's neck: *things* race around inside oneself—ants-cum-tiny-electric-racing-cars—or magic twigs scratching dust, dust-as-flesh, or dust-and-flesh. The water slides up over my toes, insteps, the undersides and oversides—I'm not sure I can bear this—"Be a man—don't twitch," Momma says: she adores her own exasperations: she has a collection of them, including ones that are oddly sensual, or pre-sensual like wool, which scratches and makes me itch and get away from it but a moment or two later, my skin is pleasantly afire or warm.

The water is over my ankles, is moving—mouthlike, closely, claspingly swallowing or taking in, in a circuit—up my legs, the backs of my knees, slides over my knees, my rump as I fold, as I sit, encircles my belly in a magnificent collar of ambiguous sensation. It is not smooth but faintly abrasive—water is (from old soap and soap powder and perhaps dirt)—I am smoother than it is: I can feel almost everything—somewhat uneasily: sensations rarely stop short of violence, of Walpurgisnacht—burning, or tickling, yells, or wild intentness—and the shout of, "Wiley, stop that!"

The water I am embedded in is formal, formidable submissive: dangerous: it fits me closely and relentlessly on its inside but it is full and oval and is itself on its outside.

I do not understand the water, its independence, its degree of subservience and then of danger-to-me. I ruffle and push at it to make it go down, as a balloon, or pillow, or woman's breast, or dog's stomach, or thick blanket, does: the water stirs—echoingly—as if it had hidden metal in it: bigger though than filings (the faint abrasive-ness that I feel)—but it returns to, it persists in returning to its outward thing. It is like a grownup who responds to you but who was a mysterious outer shape and pertinacity of being which is beyond you and your powers to affect or change in them—(to amuse or distract them, make them tender: they speak in baby-talk, they soften their voices, they smile because of you a smile reserved for—children, is it? Or for you, a child like you?)

"Lean forward, I want to do your back—I have to get you clean and pretty before your father comes home—"

(She said to people, in a sort of daring way, "Charley was tired of me—well, being a husband has its drawbacks—so I got him Wiley so he would have someone to love. . . .")

My mother's hair grows lank and partly disarranged; her eyes grow intent, crazed, distant.

If I splash her, the flying water will make irrational butterflies, leave tracks as of wind-driven twigs in snow, on her wrap or dress.

She rubs too hard: she touches me all over—apparently there is no part of me, inside or outside, that is not by law and custom, unfenced or forbidden her to touch or enter on.

I tend to lose consciousness—sometimes I become quite limp, I actually faint in a sense; at other times, I cooperate with her—but more and more and then more and more wildly—culminating often in my betraying her by being lifted on my own tempo and excitement to the dervish thing of being unconscious, of being without reason—or having a wild or mystic reason: her face is like a rosebud and keeps opening and closing; and I must splash it—or close it.

Or I chiefly sit still, hanging on to a neutrality of temper that becomes a loss-of-consciousness: I have fainted away into propriety, into feeling nothing while in process of feeling everything. My mother's hands. The wash cloth. The water.

And the soap—the thick (to me) film of soap! The soapiness and dirtiness of the water! Immersion almost in filth—so lowering, so dissolving. . . . Her hands between my legs, between my scrotum and pink-twig, between the clefts of my buttocks—and then on my back, between my shoulder blades—she bathes me because she wants to: she does not want Anne Marie to do it. This having a young child, this taking care of him, this having a boy interests her—one can see, or sense, that absorption, like a wooden board, sometimes padded but sometimes simply wooden, smacking the water, or smacking the side of one's head: and there is often, perhaps usually, a divergence between her sense of *me* and of me as a child, of there being a child there who is in her care, her keeping, whom she bathes. When that divergence becomes sharp and steep enough— excited enough—the wood of her absorption becomes something like a sandbox or an arena on which we both perch, she and I, and I watch her and myself, my other self, who is a child, the me which is particularly me being ignored—and sometimes dying away— among the sensations, the adventures of this.

When the bath is over, Momma will wrap me in a towel: I will be limp, unusually obedient by then—as if waterlogged, leached of boyhood and activity—and she will be flushed, overheated: she *often* says, "Let's get the steam out of here—I'm going to open the window. Wiley, stand out of the draft."

She and I are allies at this moment—spiritually we stand shoulder to shoulder—but she is filled with restlessness, antagonism, to things, to me; and I am passive, elusive or overly present, too dependent—it as if I swing on her arms, or hang from them, or my nakedness does. She fights to open the window which is invariably swollen from water vapor. Holding the towel over my wet, shivering shoulders, my hair dripping all over my face, I back up aimlessly—

cooperatively. When she said "window," a part of me found itself a crossroads in my head, a crossroads in a closet or basement. I am at a crossroads in my consciousness because I might know what she means—it all depends. That thing that she opens is a window then—the window I know is in my room: I know the ones in an automobile too. This one is defective—it can't be opened easily, it has no handle, it can't be seen through: it is small and pretty-ish, glazed with mist, with frosting—its size and frosting make it seem friendlier than the window in my room: I would rather play with this one. Momma tells me to hold still. Over and over, she injects me with languour—stillness—there is a heaviness in her hips, her torso: sleep chambers. She towels me as roughly as she scrubs me: I get drowsier: she shakes me: my immobility (of spirit) and the prolonged as-if-mindless staring at the newly recognized, newly enfranchised window mixes the sensations of her hands and the towel with the operations of the mind in my stilled and yet gently and genuinely enflamed body.

Thus, a window.

What did I see? A window in a wall—frosted glass—blurs of steam on it: I wait at a crossroads: waiting—mental waiting—means to be in a darkness.

What if I am wrong? What if I remember incorrectly? It does not matter. This is fiction—a game—of pleasures, of truth-and-errors, as at the sensual beginning of a sensual life.

A POSTSCRIPT TO THE BERKELEY RENAISSANCE

by Jack Spicer

from MANROOT

nominated by MANROOT

What have I lost? When shall I start to sing
A loud and idiotic song that makes
The heart rise frightened into poetry
Like birds disturbed?

I was a singer once. I sang that song.
I saw the thousands of bewildered birds
Breaking their cover into poetry
Up from the heart.

What have I lost? We lived in forests then,
Naked as jaybirds in the ever-real,
Eating our toasted buns and catching flies,
And sometimes angels, with our hooting tongues.

I was a singer once. In distant trees
We made the forests ring with sacred noise
Of gods and bears and swans and sodomy,
And no one but a bird could hear our voice.

What have I lost? The trees were full of birds.
We sat there drinking at the sour wine
In gallon bottles. Shouting song
Until the hunters came.

I was a singer once, bird-ignorant.
Time with a gun said, "Stop,
Find other forests. Teach the innocent."
God got another and a third
Birdlimed in Eloquence.

What have I lost? At night my hooting tongue,
Naked of feathers and of softening years,
Sings through the mirror at me like a whippoorwill
And then I cannot sleep.

"I was a singer once," it sings.
"I sing the song that every captured tongue
Sang once when free and wants again to sing.
But I can sing no song I have not sung."

What have I lost? Spook singer, hold your tongue.
I sing a newer song no ghost bird sings.
My tongue is sharpened on the iron's edge.
Canaries need no trees. They have their cage.

POWER

by Adrienne Rich

from THE LITTLE MAGAZINE

nominated by Joyce Carol Oates

Living   in the earth-deposits   of our history

Today a backhoe divulged   out of a crumbling flank of earth
one bottle   amber   perfect   a hundred-year-old
cure for fever   or melancholy   a tonic
for living on this earth   in the winters of this climate

Today I was reading about Marie Curie:
she must have known she suffered   from radiation sickness
her body bombarded for years   by the element
she had purified
It seems she denied to the end
the source of the cataracts on her eyes
the cracked and suppurating skin   of her finger-ends
till she could no longer hold   a test-tube or a pencil

She died   a famous woman   denying
her wounds
denying
her wounds   came   from the same source as her power

♨ ♨ ♨

XENIA

by EUGENIO MONTALE

(translated by Jonathan Galassi)

from PLOUGHSHARES

nominated by Pushcart Press

I

1
Dear little insect
—they called you Mosca, I don't know why—
this evening as I was reading
Deutero-Isaiah in the near-dark
you reappeared beside me;
but you didn't have glasses,
you couldn't see me,
and I couldn't recognize you in the dusk
without their glitter.

2
No glasses or antennae,
poor insect,
and wings only in fantasy;
a broken Bible, hardly reliable,
the dark of night,
lightning, thunder, and then
no storm. Can it be
you went that quickly, without speaking?
But it's absurd to imagine
you still had lips.

3

At the Saint James in Paris I'll have to ask
for a single room. (They don't like
solitary guests.)
And in the sham Byzantium
of your Venetian hotel; and then
go straight to the booth of your old friends
the telephone-girls; and leave again,
once the dial-tone has died—
the desire to have you back,
if only in a gesture or habit.

4

We had practiced a whistle,
a sign of recognition, for the hereafter.
I'm trying to perfect it, hoping
we've already died, all of us, and don't know it.

5

I've never understood
if I was your faithful distempered dog
or you were mine.
To others, no, you were a near-sighted insect
lost in the babble
of society. Those sophisticates
were naive not to realize
the joke was on them:
even in the dark they were under surveillance,
unmasked by some infallible sense of yours,
your bat-radar.

6

You never thought of leaving your tracks
in prose or verse. That was your magic
—and the source of my self-disgust.
It was also my fear:
that you'd consign me to the croaking
mire of the neoteroi.

7
Self-pity, unending torment, and heartache,
the lot of him who worships the *here-and-now* and hopes
without hope for another . . .(Who dares say,
          another world?)

"Strana pietà . . ." (Azucena, *Il Trovatore,* Act II).

8
Your talk, so hesitant, so reckless,
is all that's left to console me.
But the accent's different, the color's changed.
I'll get used to hearing you, deciphering you
in the ticking teletype,
in the rolling smoke
of my Brissago cigars.

9
Listening was your only way of seeing.
The phone bill is down to practically nothing.

10
"She prayed?" "Yes, she prayed to Saint Anthony,
who helps recover
lost umbrellas and other things
from the cloakroom of Sant' Ermete."
"Is that all?" "For her dead, too,
and for me."
          "Enough," said the priest.

11
Remembering your tears—mine were worse—
isn't enough to silence your explosive laughter.
It was like the prelude to your own Last Judgment,
which unfortunately never took place.

12
The night-cricket of Strasbourg, drilling
in a cleft in the cathedral;
the Maison Rouge and the bartender who taught you
         Basque;
Ruggero, limping and a little high;
Striggio, from who knows where, gorging himself
on gossip and *hor d'oeuvres*, betrayed
by a Turkish girl (his flaming nose
signalling his shame, eyes averted
from the check he can no longer put off paying);
did they come back to you *then*? Or even
slighter things. But all you said was,
"Take the sleeping pill," your last
words—and for me.

13
Your brother died young; you were
the scruffy youngster who stares at me
from the "posed" oval of your portrait.
He wrote music, unpublished, unplayed.
It's buried in a trunk, or rotting now.
Maybe someone's recreating it
without knowing, if what's written is written.
I loved him without meeting him.
Besides you, no one remembered him.
I didn't ask questions; now there's no point.
After you, I'm the only one
for whom he existed. But it's possible, you know,
to love a shadow; we ourselves shadows.

14
They say my poetry
is a poetry of unbelonging.
But if it was yours it was someone's,
yours, who are no longer form, but essence.
They say that poetry at its height
praises the fleeting Whole,

they deny that the tortoise
is faster than lightning.
You alone knew that motion
isn't different from stasis,
that void is full, and blue
is the thinnest kind of cloud.
Which helps me understand your long crossing
imprisoned in bandages and plaster.
And yet it's no consolation
knowing that one or two, we are a single thing.

II

1
Death didn't concern you.
Even your dogs had died,
and the asylum doctor they called Uncle Crazy,
and your mother, whose specialty
of frogs and rice was a Milanese triumph;
even your father, who watches over me morning
        and evening
from his little picture on the wall.
Nevertheless, death didn't concern you.

I had to go to the funerals,
hidden in a taxi, keeping my distance
from the tears and entanglements. But life, too,
and its festivals of vanity and greed,
mattered little to you, and even less
the common gangrenes that make
men wolves.

A tabula rasa; except that
there was a point I couldn't fathom,
and this point *concerned you*.

2
You often thought about Herr Cap. (I hardly ever did.)
"I only saw him once or twice, in the bus on Ischia.
He's a lawyer from Klagenfurt, the one who sends
          greetings.
He was supposed to come see us."

Finally, he comes; I tell him everything, he speechless;
it seems to be a catastrophe for him, too. He's quiet a
          long time,
mumbles, stands up stiffly and bows. He promises
to send greetings.
                    It's strange, only unlikely people
managed to understand you.
Attorney Cap! Even his name. And Celia? What became
          of her?

3
We missed the shoehorn a long time,
the rusty piece of tin we'd always
had with us. It seemed indecent to bring
such an ugly thing in among stucco and gilt.
It must have been at the Danieli that I forgot
to put it back in our luggage.
No doubt Hedia the maid threw it
into the Canalozzo. And how could I have written
to ask them to look for that sliver of tin?
Prestige (our prestige) was at stake,
and the faithful Hedia had saved it.

4
Cannily,
out of the jaws of Etna,
or from the teeth of ice,
you let drop incredible revelations.

Mangano, the good surgeon, realized it
when he was exposed as the scourge
of the Black Shirts, and smiled.

You were like that: even on the brink of the cliff
sweetness and terror in one music.

5

Arm in arm with you, I've walked down a least a million
        stairs,
and now that you're gone every step is an abyss.
Our long journey has been brief even so.
Mine still goes on, though I no longer care
about connections or reservations
or tie-ups, or the turmoil
of the man who believes
reality is what he sees.

I've gone down millions of stairs arm in arm with you,
but not because it may be we see better with four eyes.
I went down those stairs with you because I knew
that of the two of us, though your pupils were clouded,
only you could see truly.

6

The wine steward poured you a little
Inferno. You were terrified: "Do I have to drink it?
Isn't it enough to have been there, and burned?"

7

"I've never been sure of being in the world."
"Very clever," you answered, "and me?"
"Oh, you've nibbled the world to bits,
in homeopathic doses. But I . . . ."

8

"And Paradise? Is there a paradise?"
"I think so, ma'am, but no one drinks
sweet wines anymore."

9

You didn't dare look at nuns and widows,
those death-dealing, evil-smelling
professional mourners. Even he with his thousand eyes
turns from them, you were sure.
He the all-seeing . . . prudently,
you never called him god, even with a small g.

10
After searching for hours
I found you in a bar on the Avenida
da Libertade; you didn't know a word
of Portuguese, or rather, one word:
Madeira. And a glass was delivered
with a plate of shrimp.

That night I was compared to the greatest
Lusitanians with their unpronounceable names
and to Carducci.
You weren't impressed at all. I saw you crying
from laughter, hidden in a crowd
bored perhaps, but attentive.

11
Surfacing out of an infinity of time,
Celia the Phillippine called
to see how you were. I think she's fine, I say,
maybe better than before. "What do you mean,
            you think?
Isn't she there anymore?" Maybe more than before,
        only . . .
Celia, try to understand . . .
                From the other end of the line,
from Manila or some other name
in the atlas, even she
faltered. And suddenly hung up.

12
Hawks
were always out of the range of your vision,
and you rarely saw them up close.
There was one at Etretat,
watching over the gawky flights of its young.

Two more in Greece, on the road to Delphi,
a cyclone of soft feathers,
two fevered, green, inoffensive beaks.

You like life ripped to shreds,
tearing out of its impossible
web.

13
I've hung the daguerroetype of your father as a baby
in my room; it's more than a hundred years old.
In the absence of my own confused pedigree
I'm trying to reconstruct yours; but it's hopeless.
We weren't horses, our ancestors' statistics
aren't in the almanacs. Those who claimed
to know them didn't exist themselves,
as we didn't for them. So? Still, it's undeniable
that something happened, maybe some nothing
that is everything.

14
The flood has buried all the furniture,
the papers, the paintings that filled
a basement locked with a double lock.
Maybe the red morocco books struggled blindly,
and Du Bos' endless dedications,
the wax seal with Ezra's beard,
Alain's Valéry, the original
of the *Canti Orfici*—and some shaving
brushes, a thousand knick-knacks,
and all your brother Silvio's music.
Ten or twelve days exposed to the acid hunger
of naphtha and muck. They must have suffered greatly
before losing their identity.
And I'm up to my neck, too,
though my standing was doubtful from the beginning.
It's not mud that besieges me, it's the events
of an incredible reality I never believed in.
Against them, my courage was the greatest
of your gifts; maybe your didn't know it.

CALEDONIA, the type in which this book was set is one of those referred to by printers, as a "modern face". It was designed around 1939 by W.A. Dwiggins (1880–1956) and it has been called "the most popular all-purpose typeface in U.S. history".

It is an original design, but, as from the beginning, fresh and exciting designs have often evolved from variations on the old, done by competent and disciplined hands. Caledonia shows marks of the long admired Scotch roman type-letters cut by Alexander Wilson in Glasgow in the 19th century. It also shows a trace from the types that W. Bulmer & Company used, cut in London, around 1790 by William Martin.

That Dwiggins was aware of the particular needs of our time is soundly attested to by the enduring good reception his "hard working, feet-on-the-ground" type has received from countless printers, authors and readers alike.

This book was designed and produced for the publisher, by RAY FREIMAN & COMPANY.

to discriminate on a most particular level between objects previously viewed as identical or, perhaps, merely uninteresting ◆ This increased perception amply repays the student for his work & as an added attraction, he has acquired a pleasant skill ◆ ¶ Calligraphy is the art of writing beautifully & with delight, and can be the province of every man who has mastered the more difficult art of expressing himself through written symbols ◆ The student is his own teacher, and as such will learn only what he teaches himself ◆ This book can smooth his path, preventing time-consuming & discouraging errors, but can do little else ◆ Ability is best obtained through practice, the more (within reason) the better ◆ The ability to do calligraphy well is in direct proportion to the time spent in doing it ◆ Work carefully & deliberately, as haste is the enemy of good workmanship ◆ People who run for busses will never make calligraphers ◆ ¶ This book is large so that the letters will be clear & the same size as the student's ◆ It should be used as a writing pad, with the student's work opposite the page he is studying ◆ For this purpose, a fold-out writing guide is provided in the back, so that any page in the book can be copied without inconvenience ◆ ¶ In this third edition I hope to have removed the more glaring errors of the preceding, & though new mistakes may be found, the generous reader will pardon them and me ◆

abcddefgghijkklmnopqggqzrstuvvwwwx
yyz3z ◆ ABCDEFGHIJKLMNOPQRSTUVWXYZ ◆
abcdefghijklmnopqzrstuvwxyz ◆ & ◆ 1234567890 ◆